Whiteout

Whiteout

The CIA, Drugs and the Press

———————◆———————

ALEXANDER COCKBURN

AND

JEFFREY ST. CLAIR

VERSO

London · New York

First published by Verso 1998
© Alexander Cockburn and Jeffrey St. Clair 1998
All rights reserved

Verso
UK: 6 Meard Street, London W1V 3HR
USA: 180 Varick Street, 10th Floor, New York, NY 10014-4606

Verso is the imprint of New Left Books

ISBN 1 85984 897 4 (hbk)
ISBN 1 85984 139 2 (pbk)

British Library Cataloguing in Publication Data
A catalogue record for this book is available from the British Library

Library of Congress Cataloging-in-Publication Data
A catalog record for this book is available from the Library of Congress

Typeset in Times by NorthStar, San Francisco, California
Printed and bound in the USA by R. R. Donnelly & Sons Co.

Contents

Preface

This is largely a story of criminal conduct, much of it by the Central Intelligence Agency. It is a story of how many in the US press have been complicit in covering the Agency's tracks. When compelled to concede the Agency's criminal activities such journalists often take refuge in the notion of "rogue agents" or, as a last resort, of a "rogue Agency." We do not accept this separation of the CIA's activities from the policies and directives of the US government. Whether it was Truman's meddling in China, which created Burmese opium kings; or the Kennedy brothers' obsession with killing Fidel Castro; or Nixon's command for "more assassinations" in Vietnam, the CIA has always been the obedient executor of the will of the US government, starting with the White House.

Whiteout is also a record of courageous men and women who would have no truck with such conduct or with any cover-up: former CIA agents like Ralph McGehee, still maintaining an invaluable database on his old employer, which still continues to hound him; historian Al McCoy, who put his life at risk in Southeast Asia and produced perhaps the finest single book on the Agency and its relationship with drug traffickers; Bob Parry; Brian Barger; Leslie and Andrew Cockburn; Martha Honey; former DEA agents Celerino Castillo III, Michael Levine and

Richard Horn; John Marks, the former State Department official who excavated one of the CIA's darkest chapters, its efforts at mind control; Christopher Simpson and Linda Hunt, who exposed the CIA's recruitment of Nazis, including Klaus Barbie and the Nazi scientists; Gary Webb, a good reporter vilely treated by his colleagues in the profession; courageous Mexican journalists such as the late Manuel Buendía, who have exposed the ties between Mexico's drug lords and the government and Mexico's CIA-funded security apparatus, knowing that to do so was to court death.

We thank Peter Kornbluh and his colleagues at the National Security Archive for keeping the record of this era alive and available to researchers and reporters; the folks at the Sentencing Project for information on drug sentencing disparities; John Kelly; Terry Allen; Heber Jentzsch; Ralph McGehee; Douglas Valentine, who has written one of the best books on the CIA in Vietnam; Sue and Gary Webb for their hospitality; Nick Schou, an excellent reporter who generously shared information he had uncovered about the activities of CIA contractors in Southern California; Marianne McDonald; Nicholas Kozloff; Scott Handleman; Phil Connors; Becky Grant; Elinor Lindheimer; Craig Van Note; Bernardo Attias, for maintaining a useful web page on the CIA and drug trafficking; Steven Hiatt; Jonathan Lubell; Andrew Cockburn; JoAnn Wypijewski; Bryce Hoffman; Kimberly Willson-St. Clair for allowing this book to take over her house for a year and for her great skills in the library; Barbara Yaley; and Ken Silverstein, with whom we write our biweekly newsletter *CounterPunch*.

1

Webb's Big Story

Sunday, August 18, 1996, was not a major news day for most American newspapers. The big story of the hour was the preview of the Democratic convention in Chicago.

About 2,500 miles west of Chicago lies Silicon Valley. Its big newspaper is the *San Jose Mercury News,* which has a solid reputation as a good regional paper. Like other Knight-Ridder properties, such as the *Philadelphia Inquirer* and the *Detroit Free Press*, it has a middle-of-the-road political cast slightly tilted to the Democratic side.

As the citizens of Santa Clara County browsed through their newspaper that Sunday morning, many of them surely stopped at the first article of a three-part series, under the slightly sinister title "Dark Alliance," subtitled "The Story Behind the Crack Explosion." The words were superimposed on a murky picture of a black man smoking a crack pipe, said image overlaid on the seal of the Central Intelligence Agency. The first day's headline was "America's Crack Plague Has Roots in Nicaraguan War," just above the byline of the author of the series, a reporter in the *Mercury News* Sacramento bureau named Gary Webb.

Within a couple of weeks, the story that Webb laid across August 18, 19 and 20 in the *San Jose Mercury News* would convulse black America and prompt the Central Intelligence Agency first to furious denials and then to one of the most ruthless campaigns of vilification of a journalist since the Agency went after Seymour Hersh in the mid 1970s. Within three weeks, both the Justice Department and the CIA bowed to fierce demands by California Senator Barbara Boxer and Los Angeles Representative Maxine Waters for thorough a investigation. By mid-November, a crowd of 1,500 locals in Waters's own district in South Central Los Angeles would be giving CIA director John Deutch one of the hardest evenings of his life. In terms of public unease about the secret activities of the US government, Webb's series was the most significant event since the Iran/Contra affair nearly blew Ronald Reagan out of the water.

From the savage assaults on Webb by other members of his profession, those unfamiliar with the series might have assumed that Webb had made a series of wild and unsubstantiated charges, long on dramatic speculation and short on specific data or sourcing. In fact, Webb's series was succinct and narrowly focused.

Webb stuck closely to a single story line: how a group of Nicaraguan exiles set up a cocaine ring in California, establishing ties with the black street gangs of South Central Los Angeles who manufactured crack out of shipments of powder cocaine. Webb then charted how much of the profits made by the Nicaraguan exiles had been funneled back to the Contra army – created in the late 1970s by the Central Intelligence Agency, with the mission of sabotaging the Sandinista revolution that had evicted Anastasio Somoza and his corrupt clique in 1979.

The very first paragraph of the series neatly summed up the theme. It was, as they say in the business, a strong lead, but a justified one. "For the better part of a decade, a San Francisco Bay Area drug ring sold tons of cocaine to the Crips and Bloods street gangs of Los Angeles and funneled millions in drug profits to a Latin American guerrilla army run by the CIA." That San Francisco drug ring was headed by a Nicaraguan exile named Norwin Meneses Cantarero, who served "as the head of security and intelligence" for the leading organization in the Contra coalition, the FDN or Fuerza Democrático Nicaragüense. The FDN was headed by Enrique Bermúdez and Adolfo Calero, who had been installed in those positions under the oversight of the CIA. Meneses came from a family intimately linked to the Somoza dictatorship. One brother had been chief of police in Managua. Two other brothers were generals in the force most loyal to Somoza, the National Guard. While his brothers were assisting Somoza in the political dictatorship that darkened Nicaragua for many decades, Norwin Meneses applied his energies mostly to straightforwardly criminal enterprises in the civil sector. He ran a car theft ring and was also one of the top drug traffickers in Nicaragua, where he was known as *El Rey del Drogas* (the king of drugs). Meneses worked with the approval of the Somoza clan, which duly received its rake-off.

In 1977, Norwin Meneses felt it necessary to register his disquiet at a Nicaraguan customs probe into his smuggling of high-end North American cars from the US into Nicaragua. The Meneses gang murdered the chief of customs. Owing to Norwin's powerful family, the case was never prosecuted.

The US Drug Enforcement Agency and other agencies had been keeping files on Meneses since at least 1974. Yet he was granted political refugee status in July 1979, when he and other members of Somoza's elite fled to the US. Meneses landed in San Francisco as part of what became known locally as the Nicaraguan "gold rush." Here he lost no time in rebuilding his criminal enterprises in stolen cars and drugs.

Meneses's contact in Los Angeles was another Nicaraguan exile, Oscar Danilo Blandón. Blandón had left Managua in June 1979, a month before Meneses, on the eve of Somoza's downfall. The son of a Managua slumlord, Blandón had earned a master's degree in marketing from the University of Bogotá in Colombia and had headed Somoza's agricultural export program. Agricultural exports were an important component of the country's mainly ranching- and coffee-based economy, with the Somoza family itself owning no less than a quarter of the nation's agricultural land.

In his position as head of the export program, Blandón had developed close ties to the US Department of Commerce and the US State Department. He secured $27 million in USAID funding and was well known to the US military and the Central Intelligence Agency, both of which had a commanding presence in Somoza's Nicaragua. (Somoza had sent his officer corps for training in the US, and the CIA station chief was the most powerful foreigner in Managua.)

Blandón's wife, Chepita, also came from a powerful clan, the Murillo family. One of her relatives was the mayor of Managua. Like many other Somoza supporters, both the Blandón and Murillo families lost most of their fortunes in the 1979 revolution and burned with the desire to evict the popular government headed by the Sandinista commanders.

Blandón and his wife settled in Los Angeles, where he started a used-car business. He also began to involve himself in Nicaraguan émigré politics. Testifying on February 3, 1994 as a government witness before a federal grand jury investigating the Meneses family's drug ring in San Francisco, Blandón said he drove to San Francisco for several meetings with Norwin Meneses "to start the movement, the Contra revolution." Blandón had known the Meneses family in Nicaragua. In fact, Blandón said, his mother shared Meneses's last name of Cantarero, "so we are related." He said he and Meneses "met with the politics people," but couldn't find a way to raise big sums of cash.

In the spring of 1981, Blandón got a phone call from an old friend and business associate from Managua named Donald Barrios. Barrios, then living in Miami, was moving in high-level Nicaraguan émigré circles. This group included General Gustavo Medina, once an important intelligence officer in Somoza's National Guard, a position in which he had long-standing ties to the CIA. Blandón later testified that Barrios "started telling me we had to raise some money and send it to Honduras." Barrios instructed Blandón to go to Los Angeles International Airport to meet Meneses. Blandón and Meneses then flew to Honduras and, in the capital city of Tegucigalpa, met with Enrique Bermúdez, former National Guardsman and military commander of the FDN.

In Somoza's final days, President Jimmy Carter had made a last-ditch effort to maintain a US-backed regime in Nicaragua even if Somoza should be forced to quit. The plan was to preserve the bloodthirsty National Guard as the custodian of US interests. When this plan failed and the Sandinistas swept to power, Carter ordered the initial organization of what later became known as the Contras, operating out of Honduras. The CIA mustered Argentinian officers fresh from their own death squad campaigns, and these men began to organize the exiled National Guardsmen into a military force.

Bermúdez was key to this CIA-organized operation from the start. He had been a colonel in the National Guard, had trained at the US National

Defense College outside Washington, D.C., and had served from 1976 to July 1979 as Somoza's military attaché in Washington. Furnished with $300,000 in CIA money, Bermúdez took command of the fledgling Contra force in Honduras. In the summer of 1981, at the dawn of the Reagan administration, Bermúdez held a press conference in Honduras. In language drafted by his CIA handlers, Bermúdez announced the formation of the FDN and his own position as commander of its military wing. The CIA script later installed Adolfo Calero, formerly the Coca-Cola concessionaire in Managua, as the FDN's civilian head, operating mainly out of the United States, where he was under tight CIA supervision.

Blandón and Meneses arrived to meet Bermúdez at a moment of financial strain for the Contra army, then in formation. The CIA had provided seed money, but it wasn't until November 23, 1981 that Reagan approved National Security Directive 17, which provided a budget of $19.3 million for the Contras, via the CIA. The Contras, Bermúdez said, needed money urgently, and, Blandón later testified to a US federal grand jury, it was at this meeting that the need for drug money to finance the Contras was proposed. "There's a saying," Blandón testified, "that 'the ends justify the means.' And that's what Mr. Bermúdez told us in Honduras."

Bermúdez was not repelled by the moral implications of drug smuggling. In fact, evidence gathered during congressional hearings in the mid-1980s suggests that Bermúdez himself had previously had a hand in the drug trade. "Bermúdez was the target of a government-sponsored drug sting operation," said Senator John Kerry, who chaired a committee that investigated charges of Contra cocaine smuggling. "He has been involved in drug running." Kerry charged that the CIA had protected Bermúdez from arrest. "The law enforcement officials know that the sting was called back in the interest of protecting the Contras," Kerry concluded.

Back in San Francisco, Meneses began educating Blandón, the graduate in marketing, on the finer points of cocaine wholesaling. Trained in accountancy, Blandón did some work on Meneses's books and rapidly became aware of the substantial scale of his cocaine operation. In 1981 alone, Blandón later testified, the Meneses ring moved 900 kilos of cocaine. At that time the wholesale price of a kilo of cocaine was $50,000. The cocaine was coming from Colombia via Mexico and Miami and then to the Bay Area, where it was stashed in about a dozen warehouses. Meneses was also keeping cocaine at the house of his mistress, Blanca Margarita Castaño, who lived near the old Cow Palace in the Hunters Point area. Eventually Meneses's romantic complications prompted him to relocate his wife and young children to Los Angeles, with Mrs. Meneses ensconced in a silk-screening business under the eye of Blandón, who also set up a restaurant for Mrs. Meneses called Chickalina. Both the silk-screen shop and the restaurant became fronts for the drug business. As Blandón put it, "It was marketing, okay? Marketing."

As a cocaine wholesaler in Los Angeles, Blandón got off to a slow start. He'd pick up a couple of kilos from Meneses, along with a list of local buyers, and he'd do the rounds in his white Toyota. But business remained static until he made a fateful contact with a young black fellow living in South Central named Rick Ross. Ross was born in Troup, Texas and as a young child moved to Los Angeles with his mother. He'd shown promise as a tennis player in high school and had set his sights on a college scholarship, when his coach found he could neither read nor write and dropped him. Ross went to Los Angeles Trade Technical College, was number three on the tennis team, and entered a course in bookbinding. To make some money he started selling stolen car parts, was arrested, and had to quit school.

Ross first heard about cocaine, at the time a middle-class drug, from a college friend, and it wasn't long before he made a connection with a Nicaraguan dealer named Henry Corrales. Corrales gave Ross a good price, and he was able to make a decent profit in reselling to the Crips gang in South Central and Compton.

As we shall see, the economics of cocaine became a bitter issue in the uproar over Webb's series. Was it true that the cocaine prices set by the Nicaraguans rendered the drug affordable to poor people for the first time? Arguably, this was the case – and indeed there is more evidence to substantiate such a thesis than Webb was able to offer in his tightly edited series. Cheap cocaine began to appear in South Central Los Angeles in early 1982. Ross got it from Corrales, who worked for Meneses and Blandón, and it wasn't long before Ross went directly to Blandón.

As Ross later told Webb, the prices offered by Blandón gave him command of the Los Angeles market. He was buying his cocaine supplies at sometimes $10,000 less per kilo than the going rate. "It was unreal," Ross remembered. "We were just wiping everyone out." His connections to the Bloods and Crips street gangs solved the distribution problems that had previously beleaguered Blandón. By 1983, Ross – now known as "Freeway Ricky" – was buying over a 100 kilos of cocaine a week and selling as much as $3 million worth of crack a day.

Drugs weren't the only commodity Blandón was selling to Ross. The young entrepreneur was also receiving from the Nicaraguan a steady stream of weapons and surveillance equipment, including Uzi submachine guns, semi-automatic handguns, miniature videocameras, recording equipment, police scanners and Colt AR-15 assault rifles. Ross told Webb that Blandón even tried to sell his partner a grenade launcher.

Blandón's source for this equipment was a man named Ronald J. Lister. Lister, who figures prominently in the story, was a former Laguna Beach police detective who at that time was running two security firms – Mundy Security and Pyramid International Security Consultants. Blandón testified at Rick Ross's trial in March 1996 that Lister would attend meetings of Contra supporters in Southern California to demonstrate his arsenal. Lister had worked as an informant for the DEA and FBI, and boasted of his ties to the CIA during the 1980s, when the Reagan administration was waging war in Central America.

Business was indeed booming. In 1981 Meneses had, according to Blandón's reading of his account books, been moving 900 kilos a year. Two years later the numbers had surged to around 5,000 kilos a year – and the latter figure represents just the amount Blandón's LA operation was handling. Ross was a brilliant businessman. His greatest coup was to recognize the potential in recent technological innovations for the mass marketing of cocaine. Ross didn't invent the process whereby powder cocaine was converted into the "rocks" of crack that could be sold at affordable street prices; crack had first appeared in poor city neighborhoods on the West Coast in 1979. But Ross was the first to take full advantage. Crack could be bought for $4 to $5 a hit. It gave an intense, although brief, high, and was highly addictive. Consequently, as the furious black reaction to the Webb series tells us, crack engendered social disaster in neighborhoods such as South Central. Families were ravaged by addiction. Addicts stole and robbed to buy the next hit. Gangs fought bloody battles for control of turf. The plague elicited a savage response from the state. Prison sentences were a hundred times more severe for crack-related offenses than for powder cocaine.

By 1985, Ross and his affiliates in the street gangs had begun exporting their crack operation to what the DEA reckoned to be at least a dozen other cities. Obviously, the sums accruing to Danilo Blandón in the drug trade were enormous, and he testified at Ross's trial that "whatever we were running in LA, the profit was going to the Contra revolution." Duane "Dewey" Clarridge, the CIA officer in charge of covert operations in Latin America, has denied, both in the press and in his memoir, allegations that the CIA would have sanctioned or turned a blind eye to Contra drug shipments for funding reasons. The CIA's Contra operation, said Clarridge, "was funded by the US government. There was enough money to fund the operation. We didn't need, and neither did the Contras need the money from anybody else."

But from the beginning, Clarridge's plans for the Contras were much more ambitious than the initial scheme of the Reagan administration, which was to use them as part of an effort to seal off Nicaragua and try to stop it from aiding guerrilla struggles in neighboring countries. Clarridge wanted a covert war. In the summer of 1981, a week after becoming head of the CIA's Latin American operations, he took his recommendations to CIA chief William Casey: "My plan was simple. 1. Take the war to Nicaragua. 2. Start killing Cubans." This quickly evolved into a far-ranging program of assassinations, industrial sabotage and incursions into Nicaraguan territory from bases in Honduras and Costa Rica.

The problem for Clarridge and for the CIA was that the US Congress tended to be dubious of such large plans, which were not politically popular. The initial appropriation was meager, amounting to only $19 million in 1982 for the CIA's covert operations against Nicaragua. In the spring of 1982 such covert costs soared when the Argentinians who had been supervising day-to-day military training for the fledgling Contra force in Honduras pulled out at the onset of the Falklands/Malvinas War. Later that year, Congress moved to restrict CIA aid for the Contras. At the last second Rep. Edward Boland of Massachusetts introduced an amendment to the Defense Appropriations Bill for fiscal 1983, prohibiting the CIA from spending any money "for the purpose of overthrowing the government of Nicaragua." The Agency was given only $21 million outside Boland's restrictions for activities related to the Contras.

In December 1983 Congress capped Contra funding for fiscal 1984 at only $24 million, which was roughly a quarter of what the Reagan administration had claimed was necessary for a proper fighting force. The shortfall was what drove Robert McFarlane and Oliver North to hunt for alternative sources of funding – for example, asking the Saudis for $1 million a month. Clarridge went on a similar mission to South Africa. North was in the process of setting up covert bank accounts in mid-1984.

In April 1984, it emerged that the CIA had undertaken the mining of Nicaraguan harbors. The political uproar in the US resulted in the most restrictive of the Boland amendments, passed by Congress in October 1984. During fiscal 1985, the amendment read, "no funds available to the Central Intelligence Agency, the Department of Defense, or any other agency or entity of the United States involved in intelligence activities may be obligated or expended for the purpose or which have the effect of supporting, directly or indirectly, military or paramilitary operations in Nicaragua by any nation, group, organization, movement, or individual." The year 1985 also marked the peak of the Meneses-Blandón drug sales, at the time of the CIA's greatest need for money for its Contra army. The Boland amendment expired on October 17, 1986, and immediately the portion of the CIA budget allocated for the Contras rose to $100 million.

During this stressful period of desperate Contra need for cash, when Reagan secretly decreed to National Security Adviser McFarlane that whatever Congress might stipulate, the Contras had to be kept together "body and soul," the drug operation run by Contra supporters Meneses and Blandón led a charmed life, without any disruption of its activities by law enforcement. Indeed, several law enforcement officers have complained publicly that actions targeted against Meneses were blocked by NSC officers in the Reagan administration and by the CIA.

Only a few weeks after the Blandón-Meneses partnership was launched in the summer of 1981, a young DEA agent in San Francisco named Susan Smith began an investigation of Norwin Meneses. Smith had picked up rumors on the street that a group of Nicaraguan exiles headed by Meneses was selling cocaine in the Bay Area and sending money and weapons back to Central America. She checked the DEA files on Meneses and found a bulging record of the man's criminal activities, dating back to a 1978 FBI report charging that Norwin and his brother Ernest were "smuggling 20 kilos of cocaine at a time into the United States." One of the entry points for Meneses's cocaine was apparently New Orleans, where Smith came across records from the DEA's "Operation Alligator." This government sting had busted a large cocaine ring in New Orleans. One of the arrested men, Manuel Porro, told DEA agent Bill Cunningham that Meneses was the source of the cocaine. However, Meneses was never arrested.

A few months later, Smith discovered, the San Francisco DEA office received a tip that Meneses was also the supplier for cocaine seized in a major bust in Tampa, Florida in February 1980. The cocaine had apparently been flown to Tampa from Meneses's ranch in Costa Rica, to be distributed by Meneses's relatives. Smith also learned that, beginning in early June 1981, Detective Joseph Lee of the Baldwin Park Police Department in Los Angeles had been investigating a Nicaraguan dealer named Julio Bermúdez, who was making two trips a month to San Francisco, where he would pick up 20 pounds of cocaine at a time from Meneses's warehouses.

Smith mustered this information into an affidavit for a search warrant, dated November 16, 1981, and began trailing Meneses and his dealers. On one occasion, Smith followed Meneses's men to a house in Daly City, just south of San Francisco, which was owned by Carlos Cabezas, a Nicaraguan lawyer and accountant who had served as a pilot in Somoza's National Guard. Cabezas was a leading figure in the anti-Sandinista movement in California.

Then Smith's superiors abruptly terminated her investigation and she was reassigned to cover drug dealing by motorcycle gangs in Oakland. Despite her huge file on Meneses, Smith told Webb, DEA managers evinced no interest. Smith quit the DEA in 1984, asking her superiors if they wanted her extensive files on the Meneses drug ring. They declined, and the files were shredded.

What's more than a little curious about the DEA's lack of interest in Meneses in 1984 is that in February 1983 the FBI had scored one of the largest cocaine seizures in California history, in the so-called Frogman case. Members of the Meneses drug syndicate had been caught attempting to swim ashore at the San Francisco docks from a Colombian freighter, the *Ciudad de Cuta*, with 400 pounds of cocaine. According to the DEA, the drugs had a street value at that time of more than $100 million. Ultimately, thirty-five people were arrested in the Frogman case, including Julio Zavala and the man whose house Susan Smith had staked out, Carlos Cabezas. The Frogman trial was going on at the very moment the DEA was telling Susan Smith that information about Cabezas and Meneses held no interest for it.

But then again, the Frogman case was not exactly your run-of-the-mill drug trial. On November 28, 1984, Cabezas testified in that trial that this cocaine-smuggling operation was a funding source for the Contras. Furthermore, he testified that the cocaine he brought into the US came from Norwin Meneses's ranch in Costa Rica. His testimony at the trial was limited, because the judge would not allow the defense to explore the CIA's role in any detail. In a subsequent interview recorded for a British TV documentary, Cabezas said that the CIA was aware of, and in fact had supervised, a crucial phase of his drug-trafficking operation. "It wasn't until the second trip that I had to go to Costa Rica," Cabezas said, "when I met this guy [Ivan Gomez] that's supposed to be the CIA agent. They told me who he was and the reason he was there, it was to make sure that the money was given to the right people and nobody was taking advantage of the situation and nobody was taking profits that they were not supposed to. And that was it. He was making sure that the money goes to the Contra revolution."

Concerns that the drug money might have been diverted to the bank accounts of Contra leaders were not without foundation. Two of Cabezas' colleagues in this Costa Rica/San Francisco cocaine enterprise were Troilo and Ferdinand Sánchez, close relatives of Contra leader Aristides Sánchez. Sánchez was a member of the FDN's directorate. He and his relatives maintained an offshore bank account in the Dutch Antilles, which Oliver North's aide Robert Owen suspected was being refreshed with cash intended for the Contra effort. Owen wrote a memo to

North that he believed that "the CIA is being had." North took no action. Clearly, Reagan's National Security staff knew well that drug money from the Meneses syndicate was supposed to go, with CIA approval, to the Contra war effort, and they were chagrined that the money might have been diverted from that mission.

One of the other leaders of the Frogman operation was Julio Zavala, a brother-in-law of Cabezas. After his arrest, FBI agents seized $36,800 in cash from Zavala, which the government considered to be drug money and therefore subject to seizure. Zavala claimed that the money was cash meant to buy weapons for the Contras. His attorney, Judd Iverson, submitted letters to the court from two Contra leaders backing up Zavala's story. US District Attorney Joseph P. Russoniello, who had also been urged by the CIA to return the money, stipulated in a court filing on October 2, 1984 that the money would be given back. In 1987 this deal came to the attention of Jack Blum, investigator for Senator John Kerry's committee probing the stories of Contra drug running. Blum and Kerry called Russoniello to ask about the case. "We had a telephone conversation with Mr. Russoniello," Blum recalled during his testimony before the Senate Intelligence Committee on October 23, 1996, "and he shouted at us. He shouted at Senator John Kerry, who chaired the committee. He accused us of being subversives for wanting to get into it."

So Zavala got his money back, though he did spend some time in prison. Norwin Meneses, the kingpin of the operation, was never indicted or arrested for his part in the Frogman case. Witnesses testified before Kerry's committee in 1988 that Meneses had been tipped off about the planned arrest "by his sources in US law enforcement." Another witness said he believed that Meneses was working "as an FBI informant" at the time of the arrest.

In fact, the US government did not indict Norwin Meneses until 1989, after the end of the Contra war, and the indictment was for conspiracy to sell precisely 1 kilo of cocaine in 1984. By then Meneses, sensing his veil of protection might have worn thin, had left San Francisco for his ranch in Costa Rica. No attempt was made to secure Meneses's arrest or to persuade the Costa Rican government to extradite him. The indictment wasn't made public and was kept under seal in San Francisco at the request of the federal government. Interestingly enough,

1984 – the year for which the US government chose to charge Meneses with dealing in cocaine – was the very year in which he had been most conspicuous as a big figure in the Nicaraguan émigré movement supporting the Contras. During that year Meneses had been entertaining Contra leaders, hosting Contra fundraising dinners and having his photograph taken with Adolfo Calero.

Webb uncovered evidence that even Contra supporters in San Francisco were uncomfortable about the source of Meneses's disbursements in the Contra cause. The *Mercury News* series included an interview with, Dennis Ainsworth, a former Cal State/Hayward economics professor who was a well-connected Reagan Republican and active in the Contra cause. In 1985 he was told by Renato Peña, an FDN leader in San Francisco, "that the FDN is involved in drug smuggling with the aid of Norwin Meneses who also buys arms for Enrique Bermúdez, a leader of the FDN." Ainsworth finally told his friends in the Reagan administration about Meneses, and asked what they knew about the Nicaraguan. He was told that the DEA had a drug file on Meneses "two feet thick." Ainsworth gave a detailed interview to the FBI on February 27, 1987, a severely edited version of which had recently been declassified by the US National Archives. In this interview, Ainsworth not only backed the contention that Meneses was using drug profits to buy weapons for the Contras, but also gave details of how US Customs and DEA agents trying to investigate Meneses "felt threatened and intimidated by National Security interference in legitimate narcotics smuggling investigations."

Norwin Meneses was finally arrested in 1990, when Nicaraguan authorities caught him trying to transport 750 kilos of cocaine. Reporters in Managua soon unearthed the sealed San Francisco indictment. The Nicaraguan police and the Nicaraguan judge presiding over Meneses's trial expressed outrage that the United States had known about the drug lord's activities for fifteen years, but had never arrested him. "We always felt there was an unanswered question," recalled René Vita, a former narcotics investigator, to the British TV documentary crew. "How was it that this man, who was known to be involved in drug-related activities, moved so freely around Central America, the US and Mexico?"

Meneses had been turned in to the Nicaraguan police by his long-time associate Enrique Miranda, a former intelligence officer in Somoza's National Guard, who had been Meneses's link to the Bogotà cocaine cartel in Colombia. Miranda testified that from 1981 through 1985 Meneses transported his cocaine out of Colombia through the services of Marcos Aguado, a Nicaraguan who had become a senior officer in the Salvadoran air force. Aguado was a contract pilot for the US "humanitarian aid" flights to the Contras, based at Ilopango airbase in San Salvador. The overseer for such operations at this airport was a career CIA officer, Félix Rodríguez. Miranda testified that Aguado flew Salvadoran air force planes to Colombia to pick up cocaine shipments and delivered them to US Air Force bases in Texas. On the basis of Miranda's testimony, Norwin Meneses was sentenced by the Nicaraguan court to thirty years in prison.

Danilo Blandón enjoyed good fortune as far as any intrusion by law enforcement into his affairs was concerned. All the way through the first half of the 1980s, the prime wholesaler of cocaine to Los Angeles was not once raided or inconvenienced in any way by any authorities. The Boland amendment barring aid to the Contras was lifted on October 17, 1986. On October 27, 1986, warrants were issued by the FBI, IRS and Los Angeles County Sheriff's office for the arrest of Blandón and his wife. The arrest warrants from the LA Sheriff's office included an affidavit from Sergeant Tom Gordon, charging that "Danilo Blandón is in charge of a sophisticated cocaine smuggling and distribution organization operating in southern California. The moneys gained from the sales of cocaine are transported to Florida and laundered through Orlando Murillo who is a high-ranking officer of a chain of banks in Florida named Government Securities Corporation. From this bank the moneys are filtered to the Contra rebels to buy arms in the war in Nicaragua." Orlando Murillo was a cousin of Blandón's wife, Chepita. Police raided twelve warehouses suspected of being used by Blandón. No drugs were found. The police were convinced that Blandón had received a tip-off about the impending raids and had cleaned up.

One of the targets in those early morning raids on October 27 was the Mission Viejo home of Ronald Lister, the former Laguna Beach police detective who had been the arms supplier to the Blandón ring. Lister opened the door wearing his bathrobe, and sheriff's deputies flooded in. Lister became belligerent and told the deputies they were "making a big mistake." He informed the police that he didn't deal drugs, but that he did do a lot of business in Latin America for the US government, and that his friends in the government weren't going to be happy about the deputies ransacking his house.

Then Lister picked up the phone and said he was calling his friend "Scott Weekly of the CIA." The cops continued in the search, and though they found no cocaine, they did turn up an amazing cache of weapons, military manuals and training videotapes. Even though Lister escaped arrest, the police seized boxes of military material. Again, the police were convinced that someone had tipped Lister to the impending raid. These suspicions magnified when, less than a week later, all of the evidence carted from Lister's house mysteriously disappeared from the Sheriff's Department's property room.

The Lister investigation went nowhere for ten years. Then Gary Webb came across Lister's name and details of his ties to Blandón and Rick Ross. Webb asked the LA Sheriff's office for information on their raid of Lister's house. The Sheriff's Department denied there had ever been any such raid, and also denied that the department had been involved in the 1986 investigation into the Blandón drug ring. The documents regarding the raid on Lister's house surfaced only after Rep. Maxine Waters paid a surprise visit to the LA Sheriff's office in September 1996, in the aftermath of the Webb series. The Sheriff's Department handed over to Waters a partial inventory of what had been seized from Lister's house. It included films of military operations in Central America, technical manuals, information on assorted military hardware and communications, and numerous documents indicating that drug money was being used to buy military equipment for US-backed troops in Central America. There were also pictures of Lister with the Contras in El Salvador, featuring equipment and military bases, and the names and addresses of CIA officers and CIA contractors in Central America.

Even with these documents the *Los Angeles Times* did not advance the Lister part of the story in the wake of the *Mercury News* series. The sole mission of the *Times* was to destroy Webb. However, reporter Nick Schou of the *Orange County Weekly* discovered that Lister's company,

Pyramid International Security Consultants, had been a contractor with the CIA, helping funnel weapons from El Salvador to Contra bases in Honduras.

One of Lister's partners in this operation was Timothy LaFrance, a weapons manufacturer based in San Diego. Lister and LaFrance, the latter told Schou, built a munitions plant for the CIA in San Salvador. Schou also quoted from Lister's notes describing his relationship to Scott Weekly, who was at various times a contractor with the Defense Intelligence Agency and the CIA, and with a man named Bill Nelson. Back in the 1980s, Nelson, now dead, was the executive vice president for security for the Fluor Corporation, which is based in Orange County. More intriguingly, Nelson had worked for the CIA from 1948 to 1976. He was chief of covert operations in the early 1970s, then resigned from the Agency after coming under congressional criticism for his role in CIA operations in Chile and Angola.

Also part of Lister's arms supply network was a man called Richard Wilker, whom LaFrance described to Schou as another former CIA officer and later contractor for the Agency. "The whole idea was to set up an operation in El Salvador that would allow us to get around US laws and supply the contras with guns," LaFrance said. "The smart way to do this was to find a military base. It's much easier to just build the weapons down there." LaFrance said he'd gone to El Salvador with "two giant boxes full of machine guns and ammunition." Quartered with the Atlacatl Battalion, one of the US-trained Salvadoran units, they set up their operation at a military depot in downtown San Salvador. An October 1982 contract for this work was found in Lister's files. It showed that Lister's contact in El Salvador was Defense Minister General José Guillermo García. (Guillermo García has been linked to numerous atrocities, including the El Mozote massacre during which the Atlacatl Battalion killed over 1,000 Salvadoran peasants.)

By the end of 1986, there was no longer any need for the services of people like Lister, LaFrance and Blandón. This had certainly become apparent to Blandón. Webb was able to get a copy of an FBI teletype recording a conversation in which one party was Blandón's lawyer, Brad Brunon. The teletype reads, "CIA winked at this sort of thing … Brunon indicated that now that US Congress had voted funds for Nicaraguan Contra movement US Government now appears to be turning against organizations like this."

In 1986 Blandón left Los Angeles and with over a million dollars in cash moved to Miami, where he started a restaurant and a car dealership. Within two years Blandón's business enterprises in Miami were failing, and he and his wife moved back to California and attempted to rebuild their cocaine empire. In 1990 an undercover DEA agent taped a conversation between Blandón and another drug dealer in which Blandón described his relationship with Rick Ross: "I've sold them about two thousand to four thousand kilos. These are black people, the people that control LA." Over the next sixteen months Blandón sold 425 kilos of cocaine, worth about $10.5 million. By now Ross was sitting in an Ohio prison, serving a ten-year sentence for drug trafficking after he had relocated to Cincinnati. In 1991, the DEA arrested Blandón and his wife for cocaine trafficking. During the trial, Assistant US District Attorney L. J. O'Neale described Blandón as "the biggest Nicaraguan cocaine dealer." The US Probation Office recommended a sentence of life in prison and a $4 million fine. On May 2, 1992 Blandón was sentenced to only four years in prison. This indulgence was compounded in 1993, when O'Neale filed a motion with the court stating that Blandón had agreed to become an informant for the Department of Justice and the DEA. In exchange for his cooperation, O'Neale requested that Blandón's sentence be reduced to time served and that he be released without parole or fine. The court approved the request and Blandón was freed from prison on September 19, 1994. He had served only twenty-eight months, and had spent almost that entire spell briefing the DEA and the Department of Justice and appearing as a government witness in trials such as that of Rafael Corñejo. The stage for the final denouncement of the LA ring was set.

In the spring of 1995, the DEA approached Blandón about setting up a sting operation that would snare his former client Rick Ross. The operation was planned while Ross was awaiting early release from his Ohio prison. He had won reduced time by testifying about corruption in the Los Angeles Sheriff's Department. Ross returned to Los Angeles and was contacted by Blandón, who asked him if he wanted to start buying cocaine from him again. Ross said no; he wanted to stay clean.

Blandón pressed Ross to give him names of other potential buyers, pleading he was desperate for cash. Ross agreed to see Blandón at a mall in San Diego on March 2. When Ross approached Blandón's van, he found himself surrounded by law enforcement officers. He made a run for it, crashed his light truck into a hedge, and was arrested.

Ross was charged with conspiracy to purchase cocaine with the intent to distribute and convicted on the testimony of Blandón, and finally sentenced to life without the possibility of parole. Blandón received at least $166,000 for his services as a DEA agent and returned to postrevolutionary Nicaragua, where he now commands a profitable timber export business.

The man who pieced this saga together, Gary Webb, looks a straight-arrow type, like many other reporters who cut their teeth in the Midwest. He grew up on the road, the son of a marine. "We were straight-up pro–Marine Corps," Webb remembers. "My brother and I were brought up to despise hippies."

In 1978 he got a job at the *Kentucky Post*. There Webb was broken in as a reporter by Gene Goltz, a Pulitzer Prize–winning investigative reporter near the end of a long career. After five years at the *Kentucky Post*, Webb was hired as an investigative reporter by the *Cleveland Plain Dealer* in 1983, writing stories on state politics and union corruption. Then in 1988 he went to work at the *San Jose Mercury News*. Again Webb was assigned to statewide investigations covering corruption in California state government.

In 1995 Webb wrote a series of articles on drug forfeiture laws. It was this story that led him to the whole CIA/crack/Contra nexus. "I'd written a story about a drug forfeiture case, a big important case that was going to throw out the Justice Department's assets forfeiture program," Webb remembers. The case had been filed by a jailhouse lawyer named Michael Montalbo who turned out to have found the Achilles heel in the law. The case had the potential to overturn all the forfeitures that had taken place since 1991. "I thought this was an amazing story," Webb recalls, "that this guy was in jail serving life without parole for cocaine trafficking. I went to Lompoc Prison to interview him and wrote the story."

After the story on Montalbo appeared in the *Mercury News*, Webb got a call from a woman in Oakland. She told the reporter that she had been intrigued by his story. She said she had called Montalbo to ask him about Webb, and the drug dealer had told her that Webb was trustworthy. The woman told Webb that he might be interested in the case of her boyfriend, Rafael Corñejo. Corñejo had been arrested for drug trafficking in 1992, and he had been sitting in jail for three years without a trial. The woman was convinced that Corñejo's case would never come to trial because he worked for a man who was tied to the CIA and the Nicaraguan Contras. That man was named Norwin Meneses.

"This was the first time I heard the name Meneses," Webb recalls. "She said the only person that had been let out of jail in this drug ring had been the percussion player for the rock group Santana, who was apparently another Nicaraguan."

Corñejo's girlfriend, Coral, told Webb that she had some damaging information against the chief witness against Corñejo, a Nicaraguan named Oscar Danilo Blandón. The information suggested that Blandón was associated with the CIA and that he had been smuggling cocaine for the Contras. Coral said the allegations about Blandón's ties to the CIA were contained in federal grand jury transcripts.

"I don't know how she got these things," Webb says. "I've been doing this type of work for nineteen years and I've only seen federal grand jury transcripts once in my life." The government had accidentally turned over the transcripts, Drug Enforcement Agency reports, FBI documents and other information on Blandón's CIA ties as part of the discovery process.

"Somebody fucked up somewhere," Webb says. "But when I saw those documents, I thought, this is a different story. We're not doing a story about some poor guy in jail with his property taken away. We're doing a story about some CIA-connected drug dealer." Webb took the story idea to his editor, Dawn Garcia, who ran the state desk at the *Mercury News*. She encouraged Webb to pursue the story.

Webb went back to the material unearthed about Blandón in the Corñejo case. In the documents, Blandón had testified that he had been running drugs for the Contras and that he was told by the CIA at one point they didn't need any more drug money because Congress had just appropriated new funds for the Contras. It was then, Blandón said, that he went into the drug business for himself.

"The thing that struck me about Blandón was that he was appearing as a government witness," Webb said. "He was not there to do anything but to give testimony as a DEA informant about the history of the Meneses family. What made it believable to me was that he wasn't there trying to beat a rap. He was there as a cooperating witness for the government."

Webb asked Coral what she knew about the Nicaraguan drug dealers and their backgrounds. Coral said she had grown up with and dated many of them. She told Webb that the man he really needed to be looking at was Norwin Meneses. Her boyfriend worked for Meneses. So did Danilo Blandón. "Meneses was the big man of the drug ring," Coral told Webb. So Webb began looking into Meneses's past. He found a story about Meneses's arrest and trial on drug charges in Nicaragua in 1992. Then he came across a long story by Seth Rosenfeld that ran in the *San Francisco Chronicle* in 1986. It described in detail Meneses's connection to the Contra faction based in Honduras.

"I thought, somebody was on this story ten years ago," Webb says. He continued researching the story until December 1995, describing it as a matter of gathering up the loose ends, getting lists of names and finding out all he could about those involved, scouring court records and interviewing police and prosecutors.

By the end of December he went back to Garcia and told her that the story was at the point where he needed to start traveling. He wanted to go to San Diego and to Nicaragua to locate Blandón and Meneses. Garcia and Webb then went to see the *Mercury News*'s managing editor, David Yarnold. They laid the entire story out for him, and Yarnold gave Webb the green light to go to Nicaragua.

Webb didn't speak Spanish, so he called Martha Honey, an investigative journalist with many years of experience in Nicaragua. Honey suggested that Webb team up with Georg Hodel, with whom she had coauthored a book on Central America. Hodel is a Swiss reporter who had covered the Contra War for *Der Spiegel;* he had married a Nicaraguan woman and had stayed on in Nicaragua after the Sandinista defeat. Webb contacted Hodel and outlined the story for him. It turned out that Hodel already had a pretty good background on the situation and was familiar with many of the key players. "Georg knew everybody down in Nicaragua," Webb recalls. "He was great." So Webb went down to Managua and together with Hodel combed through court records and newspaper stories. They also interviewed Meneses. But they were unable to locate the man Webb had gone to Nicaragua to find – Danilo Blandón.

Webb returned to California. His next visit was to San Diego. And here, at last, the elusive Blandón's name popped up in a 1992 court case. "I just started going down the list of attorneys who had represented Blandón and his codefendants," Webb says. "I just started calling them up and asking, 'Have you seen Blandón? Do you know where he is? Have you heard anything from him?'" Webb didn't have much luck. It was as if Blandón had simply disappeared. Then he called a lawyer named Juanita Brooks who had represented Blandón's wife in a drug case. She told Webb that Blandón was scheduled to be in San Diego in a couple of months to testify in a court case involving one of her clients. "Blandón's testifying as a government witness," Brooks told Webb. "He's working for the DEA now." Webb was incredulous. "Are you sure this is the same guy?" "Yeah," Brooks said. "I represented his wife and then he disappeared out of the case and turned up working for the government. Now he's set up one of his old customers in a sting operation."

The man Blandón was taking down was Rick Ross, "Freeway" Rick, the same name Webb had come across during his investigations into the drug forfeiture story. Ross was known as one of California's biggest drug kingpins, a crack lord. When Webb looked at Ross's arrest record he found what seemed to be a typical pattern. Ross had been busted, but had never lost any property. It also appeared to Webb that the big players went free and that the street-corner peddlers and welfare mothers lost everything. At first Webb didn't catch the significance of the connection between Blandón and Ross. Then Brooks filled in the blanks. "Danilo Blandón was one of Ross's biggest suppliers," Brooks said. "He's been supplying Ross for a long time. My impression is that Blandón may have started Ross out in the business."

Unlike Blandón, Ricky Ross was easy to find. He was locked up in the Metropolitan Correctional Center in San Diego awaiting trial. Webb wrote Ross a letter asking the drug dealer for an interview. "Then the weirdest thing happened," Webb says. "I got a call from Jesse Katz at the *Los Angeles Times*. Katz asked me what I wanted to talk to Ross about." It turned out that Katz had written a profile of Ross for the *Los Angeles Times*. In his story Katz had described Ross as the "crack king" of Los Angeles. After the story ran, Ross and Katz kept up a correspondence. When Ross received Webb's letter requesting an interview, he contacted Katz and asked him if Webb was a real reporter and whether he should talk to him.

A few days later Webb went down to San Diego for his first interview of Ross. Webb was surprised to discover that Ross and his lawyers were unaware that Blandón was going to appear as a witness against the crack dealer. The government hadn't given Ross's defense team a list of its witnesses. "When I mentioned it was Blandón," Webb said. "Ross suddenly knew that he'd been set up."

Ross told Webb that when his arrest went down, he was hustled off in one direction and Blandón in the other. As soon as Ross learned that Blandón had been working for the DEA, he opened up. He told Webb everything he knew about the Nicaraguan – how they met, their drug and money relationship, Blandón's associates. "That's when I put two and two together and figured out that this Contra drug ring was selling dope to the Crips and the Bloods," Webb says. "Because Ricky Ross was the biggest gang wholesaler in South Central LA."

Now Webb had a decision to make.

A few weeks later Webb flew to San Diego for a hearing in the Ross case. The hearing was to determine whether Ross's lawyer, Alan Fenster, could question Danilo Blandón about his possible ties to the Central Intelligence Agency. The federal prosecutors had filed a motion with the court to keep the defense from exploring the CIA and Contra issues. Webb was one of the only people in the courtroom when the door opened and in walked Jesse Katz. Katz sat down next to Webb. "Hey, Gary, how you doing?"

"Fine."

"They're going to have a hearing today on that CIA stuff you've been sitting on, right?"

At that moment US Assistant District Attorney L. J. O'Neale got up and looked at Webb and Katz. He conferred with his colleagues and then approached the judge and whispered to her. The judge signaled to Ross's lawyer. "Mr. Fenster, we're going to have this hearing at side-bar," the judge said. "Please approach the bench." For about forty-five minutes the lawyers and the judge debated whether Blandón's relationship with the CIA could be brought into the case. "All this time Katz was going crazy," Webb remembers. "He was straining to hear what they were saying. But it was impossible. Finally he got pissed off and left. He never came back to cover the trial."

Webb stayed in San Diego for the Ross trial and heard Danilo Blandón give his testimony against Freeway Rick. Afterward, Webb was approached by Ross's lawyer, Alan Fenster, who invited him to lunch. The lawyer told Webb that he was at a loss as to how to conduct the cross-examination of Blandón. "The prosecution hasn't told me anything about this Contra stuff," Fenster said. "They haven't said anything about the CIA. I don't know enough to even raise any of this shit in court."

Fenster asked Webb if he knew of any questions he could ask Blandón. Webb didn't miss a beat. "Man, I'd ask him a lot of questions." Webb told Fenster to look at the DEA records and the grand jury transcripts that had been turned over as part of the discovery process in the investigation into the Meneses drug ring in the Bay Area. Fenster immediately reviewed the documents and was able to lead Blandón through a series of questions about his ties to the Contras, his meetings with Col. Enrique Bermúdez and his relationship to Norwin Meneses. "O'Neale, the prosecutor, kept jumping up and objecting to every question," Webb recalls. "But the judge was just sitting there doing her nails or something. She kept saying, 'Overruled, overruled.' Blandón testified how he became involved in the cocaine business. He recounted his meeting with Enrique Bermúdez and how the Contra leader had instructed him to return to the US, begin selling cheap cocaine and cycle the profits back to the Contra effort. Blandón described in some detail the inner workings of his drug ring, where he got the cocaine, how many kilos he sold and how much he sold it for.

Blandón's testimony didn't end up helping Ricky Ross stave off a conviction that left him facing a life sentence. But it did provide Gary Webb with the centerpiece for his story. Here was a government witness who admitted under oath that he had sold cocaine for the Contras and that he had received his instructions from Col. Enrique Bermúdez, a paid agent of the CIA.

After the trial, Webb sat down and wrote his story. By the end of March he had turned in to his editor Dawn Garcia about 25,000 words of prose. Then the editors went to work. "The story went through, it seems like 50,000 rewrites," Webb says. It was shuttled back and forth between Garcia, managing editor Yarnold and the paper's editor-in-chief, Jerry Ceppos. None of them raised any objections to the articles. Nobody came to Webb and said that this was risky stuff he was writing. Certainly the reaction would have been different if the story had come out at the height of the Contra War or even during the 1992 presidential election pitting Bill Clinton against George Bush. Now, Webb thought, perhaps it was safe to write about these issues.

The desire to get everything out is one reason Webb came up with the idea of developing an Internet web site for the series. "I wrote a memo saying this story has a very high unbelievability factor built into it," Webb says. "The best way to protect it is to release other source documents and we can do this easily with hyperlinks on the Net. And management of the paper had been drumming into reporters that they should always think of ways to use the vast resources of the Internet to interface with the reader. They saw the *Mercury News* as Silicon Valley's newspaper." So before the series ran Webb went to talk to the people at Mercury Center, the paper's web site. Access to Mercury Center was a feature of America Online, the nation's largest Internet service. Webb told the Mercury Center people that he wanted to use the web site to display all of the source material he had used for the story – the court transcripts, the DEA and FBI reports, and the grand jury transcripts. They even developed sound chips of Blandón's testimony at Ross's trial. The web site also featured a detailed timeline, photos and bios of the key players in the story and links to government documents, such as the report published by Senator John Kerry after his 1988 hearing on Contra drug running.

Webb's stories finally began appearing on the front page of the *San Jose Mercury News* on August 18, 1996. At first they didn't spark much national interest. Webb got a call from syndicated columnist Norman Solomon, who wrote a complimentary piece about the series, and he was asked to appear on Dennis Bernstein's show on Berkeley's KPFA radio station. The first bigtime reporter to contact Webb was Michael Jackson, host of a popular syndicated talk show on KABC out of Los Angeles. Webb's appearance on Jackson's show was the first time the people of South Central Los Angeles heard the story about the CIA's ties to the crack plague that had ravaged their neighborhoods. "Then all hell broke loose," Webb says. "It was suddenly on radio shows all over the country. When I was on the talk shows I gave out the web site address, so that anybody across the country could read the story. The furor really started when people began reading this for themselves." The Mercury Center web site soon began getting more than 1.3 million hits a day.

The publication of Webb's "Dark Alliance" series came just at the start of the Democratic National Convention. That's one reason the story didn't get as much initial attention as it might have otherwise received. But when Rep. Maxine Waters, who represents South Central Los Angeles, returned to her district, she found that her office had been flooded with calls about the stories. Her constituents were demanding that she investigate the CIA role in the city's crack epidemic. Waters called Webb, who accepted her invitation to address a town meeting in South Central about his story.

So, the first wave of publicity about the "Dark Alliance" stories was extremely favorable. Webb was invited onto the TV talk shows hosted by Jesse Jackson and Montel Williams. And it continued to be a hot topic on radio. Looking back on it, Webb believes that the attack on him was launched just as the story was primed to break out into the mainstream. In late September he had appeared on the *CBS Morning News* with Maxine Waters and was positively received.

Then on September 20 he was invited to appear on a CNN program hosted by Lou Waters. Appearing with Webb that afternoon was Ronald Kessler, author of *Inside the CIA*. Waters opened by asking Webb to describe his story and then pressed him on some of its softer elements, such as how Webb knew the crack money was converted to weapons for the Contras. Webb was in the midst of answering Waters's queries when the CNN transmission from San Francisco broke down.

At that point, Waters said, "OK. We have a little satellite problem there. So let's call on Ronald Kessler, who's in our Washington Bureau.

Perhaps there are no satellite problems there. Are you buying this?"

Kessler, who has a reputation as a liberal investigative reporter, leaped into a denunciation of Webb that would prefigure the attacks to come, claiming that Webb had "no evidence" to back up his story.

Webb, now relinked, responded fiercely. "He says there was no documentation. We posted it all on the Internet. We've got declassified FBI reports; we've got DEA reports. The thing to bear in mind is that there are no facts in dispute. Danilo Blandón admits selling cocaine for the Contras. Freeway Rick Ross admits buying it and turning it into crack and selling it to the gangs. We have pictures of Meneses meeting with Adolfo Calero. And we have testimony that they met with Enrique Bermúdez, who are the top CIA officials running the Contras. So to claim there's no documentation is idiotic."

Then Kessler quickly shifted the angle of his attack, stating that "there's no evidence to begin with to show that there's any reason to go into CIA involvement."

"That's absolutely, flatly untrue," Webb said. "I mean clearly the guy hasn't looked at the documents. We've got a 1986 FBI report. We've got a sworn statement that was filed in Los Angeles by a detective who was investigating Blandón in 1986. So this isn't a convicted drug dealer. This is a cop saying it; this is the guy's own attorney saying it. And this is a guy admitting it under oath."

"Admitting what?" Kessler prodded. "Admitting what? What's the connection with the CIA?"

"Admitting the CIA ran the operation," Webb replied. "Blandón said that before a federal grand jury. He testified in San Diego that he met with Enrique Bermúdez to discuss this, and Enrique Bermúdez clearly was on the CIA payroll."

Webb may have won that skirmish. But the battle was just beginning.

Sources

This chapter is largely based on three sources: the "Dark Alliance" stories by Gary Webb and his colleagues at the *San Jose Mercury News*, Pete Carey, Pamela Kramer, and Thomas Farragher; an extensive interview by the authors with Webb and off-the-record interviews with several of his editors and fellow reporters at the *Merc;* and stories by Nick Schou, a fine investigative reporter at the *Orange County Weekly.* Schou was also extremely generous in sharing information he had excavated on the arms operation of Ronald Lister and Tim LaFrance. Other sources for this chapter were the several legal cases involving Ross, Danilo Blandón and other Nicaraguan exiles. The source for the Ricky Ross trial in San Diego, which includes the testimony of Danilo Blandón, is *United States* v. *James.* Also useful was Blandón's testimony before a federal grand jury investigating the Meneses drug ring and the transcripts and motions from the trial of Julio Zavala.

Associated Press. "Ex-Contras Say CIA Cleared Planes, Cash From Narcotics Suspect." *San Jose Mercury News,* Oct. 31, 1996.

Bernstein, Dennis, and Robert Knight. "Federal Court Cases Offer Plenty of Leads on CIA–Contra Drug Trafficking." *Pacific News Service,* Nov. 15, 1996.

Blum, Jack. "Former Senate Special Counsel Discusses Controversy." *Baltimore Sun,* Oct. 23, 1996.

Carey, Pete. "'Dark Alliance' Series Takes On a Life of Its Own." *San Jose Mercury News,* Oct. 13, 1996.

Diamond, John. "CIA Promises Independent Probe of Drug Link." *San Jose Mercury News,* Sept. 20, 1996.

Early, David. "MN Series Stirs National Debate." *San Jose Mercury News,* Oct. 6, 1996.

Farragher, Thomas. "Capital Hill Probes of Alleged CIA–Crack Link Begin." *San Jose Mercury News,* Oct. 24, 1996.

Kramer, Pamela, and Pete Carey. "Results Released from Los Angeles Sheriff's Investigation." *San Jose Mercury News,* Dec. 11, 1996.

Kramer, Pamela. "Cheers, Jeers at 'Crack' Inquiry." *San Jose Mercury News,* Oct. 20, 1996.

——. "CIA Chief Braves South-Central's Anger." *San Jose Mercury News,* Nov. 16, 1996.

Kramer, Pamela, and Gary Webb. "No Proof of CIA–Drug Link, Sheriff Says." *San Jose Mercury News,* Oct. 8, 1996.

Los Angeles Sheriff's Office. "Report on Nov. 19, 1996 Interview with L. J. O'Neale."

Los Angeles Times, staff report. "CIA Says It Finds No Link to Nicaraguan Cocaine Ring in Its Records." *Los Angeles Times,* Nov. 6, 1996.

New York Times, editorial. "The CIA and Drugs." *New York Times,* Nov. 5, 1996.

Perry, Tony. "Ross Gets Life; His Case Fueled CIA Crack Furor." *Los Angeles Times,* Nov. 20, 1996.

San Jose Mercury News, editorial. "Another CIA Disgrace: Helping the Crack Flow." *San Jose Mercury News,* August 21, 1996.

Schou, Nick. "Secret Agent Men." *Orange County Weekly,* Nov. 5, 1997.

——. "Who Is Ron Lister?" *LA Weekly,* Nov. 22, 1996.

——. "New Dope on the Contra–Crack Connection: Mystery Man Lister Had Ties to US Intelligence, as Did His Partners." *LA Weekly,* Dec. 20, 1996.

——. "Tracks in the Snow." *LA Weekly,* May 22, 1997.

United States District Court, Northern District of California. "Grand Jury Testimony of Danilo Blandón." Federal Grand Jury Investigation 9301035. Feb. 3, 1994.

United States District Court, Northern District of California. *United States* v. *Julio Zavala, et al.* No. 83-CR-0154.

United States District Court, Southern District of California. "Testimony of Danilo Blandón." *United States of America* v. *Curtis James, Ricky Ross, Michael Ross.* Case No. 95-0353-H-Crim. March 6 and 7, 1996.

——. "Motion in Limine to Preclude Reference to the Central Intelligence Agency and for Reciprocal Discovery." *United States of America* v. *Curtis James, Ricky Ross, Michael Ross.* March 4, 1996.

Webb, Gary. "America's 'Crack' Plague Has Roots in Nicaraguan War." *San Jose Mercury News,* August 18, 1996.

——. "Testimony Links US to Drugs-Guns Trade." *San Jose Mercury News,* August 18, 1996.

——. "Shadowy Origins of 'Crack' Epidemic." *San Jose Mercury News,* August 19, 1996.

——. "Drug Agent Thought She Was on to Something Big." *San Jose Mercury News,* August 19, 1996.

——. "Drug Expert: 'Crack' Born in SF Bay Area in '74." *San Jose Mercury News,* August 19, 1996.

——. "War on Drugs Has Unequal Impact on Black Americans." *San Jose Mercury News,* August 20, 1996.

——. "SF Bay Area Man Tangled in Drug Web." *San Jose Mercury News,* August 20, 1996.

——. "'Dark Alliance' Series Leads to CIA Probe." *San Jose Mercury News,* Sept. 6, 1996.

——. "Dealer's Sentencing Postponed; Lawyer Gets Time to Seek Documents on Alleged CIA-Crack Link." *San Jose Mercury News,* Sept. 14, 1996.

——. "Legendary Drug Dealer Gets Life." *San Jose Mercury News,* Nov. 20, 1996.

——. "US Gave Visa to Nicaraguan Drug Trafficker." *San Jose Mercury News,* Dec. 31, 1996.

Webb, Gary, and Pamela Kramer. "Black Groups Seek Probe of CIA Drug Links." *San Jose Mercury News,* August 24, 1996.

——. "Gag Order Concealed Possible Drug Link." *San Jose Mercury News,* Sept. 29, 1996.

——. "Affidavit: Cops Knew of Drug Ring." *San Jose Mercury News,* Oct. 3, 1996.

——. "Drug Raid Documents Reveal Allegations of CIA Involvement." *San Jose Mercury News,* Oct. 6, 1996.

Webb, Gary, and Thomas Farragher. "Ex-Contras: We Saw No CIA Link to Drugs." *San Jose Mercury News,* Nov. 27, 1996.

2

Counterattack

The attack on Gary Webb and his series in the *San Jose Mercury News* remains one of the most venomous and factually inane assaults on a professional journalist's competence in living memory. In the mainstream press he found virtually no defenders, and those who dared stand up for him themselves became the object of virulent abuse and misrepresentation. L. J. O'Neale, the prosecutor for the Justice Department who was Danilo Blandón's patron and Rick Ross's prosecutor, initially formulated the polemical program against him. When one looks back on the assault in the calm of hindsight, what is astounding is the way Webb's foes in the press mechanically reiterated those attacks.

There was a disturbing racist thread underlying the attacks on Webb's series, and on those who took his findings seriously. It's clear, looking through the onslaughts on Webb in the *Los Angeles Times,* the *Washington Post,* and the *New York Times,* that the reaction in black communities to the series was extremely disturbing to elite opinion. This was an eruption of outrage, an insurgency not just of very poor people in South Central and kindred areas, but of almost all blacks and many whites as well. In the counterattacks, one gets the sense that a kind of pacification program was in progress. Karen De Young, an assistant editor at the *Washington Post,* evoked just such an impulse when Alicia Shepard of the *American Journalism Review* interviewed her. "I looked at [the *Mercury News* series] when it initially came out and decided it was something we needed to follow up on. When it became an issue in the black community and on talk shows, that seemed to be a different phenomenon." Remember too that the O. J. Simpson jury decision had also been deeply disturbing to white opinion. In that case, blacks had rallied around a man most whites believed to be a vicious killer, and there was a "white opinion riot" in response. Now blacks were mustering in support of a story charging that their profoundest suspicions of white malfeasance were true. So in the counterattack there were constant, patronizing references to "black paranoia," decorously salted with the occasional concession that there was evidence from the past to support the notion that such paranoia might have some sound foundation.

Another factor lent a particular edge to the onslaughts. This was the first occasion on which the established press had to face the changing circumstances of the news business, in terms of registering mass opinion and allowing popular access. Webb's series coincided with the coming of age of the Internet. The *Miami Herald,* another Knight-Ridder paper in the same corporate family as the *Mercury News,* had been forced to change editorial course in the mid-1980s by the vociferous, highly conservative Cuban American presence in Miami. The *Herald* chose not to reprint Webb's series. However, this didn't prevent anyone in south Florida from finding the entire series on the Internet, along with all the supporting documents.

The word "pacification" is not inappropriate to describe the responses to Webb's story. Back in the 1980s, allegations about Contra drug running, also backed by documentary evidence, could be ignored with impunity. Given the Internet and black radio reaction, in the mid-1990s this was no longer possible, and the established organs of public opinion had to launch the fiercest of attacks on Webb and on his employer. This was a campaign of extermination: the aim was to destroy Webb and to force the *Mercury News* into backing away from the story's central premise. At the same time, these media manipulators attempted to minimize the impact of Webb's story on the black community.

Another important point in the politics of this campaign is that Webb's fiercest assailants were not on the right. They were mainstream liberals, such as Walter Pincus and Richard Cohen of the *Washington Post* and David Corn of the *Nation,* There has always been a certain conservative suspicion of the CIA, even if conservatives – outside the libertarian wing – heartily applaud the Agency's imperial role. The CIA's most effective friends have always been the liberal center, on the editorial pages of the *Washington Post* and the *New York Times* and in the endorsement of a person like the *Washington Post*'s president, Katharine Graham. In 1988 Graham had told CIA recruits, "We live in a dirty and dangerous world. There are some things the general public does not need to know, and shouldn't. I believe democracy flourishes when the government can take legitimate steps to keep its secrets and when the press can decide whether to print what it knows."

By mid-September of 1996 the energy waves created by Webb's series were approaching critical mass and beginning to become an unavoidable part of the national news agenda. For example, *NBC Dateline,* a prime-time news show, had shot interviews with Webb and Rick Ross and had sent a team down to Nicaragua, where they filmed an interview with Norwin Meneses and other figures in the saga. Webb tells of a conversation with one of the *Dateline* producers, who asked him, "Why hasn't this shit been on TV before?" "You tell me," Webb answered. "You're the TV man."

A couple of weeks after this exchange, the program was telling Webb that it didn't look as though they would be going forward with the story after all. In the intervening weeks, the counterattack had been launched, and throughout the networks the mood had abruptly shifted. On November 15, NBC's Andrea Mitchell (partner of Federal Reserve chairman Alan Greenspan, about as snugly ensconced a member of the Washington elite as you could hope to find) was saying on *NBC News in Depth* that Webb's story "was a conspiracy theory" that had been "spread by talk radio."

The storm clouds began to gather with the CNN-brokered exchange between Webb and Ron Kessler. Kessler had had his own dealings with the Agency. In 1992 he had published *Inside the CIA,* a highly anecdotal and relatively sympathetic book about the Agency, entirely devoid of the sharp critical edge that had characterized Kessler's *The FBI.* A couple of CIA memos written in 1991 and 1992 record the Agency's view of the experience of working with Kessler and other reporters.

The 1991 CIA note discusses Kessler's request for information and brags that a close relationship had been formed with Kessler, "which helped turn some 'intelligence failure' stories into 'intelligence success' stories." Of course this could have been merely self-serving fluff by an Agency officer, but it is certainly true that Kessler was far from hard on the Agency. That same CIA memo goes on to explain that the Agency maintains "relationships with reporters from every major wire service, newspaper, news weekly and TV network." The memo continues, "In many instances we have persuaded reporters to postpone, change, hold or even scrap stories that could have adversely affected national security interests or jeopardized sources or methods."

The next attack on Webb came from another long-time friend of the Agency, Arnaud de Borchgrave. De Borchgrave had worked for *Newsweek* as a columnist for many years and made no secret of the fact that he regarded many of his colleagues as KGB dupes. He himself boasted of intimate relations with French, British and US intelligence agencies and was violently right-wing in his views. In recent years he has written for the sprightly *Washington Times,* a conservative paper owned by the Rev. Sun Myung Moon.

The thrust of de Borchgrave's attack, which appeared in the *Washington Times* on September 24, 1996, was that Webb's basic thesis was wrong, because the Contras had been rolling in CIA money. Like almost all other critics, de Borchgrave made no effort to deal with the plentiful documents, such as federal grand jury transcripts, that Webb had secured and that were available on the *Mercury News* website. Indeed, some of the most experienced reporters in Washington displayed, amid their criticisms, a marked aversion to studying such source documents. De Borchgrave did remark that when all the investigations were done, the most that would emerge would be that a couple of CIA officers might have been lining their own pockets.

That same September 24, 1996, a more insidious assault came in the form of an interview of Webb by Christopher Matthews on the CNBC cable station. There are some ironies here. Matthews had once worked for Speaker of the House Tip O'Neill. O'Neill had been sympathetic to the amendment against Contra funding offered by his Massachusetts colleague, Edward Boland. On the other hand, O'Neill had swiftly reacted to a firestorm of outrage about cocaine after the death of the Celtics' draftee Len Bias, a star basketball player at the University of Maryland. At that time, he rushed through the House some appalling "War on Drugs" legislation whose dire effects are still with us today.

Matthews left O'Neill's office with a carefully calculated career plan to market himself as a syndicated columnist and telepundit. Positioning himself as a right-of-center liberal, Matthews habitually eschewed fact for opinion, and is regarded by many op-ed editors as a self-serving blowhard with an exceptionally keen eye for the main chance. Clearly sensing where the wind was blowing, Matthews used his show to launch a fierce attack on Webb. First, he badgered the reporter for supposedly producing no evidence of "the direct involvement of American CIA officers." "Who said anything about American CIA agents?" Webb responded. "That's the most ethnocentric viewpoint I've ever seen in my life. The CIA used foreign nationals all the time. In this operation they were using Nicaraguan exiles."

Matthews had clearly prepped himself with de Borchgrave's article that morning. His next challenge to Webb was on whether or not the Contras needed drug money. Matthews's research assistants had prepared a timeline purporting to show that the Contras were flush with cash during the period when Webb's stories said they were desperate for money from any source.

But Webb, who had lived the chronology for eighteen months, stood his ground. He patiently expounded to Matthews's audience how Meneses and Blandón's drugs-for-guns operation was at its peak during the period when Congress had first restricted, then later totally cut off US funding to the Contra army based in Honduras. Webb told Matthews, "When the CIA funding was restored, all these guys got busted." After the interview, Webb says Matthews stormed off the set, berating his staff, "This is outrageous. I've been sabotaged."

The tempo now began to pick up. On October 1, Webb got a call in San Diego from Howard Kurtz, the *Washington Post* media reporter. "Kurtz called me," Webb remembers, "and after a few innocuous questions I thought that was that." It wasn't. Kurtz's critique came out on October 2 and became a paradigm for many of the assaults that followed. The method was simplicity itself: a series of straw men swiftly raised up, and as swiftly demolished. Kurtz opened by describing how blacks, liberal politicians and "some" journalists "have been trumpeting a *Mercury News* story that they say links the CIA to drug trafficking in the United States." Kurtz told how Webb's story had become "a hot topic," through the unreliable mediums of the Internet and black talk radio. "There's just one problem," Kurtz went on. "The series doesn't actually say the CIA knew about the drug trafficking." To buttress this claim, Kurtz then wrote that Webb had "admitted" as much in their brief chat with the statement, "We'd never pretended otherwise. This doesn't prove the CIA targeted black people. It doesn't say this was ordered by the CIA. Essentially, our trail stopped at the door of the CIA. They wouldn't return my phone calls."

What Webb had done in the series was show in great detail how a Contra funding crisis had engendered enormous sales of crack in South Central, how the wholesalers of that cocaine were protected from prosecution until the funding crisis ended, and how these same wholesalers were never locked away in prison, but were hired as informants by federal prosecutors. It could be argued that Webb's case is often circumstantial, but prosecutions on this same amount of circumstantial evidence have seen people put away on life sentences. Webb was telling the truth on another point as well: the CIA did not return his phone calls. And unlike Kurtz's colleagues at the *Washington Post* or *New York Times* reporter Tim Golden, who offered twenty-four off-the-record interviews in his attack, Webb refused to run quotes from officials without attribution. In fact, Webb did have a CIA source. "He told me," Webb remembers, "he knew who these guys were and he knew they were cocaine dealers. But he wouldn't go on the record so I didn't use his stuff in the story. I mean, one of the criticisms is we didn't include CIA comments in [the] story. And the reason we didn't is because they wouldn't return my phone calls and they denied my Freedom of Information Act requests."

But suppose the CIA had returned Webb's calls? What would a spokesperson have said, other than that Webb's allegations were outrageous and untrue? The CIA is a government entity pledged to secrecy about its activities. On scores of occasions, it has remained deceptive when under subpoena before a government committee. Why should the Agency be expected to answer frankly a bothersome question from a reporter? Yet it became a fetish for Webb's assailants to repeat, time after time, that the CIA denied his charges and that he had never given this denial as the Agency's point of view.

The CIA is not a kindergarten. The Agency has been responsible for many horrible deeds, including killings. Yet journalists kept treating it as though it was some above-board body, like the US Supreme Court. Many of the attackers assumed that Webb had been somehow derelict in not unearthing a signed order from William Casey mandating Agency officers to instruct Enrique Bermúdez to arrange with Norwin Meneses and Danilo Blandón to sell "x kilos of cocaine." This is an old tactic, known as "the hunt for the smoking gun." But of course, such a direct order would never be found by a journalist. Even when there is a clearly smoking gun, like the references to cocaine paste in Oliver North's notebooks, the gun rarely shows up in the news stories. North's notebooks were released to the public in the early 1990s. There for all to see was an entry on July 9, 1984, describing a conversation with CIA man Dewey Clarridge: "Wanted aircraft to go to Bolivia to pick up paste." Another entry on the same day stated, "Want aircraft to pick up 1,500 kilos."

"In Bolivia they have only one kind of paste," says former DEA agent Michael Levine, who spent more than a decade tracking down drug smugglers in Mexico, Southeast Asia and Bolivia. "That's cocaine paste. We have a guy working for the NSC talking to a CIA agent about a phone call to Adolfo Calero. In this phone call they discuss picking up cocaine paste from Bolivia and wanting an aircraft to pick up 1,500 kilos." None of Webb's attackers mentioned these diary entries.

A sort of manic literalism permeated the attacks modeled on Kurtz's chop job. For instance, critics repeatedly returned to Webb's implied accusation that the CIA had targeted blacks. As we have noted, Webb didn't actually say this, but merely described the sequence which had led to blacks being targeted by the wholesaler. However, we shall see that there have been many instances where the CIA, along with other government bodies, has targeted blacks quite explicitly – in testing the toxicity of disease organisms, or the effects of radiation and mind-altering drugs. Yet Webb's critics never went anywhere near the well-established details of such targeting. Instead, they relied on talk about "black paranoia," which liberals kindly suggested could be traced to the black historical experience, and which conservatives more brusquely identified as "black irrationality."

Kurtz lost no time in going after Webb's journalistic ethics and denouncing the *Mercury News* for exploitative marketing of the series. As an arbiter of journalistic morals, Kurtz castigated Webb for referring to the Contras as "the CIA's army," suggesting that Webb used this phrase merely to implicate the Agency. This charge recurs endlessly in the onslaughts on Webb, and it is by far the silliest. One fact is agreed upon by everyone except a few berserk Maoists-turned-Reaganites, like Robert Leiken of Harvard. That fact is that the Contras were indeed the CIA's army, and that they had been recruited, trained and funded under the Agency's supervision. It's true that in the biggest raids of all – the mining of the Nicaraguan harbors and the raids on the Nicaraguan oil refineries – the Agency used its own men, not trusting its proxies. But for a decade the main Contra force was indeed the CIA's army, and followed its orders obediently.

In attacks on reporters who have overstepped the bounds of political good taste, the assailants will often make an effort to drive a wedge between the reporter and the institution for which the reporter works. For example, when Ray Bonner, working in Central America for the *New York Times,* sent a dispatch saying the unsayable – that US personnel had been present at a torture session – the *Wall Street Journal* and politicians in Washington attacked the *Times* as irresponsible for running such a report. The *Times* did not stand behind Bonner, and allowed his professional credentials to be successfully challenged.

The fissure between Webb and his paper opened when Kurtz elicited a statement from Jerry Ceppos, executive editor of the *Mercury News,* that he was "disturbed that so many people have leaped to the conclusion that the CIA was involved." This apologetic note from Ceppos was not lost on Webb's attackers, who successfully worked to widen the gap between reporter and editor.

Another time-hallowed technique in such demolition jobs is to charge that this is all "old news" – as opposed to that other derided commodity, "ill-founded speculation." Kurtz used the "old news" ploy when he wrote, "The fact that Nicaraguan rebels were involved in drug trafficking has been known for a decade. " Kurtz should have felt some sense of shame in writing these lines, since his own paper had sedulously avoided acquainting its readers with this fact. Kurtz claimed, ludicrously, that "the Reagan Administration acknowledged as much in the 1980s, but subsequent investigations failed to prove that the CIA condoned or even knew about it." This odd sentence raised some intriguing questions. When had the Reagan administration "acknowledged as much"? And if the Reagan administration knew, how could the CIA have remained in ignorance? Recall that in the 1980s, the Reagan administration was referring to the Contras as the "moral equivalent of the Founding Fathers," and accusing the Sandinistas of being drug runners.

Kurtz also slashed at Webb personally, stating that he "appeared conscious of making the news." As illustration, Kurtz quoted a letter that Webb had written to Rick Ross in July 1996 about the timing of the series. Webb told Ross that it would probably be run around the time of his sentencing, in order to "generate as much public interest as possible." As Webb candidly told Ross, this was the way the news business worked. So indeed it does, at the *Washington Post* far more than at the *Mercury News*, as anyone following the *Post*'s promotion of Bob Woodward's books will acknowledge. But Webb is somehow painted as guilty of self-inflation for telling Ross a journalistic fact of life.

On Friday, October 4, the *Washington Post* went to town on Webb and on the *Mercury News,* The onslaught carried no less than 5,000 words in five articles. The front page featured a lead article by Roberto Suro and Walter Pincus, headlined "CIA and Crack: Evidence Is Lacking of Contra-Tied Plot." Also on the front page was a piece by Michael Fletcher on black paranoia. The A section carried another piece on an inside page, a profile of Norwin Meneses by Douglas Farah. A brief sidebar by Walter Pincus was titled, "A Long History of Drug Allegations," compressing the entire history of the CIA's involvement with drug production in Southeast Asia – a saga that Al McCoy took 634 pages to chart – into 300 words. Finally, the front page of the *Post*'s Style section that Friday morning contained an article by Donna Britt headlined, "Finding the Truest Truth." Britt's topic was how blacks tell stories to each other and screw things up in the process.

Connections between Walter Pincus and the intelligence sector are long-standing and well-known. From 1955 to 1957, he worked for US Army Counter-Intelligence in Washington, D.C. Pincus himself is a useful source about his first connections with the CIA. In 1968, when the stories about the CIA's penetration of the National Student Association had been broken by the radical magazine *Ramparts,* Pincus wrote a rather solemn expose of himself in the *Washington Post.* In a confessional style, he reported how the Agency had sponsored three trips for him, starting in 1960. He had gone to conferences in Vienna, Accra and New Delhi, acting as a CIA observer. It was clearly an apprenticeship in which – as he well knew – Pincus was being assessed as officer material. He evidently made a good impression, because the CIA asked him to do additional work. Pincus says he declined, though it would be hard to discern from his reporting that he was not, at the least, an Agency asset. The *Washington Times* describes Pincus as a person "who some in the Agency refer to as 'the CIA's house reporter.'"

Since Webb's narrative revolved around the central figures of Blandón and Meneses, Pincus and Suro understandably focused on the Nicaraguans, claiming that they were never important players in Contra circles. To buttress this view, the *Post* writers hauled out the somewhat dubious assertions of Adolfo Calero. As with other CIA denials, one enters a certain zone of unreality here. Journalists were using as a supposedly reliable source someone with a strong motivation to deny that his organization had anything to do with the cocaine trafficking of which it was accused. Pincus and Suro solemnly cited Calero as saying that when he met with Meneses and Blandón, "We had no crystal ball to know who they were or what they were doing." Calero's view was emphasized as reliable, whereas Blandón and Meneses were held to be exaggerating their status in the FDN.

Thus, we have Webb, based on Blandón's sworn testimony as a government witness before a federal grand jury, reporting that FDN leader Colonel Enrique Bermúdez had bestowed on Meneses the title of head of intelligence and security for the FDN in California. On the other hand, we have the self-interested denials to Pincus and Suro of a man who has been denounced to the FBI as "a pathological liar" by a former professor at California State University, Hayward, Dennis Ainsworth.

Just as Kurtz had done, Pincus and Suro homed in on the charge that Webb had behaved unethically. This time the charge was suggesting certain questions that Ross's lawyer, Alan Fenster, could ask Blandón. Webb's retort has always been that it would be hard to imagine a better venue for reliable responses than a courtroom with the witness under oath.

But how did all the *Washington Post* writers come to focus in so knowledgeably on this particular courtroom scene?

Kurtz never mentions his name, and Pincus and Suro refer to him only in passing, but Assistant US District Attorney L. J. O'Neale was himself being questioned by Los Angeles Sheriff's Department investigators on November 19, 1996. The department's transcript of the interview shows O'Neale reveling in his top-secret security clearance with the CIA, and saying that "his personal feelings were that Mr. Webb had become an active part of Ricky Ross's defense team. He said that it was his personal opinion that Webb's involvement was on the verge of complicity." While he was speaking, O'Neale was searching for a document. As the investigators put it in their report, "In our presence he called Howard Kurtz, the author of the first *Washington Post* article, but nobody answered." Thereupon, also in their presence, he talked to Walter Pincus.

This hint of pre-existing relations between the *Washington Post* and the federal prosecutor suggests that O'Neale had rather more input into the *Post*'s attacks on Webb than the passing mention of his name might suggest. And indeed, a comparison between O'Neale's court filings and the piece by Pincus and Suro shows that the *Washington Post* duo faithfully followed the line of O'Neale's attack. Once again, motive is important. O'Neale had every reason to try to subvert a reporter who had described in great detail how the US District Attorney had become the patron and handler of Danilo Blandón. Webb had described how O'Neale had saved Blandón from a life term in prison, found him a job as a government agent and used him as his chief witness in a series of trials. O'Neale had an enormous stake in discrediting Webb.

O'Neale's claim, reiterated by Pincus and Suro, is that Blandón mainly engaged in sending cocaine profits to the Contras in late 1981 and 1982, before hooking up with Rick Ross. Furthermore, the amount of cocaine sold by Blandón was a mere fraction of the national market for the drug, and thus could not have played a decisive role in sparking a crack plague in Los Angeles. In other words, according to the O'Neale line in the *Post*, Blandón had sold only a relatively insignificant amount of cocaine in 1981 and 1982 (later the magical figure $50,000 worth became holy writ among Webb's critics). His association with Ross had begun after Blandón had given up his charitable dispensations to the Contras, and thus was a purely criminal enterprise with no political ramifications. Therefore, even by implication, there could be no connection between the CIA and the rise of crack.

O'Neale had reversed the position he had taken in the days when he was prosecuting Blandón and calling him "the largest Nicaraguan cocaine dealer in the United States." Now he was claiming that Blandón's total sales of cocaine amounted to only 5 tons, and thus he could not be held accountable for the rise of crack. This specific argument was seized gratefully by Pincus and Suro. "Law enforcement estimates," Pincus and Suro wrote, "say Blandón handled a total of only about five tons of cocaine during a decade-long career."

Imagine if the *Washington Post* had been dealing with a claim by Mayor Marion Barry that during his mayoral terms "only" about 10,000 pounds of crack had been handled by traffickers in the blocks surrounding his office!

Webb was attacked for claiming, in the opening lines of his series, that "millions" had been funneled back to the Contras. In his statements to the Los Angeles Sheriff's Department investigators, O'Neale said, "... Blandón dealt with a total of 40 kilos of cocaine from January to December 1982. The profits of the sales were used to purchase weapons and equipment for the Contras." O'Neale was trying to narrow the window of "political" cocaine sales. However, during that time Blandón was selling cocaine worth over $2 million – in only a fraction of the period that Webb identified as the time the cocaine profits were being remitted to Honduras.

The degree of enmity directed toward Webb can be gauged not only by O'Neale's diligent briefings of Webb's antagonists, but also by the raid on the office of Gary Webb's literary agent, Jody Hotchkiss of the Sterling Lord Agency, by agents of the Department of Justice and the

DEA. The government men came brandishing subpoenas for copies of all correspondence between the Sterling Lord Agency, Rick Ross, Ross's lawyer Alan Fenster, and Webb. The DEA justified the search on the grounds that it wanted to see if Ross had any assets it could seize to pay his hefty fines. But Webb reckons "they were really looking for some sort of business deal between me and Ross. They wanted to discredit me as a reporter by saying he's making deals with drug dealers." The raid produced no evidence of any such deal, because there was none.

Cheek by jowl with Pincus and Suro on the *Washington Post*'s front page that October 4 was Fletcher's essay on the sociology of black paranoia. Blacks, Fletcher claimed, cling to beliefs regardless of "the shortage of factual substantiation" and of "denials by government officials." Fletcher duly stated some pieties about the "bitter" history of American blacks. Then he bundled together some supposed conspiracies (that the government deliberately infected blacks with the AIDS virus, that Church's fried chicken and Snapple drinks had been laced with chemicals designed to sterilize black men) and implied that allegations about the CIA and cocaine trafficking were of the same order. It is true, Fletcher conceded, that blacks had reasons to be paranoid. "Many southern police departments," he wrote delicately, "were suspected of having ties to the Ku Klux Klan." He mentioned in passing the FBI snooping on Martin Luther King Jr. and the sting operation on Washington, D.C.'s Mayor Marion Barry. He also touched on the syphilis experiments conducted by the government on blacks in Tuskegee, Alabama. "The history of victimization of black people allows myths – and, at times, outright paranoia – to flourish." In other words, the black folk get it coming and going. Terrible things happen to them, and then they're patronized in the *Washington Post* for imagining that such terrible things might happen again. "Even if a major investigation is done," Fletcher concluded, "it is unlikely to quell the certainty among many African Americans that the government played a role in bringing the crack epidemic to black communities."

A few days later, a *Post* editorial followed through on this notion of black irrationality and the lack of substance in Webb's thesis. The writer observed that "The *Mercury* [had] borrowed heavily from a certain view of CIA rogue conduct that was widespread ten years ago." The "biggest shock," the editorial went on, "wasn't the story but the credibility the story seems to have generated when it reached some parts of the black community." This amazing sentence was an accurate rendition of what really bothered the *Washington Post,* which was not charges that the CIA had been complicit in drug running, but that black people might be suspicious of the government's intentions toward them. The *Post*'s editorial said solemnly that "[i]f the CIA did associate with drug pushers its aim was not to infect Americans but to advance the CIA' s foreign project and purposes."

In the weeks that followed, *Post* columnists piled on the heat. Mary McGrory, the doyenne of liberal punditry, said that the *Post* had successfully "discredited" the *Mercury News.* Richard Cohen, always edgy on the topic of black America, denounced Rep. Maxine Waters for demanding an investigation after the *Washington Post* had concluded that Webb's charges were "baseless." "When it comes to sheer gullibility – or is it mere political opportunism? – Waters is in a class of her own."

One story in that October 4 onslaught in the *Post* differed markedly from its companion pieces. That was the profile of Meneses by Douglas Farah, which actually advanced Webb's story. Farah, the *Post*'s man in Central America, filed a dispatch from Managua giving a detailed account of Meneses's career as a drug trafficker, going back to 1974. Farah described how Meneses had "worked for the Contras for five years, fundraising, training and sending people down to Honduras." He confirmed Meneses's encounter with Enrique Bermúdez and added a detail – the gift of a crossbow by Meneses to the colonel. Then Farah produced a stunner, lurking in the twelfth paragraph of his story. Citing "knowledgeable sources," he reported that the DEA had hired Meneses in 1988 to try to set up Sandinista political and military leaders in drug stings. Farah named the DEA agent involved as Federico Villareal. The DEA did not dispute this version of events. In other words, Farah had Meneses performing a political mission for the US government, side by side with the story by his colleagues Pincus and Suro claiming Meneses had no such connections.

Shortly after the *Post*'s offensives on October 2 and October 4, the *Mercury News*'s editor, Jerry Ceppos, sent a detailed letter to the *Post* aggressively defending Webb and rebutting the criticisms. "The *Post* has every right to reach different conclusions from those of the *Mercury News*," Ceppos wrote. "But I'm disappointed in the 'what's the big deal' tone running through the *Post*'s critique. If the CIA knew about illegal activities being conducted by its associates, federal law and basic morality required that it notify domestic authorities. It seems to me that this is exactly the kind of story that a newspaper should shine a light on."

The *Post* refused to print Ceppos's letter. Ceppos called Stephen Rosenfeld, the deputy editor of the editorial page, who suggested that Ceppos revise his letter and resubmit it. Ceppos promptly did this, and again the *Post* refused to print his response. Rosenfeld said Ceppos's letter was "misinformation." Ceppos later wrote in the *Mercury News:* "I was stunned when the *Washington Post* rejected my request to reply to its long critique of 'Dark Alliance.' The *Post* at first encouraged me, asking me to rewrite the article and then to agree to other changes. I did. Then, a few days ago, I received a one-paragraph fax saying that the *Post* is 'not able to publish' my response. Among other reasons, the *Post* said [that] other papers 'essentially' confirmed the *Post*'s criticism of our series. I've insisted for years that newspapers don't practice 'groupthink.' I'm still sure that most don't. But the *Post*'s argument certainly gives ammunition to the most virulent critics of American journalism. The *Post* also said I had backed down 'elsewhere' from positions I took in the piece I wrote for the *Post*. But I didn't. I shouted to anyone who would listen (and wrote that, in another letter to the *Post*). It was too late. On the day that the *Post* faxed me, the *Los Angeles Times* incorrectly had written that reporter Gary Webb, who wrote the 'Dark Alliance' series, and I had backed down on several key points. Fiction became fact. As if I had no tongue, and no typewriter, I suddenly had lost access to the newspaper that first bitterly criticized our series."

The *Post*'s sordid procedures in savaging Webb were examined by its ombudsman, Geneva Overholzer, on November 10. Ultimately she found her own paper guilty of "misdirected zeal," but first she took the opportunity to stick a few more knives into poor Webb. "The San Jose series was seriously flawed. It was reported by a seemingly hot-headed fellow willing to have people leap to conclusions his reporting couldn't back up – principally that the CIA was knowingly involved in the introduction of drugs into the United States." That said, Overholzer then turned her sights on the *Post*'s editors, saying that the *Post* showed more energy for protecting the CIA than for protecting the people from government excesses. "*Post* editors and reporters knew there was strong evidence that the CIA at least chose to overlook Contra involvement in the drug trade. Yet when those revelations came out in the 1980s they had caused 'little stir,' as the *Post* delicately noted. Would that we had welcomed the surge of public interest as an occasion to return to a subject the *Post* and the public had given short shrift. Alas, dismissing someone else's story as old news comes more naturally."

Despite Ceppos's anger at the *Washington Post,* the unrelenting attacks from organizations that he held in great professional esteem were beginning to take their toll. It is also quite possible that he was feeling pressure from within the Knight-Ridder empire. To judge from the bleating tone of his pieces about the Webb series in the *Mercury News* – the November 4 article, for example – Ceppos may not have had quite the necessary backbone to hold up under pressure.

Ceppos assigned another *Mercury News* investigative reporter, Pete Carey, to review Webb's reporting against the charges of the media critics. On October 12 the *Mercury News* published Carey's findings, which backed up Webb's work and actually added new information, particularly regarding the 1986 search warrant against Blandón and his arms-dealing associate, Ronald Lister. But though Webb's reporting was vindicated, the assignment to Carey was an omen of the paper's increasing defensiveness.

Another omen was Ceppos's reaction to charges that Webb had a vested interest in the story because he had a book offer and film offers. The *Los Angeles Times* reported, inaccurately, that Webb had signed a deal. "This story really pissed off Ceppos," Webb recalls. "He said it made the paper look bad." Webb told Ceppos he didn't have any deals. Ceppos then told Webb, "I don't want you to sign any deals and if you sign any book deals or movie deals you can't work on this story for us anymore."

"That's kind of asking a lot," Webb says he answered. "This is what most reporters dream of."

"Well, you'll have to make up your mind," Ceppos said. "You can either do a book deal or you can work on it for us."

Webb went home to talk over the ultimatum with his wife, Sue, a respiratory therapist. She told him, "Screw them. Do the book. Do the movie and let the *Mercury News* worry about itself."

"I owe it to the paper," Webb answered. "They're being sniped at." So he called up Hotchkiss at Sterling Lord and told him, "Forget the books. Forget the movie deals. They want me to do more stories. Then I'll do the book."

Sue had better instincts about the *Mercury News* than her husband. Having told Webb to give up the deals and write the stories for the paper, Ceppos thus did his reporter out of book and movie advances, then failed to run the stories and finally tried to ruin his career.

The next assault was a double-barreled one from either side of the continent, on Sunday, October 17, in the *New York Times,* staff reporter Tim Golden was given an entire page on which to flail away at Webb. In the *Los Angeles Times,* an army of fourteen reporters and three editors put out a three-part series, intended to finish off Webb forever.

Golden's piece, entitled "The Tale of CIA and Drugs Has Life of Its Own," was remarkable, among other reasons, for the pullulating anonymity of its sources. Golden claimed to have interviewed "more than two dozen current and former rebels, CIA officers and narcotics agents." From these informants, Golden had concluded that there was "scant" proof to support the paper's contention that Nicaraguan rebel officials linked to the CIA played a central role in spreading crack through Los Angeles and other cities. One conspicuous common link between all the officials quoted by Golden as being critical of Webb is that they remained anonymous. Only Adolfo Calero permitted himself to be identified. Golden's editors at the *New York Times* allowed him to offer scores of blind quotes without any identification. The *Mercury News* never offered Webb that indulgence, nor did he request it.

In truth, Golden's story had no substance whatsoever. He got his final word on the story from that well-known Uncle Tom to the thumb-sucking crowd, Dr. Alvin Poussaint, a black professor from the Harvard University Medical School. Poussaint, who is always being wheeled out in these situations, ascribed the reaction of black America to the *Mercury News* story as another case of black paranoia. This tendresse for the CIA's reputation was nothing new for the *New York Times*. In 1987, its reporter Keith Schneider weighed in with a three-part series dismissing allegations of Contra drug trafficking. A month later Schneider explained to *In These Times* magazine why he took that approach. He said such a story could "shatter the Republic. I think it is so damaging, the implications are so extraordinary, that for us to run the story, it had better be based on the most solid evidence we could amass." In other words, it would have to be approved by the Agency.

Of all the attacks on Webb, the *Los Angeles Times* series was the most elaborate and the most disingenuous. For two months the dominant newspaper in Southern California had been derided for missing the big story on its own doorstep. The only way it could salvage its reputation was to claim that there'd been no big story to miss. This is the path it took. It would have been extraordinary if the *Times* had the decency to clap the *Mercury News* on the back and praise it for good work, particularly given the disposition of its editor-in-chief at the time, Shelby Coffee III. Coffee came to Los Angeles from the *Washington Post*, where he had been editor of the Style section. He was regarded there as a smooth courtier in the retinue of Katharine Graham and not in any way as a boat rocker. It would have gone against every instinct for Coffee to have endorsed a story so displeasing to liberal elites. "He is the dictionary definition of someone who wants to protect the status quo," said Dennis McDougal, a former *Los Angeles Times* reporter, in an interview with *New Times,* "He weighs whether or not an investigative piece will have repercussions among the ruling elites and if it will, the chances of seeing it in print in the *LA Times* decrease accordingly."

The mood of the group doing the series, under the leadership of Doyle McManus, could scarcely be described as one of objective dispassion. They referred to themselves as the "Get Gary Webb Team," as Peter Kornbluh reported in the *Columbia Journalism Review*, and bragged in the office about denying Webb his Pulitzer.

The most important task for the hit squad was to deal with its own backyard. They assigned Webb's old nemesis Jesse Katz the task of undermining Webb's assertion that the Blandón/Ross cocaine ring helped spark the crack epidemic in Los Angeles. Katz duly turned in an article claiming that "the explosion of cheap smokable cocaine in the 1980s was a uniquely egalitarian phenomenon, one that lent itself more to makeshift mom and pop operations than to the sinister hand of a government-sanctioned plot." Katz went on to minimize the role of Rick Ross: "How the crack epidemic reached that extreme, on some level, had nothing to do with Ricky Ross." Katz then asserted that gangs had little or nothing to do with the crack trade, stating flatly that crack sales did not "fill the coffers of the Bloods and the Crips." He also disputed the idea that crack use had spread across the country from Los Angeles.

This was a substantial turnaround from what the *Los Angeles Times* and Katz had previously reported, before the task of demolishing the *Mercury News* became paramount. The drumbeat of the newspaper during the mid- and late 1980s was that the Los Angeles Police Department had to crush the gangs. In a 1987 news story, the *Times* described the gangs as "the foot soldiers of the Colombian cartels." On August 4, 1989, another news story sympathetically relayed a Justice Department report: "Los Angeles street gangs now dominate the rock cocaine trade in Los Angeles and elsewhere, due in part to their steady recourse to murderous violence to enforce territorial dealing supremacy, to deter cheating and to punish rival gang members. The LAPD has identified 47 cities, from Seattle to Kansas City, to Baltimore, where Los Angeles street gang traffickers have appeared."

As for Ross, on December 20, 1994 the *Los Angeles Times* had published a 2,400-word investigative report by Katz entitled "Deposed King of Crack Now Freed After Five Years in Prison. This Master Marketer Was Key to the Drug's Spread in LA." Katz pulled out all the stops in his lead. "If there was an eye to the storm, if there was a criminal mastermind behind crack's decade-long reign, if there was an outlaw capitalist most responsible for flooding Los Angeles' streets with mass-marketed cocaine, his name was Freeway Rick." Katz reported that "Ross did more than anyone else to democratize it, boosting volume, slashing prices, and spreading disease on a scale never before conceived." Katz called Ross "South Central's first multi-millionaire crack lord" and said "his coast-to-coast conglomerate was selling more than $500,000 a day, a staggering turnover that put the drug within reach of anyone with a few dollars."

A day later, it was Doyle McManus who tried to undermine Webb's work on the Contra connection. One hopes that McManus felt some slight tinge of embarrassment at his newspaper's attack on Webb for unethical behavior in signing a book deal (which, as we have seen, Webb had not in fact done). McManus himself had reported on the Iran/Contra scandal, and simultaneously put out a book on the affair, co-written with Jane Mayer. McManus went the familiar route of larding his story with unattributed quotes from Contras, CIA men and associates of Blandón, all of them naturally enough protesting their innocence. "I wish we had been able to identify them by names of course," McManus piously told Alicia Shepard of the *American Journalism Review*. McManus, apparently in some sort of journalistic race to the bottom with his co-assailants Pincus and Golden, contended that Meneses gave the Contras only $20 to $30 at a time, and asserted that Meneses's and Blandón's total contribution was far less than $50,000. This conclusion is derived from McManus's unnamed informants, and has to be set against court testimony, under oath, from numerous named sources cited by Webb. No less an authority than assistant federal prosecutor L. J. O'Neale, who lowballed the dollar figures for reasons noted earlier, had still produced a number of more than $2 million in a single year.

McManus tried to establish a scenario in which Blandón and Meneses gave very little to the Contras, to whom they were not connected in any official capacity, and in which Meneses's cocaine never made it to Rick Ross to be transformed into crack. McManus claimed Ross's crack came from Colombian cocaine and had nothing to do with the Nicaraguans. In McManus's version, Blandón and Meneses were incompetent stooges. However, amid all this dogged effort to subvert Webb's chronology, McManus tripped himself up badly. He alleged that Blandón and Meneses had severed their relationship "entirely by 1983." A few paragraphs later, amid an anecdote designed to establish Meneses as head of a gang-that-couldn't-shoot-straight, McManus quoted at length a description of a scene at Meneses's house in San Francisco in November 1984. The unnamed source is identified as a member of the Blandón cocaine ring. He is describing the reaction of Meneses and Blandón to the news that Jairo Meneses, Meneses's cousin, and Renato Peña Cabrerra, official spokesman for the FDN's San Francisco group, had just been busted on cocaine charges. Although McManus had just said that Meneses and Blandón had split two years earlier, he now had them in the midst of a division of cash from a cocaine deal. "Danilo and Norwin had done some business deal. The deal is 40 to 50 kilos. The money was all divvied up. There was cash all over the place. Norwin had steaks on the grill. It was going to be a big party. The phone rings and Margarita shrieks, 'Jairo's been arrested!' Well, everybody cleared out in a heartbeat. They grabbed the money and ran. I don't think anyone turned off the steaks."

It's hard to imagine an anecdote that could more effectively rebut everything McManus had previously labored to establish.

McManus's other objective was to assert the moral purity of the CIA. To this end he interviewed Vincent Cannistraro, a former CIA officer and staffer at the National Security Council at the time Oliver North was manfully toiling at Reagan's behest to keep the Contras afloat. Cannistraro told McManus that sometimes CIA station chiefs turn a blind eye to "misdeeds by the foreign collaborators they recruit." Cannistraro referred to this trait as "falling in love with your agent." Cannistraro adamantly insisted, however, that there's "no tendency to turn a blind eye to drug trafficking. It's too sensitive. It's not a fine line. It's not a shaded area where you can turn away from the rules." (In 1998 the CIA Inspector General finally admitted to Congress that in 1982 the Agency had received clearance from the Justice Department *not* to report drug trafficking by CIA assets.) What McManus failed to confide to his readers was that Cannistraro had a deep personal interest in denying any Agency tolerance for trafficking. He had supervised many of the CIA/Contra operations and was then transferred to the NSC, where he oversaw US aid to the Afghan mujahidin. As we shall see, the mujahidin were heavily engaged in the trafficking of opium and heroin. Perhaps the most piquant bit of effrontery in McManus's attack was his assertion that even if Meneses had been selling drugs in California and remitting the profits to the Contras, the CIA would have had to turn a blind eye, because the Agency was prohibited from domestic spying!

Even after his pummeling by the two big West and East Coast papers, Webb felt he still retained the support of his editors. "They urged me to continue digging on the story so that we could stick to the *Washington Post*," For the next two months, Webb continued his research. He flushed out more evidence of direct CIA knowledge of Meneses's operations in Costa Rica and El Salvador. He traced how the DEA made Meneses one of their informer/assets as early as 1985. And he secured more evidence on the controversial money angle, finding that as much as $5 million was channeled back to the Contras from the Blandón/Meneses ring in 1983 alone. Webb turned the stories in to his editor, Dawn Garcia, in January 1997, and the newspaper sat on them. "They didn't edit them," Webb recalls. "They told me that they had read them, but they never asked me for any supporting documentation. They never asked any questions about them."

Then Webb got a call from a friend, saying that a reporter had requested copies of all of Webb's clippings. The reporter seemed interested in digging into Webb's personal background. She particularly asked about an incident in which Webb had fired his .22 at a man who had been trying to steal his prized TR6 and who threatened Webb and his then-pregnant wife. (The man turned out to be a known local crook already convicted of manslaughter.) The reporter pursuing this story was Alicia Shepard of the *American Journalism Review*. Shepard had formerly worked as a reporter for the *San Jose Mercury News*. Her story was another smear on Webb's journalistic ethics, but this time the smears were coming from a source much closer to home. Shepard recounted how Sharon Rosenhause, managing editor of the *San Francisco Examiner* (a paper boasting Chris Matthews as its Washington, D.C. correspondent), had filed a petition with the Society of Professional Journalists to have Webb stripped of the Journalist of the Year Award that had just been bestowed on him. This had elicited a stinging letter from the director of the Society of Professional Journalists, emphasizing how Rosenhause had a private agenda, and how the society stood behind Webb.

Shepard got several *Mercury News* staffers to go on record with their criticism of Webb and his stories. Economics writer Scott Thrum, investigative editors Jonathan Krim and Chriss Schmitt, editorial page editor Rob Elder, and the most virulent critic of all, Phil Yost, who is the chief editorial writer for the *Mercury News*. The criticisms consisted mostly of hand-wringing by nervous colleagues who felt that Webb had compromised the newspaper's "hard-won credibility." Yost simply reiterated the charges made by other newspapers. It was a disgusting demonstration of backstabbing. And it showed clearly that the *Mercury News* was beginning to distance itself from Webb.

What accounts for the vicious edge to many of these attacks on Webb? One reason for the animosity of the California reporters can be traced back to one of Webb's earliest investigations for the *Mercury News*. His story revealed that a number of reporters were moonlighting for the very agencies they were supposed to be covering – for example, how a TV reporter in Sacramento was being paid by the California Highway Patrol for coaching officers on how to deal with the press. He uncovered a curriculum for the TV reporter's class describing how the CHP should call up editors and complain about unfavorable stories. Webb also exposed reporters at the *Sacramento Bee* and United Press International, who had received state contracts from the California Lottery Commission. Webb says that after this story appeared, his colleagues regarded him as an outsider.

Another reason for ostracism by his colleagues could be what Webb describes as racist attitudes among the *Mercury News* staff toward the editor of his series, Dawn Garcia. "I don't think she has a lot of friends in that newsroom, because she came in and she was regarded as one of the Hispanic hires, a quota hire. That's unfair. She's a good newsperson. She took a job from someone that was widely liked in the newsroom."

With his stories sitting unpublished on his editor's desk, some time in early 1997 Webb got a call from Georg Hodel, who had done legwork for him in Nicaragua. Hodel said that he had located four other members of the Meneses/Blandón operation who were willing to talk to Webb. Webb called his editors and said he was going to Nicaragua. They told him they didn't want him to go until they figured out what to do with his stories. Worried that the drug dealers might disappear, Webb said he'd go anyway, on his own time and money.

Soon after he returned to Sacramento from Nicaragua, Webb got a call from Jerry Ceppos, who had spent much of the winter months being treated for prostate cancer. Ceppos told Webb that he was going to publish a letter in the *Mercury News* admitting that "mistakes had been made" in the "Dark Alliance" series. Ceppos originally wanted to run the apologia in the Easter Sunday edition. When Webb saw a draft of the column, he was outraged. "This is idiotic," Webb recalls telling Ceppos.

"Half this stuff isn't even true. It's unconscionable to run this." Ceppos told Webb not to take it personally, that it was just a column and it didn't mean the paper was trying to hang him out to dry.

Webb insisted that he thought Ceppos's column was unethical for a number of reasons, including the fact that though it said there had been shortcomings in the series, it made no reference to the fact that six months of further research had substantiated and advanced most of Webb's original findings. Ceppos replied that they didn't "want to get into that kind of detail."

Ceppos's column ran on May 11. It was a retreat on every front, and a shameful day for American journalism. It accused Webb of leaving out contradictory information, of failing to emphasize that the multimillion-dollar figure was an estimate, and of not including the obligatory denials of the CIA. The series, Ceppos said, had oversimplified the origins of the crack epidemic. Ceppos also declared that the series had wrongly implied CIA knowledge of the Contra drug ring.

Predictably, Ceppos's appalling betrayal of his own reporter was greeted with exuberance by the *New York Times,* where Todd Purdum used it to legitimize the *New York Times*'s original attack and to lash out at Webb as a paranoid. Purdum also alleged that Ceppos's column had been based on "an exhaustive review" written by a seven-member *Mercury News* team of reporters and editors. Both the "exhaustive review" and the team had never existed, according to Webb. Though Webb had submitted four stories totaling 14,000 words, Ceppos told Purdum that the reporter had only submitted "notes and ideas." Purdum also marshalled disobliging blind quotes from Webb's *Mercury News* colleagues.

The Ceppos column was also greeted with glee on the *New York Times* editorial page, where Ceppos got a patronizing clap on the back for his "courageous gesture." The editorial again affixed blame on Webb, saying that Ceppos's action "sets a high standard for cases in which journalists make egregious errors." Webb had made no such errors. Down at Langley, the CIA was quick to use Ceppos's letter to assert that the Agency had been absolved. "It's gratifying to see," said the Agency's Mark Mansfield, "that a large segment of the media, including the *San Jose Mercury News*, has taken an objective look at how this story was constructed and reported."

Nor did the Ceppos letter escape notice by Nicaragua's right wing, with perilous consequences for those who had worked on the story with Webb and who had been interviewed by him. The Nicaraguan press, chiefly *La Prensa,* which had been funded for years by the CIA, ran stories denouncing Webb and urging people to sue him, as well as Hodel and others associated with the story. The Nicaraguan papers alleged that the *Mercury News* would not mount a defense against such libel actions.

It wasn't long before Georg Hodel became the target of harassment and a possible murder attempt. In mid-June 1997, about a month after Ceppos disowned Webb, Hodel and an attorney for several of the men he and Webb had interviewed were run off the road in Nicaragua and threatened by a group of armed thugs. Hodel and the lawyer escaped and went to a police station to file a complaint. A few days later, a story appeared in one of Nicaragua's right-wing papers saying that Hodel and his companions had gotten drunk and driven off the road themselves.

Meanwhile, the *Mercury News* had told Webb that his follow-up stories were being killed and that he was being reassigned to the paper's Cupertino bureau, 150 miles from Sacramento. Webb filed a grievance against the paper.

The *New York Times* continued its vendetta. In perhaps the lowest of all the attacks, Iver Peterson, one of the newspaper's more undistinguished reporters, went back over Webb's investigative pieces before he embarked on the "Dark Alliance" series. Peterson charged that Webb had a history of playing loose with the facts and having "a penchant for self-promotion." He reached this conclusion after dredging up four libel suits, two of which had been dismissed and two of which had been settled. Webb says no major corrections were ever required. (The *Times* refused to print Webb's letter correcting the record, which is reproduced below.) Peterson also quoted from the targets of Webb's investigations, who, predictably, were not appreciative of the reporter. Back in his Ohio days as a reporter at the *Cleveland Plain Dealer,* Webb had exposed Ohio Supreme Court Judge Frank D. Celebrezze as being in receipt of political contributions from organizations tied to the mob. Celebrezze had sued. There was a settlement and no retraction. Peterson dutifully cited Celebrezze's eager comment that Webb "lied about me and whatever happens to him I think he deserves." It was as if some reporter had used Richard Nixon as a reliable source on the quality of reporting by the *New York Times*.

However, the coverup and counterattacks had not yet ended. There was the delicate matter of how to deal with the CIA's own internal probe. It's a neat trick to get great coverage for a report you haven't published and that no journalist has actually seen. You need accomplices. The CIA once again used its friends in the press to issue a self-serving news release on its internal investigation of charges that the Agency had connived in Contra drug smuggling into Los Angeles in the early 1980s.

In this particular piece of news management, the CIA outdid itself. In the past, it has relied on its journalistic allies to put the best face on probes that, albeit heavily censored, displayed the Agency in an unpleasing light. But in late December 1997, the CIA elicited friendly coverage, even though the report by the CIA's own Inspector General remained unpublished and under heavy security wraps.

It will be recalled that a month after Webb's story first appeared, the CIA's director John Deutch announced that the Agency's Inspector General, Frederick Hitz, was launching "the most comprehensive analysis ever done" of CIA activities in this sphere. The gambit of the internal probe was initially confined to the allegations made by Webb, but was then widened to take in any references to drug connections in the CIA's files. Also launched in the fall of 1996 was a Justice Department review of Webb's charges. Deutch initially pledged that the CIA report would be finished and released to the public by the end of December 1996. Sixteen months went by.

Then on December 18, 1997 came stories in the *Los Angeles Times* and the *San Jose Mercury News* under headlines such as "CIA Clears Itself in Crack Investigation." CNN picked up the *Mercury News*'s story immediately, telling viewers that the very paper that had made the initial charges against the CIA was now reporting that "an investigation" had absolved the Agency.

But where was the CIA report that had prompted the stories in the *LA Times* and *Mercury News*? Unavailable. Reason? It depended who one called. The stories in the *LA Times* and *Mercury News* about the mysterious report were filed on Wednesday, December 17 and appeared in print the next day. Then on Thursday, the Justice Department announced its view that public release of the CIA report would damage current criminal investigations. When called, the CIA's press department stated that the CIA now wanted to wait until mid-January, when the second part of the Inspector General's report was supposedly to be finished. Later that Thursday, the Justice Department stated that it would edit the CIA's and its own probes to purge them of any compromising material.

In other words, one was being asked to believe that after sixteen months the CIA and Justice Department had somehow, entirely by accident, contrived a news "event" that exonerated the CIA in major headlines, without providing any evidence to support such a conclusion. Imagine the fury that would have been unleashed if Webb had written a news story thus shorn of any documentary substantiation.

Friday, December 19 brought stories in the *New York Times* by Tim Weiner and in the *Washington Post* by Walter Pincus, who had started the press onslaught on Webb in the fall of 1996. Weiner's story ran under the headline, "CIA Says It Has Found No Link Between Itself and Crack Trade." Weiner quoted no named sources and relied entirely on our old friend, "a government official who would not allow his name to be used." Pincus quoted three anonymous officials who claimed that the CIA report shows "no direct or indirect link" between the CIA and cocaine traffickers.

Just how thorough was the CIA's much-touted probe of itself? All indications are that the investigation was far from fierce. The Inspector General had no subpoena power. The CIA's former chief officer in Central America, Dewey Clarridge, now retired and working for General Dynamics, told the *Los Angeles Times* that the CIA "sent me questions that were a bunch of bullshit." He refused to be interviewed by the CIA's investigators. Clarridge, it should be noted, was a central figure in CIA operations with the Contras, whom he conjured into being from an initial recruitment of Argentinian military torturers, and whose assassination schemes he boasts of having recommended. Other people interviewed by the CIA claim to have been bullied by the Agency's investigators whenever they showed signs of supporting Webb. And what about the author of the stories, Gary Webb? He was never interviewed.

With Webb, we get to the heart of the dust storm. On Saturday, December 13, the *San Jose Mercury News* announced that Gary Webb had resigned from the paper, after reaching a settlement on a grievance he had filed about his transfer from Sacramento to Cupertino. In the *Washington Post* and *New York Times,* Webb's departure from the *Mercury News* was flagged, with the implication that somehow it offered further evidence of the conclusiveness of the CIA's self-examination.

It looks as though the Agency took the opportunity of Webb's departure to leak a self-serving press release about its conduct. This item was eagerly seized upon by the papers who had been after Webb, and by the *Mercury News,* which had been terrorized into betraying a fine reporter.

Looking back at the series in mid-1997, Webb said he had nothing to apologize for. "If anything, we pussy-footed around some stuff we shouldn't have, like CIA involvement and their level of knowledge. I'm glad I did the series because this is a story that gutless papers on the East Coast have been ducking for ten years. And now they're forced to confront it. However they chose to confront it, they still have to say what the story's about."

Sources

The attack on Gary Webb by his colleagues in the national press was relentless. There are a lot of examples, but perhaps none more blatant than Iver Peterson's smear on Webb in the *New York Times,* nearly a year after Webb's story had appeared. The initial assault was led by four "star" reporters at the nation's biggest papers: Howard Kurtz and Walter Pincus at the *Washington Post,* Tim Golden at the *New York Times* and Doyle McManus (Lt. Colonel of a "Get Webb Team") at the *Los Angeles Times.* Once these heavyweights drew blood, the editorial pages from across the country came in for the kill. The behavior of the top editors at Webb's own paper, the *San Jose Mercury News,* was despicable and cowardly. Even the so-called progressive press took shots at Webb, most notably the *Nation,* whose David Corn sniped that Webb's reporting was flawed.

On the other hand, Webb had his defenders. The *LA Weekly* was quick to reveal the gaping holes in the *Los Angeles Times*'s saturation bombing of the "Dark Alliance" series. Norman Soloman's article "Snow Job" for *Extra!,* the magazine of the media watchdog group FAIR, was a fine piece of work that was useful to us. Robert Parry and his colleagues at *The Consortium* wrote good press criticism and worked to advance the story. *The Consortium* also printed a harrowing account from Nicaragua by Webb's partner, Georg Hodel, showing the dangers of writing about these forbidden topics in a hostile landscape. Similarly, Peter Kornbluh, the investigator at the National Security Archives, wrote a fine piece for the *Columbia Journalism Review.* Alicia Shepard's story in the *American Journalism Review* is neither kind nor fair to Webb, but it does expose the biases and petty jealousies of his colleagues.

As an example of the obdurate and spiteful hostility of the *New York Times* toward Webb, we include here two letters to the *Times* correcting serious inaccuracies and exhibitions of bias in the paper's reporting. The first is a response by Webb to Peterson's attack noted above. The *Times* refused to print it. The second is another commentary, which speaks for itself, on Peterson's story. The *Times* likewise had refused to print this letter.

To the editor:

Since the *New York Times* allegedly places such a high value on accuracy, I would like to point out some factual errors and omissions in your June 3 story about me and the "Dark Alliance" series I authored last year.

The statement that a state audit "cleared" Tandem Computers for its part in a $50 million computer debacle at the California Department of Motor Vehicles is incorrect. The audit, by California Auditor General Kurt Sjoberg, corroborated the findings of my investigation and the Tandem project was scrapped at considerable cost to the state's taxpayers. Moreover, two state officials who approved and oversaw this project – and then went to work for Tandem – paid large fees to settle conflict of interest charges lodged by the state Fair Political Practices Commission. These charges were filed as a result of my reporting, which won the California Journalism Award in 1994.

The statement that the *Mercury News* "never published a follow-up story" to the Tandem series is also false. Several follow-ups were published, including stories I wrote about the Auditor General's report and the fines paid by the former state officials.

(It might have been useful to note that the reporter who criticized my Tandem stories, Lee Gomes, was covering Tandem while its much-ballyhooed DMV project was collapsing, yet somehow managed to miss the story entirely.)

Since your reporter, Iver Peterson, did not question me about my Tandem stories, perhaps it's not surprising that these errors and omissions occurred.

Finally, I found it amusing that while Mr. Peterson spent many inches airing vague complaints from people I've investigated, he would neglect to mention that I have won more than 30 journalism awards, been nominated for a Pulitzer Prize half a dozen times, and sent a number of corrupt or incompetent government officials and businessmen to jail or early retirement by exposing their misdeeds.

Granted, this kind of reporting makes few friends and prompts libel suits, but being well-loved and lawsuit-free has never been part of a reporter's duties as I understand them.

Gary Webb,
June 3, 1997

To the editor:

A *Times* reporter [Iver Peterson] has seen fit to lead a story (6/3) on the *San Jose Mercury New*'s "Dark Alliance" series with the *stunning* news that a request was placed on the agenda of the Northern California chapter of the Society of Professional Journalists (SPJ) to strip the series' author, Gary Webb, of his 1996 Journalist of the Year award. Gratified as I am, as president of the organization, to see that our monthly agenda is of such interest to a national newspaper, in the interests of ethical journalism, which SPJ is dedicated to furthering, please allow me to correct the misleading impression that you have knowingly fostered with that lead paragraph.

Putting an anecdote in the lead paragraph of a news story implies that it has some representative significance, and indeed your writer goes on to state that the agenda item "illustrates" how Webb's series "continues to echo among journalists."

Actually, it illustrates no such thing. One person, an editor at a competing newspaper, has been insisting for nearly a year that the award be withdrawn, and she reiterated her request after appearance of the *Mercury News* column clarifying (not retracting) its series. As a courtesy to that one person, the item was placed on our agenda. But as your writer was aware – because he asked me – that person was in no way representative. In fact, she is the *only* person who has expressed such a view to us, and she acknowledges that she has other reasons to be angry with the *San Jose Mercury News.*

When the board finally discussed the issue at the member's request, there was no sentiment for withdrawal of the award. The discussion was brief, mostly centered on the irresponsibility of the *Times*'s story.

Your reporter's determination to prove a point with a misguided example is disturbing, but even more so is the fact that he knew in advance that it was misleading and even wrote that "Chances are remote that Webb will lose the award because of one request." The reporter knew that the person who brought our meeting to his attention had an interest in inflating the significance of her own request. In other words, his informant's interest illustrated his informant's interest. Period.

Indeed, if the SPJ chapter meeting had had the importance that the *Times*'s article implied, shouldn't the paper have reported the results of the meeting after it was held?

If the suggestion of potential retraction of Gary Webb's SPJ award continues to echo among journalists, it echoes because those journalists have read it in the *New York Times* and perpetuated the misimpression by calling us to find out what happened at the meeting, hyped by the *Times* and its source.

I suggested that the *Times*'s energy in bludgeoning flaws in the *Mercury News* series and personally attacking its author be matched by an equal or greater determination to explore the far more important story of the degree of US government complicity in the Contras' dealing in drugs that have devastated so many American communities. That is the story that the major news media have downplayed for more than a decade, while newspapers such as yours devote unprecedented lineage to debunking, in the most personal terms, the efforts of a reporter at another newspaper.

Peter Y. Sussman, President,
Northern California Chapter,
Society of Professional Journalists
June 6, 1997

Associated Press. "Oliver North Labels CIA-Drug Allegations 'Garbage.'" *San Jose Mercury News,* Sept. 22, 1996.
Barris, Rick. "A Barracuda Tries to Eat the Messenger." *New Times,* Oct. 31, 1996.
Bernstein, Dennis, and Julie Light. "Closing the Loop on the Contra-CIA Connection." *Pacifica,* Nov. 1996.
Billiter, Bill, Ralph Frammolino and Jim Newton. "Deputies Said in '86 Drug Ring Was Tied to the Contras." *Los Angeles Times,* Oct. 8, 1996.
Boston Herald, editorial. "Courage at the Merc." *Boston Herald,* May 14, 1997.
Britt, Donna. "Finding the Truest Truth." *Washington Post,* Oct. 4, 1996.
Brown, Joseph. "Typecast for Genocide or Suicide?" *Tampa Tribune,* Sept. 29, 1996.
Carey, Peter. "CIA Clears Itself in Crack Investigation." *San Jose Mercury News,* Dec. 18, 1997.
Ceppos, Jerry. "Perspective: In the Eye of the Storm." *San Jose Mercury News,* Nov. 3, 1996.
——. "A Letter to the Washington Post," *San Jose Mercury News,* Oct. 18, 1996.
——. "A Letter to Our Readers." *San Jose Mercury News,* May 11, 1997.
Chicago Tribune, editorial. "A Newspaper Says 'Mea Culpa,'" *Chicago Tribune.* May 14, 1997.
Ciolli, Rita. "Paper Admits Flaws." *Newsday,* May 13, 1997.
Clairborne, William. "Hearing on CIA Drug Allegations Turns into Rally." *Washington Post,* Oct. 20, 1996.
Cockburn, Alexander, and Jeffrey St. Clair. "Drugs, Contras, and the CIA: Covering Up for the Agency." *CounterPunch,* Nov. 1–15, 1996.
——. "The CIA's Latest Coup." *CounterPunch,* Dec. 16–30, 1997.
Cohen, Richard. "A Racist Past and a Wary Present." *Washington Post,* Oct. 27, 1996.
Connell, Rich. "Congressional Inquiry Probes CIA Allegations." *Los Angeles Times,* Oct. 20, 1996.
Corn, David. "Crack Reporting." *Nation,* Nov. 18, 1996.
Crogan, Jim. "Snow Hits Spring Street." *LA Weekly,* Feb. 21, 1997.
Davis, Deborah. *Katharine the Great: Katharine Graham and Her Washington Post Empire.* Sheridan Square Press, 1991.
Diamond, John. "CIA Promises Independent Probe of Drug Link." AP Wire, Sept. 20, 1996.
——. "Questions Arise About Series on CIA-Crack Link." AP Wire, Oct. 4, 1996.
Deutch, John. "The CIA Fights Drugs." *Baltimore Sun,* Nov. 24, 1996.
Daughen, Joseph. "Belief May Persist." *Milwaukee Journal Sentinel,* May 18, 1997.
Dokes, Jennifer. "Media Need to Fill Holes in CIA-Contra Crack Story." *Arizona Republic,* Oct. 24, 1996.
Early, David E. "Contra-Drug Story Stirs National Debate." *San Jose Mercury News,* Oct. 6, 1996.

Farragher, Thomas. "Justice Department to Continue Crack/CIA Inquiry." *San Jose Mercury News,* May 14, 1997.

Fletcher, Michael. "Deutch Assures Caucus on Drug Charges." *Washington Post,* Sept. 20, 1996.

———. "Black Caucus Urges Probe of CIA Drug Charge." *Washington Post,* Sept. 13, 1996.

———. "History Lends Credence to Conspiracy Theories." *Washington Post,* Oct. 4, 1996.

Flynn, Kitson. "Arresting Talker." *Washington Times,* Sept. 16, 1996.

Glassman, Jim, host. "CIA and Crack." *CNN Capital Gang Sunday,* Nov. 17, 1996.

Golden, Tim. "Tale of CIA and Drugs Has Life of Its Own." *New York Times,* Oct. 17, 1996.

Goulden, Joseph. "Wake Up, Associated Press! The CIA Did Not Introduce Crack into LA." *Washington Times,* Dec. 20, 1996.

Graham, Katharine. "Secrecy and the Press." Speech at the CIA, Nov. 16, 1988.

Greene, Leonard. "Editor's Apology for Paper's Crack–CIA Series Clouds Truth." *Boston Herald,* May 14, 1997.

Gregory, Dick. "White Press Doesn't Believe It? What Else Is New?" *Baltimore Sun,* Nov. 24, 1996.

Hackett, Thomas. "The CIA–Crack Story – Anatomy of a Journalistic Train Wreck." *Salon,* May 30, 1997.

Herman, Edward S. "Gary Webb and the Media's Rush to Judgment." *Z Magazine,* Feb. 1997.

Hinckle, Pia. "Soul Searching in San Jose: How the *Mercury News* Painfully Distanced Itself from a Big But Flawed Story." *Columbia Journalism Review,* August 1997.

Hodel, Georg. "Hung Out to Dry: 'Dark Alliance' Series Dies." *The Consortium,* June 30, 1997.

Holmes, Steven. "CIA Critics Seek Study of Implied Cocaine Link." *New York Times,* April 15, 1997.

Horgan, John. "Credibility and America's Fourth Estate." *Tampa Tribune,* Oct. 5, 1996.

Irvine, Reed, and Joseph Goulden. "Partnership for Public Profits." *Washington Times,* Nov. 14, 1996.

———. "Knight-Ridder Defends Botched Stories." *Washington Inquirer,* Dec. 9, 1996.

Jones, Christopher. "Colorblind Drug Hurts All People." *Arizona Republic,* Oct. 13, 1996.

Katz, Jesse. "Deposed King of Crack." *Los Angeles Times,* Dec. 20, 1994.

———. "Tracking the Genesis of the Crack Trade." *Los Angeles Times,* Oct. 20, 1996.

Kaye, Jeffrey. "Drug Conspiracy?" *The Newshour with Jim Lehrer.* PBS, Nov. 18, 1996.

Kornbluh, Peter. "Crack, Contras and the CIA: The Storm over Dark Alliance." *Columbia Journalism Review,* Jan./Feb. 1997.

Kurtz, Howard. "Running with the CIA Story." *Washington Post,* Oct. 2, 1996.

———. "CIA Hooking Blacks on Crack? That's Not Quite the Story." *Washington Post,* Oct. 4, 1996.

———. "Editor Criticizes His Paper's CIA Series." *Washington Post,* May 14, 1997.

Lane, Charles. "An Imaginary Conspiracy." *Baltimore Sun,* Nov. 8, 1996.

Lewis, Claude. "CIA Drug Plot? Blacks Didn't Have to Use Them." *Philadelphia Inquirer,* Sept. 30, 1996.

McManus, Doyle. "Examining Charges of CIA Role in Crack Sales." *Los Angeles Times,* Oct. 21, 1996.

Maxwell, Bill. "It's Time to Put the Scapegoats out to Pasture." *Memphis Commercial Appeal*, Oct. 20, 1996.

Memphis Commercial Appeal, editorial. "A Destructive Newspaper Series." *Memphis Commercial Appeal*, May 14, 1997.

Merina, Victor, and William Rempel. "Ex-Associates Doubt Onetime Drug Trafficker's Claim of CIA Ties." *Los Angeles Times*, Oct. 21, 1996.

Mitchell, Andrea. "Crack Cocaine, the CIA and Oliver North." *NBC News: In Depth*, Nov. 16, 1996.

Mitchell, John, and Sam Fullwood III. "History Fuels Outrage over Crack Allegations." *Los Angeles Times*, Oct. 23, 1996.

Muller, Judy. "Crack and the CIA: Conspiracy or Myth?" *ABC News Nightline*, Nov. 15, 1996.

Nation, editorial. "CIA Crack and the Media." *Nation*, June 2, 1997.

Orrick, Phyllis, and Susan Rasky. "Unspun: Heard It Through the Grapevine." *Dallas Observer*, Sept. 25, 1996.

Osborne, Barbara. "Are You Sure You Want to Ruin Your Career?" *Extra!* April 1998.

Overholser, Geneva. "The CIA, Drugs and the Press." *Washington Post*, Nov. 18, 1996.

Page, Clarence. "Crack: CIA Is Not Alone as Drug Suspect." *Phoenix Gazette*, Sept. 24, 1996.

——. "What Did the CIA Know and When Did It Know It?" *Baltimore Sun*, Nov. 16, 1996.

Parry, Robert. "Contras, Crack, The CIA." *Nation*, Oct. 21, 1996.

——. "CIA, Drugs and the National Press." *Consortium*, Dec. 23, 1996.

Parry, Sam. "Contra–Crack: Investigators v. Brick Wall." *The Consortium*, Feb. 3, 1997.

——. "Contra–Crack Controversy Continues." *The Consortium*, Jan. 6, 1997.

Parry, Sam, and Nat Parry. "'Conspiracism': Who's at Fault for the Distrust?" *The Consortium*, Jan. 20, 1997.

Peterson, Iver. "Repercussions from Flawed News Articles." *New York Times*, May 13, 1997.

Pincus, Walter. "How I Traveled Abroad on a CIA Subsidy." *San Jose Mercury News*, Feb. 16, 1967.

——. "Internal Investigator Extends Probe of CIA-Contra Crack Cocaine Allegations." *Washington Post*, Oct. 12, 1996.

——. "A Long History of Drug Allegations." *Washington Post*, Sept. 23, 1996.

——. "Justice Opens Probe on CIA Drug Charges." *Washington Post*, Sept. 13, 1996.

——. "CIA Finds No Link to Cocaine Sales." *Washington Post*, Dec. 18, 1997.

Purdum, Todd. "Exposé on Crack was Flawed, Paper Says." *New York Times*, May 13, 1997.

Randolph, Eleanor, and John M. Broder. "Cyberspace Contributes to Volatility of Allegations." *Los Angeles Times*, Oct. 22, 1996.

Rappleye, Charles. "The Times Cracks Back." *LA Weekly*, Nov. 1, 1996.

Raspberry, William. "The Crack Story: Who's Buying It?" *Washington Post*, Sept. 23, 1996.

Reed, Christopher. "Dirty Hands and Finger of Guilt." *Guardian* [London], Nov. 10, 1996.

Reeves, Richard. "A Pacification Plan for the Troublemakers." *Baltimore Sun*, Nov. 22, 1996.

St. Petersburg Times, editorial. "An Editor Comes Clean." *St. Petersburg Times*, May 15, 1997.

San Jose Mercury News, staff report. "'Dark Alliance' Reporter Resigns." *San Jose Mercury News,* Dec. 13, 1997.

Schiraldi, Vincent. "Black Paranoia – or Common Sense?" *Pacific News Service*, Dec. 18, 1996.

Schorr, Daniel. "Weekly Review." *Weekend Edition*, NPR, Oct. 26, 1996.

Shepard, Alicia. "The Web Gary Spun." *American Journalism Review*, Jan./Feb. 1997.

Solomon, Norman. "Snow Job." *Extra!* Jan./Feb. 1997.

Stewart, Jill. "Bah-Bah-Bah." *New Times*, June 5, 1997.

Stein, M. L. "Reporter Reined In." *Editor and Publisher,* June 21, 1997.

Suro, Roberto, and Walter Pincus. "The CIA and Crack: Evidence Is Lacking of Contra-Tied Plot." *Washington Post*, Oct. 4, 1996.

Terzian, Philip. "CIA Rumors Not All They're Cracked Up to Be? Familiar Thesis." *Washington Times*, Oct. 19, 1996.

Tucker, Cynthia. "CIA's Drug Dealing Role." *San Francisco Chronicle,* Sept. 21, 1996.

Waters, Lou. "Journalist Points to CIA Involvement in Drugs." (Interview with Gary Webb and Ronald Kessler.) *CNN Today*, Sept. 20, 1996.

Washington Post, editorial. "The Story of the Crack Explosion." *Washington Post,* Oct. 9, 1996.

Washington Times, editorial. "The CIA and Drugs." *Washington Times,* Oct. 23, 1996.

Webb, Gary. "Webb on 'Dark Alliance.'" (Letter) *American Journalism Review,* April 1997.

Weise, Elizabeth. "Series Draws Black Community to the Web." AP Wire, Dec. 9, 1996.

Weinberg, Steve. "Crack and the Contras." *Baltimore Sun,* Nov. 17, 1996.

Weiner, Tim. "CIA Says It Has Found No Link Between Itself and Crack Trade." *New York Times,* Dec. 19, 1997.

White, Jack E. "Crack, Contras and Cyberspace." *Time,* Sept. 30, 1996.

——. "Caught in the Middle: The CIA–Crack Story Put Black Reporters in a Bind." *Time*. May 26, 1997.

Wickham, DeWayne. "Clinton Must Act on CIA/Crack Case." *Tampa Tribune,* Oct. 21, 1996.

3

The History of Black "Paranoia"

The fury among American blacks sparked by Webb's "Dark Alliance" series was powerful enough to cause serious concern to the US government, urban mayors and major newspapers, and even prompted CIA director John Deutch to make an extraordinary appearance at a town meeting in South Central Los Angeles.

One of the first to seize on the significance of Webb's series was Joe Madison, the black host of a syndicated talk show on WWRC based in Washington, D.C. Madison read Webb's series on the air and devoted two full weeks of his show to an explanation of the charges, and a detailed examination of the CIA, its history of domestic spying and its role in toppling black leaders round the world. Madison's shows were not Rush Limbaugh–style rants but thoughtful attempts to push the story forward. Gary Webb was interviewed on the show several times, as were black historians explaining the rise of the national security state and urban sociologists exploring the history of the crack epidemic in the 1980s. Madison also brought on to his show former DEA man Celerino Castillo III, who had worked as a narcotics agent in El Salvador at the height of the Contra War. Castillo described for Madison's audience how he had watched Contra supply planes at the Ilopango air base outside San Salvador arrive loaded with weapons and leave for the United

States packed with cocaine. He also recounted how he developed extensive case files on the smuggling operations of the CIA-backed Contras, including the serial numbers of the airplanes used and the names of the pilots and his informants. He had sent this information back to DEA headquarters: "All of my reports went into a black hole and I was told by my superiors, your career is going to end in Central America if you keep this up." Castillo persisted in his investigation and the DEA carried out its threat by transferring him from El Salvador and then by launching an investigation of him.

Madison also teamed up with the black activist Dick Gregory. On September 11, the two held a press conference at the National Press Club to demand a federal investigation into the charges made in the *San Jose Mercury News,* and also that the CIA be compelled to declassify and release all documents relating to activities involving drug traffickers. Madison and Gregory then left the Press Club, crossed the Potomac and showed up at CIA headquarters in Langley, Virginia. Their plan was to make a personal delivery of copies of the *Mercury News* series to John Deutch. They were stopped at the entrance by CIA internal security. Madison and Gregory refused to leave without a personal meeting with Deutch, were then arrested and taken away.

On the political side, Rep. Maxine Waters, who represents South Central Los Angeles in Congress, seized on the *Mercury News* series. She pressed House Speaker Newt Gingrich to order a congressional investigation into the charges and petitioned both Deutch and US Attorney General Janet Reno to launch probes. She then organized a session at the Congressional Black Caucus legislative conference entitled "Cocaine, Contras and the CIA: How They Introduced Crack into the Inner Cities." The session drew a crowd of 2,000 in Washington, D.C.

Waters used the floor of the House aggressively to put the story before C-SPAN viewers, and she organized town meetings not only in Los Angeles but in Detroit, Denver and Atlanta where, despite constant jibes inside the Beltway, her efforts met with a sympathetic hearing. In Los Angeles she extracted important corroborating evidence that had been deep-sixed by the Los Angeles Sheriff's Department; she also went to the San Diego jail and interviewed Rick Ross. In addition, she traveled to Managua, where she tracked down Enrique Miranda, the former Somocista intelligence officer who was Meneses's link to the Calí cocaine cartel. Waters said Miranda "gave me information about the connection between Meneses and Blandón and he indicated he had been involved in drug running with Meneses and the Calí Cartel."

Waters was also a constant thorn in the side of her hometown newspaper, continually berating the *Los Angeles Times* for its hostile stance toward the whole story. This hostility, she explains, left her no option but to go on the road and spread the story by meeting with church groups and alternative media and appearing on talk radio. "In South Central Los Angeles we wondered where these guns were coming from," she recalls. "They were not simply handguns, they were Uzis and AK-47s, sophisticated weapons brought in by the same CIA operatives who were selling the cocaine because they had to enforce bringing the profits back in. It was at about this time when you saw all these guns coming into the community, that you saw more and more killing, more and more violence. Now we know what was going on. The drugs were put in our communities on consignment, out to the gangs and others. If they did not bring the profits back, the guns were brought in so they could enforce their control. The killings just mounted and people said, 'What are they fighting about? What are these drive-by shootings about? What is this gang warfare?' And the press said, 'Oh, it's the colors. Some like red, some like blue.' Well, you know it was about the drugs, it was about crack cocaine, introduced into our communities by people who brought it in with a purpose."

As for the attacks on Webb by the *New York Times* and *Los Angeles Times,* Waters notes that at least they had admitted that money had gone to the Contras: "I never cared how much money was involved. Just that it happened."

Waters was not deterred by the mean-spirited and often racist attacks of her journalistic critics, particularly those at the *New Republic*. Shortly after the CIA finally unveiled the hitherto secret annual intelligence budget – $26.7 billion – Waters took to the floor of the House of Representatives and in a sixty-minute speech called for the Agency to be "zeroed out": "I know that there are some who will say that this is a very, very harsh recommendation, but it is no harsher than the recommendation that came to this House from the other side of the aisle when they said to get rid of the Department of Education."

And, of course, Waters was accused of fanning the flames of "black paranoia." The following sections briefly outline why this "paranoia" is amply justified and why Webb's series very reasonably struck a chord in the black community.

In all discussions of "black paranoia" during the Webb affair, white commentators invariably conceded – as indeed they had to – that the one instance where such fears were entirely justified was the infamous Tuskegee experiments. Yet in all of the press coverage no more than a sentence or two was devoted to any account of what actually happened at Tuskegee.

The facts are terrible. In 1932, 600 poor black men from rural Macon County, Alabama were recruited for a study by the United States Public Health Service and the Tuskegee Institute. The researchers found 400 out of the 600 infected with syphilis, and the 200 uninfected men were monitored as the control group. The other 400 men were told they were being treated for "bad blood" and were given a treatment the doctors called "pink medicine," which was actually nothing more than aspirin and an iron supplement. No effective medical treatment was ever given to the Tuskegee victims because the researchers wanted to study the natural progress of venereal disease. When other physicians diagnosed syphilis in some of the men, the Public Health Service researchers intervened to prevent any treatment. When penicillin was developed as a cure for syphilis in 1943 it was not provided to the patients. Indeed, the development of a cure only seemed to spur on the Tuskegee researchers, who, in the words of historian James Jones, author of *Bad Blood,* saw Tuskegee as a "never-again-to-be-repeated opportunity."

As an inducement to continue in the program over several decades the men were given hot meals, a certificate signed by the surgeon general, the promise of free medical care and a $50 burial stipend. This stipend was far from altruistic because it allowed the Health Service researchers to perform their own autopsies on the men after they died. The experiments continued until 1972, and were canceled only after information about them had leaked to the press. Over the course of the experiments more than 100 of the men died of causes related to syphilis, but even after exposure, the lead researchers remained unapologetic. "For the most part, doctors and civil servants simply did their job," said Dr. John Heller, who had headed the US Public Health Services Division of Venereal Diseases: "Some merely followed orders, others worked for the glory of science."

In 1996 President Clinton issued a public apology to the Tuskegee victims. Nor was this an entirely disinterested act of governmental contrition. Earlier in the year Clinton had been approached by Secretary of Health and Human Services Donna Shalala regarding the scarcity of blacks willing to volunteer as research subjects. Shalala attributed this reluctance to "unnatural fears" arising from the Tuskegee experiments. George Annas, who runs the Law, Ethics and Medicine program at Boston University, notes that the apology was skewed and that Clinton and Shalala should have been finding ways of recruiting more blacks as medical students rather than research subjects. "If you were to look at the historical record, you will see that blacks' distrust predated Tuskegee," according to Dr. Vanessa Gamble, an associate professor of the history of medicine at the University of Wisconsin at Madison. "There were experiments dating back to more than a hundred years that were more often done by whites on slaves and free blacks than on poor whites."

Another oft-cited explanation for the readiness of blacks to believe the worst about the white man's intentions is briskly referred to as "the FBI's snooping on Martin Luther King Jr.," as Tim Golden put it amid his reflections on black paranoia in the *New York Times*. The government's interest in Dr. King went considerably beyond "snooping," however, to constitute one of the most prolonged surveillances of any family in American history. In the early years of the century, Lieut.-Col. Ralph Van Deman created an Army Intelligence network targeting four prime foes: the Industrial Workers of the World, opponents of the draft, Socialists and "Negro unrest." Fear that the Germans would take advantage of black grievances was great, and Van Deman was much preoccupied with the role of black churches as possible centers of sedition.

By the end of 1917 the War Department's Military Intelligence Division had opened a file on Martin Luther King Jr.'s maternal grandfather, the Rev. A. D. Williams, pastor of Ebenezer Baptist Church and first president of the Atlanta NAACP. King's father, Martin Sr., Williams's successor at Ebenezer Baptist, also entered the army files. Martin Jr. first shows up in these files (kept by the 111th Military Intelligence Group at Fort McPherson in Atlanta) in 1947, when he attended Dorothy Lilley's Intercollegiate School; the army suspected Lilley of having ties to the Communist Party.

Army Intelligence officers became convinced of Martin Luther King Jr.'s own Communist ties when he spoke in 1950 at the twenty-fifth anniversary of the integrated Highlander Folk School in Monteagle, Tennessee. Ten years earlier, an Army Intelligence officer had reported to his superiors that the Highlander school was teaching a course of instruction to develop Negro organizers in the southern cotton states.

By 1963, so Tennessee journalist Stephen Tompkins reported in the *Memphis Commercial Appeal,* U-2 planes were photographing disturbances in Birmingham, Alabama, capping a multilayered spy system that by 1968 included 304 intelligence offices across the country, "subversive national security dossiers" on 80,731 Americans, plus 19 million personnel dossiers lodged at the Defense Department's Central Index of Investigations.

A more sinister thread derives from the anger and fear with which the army high command greeted King's denunciation of the Vietnam War at Riverside Church in 1967. Army spies recorded Stokely Carmichael telling King, "The Man don't care you call ghettos concentration camps, but when you tell him his war machine is nothing but hired killers you got trouble."

After the 1967 Detroit riots, 496 black men under arrest were interviewed by agents of the army's Psychological Operations group, dressed as civilians. It turned out King was by far the most popular black leader. That same year Maj. Gen. William Yarborough, assistant chief of staff for intelligence, observing the great antiwar march on Washington from the roof of the Pentagon, concluded that the empire was coming apart at the seams. There were, Yarborough reckoned, too few reliable troops to fight in Vietnam and hold the line at home.

In response, the army increased its surveillance of King. Green Berets and other Special Forces veterans from Vietnam began making street maps and identifying landing zones and potential sniper sites in major US cities. The Ku Klux Klan was recruited by the 20th Special Forces Group, headquartered in Alabama as a subsidiary intelligence network. The army began offering 30.06 sniper rifles to police departments, including that of Memphis.

In his fine investigation, Tompkins detailed the increasing hysteria of Army Intelligence chiefs over the threat they considered King to pose to national stability. The FBI's J. Edgar Hoover was similarly obsessed, and King was dogged by spy units through early 1967. A Green Beret special unit was operating in Memphis on the day he was shot. He died from a bullet from a 30.06 rifle purchased in a Memphis store, a murder for which James Earl Ray was given a 99-year sentence in a Tennessee prison. A court-ordered test of James Earl Ray's rifle raised questions as to whether it in fact had fired the bullet that killed King.

Notable black Americans, from the boxing champion Jack Johnson to Paul Robeson to W. E. B. Du Bois were all the object of relentless harassment by the FBI. Johnson, the first black superstar, was framed by the FBI's predecessor under the Mann Act. Johnson ultimately served a year for crossing state lines with his white girlfriend (who later became his wife). Du Bois, founder of the NAACP, was himself under surveillance for nearly seventy years and was arrested and shackled for urging peace talks with North Korea.

Still fresh in the minds of many blacks is the FBI's COINTELPRO program, started in 1956 and conceived as a domestic counterinsurgency program. Though its ambit extended to the New Left, Puerto Rican revolutionaries and Native Americans, the most vigorous persecutions under COINTELPRO were those of black leaders. A memo from FBI director J. Edgar Hoover described the program as it stood in August 1967: the purpose of COINTELPRO was to "expose, disrupt, misdirect, discredit or otherwise neutralize" black organizations the FBI didn't care for. And if any black leader emerged, Hoover's order was that the Bureau should "pinpoint potential troublemakers and neutralize them before they exercised their potential for violence."

"Neutralize" has long been government-speak for assassination. At least six or seven Black Panther leaders were killed at the instigation of the FBI, the most infamous episode being the assassination of Fred

Hampton and Mark Clark in Chicago. These two Panther leaders were shot in their beds while asleep, by Chicago police who had been given a detailed floor plan of the house by an FBI informant who had also drugged Hampton and Clark.

During the mid-1970s hearings chaired by Idaho Senator Frank Church, the FBI was found to have undertaken more than 200 so-called "black bag" jobs, in which FBI agents broke into offices, homes and apartments to destroy equipment, steal and copy files, take money and plant drugs. The FBI was also linked to the arson fire that destroyed the Watts Writers Workshop in Los Angeles.

In all the stories about "black paranoia" trolled forth by Webb's assailants one topic was conspicuously ignored: the long history of the racist application of US drug laws.

The first racist application of drug laws in the United States was against Chinese laborers. After the US Civil War opium addiction was a major problem: wounded soldiers used it to dull pain and then became habituated. One study estimates that by 1880, 1 in every 400 adults in the United States had such an addiction to opium. Chinese laborers had been brought into the United States in the wake of the Civil War to build the transcontinental railroad and, in California, to haul rock in the gold mines in the Sierras. Thousands of Chinese were also brought into the South to replace slave labor on the cotton and rice plantations. The Chinese brought opium smoking with them, their addiction having actively fostered in the Opium Wars by the British, who had successfully beaten down efforts by the Chinese government to curb the habit.

Then came the recession of the 1870s. The Chinese were now viewed as competitors for the dwindling number of jobs available. In 1875 San Francisco became the first city to outlaw opium smoking with legislation clearly aimed at the Chinese, who smoked the narcotic, as opposed to the main group of users, white men and women, who took opium in liquid form. This was the era when the use of opium-based patent medicines was pervasive. Women used them in "tonics" to alleviate pain in childbirth, and also to "soothe" their nerves. Unlike the "yellow dope fiends," however, the white users were politely termed "habitués." In 1887 the US Congress weighed in with the Chinese Exclusion Act, which among other things, allowing Chinese opium addicts to be arrested and deported.

Similarly racist attitudes accompanied the rise of cocaine use. Cocaine had been mass marketed in the United States in the late 1880s by the Parke-Davis Company (which many decades later had contracts to provide the CIA with drugs in the MK-ULTRA program). The company also sold a precursor to crack, marketing cocaine-laden cigarettes in the 1890s. In that same decade the Sears & Roebuck catalogue, which was distributed to millions of homes, offered a syringe and a small amount of cocaine for $1.50. But by the turn of the century the attitude of the medical and legal establishment to cocaine was beginning to change. In 1900 the *Journal of the American Medical Association* printed an editorial alerting its leaders to a new peril: "Negroes in the South are reported as being addicted to a new form of vice – that of 'cocaine sniffing' or the 'coke habit.'"

President Theodore Roosevelt responded to the new scare by creating the nation's first drug czar, Dr. Hamilton Wright. Wright was a fanatic racist, announcing that "[i]t is been authoritatively stated that cocaine is often the direct incentive to the crime of rape by the Negroes of the South and other regions." One of Wright's favored authorities was Dr. Christopher Koch of the State Pharmacy Board of Pennsylvania. Koch testified before Congress in 1914 in support of the Harrison Bill, shortly to pass into law as the first criminalization of drug use. Said Koch: "Most of the attacks upon the white women of the South are the direct result of a cocaine-crazed Negro brain." At the same hearing, Wright alleged that drugs made blacks uncontrollable, gave them superhuman powers and prompted them to rebel against white authority. These hysterical charges were trumpeted by the press, in particular the *New York Times,* which on February 8, 1914, ran an article by Edward Hunting Williams reporting how Southern sheriffs had upped the caliber of their weapons from .32 to .38 in order to bring down black men under the influence of cocaine. The *Times'*s headline for the article read, "Negro Cocaine 'Fiends' Are New Southern Menace: Murder and Insanity Increasing Among Lower-Class Blacks." Amid these salvoes, the Harrison Act passed into law.

In 1930 a new department of the federal government, the Bureau of

Narcotics and Dangerous Drugs, was formed under the leadership of Harry Anslinger to carry on the war against drug users. Anslinger, another racist, was an adroit publicist and became the prime shaper of American attitudes to drug addiction, hammering home his view that this was not a treatable addiction but one that could only be suppressed by harsh criminal sanctions. Anslinger's first major campaign was to criminalize the drug commonly known at the time as hemp. But Anslinger renamed it "marijuana" to associate it with Mexican laborers who, like the Chinese before them, were unwelcome competitors for scarce jobs in the Depression. Anslinger claimed that marijuana "can arouse in blacks and Hispanics a state of menacing fury or homicidal attack. During this period, addicts have perpetrated some of the most bizarre and fantastic offenses and sex crimes known to police annals."

Anslinger linked marijuana with jazz and persecuted many black musicians, including Thelonius Monk, Dizzy Gillespie and Duke Ellington. Louis Armstrong was also arrested on drug charges, and Anslinger made sure his name was smeared in the press. In Congress he testified that "[c]oloreds with big lips lure white women with jazz and marijuana."

By the 1950s, amid the full blast of the Cold War, Anslinger was working with the CIA to charge that the new-born People's Republic of China was attempting to undermine America by selling opium to US crime syndicates. (This took a good deal of chutzpa on the part of the CIA, whose planes, as we show in a later chapter, were then flying opium from Chiang Kai-shek's bases in Burma to Thailand and the Philippines for processing and export to the US.) Anslinger convinced the US Senate to approve a resolution stating that "subversion through drug addiction is an established aim of Communist China."

In 1951 Anslinger worked with Democrat Hale Boggs to marshall through Congress the first minimum mandatory sentences for drug possession: two years for the first conviction of possession of a Schedule 1 drug (marijuana, cocaine), five to ten years for a second offense, and ten to twenty years for a third conviction.) In 1956 Anslinger once again enlisted the help of Boggs to pass a law allowing the death penalty to be imposed on anyone selling heroin to a minor, the first linking of drugs with Death Row.

This was Anslinger's last hurrah. Along John Kennedy's New Frontier cantered sociologists attacking Anslinger's punitive philosophy. The tempo of the times changed, and federal money began to target treatment and prevention as much as enforcement and prison. But the interim did not last long. With the waning of the war in Southeast Asia millions of addicted GIs came home to meet the fury of Nixon's War on Drugs program. Nixon picked up Anslinger's techniques of threat inflation, declaring in Los Angeles that "as I look over the problems of this country I see that one stands out particularly: the problem of narcotics."

Nixon pledged to launch a war on drugs, to return to the punitive approach and not let any quaint notions of civil liberties and constitutional rights stand in the way. After a Nixon briefing in 1969, his top aide, H. R. Haldeman noted in his diary: "Nixon emphasized that you have to face the fact that the whole problem is really the blacks. The key is to devise a system that recognizes this while not appearing to."

But for all his bluster, Nixon was a mere prelude to the full fury of the Reagan-Bush-Clinton years, when the War on Drugs became explicitly a war on blacks. The first move of the Reagan administration was to expand the forfeiture laws passed during the Carter administration. In 1981 Reagan's drug policy advisers outlined a plan they thought would be little more than good PR, a public display of the required toughness. They proposed allowing the Justice Department to seize real property and so-called "substitute property" (that is, legally acquired assets equal in value to illegal monetary gains). They also proposed that the federal government seize attorneys' fees that they suspected might have been funded by drug proceeds. They even proposed to allow attorneys to be summoned by federal prosecutors before grand juries to testify about the source of their clients' money. The Reagan plan was to permit forfeitures on the basis of a "probable cause showing" before a federal judge. This meant that seizures could be made against people neither charged nor convicted, but only suspected, of drug crimes.

Contrary to the administration's expectations this plan sailed through Congress, eagerly supported by two Democratic Party liberals, Senators Hubert H. Humphrey and Joe Biden, the latter being the artificer, in the Carter era, of a revision to the RICO act, a huge extension of the federal conspiracy laws. Over the next few years the press would occasionally report on some exceptionally bizarre applications of the new forfeiture laws, such as the confiscation of a $2.5 million yacht in a drug bust that netted only a handful of marijuana stems and seeds. But typically the press ignored the essential pattern of humdrum seizures, which more often focused on such ordinary assets as houses and cars. In Orange County, California, fifty-seven cars were seized in drug-related cases in 1989: "Even if only a small amount of drugs is found inside," an Orange County narcotics detective explained, "the law permits seized vehicles to be sold by law enforcement agencies to finance anti-drug law enforcement programs."

In fact, the forfeiture program became a tremendous revenue stream for the police. From 1982 to 1991 the US Department of Justice seized more than $2.5 billion in assets. The Justice Department confiscated $500 million in property in 1991 alone, and 80 percent of these seizures were from people who were never charged with a crime.

On June 17, 1986 University of Maryland basketball star Len Bias died, reportedly from an overdose of cocaine. As Dan Baum put it in his excellent *Smoke and Mirrors: The War on Drugs and the Politics of Failure,* "In life, Len Bias was a terrific basketball player. In death he became the Archduke Ferdinand of the Total War on Drugs." It was falsely reported that Bias had smoked crack cocaine the night before his death. (He had in fact used powder cocaine and, according to the coroner, there was no clear link between this use and the failure of his heart.)

Bias had signed with the Boston Celtics and amid Boston's rage and grief, Speaker of the House Tip O'Neill, a representative from Massachusetts, rushed into action. In early July he convened a meeting of the Democratic Party leadership: "Write me some goddam legislation," he ordered. "All anybody in Boston is talking about is Len Bias. They want blood. If we move fast enough we can get out in front of the White House." The White House was itself moving fast. Among other things the DEA had been instructed to allow ABC News to accompany it on raids against crack houses. "Crack is the hottest combat-reporting story to come along since the end of the Vietnam War," the head of the the the New York office of the DEA exulted.

All this fed into congressional frenzy to write tougher laws. House majority leader Jim Wright called drug abuse "a menace draining away our economy of some $230 billion this year, slowly rotting away the fabric of our society and seducing and killing our young." Not to be outdone, South Carolina Republican Thomas Arnett proclaimed that "drugs are a threat worse than nuclear warfare or any chemical warfare waged on any battlefield." The 1986 Anti-Drug Abuse Act was duly passed. It contained twenty-nine new minimum mandatory sentences. Up until that time in the history of the Republic there had been only fifty-six mandatory minimum sentences. The new law had a death penalty provision for drug "king pins" and prohibited parole for even minor possession offenses. But the chief target of the bill was crack cocaine. Congress established a 100-to-1 sentencing ratio between possession of crack and powder cocaine. Under this provision possession of 5 grams of crack carries a minimum five-year federal prison sentence. The same mandatory minimum is not reached for any amount of powder cocaine under 500 grams. This sentencing disproportion was based on faulty testimony that crack was fifty times as addictive as powder cocaine. Congress then doubled this ratio as a so-called "violence penalty." There is no inherent difference in the drugs, as Clinton drug czar Barry McCaffery conceded. The federal Sentencing Commission, established by Congress to review sentencing guidelines, found that so-called "crack violence" is attributable to the drug trade and has more to do with the setting in which crack is sold: crack is sold on the street, while powder cocaine is vended by house calls. As Nixon and Haldeman would have approvingly noted about the new drug law, it was transparently aimed at blacks, reminiscent of the early targeting of Chinese smoking opium rather than ladies sipping their laudanum-laced tonics.

In 1995 the US Sentencing Commission reviewed eight years of application of this provision and found it to be undeniably racist in practice: 84 percent of those arrested for crack possession were black, while only 10 percent were white and 5 percent Hispanic. The disparity for crack-trafficking prosecutions was even wider: 88 percent blacks, 7 percent Hispanics, 4 percent whites. By comparison, defendants arrested for powder cocaine possession were 58 percent white, 26 percent black and 15 percent Hispanic.

In Los Angeles all twenty-four federal defendants in crack cases in 1991 were black. The Sentencing Commission recommended to Congress and the Clinton administration that the ratio should be one-to-one between sentences for offenses involving crack and powder cocaine, arguing that federal law allows for other factors to be considered by judges in lengthening sentences (such as whether violence was associated with the offense). But for the first time in its history the Congress rejected the Sentencing Commission's recommendation and retained the 100-to-1 ratio. Clinton likewise declined the advice of his drug czar and his attorney general, and signed the bill.

One need only look at the racial make-up of federal prisons to appreciate the consequences of the 1986 drug law. In 1983 the total number of prisoners in federal, state and local prisons and jails was 660,800. Of those, 57,975 – 8.8 percent – were incarcerated for drug-related offenses. In 1993 the total prison population was 1,408,000, of whom 353,564 – 25.1 percent – were inside for drug offenses. The Sentencing Project, a Washington, D.C.–based watchdog group, found that the increase was far from racially balanced. Between 1986 and 1991 the incarceration rate for white males convicted on drug crimes increased by 106 percent. But the number of black males in prison for kindred offenses soared by a factor of 429 percent, and the rate for black women went up by an incredible 828 percent.

The queen of the drug war, Nancy Reagan, said amid one of her innumerable sermons on the issue, "If you're a casual drug user, you're an accomplice to murder." In tune with this line of thinking, Congress moved in 1988 to expand the crimes for which the federal death penalty could be imposed. These included drug-related murders, and murders committed by drug gangs, which would allow any gang member to face the death penalty if one member of the gang was linked to a drug killing. The new penalties were inscribed in an update of the Continuing Criminal Enterprises Act. The figures arising from implementation of the act suggest that "black paranoia" has in fact a sound basis in reality.

Convictions under the act between 1989 and 1996 were 70 percent white and 24 percent black – but 90 percent of the times the federal prosecutors sought the death penalty it was against non-whites: of these, 78 percent were black and the rest Hispanic. From 1930 to 1972 (when the US Supreme Court found the federal death penalty unconstitutional) 85 percent of those given death sentences were white. When it was reapplied in 1984, with the Anti-Drug Abuse Act, the numbers for black death penalty convictions soared. Whether the offense is drug-related or not, a black is far more likely to end up on Death Row. Of those on Death Row, both federal and state, 50 percent are black. Blacks constitute 16 percent of the population. Since 1976 40 percent of the nation's homicide victims have been black, but 90 percent of death sentences handed down for homicide involved white victims.

In the drug war, Los Angeles was Ground Zero. On the streets of Los Angeles, gang-related killings were a constant presence to the residents of the mostly poor areas in which they occurred, as gangs fought out turf battles for distribution rights to the crack supplied by Rick Ross and his associates in an operation connived at by the CIA. As long as it was confined to black areas of Los Angeles, little official attention was paid to this slaughter – an average of one murder per day from 1988 through 1990. However, in December 1987 a gang mistakenly killed 27-year-old Karen Toshima outside a cinema complex in Westwood, near the UCLA campus, prompting outrage from the city's government: "The continued protection of gang activity under the guise of upholding our constitution is causing a deadly blight on our city," cried Los Angeles City Attorney Kenneth Hahn.

LAPD Chief Darryl Gates promptly rolled out his campaign to pacify inner-city Los Angeles, Operation Hammer. Even before this campaign the LAPD was not known for its sensitivity to black people. In the 1970s there had been more than 300 killings of non-whites by the LAPD, and Gate's own racism was notorious. Responding to complaints about a string of choke-hold deaths, Gates blamed them on the physiology of blacks: "We may be finding that in some blacks, when [the choke-hold] is applied, the veins or arteries do not open as fast as they do on normal people."

Operation Hammer was a counterinsurgency program that sometimes resembled the Phoenix program in Vietnam. There were hundreds of commando-style raids on "gang houses." More than 50,000 suspected gang members were swept up for interrogation based on factors such as style of dress and whether the suspect was a young black male on the street past curfew. Of those caught up in such Hammer sweeps, 90 percent were later released without charge, but their names were held in a computer database of gang members that was later shown to have included twice as many names as there were black youths in Los Angeles. Gates sealed off large areas of South Central as "narcotics enforcement zones." There was a strict curfew, constant police presence and on-the-spot strip searches for those caught outside after curfew.

In this war there were many innocent casualties. In 1989 the LAPD shotgunned to death an 81-year-old man they wrongly believed to be a crack dealer. Witnesses claimed that the old man had his hands up when he was blown away. In 1989, 75 percent of all cases in the Los Angeles criminal courts were drug-related.

It would be difficult to find any documentary evidence that this war on drugs had anything other than a deleterious effect. By 1990 black youth unemployment in the greater Los Angeles area was 45 percent. Nearly half of all black males under the age of twenty-five had been in the criminal justice system. Life expectancy for blacks was falling for the first time in this century, and infant mortality in the city was rising. Some 40 percent of black children were born into poverty.

Among those white people concerned by the awful conditions of life in the inner cities was government psychiatrist Fred Goodwin. In 1992 he was director of the umbrella agency ADAMHA, the Alcohol, Drug Abuse, and Mental Health Administration. Goodwin was an eager crusader for a national biomedical program to control violence, the core notion being the search for a "violence" gene. In the quest for this supposed biological basis for social crisis in the poverty-stricken and crime-ridden ghettoes Goodwin was replicating all the Malthusian obsessions of late-nineteenth and early-twentieth-century white American intellectuals and politicians. Many of supposedly enlightened people like Woodrow Wilson believed that sterilization was the best way to maintain the cleanliness in the national gene pool. It was too late to stop the arrival of Africans, but these Malthusians inspired the race exclusion laws of 1923, designed to keep out genetically dubious Slavs, Jews, Italians and other rabble – legislation admired by the Nazis.

On February 11, 1992, Goodwin gave a speech to the National Mental Health Advisory Council on the future of federal mental health policy, calling for an approach that would focus on presumed genetic and biomedical factors. Among Goodwin's observations in his address:

There are discussions of "biological correlates" and "biological markers." The individuals have defective brains with detectable 'prefrontal changes that may well be predictive of later violence. The individuals have impaired intelligence, in this case "cognitive deficit." ... Now, one could say that if some of the loss of social structure in this society, and particularly within the high impact inner city areas, has removed some of the civilizing evolutionary things that we have built up and that maybe it isn't just the careless use of the word when people call certain areas of certain cities jungles, that we may have gone back to what might be more natural, without all of the social controls that we have imposed upon ourselves as a civilization over thousands of years in our evolution.

If you look, for example, at male monkeys, especially in the wild, roughly half of them survive to adulthood. The other half die by violence. That is the natural way of it for males, to knock each other off and, in fact, there are some interesting evolutionary implications of that because the same hyperaggressive monkeys who kill each other are also hypersexual, so they copulate more and therefore they reproduce more to offset the fact that half of them are dying.

Goodwin called for early identification of these dangerous monkey-men. "There will be emphasis on the earliest detection of behavioral patterns which have predictor value, and two, what do we know and what can we learn about preventive interventions."

Goodwin did not address treatment issues further, but a news story in the *Washington Post* by Boyce Rensberger noted that NIMH psychiatrists who supported Goodwin and his violence initiative were testing new medications to correct the biochemical imbalances supposedly found in both violent monkeys and men.

Goodwin's remarks were reported in the press and created a commotion. There was a brief spasm of official admonition, and he was "demoted" to the post of director of the National Institute of Mental Health, a position for which he had been already slated.

Would a black man or woman already "paranoid" about the idea of the problem of poverty being addressed by government chemists carrying "rebalancing" agents in their syringes have been hyperbolically paranoid in seeing traces of a longer obsession on the part of the government agencies such as the CIA?

Goodwin was himself only following in the footsteps of "Jolly" West. West is a psychiatrist in UCLA who is well known for his suzerainty over the university's Neuropsychiatric Institute. Back in 1969 he leaped to prominence with disclosure of his plan to put electrodes in the brains of suspected violent offenders at a spin-off of the institute called the Center for the Study and Reduction of Violence. Public uproar forced West to abandon this scheme. In 1973 West once again sought to set up a center for human experimentation, this time at a former Nike missile base in the Santa Monica Mountains. In this pastoral setting the work of scientific experimentation would proceed undisturbed: "The site is securely fenced," West wrote excitedly to the California state legislature. "Comparative studies could be carried out there, in an isolated but convenient location, of experimental model programs, for alteration of undesirable behavior."

West had long worked with CIA chemists and kindred boffins on the use of LSD in altering human behavior – and not just that of humans, either. In 1962 West killed Tusko, a renowned elephant at the Oklahoma City zoo. He shot the mighty pachyderm full of LSD and Tusko swiftly succumbed. West claimed that the zookeeper had brought him the elephant for treatment.

In the late 1960s and early 1970s neurologists and psychiatrists were much taken with the problems of urban violence. One of West's mentors was Dr. Ernst Rodin, a Dr. Strangelove–type heading up the Neurology Department at the Lafayette Clinic, who recommended psychosurgery and castration as appropriate medical technologies to apply to the dangerous classes.

Rodin equated "dumb young males who riot" to oxen and declared that "the castrated ox will pull his plow" and that "human eunuchs, although at times quite scheming entrepreneurs are not given to physical violence. Our scientific age tends to disregard this wisdom of the past."

West made similar statements after the Watts rebellion, but for the castrator's sickle he recommended the substitution of cyproterone acetate, a sterilizing chemical developed by the East Germans. By 1972 West was suggesting the use of prisoners as "subjects" in such treatment. There was a big stink about this, and in 1974 statewide protests led to cuts of state funding to West's project. In his *Operation Mind Control* Walter Bowart wrote that West is "perhaps the chief advocate of mind control in America today."

West put his finger unerringly on the usefulness of drug laws as a way of imposing selective social control. "The role of drugs in the exercise of political control is also coming under increasing discussion," he wrote in *Hallucinations: Behavior, Experience and Theory,* a book he edited in 1975. "Control can be imposed either through prohibition or supply. The total or even partial prohibition of drugs gives government considerable leverage for other types of control. An example would be the selective application of drug laws ... against selected components of the population such as members of certain minority groups or political organizations." As we have seen, sentencing patterns vindicate West's analysis.

It is not in the least paranoid for any black person to conclude that since the late nineteenth century prominent white intellectuals and politicians have devoted much effort to reducing the number of black people by the expedient of sterilization, or selective medical assault, often chastely described as the "science" of eugenics.

Back in 1910, blunt as always, Home Secretary Winston Churchill used his position to secretly propose the sterilization of 100,000 "mental degenerates" in the UK, using as intellectual buttress a book by Dr. H. C. Sharp of the Indiana Reformatory in the US. In the first couple of decades of the twentieth-century American elites also were much concerned about the national gene pool (the founders of Cal Tech, for example, were rabid eugenicists). Between 1907 and 1913, starting with Indiana, twelve states put sterilization statutes on their books, Indiana's Governor J. Frank Hanley, signed a law authorizing the compulsory sterilization of any confirmed criminal, idiot, rapist or imbecile in a state institution whose condition was determined to be "unimprovable" by a panel of physicians.

Allan Chase in *The Legacy of Malthus* reports that 63,678 people were compulsorily sterilized between 1907 and 1964 in thirty states and one colony with such laws. But he also points out that these victims represent "the smallest part of the actual number of Americans who have this century been subjected to forced eugenic sterilization operations by state and federal agencies." Chase quotes federal judge Gerhard Gessell as saying in 1974 in a suit brought on behalf of poor victims of involuntary sterilization: "Over the last few years an estimated 100,000 to 150,000 low-income persons have been sterilized annually in federally funded programs." This rate, as Chase points out, equals that achieved in Nazi Germany. Across the twelve years of the Third Reich, after the German Sterilization Act of 1933 (inspired by US laws) went into effect, 2 million Germans were sterilized as social inadequates.

Gesell said that though Congress had been insistent that all family planning programs function on a purely voluntary basis, " an indefinite number of poor people have been improperly coerced into accepting a sterilization operation under the threat that various federally supported welfare benefits would be withdrawn unless they submitted to irreversible sterilization. Patients receiving Medicaid assistance at childbirth are evidently the most frequent targets of this pressure." Among the plaintiffs in this action was Katie Relf of Alabama, who fought off the advancing sterilizers by locking herself in her room. Writing toward the end of the 1970s, Chase reckoned that probably at least 200,000 Americans per year were the victims of involuntary and irreversible sterilization.

In the great program of sterilization, the note of commonsensical do-goodism was relentlessly sounded. Take the California sterilizer and racist Paul Popenoe, a man close to the Chandler family, who owned the *Los Angeles Times.* In a 1930 pamphlet, "Sterilization for Human Betterment," Popenoe and his co-author E. S. Gosney cautioned thus: "One of the greatest dangers in the use of sterilization is that overzealous persons who have not thought through the subject will look on it as a cure-all, and apply it to all sorts of ends for which it is not adapted. It is only one of many measures that the state can and must use to protect itself from racial deterioration. Ordinarily it is merely adjunct to supervision of the defective or diseased.

"The objection is sometimes made that sterilization will at least deprive the world of many useful, law-abiding, self-supporting citizens. They may not be brilliant, it is admitted; but isn't there a need for a large portion of dull people in modern civilization, to do the rough and routine work that the intellectuals are unwilling to do? If the breeding of all the morons is stopped, who will dig the sewers and collect the garbage?

"Fortunately or unfortunately, there is no possibility of stopping production of morons altogether. Many of them are born in families of normal intelligence, simply through unfavorable combination of genes which carry the heredity. There will always be enough of them produced to dig sewers and collect the garbage, without encouraging the reproduction of people who are likely to produce only morons."

Though race-specific terms were usually avoided by eugenicists, who preferred words like "weak-minded," or "imbeciles" (a favorite of that enthusiast for sterilizing, Oliver Wendell Holmes, a jurist much admired by liberals), the target was, by and large, blacks. What direct sterilization could not prevent, incarceration or medically justified confinement has also sought to achieve.

So far as medical confinement is concerned, the magazine *Southern Exposure* has documented the excessively large number of blacks locked up in state-run mental hospitals in the southern US. In 1987 nearly 37 percent of those involuntarily committed were black. The blacks were consistently diagnosed with more serious illnesses, more frequently subjected to sedative medicine, and held in greater numbers for indefinite confinement without judicial review. The pattern, so the article suggested, may extend beyond the South.

The history of bio-chemical warfare is also suggestive.

The US use of bio-weapons goes back to the distribution of cholera-infected blankets to American Indian tribes in the 1860s. In 1900, US Army doctors in the Philippines infected five prisoners with a variety of plague and 29 prisoners with beriberi. At least four of the subjects died. In 1915, a doctor working with government grants exposed 12 prisoners in Mississippi to pellagra, an incapacitating condition that attacks the nervous system.

In 1942 US Army and Navy doctors infected 400 prisoners in Chicago with malaria in experiments designed to get "a profile of the disease and develop a treatment for it." Most of the inmates were black and none was informed of the risks of the experiment. Nazi doctors on trial at Nuremberg cited the Chicago malaria experiments as part of their defense.

In 1951 the US Army secretly contaminated the Norfolk Naval Supply Center in Virginia with infectious bacteria. One type of bacterium was chosen because blacks were believed to be more susceptible than whites. Savannah, Georgia and Avon Park, Florida were the targets of repeated army bio-weapons experiments in 1956 and 1957. Army CBW researchers released millions of mosquitoes on the two towns in order to test the ability of insects to carry and deliver yellow fever and dengue fever. Hundreds of residents fell ill, suffering from fevers, respiratory distress, stillbirths, and encephalitis. Several deaths were reported.

The harmonious collaboration between the CIA and racist regimes of an overall Nazi outlook began with the importing of Nazi scientists. Among the CIA's friends in later years was South Africa's apartheid regime. It was, for example, a CIA tip that led the arrest of Nelson Mandela and his imprisonment for more than twenty years. Close CIA cooperation with South Africa's intelligence agencies continued unabated and indeed mounted during the Reagan years, with close collaboration in attacks on Mozambique and other neighbors of South Africa deemed to be threats to South African and US interests.

In a 1970 article in *Military Review,* a journal published by the US Army Command and General Staff College, a Swedish geneticist at the University of Lund named Carl Larson discussed genetically selective weapons. Larson stated that though the study of drug metabolizing enzymes was in its infancy, "observed variations in drug responses have pointed to the possibility of great innate differences in vulnerability to chemical agents between different populations." Larson went on to speculate that in a process similar to mapping the world's blood groups, "we may soon have a grid where new observations of this kind can be pinpointed." In the same vein, a January 1975 US Army report noted in its conclusion that "[i]t is theoretically possible to develop so-called 'ethnic weapons' which would be designed to exploit naturally occurring differences in vulnerability among specific population groups."

November 14, 1996, was the night Congresswomen Juanita Millender-McDonald and Maxine Waters, jointly representing South Central Los Angeles, had invited CIA director John Deutch to attend a townhall meeting at a high school in Watts. A thousand angry people were on hand to confront the former MIT professor, turned assistant secretary of defense, turned chief spook. If Webb's initial stories had not sparked the full attention of the mainstream press, this event certainly did. On hand were the big guns: Ted Koppel's *Nightline* crew, the major network news teams and the major papers.

Rep. Millender-McDonald, a former school teacher freshly elected to

Congress, struck a tough tone from the outset: "It's not up to us to prove the CIA was involved in drug trafficking in South Central Los Angeles. Rather, it's up to them to prove they were not," she told the crowd. Then she signaled for Deutch to approach the microphone, and the crowd erupted with jeers and hoots. Millender-McDonald cautioned the barrackers, and Deutch then launched a well-conceived effort at exculpation of the Agency. "I'm going to be brief," he began. "I want to make four points, and only four points. First, the people of the CIA and I understand the tremendous horror that drugs have been to Americans, what drugs do to families and communities, and the way drugs kill babies. We understand how ravaging drugs are in this country. CIA employees and I share your anger at the injustice and lack of compassion that drug victims encounter."

There was more hooting, and a cry of "He sounds just like Clinton."

"During the past two years," Deutch went on, "while I have been director of Central Intelligence, our case officers' intelligence operations have directly worked to capture all of the Calí cartel drug lords. We have seriously disrupted the flow of coca paste between the growing areas of Peru and Bolivia to the cocaine processing facilities in Colombia. We have seized huge amounts of heroin grown in the poppy fields of Southwest Asia. Our purpose is to stop drugs from coming into the US. So my second point is that the CIA is fighting against drugs." To the knowledgeable ear Deutch's litany sounded like a nostalgic return to the scene of various CIA crimes, and to judge by the grumbles the South Central audience was mightily unimpressed.

"Our activities are secret," Deutch continued in somewhat patronizing tones. "Accordingly, there's not a lot of public understanding of what we do. I understand that people are suspicious of the CIA and in the course of recruiting agents to break up those groups that bring drugs into the US, our case officers, our men and women deal with bad people, very bad people, sometimes at great risks to their lives. These are criminals with which we must deal, if we are going to stop drugs from coming to the country. They frequently lie about their relationships with us for their own purpose. So it is hard for members of the public to know what is true and what is not true."

Deutch simply asserted that the Agency had never put a foot wrong.

"Now we all know that the US government and the CIA supported the Contras in their efforts to overthrow the Sandinista government in Nicaragua in the mid-eighties. It is alleged that the CIA also helped the Contras raise money for arms by introducing crack cocaine into California. It is an appalling charge that goes to the heart of this country. It is a charge that cannot go unanswered." By now Deutch was pounding on the table. "It says that the CIA, an agency of the United States government founded to protect Americans, helped introduce drugs and poison into our children and helped kill their future. No one who heads a government agency – not myself or anyone else – can let such an allegation stand. I will get to the bottom of it and I will let you know the results of what I have found."

Deutch promptly made a pledge that duly met the same fate as many other CIA promises of full disclosure: "I've ordered an independent investigation of these charges. The third point I want to make to you is to explain the nature of the investigation. I've ordered the CIA Inspector General to undertake a full investigation." The heckling grew in intensity, and Deutch could not make himself heard for a full minute before he was able to resume: "Let me tell you why he's the right official to do the job. First, the IG is established by law of Congress to be independent, to carry out activities, to look for fraud and crimes within the CIA. Secondly, the Inspector General has access to all CIA records and documents, no matter how secret. Third, the IG has the authority to interview the right people. Fourth, he is able to cooperate with other government departments. For example, the Department of Justice, the DEA, the Department of Defense, all of which had operations ongoing in Nicaragua at the time. Finally, the IG has a good track record of being a whistle-blower on past misdeeds of the CIA. For example, just last month he uncovered that some CIA employees were misusing credit cards and they are now in jail." Another interruption: "What about Guatemala, what about those murders ..."

Deutch continued with his pledge: "Most importantly, when this investigation is complete I intend to make the results public so that any person can judge the adequacy of the investigation. Anyone in the public who has a wish to look at the report will be able to do so. I want to stress that I am not the only person in the CIA who wants any American to believe that the CIA was responsible for this kind of disgusting charge. Finally, I want to say to you that as of today, we have no evidence of conspiracy by the CIA to engage in encouraging drug traffickers in Nicaragua or elsewhere in Latin America during this or any other period."

Deutch now endured a grilling of the sort an MIT prof might have had to submit to in the Vietnam War era during a student sit-in. One of the first questions came from a graduate of Tuskegee Institute in Alabama. She wanted to know why anyone should trust the US government on the crack issue after it had covered up for forty years the medical experiments on black men with syphilis. "I'd like to know how this incident differs from what happened at my school where, for forty years, the government denied inflicting syphilis on African-American men."

Clearly taken aback, Deutch said that he too thought what had happened at Tuskegee was terrible, and then snatched at the silver lining: "Let me say something else. There was no one who came forward forty years ago and said they were going to investigate."

From the audience now came some harrowing personal accounts of the ravages of crack in their neighborhoods. A woman said, "In Baldwin Village where I live there are no jobs for the children and our kids are just seen as commodities. They are being cycled through the prisons. They come back to the street and are marked and scarred for the rest of their life. You, the President and everybody else should be highly upset. You should be saying, how did this cancer get here?"

Deutch had no response. Then a man stood up and said, "And now we are supposed to trust the CIA to investigate itself?" Deutch responded with an assertion of the Inspector General's independence, and the crowd grew angrier. "Why don't you turn it over to an independent counsel, someone who has the power to issues subpoenas. It would have more credibility." The best Deutch could do with this one was to say that the reason there was no independent counsel was because no criminal complaint had been filed.

Now came one of the most interesting exchanges of the evening. A former Los Angeles police narcotics officer, Michael Ruppert, rose to confront Deutch. "I will tell you, director Deutch, as a former LAPD narcotics detective, that your Agency has dealt drugs throughout this country for a long time." Roars of applause. Deutch: "If you have information about the CIA [and] illegal activity and drugs you should immediately bring that information to wherever you want. But let me suggest three places: the Los Angeles Police Department ..." Cries of "No, no." Then a question: "If in the course of the Inspector General's investigation you came across evidence of severely criminal activity and it is classified, will you use that classification to hide the criminal activity, or will you tell the American people the truth?"

Amid continued hostility from the crowd Deutch promised that if such information turned up wrong-doing, "We'll bring the people to justice."

Another confrontation, from an obviously middle-class black man: "My question to you is, If you know all this stuff that the Agency has done historically, then why should we believe you today, when you say certainly this could never happen in Los Angeles, when the CIA's done this stuff all over the world?"

"I didn't come here thinking everyone was going to believe me," Deutch replied. "I came here for a much simpler task. I came here to stand up on my legs and tell you I was going to investigate these horrible allegations. All you can do is listen to what I have to say and wait to see the results."

"But how can we know how many viable documents have been shredded and how can we be certain that more documents won't be shredded?" asked another black member of the audience. "I don't know that anybody has found any lost documents in the operational files," Deutch answered oddly. "I know of nobody who has found any gaps in sequences, any missing files, any missing papers for any period of that time. That may come up ..." Deutch was interrupted here by a man who said, "Hey, do you know Walter Pincus?" Deutch said yes, he had heard of Walter Pincus. Why? "Is he an asset of the CIA?" Deutch put his head in his hands and shook it.

Now the crowd was smelling blood and beginning to get testy with Rep. Millender-McDonald for inviting the CIA boss to South Central. "I don't know why this lady is saluting Deutch's courage for coming here today," someone in the crowd cried, "when everybody knows this building has got hundreds of pigs in it. There's pigs behind those curtains.

There's pigs on the roof. We're not going to get no ghetto justice today."

Millender-McDonald shouted the man down, but his sentiments seemed to resonate with the crowd. The next black person to stand up pointed at Deutch and said, "To see you coming in this community today in this way is nothing more than a public relations move for the white people of this country. So you are going to come into this community today and insult us, and tell us you're going to investigate yourself. You've got to be crazy."

This was the last straw for John Deutch. The questioning was called off and the CIA man spoke a few words to the crowd before leaving: "You know, I've learned how important it is for our government and our Agency to get on top of this problem and stop it. I came today to try and describe the approach and have left with a better appreciation of what is on your mind."

He may have had an uncomfortable moment or two, but John Deutch knew what he was doing and after a glance at the coverage of the occasion, he surely must have felt his calculation had been correct. That very evening Ted Koppel used the meeting as a hook for his first mention of the CIA–drug connection on his *Nightline* show – three months after the story broke. Koppel spent half an hour interviewing members of the South Central audience via satellite from his control booth in Washington, D.C. He sought desperately to find someone who would say that Deutch's visit had been worthwhile, that it was a useful first step in the process of allaying suspicion. But he was disappointed. The great interrogator was mostly met with sharp-pointed questions himself, such as "You come down here and talk about solutions. We have kids that are dying, we have hospitals for babies born drug addicted. When are you guys going to come down and bring cameras to our neighborhood?" Koppel: "I'm not sure that anybody even thought that was why Director Deutch came there today. He's coming here because a lot of you are in anguish. A lot of you are angry. A lot of you are frustrated by what you believe to be the CIA's involvement in bringing drugs to South Central LA. Now, I want to hear from someone who thought it did some good."

The closest Koppel could get to this objective was Marcine Shaw, the mayor pro tem of Compton: "Well, I am glad Mr. Deutch was here today. I'm glad Congresswoman McDonald had him here because that's what it took to get your cameras here, Mr. Koppel." Koppel shook his head and answered, "Yes, but that's not the question." He wrapped up his show with the doleful thought that "if any suspicions were put to rest or minds changed, there was no evidence of it in South Central this evening."

By and large, the commentary in the white press on the Deutch's visit was positive. He had reached out. He had confronted "black paranoia" head on. The only sour note was from *Washington Post* columnist James Glassman, who argued that Deutch had demeaned government by going out to South Central and "listening passively as paranoids and lunatics shouted epithets at him. That's not the way a top government official should behave in the face of vicious insults."

But aside from Glassman's diatribe on *Capitol Gang,* a TV show, Deutch vindicated a proposal he and the Council on Foreign Relations had made some months before, which attracted remarkably little criticism. Deutch had said in congressional testimony that he wanted to change the twenty-year-old policy of the Agency not using journalists accredited to American news organizations, nor clergy or members of the Peace Corps. He argued that American journalists should feel a civic responsibility to step outside their role as journalists. (The ban may have been official policy, though the CIA has always retained journalistic assets.) To his credit, Koppel testified in Congress against Deutch's proposal, though he certainly didn't repeat on the night of Deutch's town meeting what he said in Congress: "I'm opposed to having the legal option of using journalistic cover. The CIA has broken laws. It will again. When an intelligence official breaks US laws, if their argument is persuasive Congress can be lenient. If the CIA must use journalists, it will do so, but it should have to be breaking the law in doing so."

Sources

Maxine Waters has been one of the heroes of this story. We are grateful to Waters and her resourceful staff for providing crucial documents and copies of the congresswoman's numerous speeches on the CIA, urban America, money laundering and the drug trade. James Jones has written the most thorough account of the Tuskegee syphilis experiments, *Bad Blood*. For information on the Justice Department's snooping into the life of Martin Luther King and his family we turned to Stephen Tompkins's amazing investigation in the *Memphis Commercial Appeal*, Taylor Branch's *Pillar of Fire* (the second volume of his biography of King), and David Garrow's *The FBI and Martin Luther King*. Ward Churchill and Jay Vander Wall's books tell the story of the FBI's COINTELPRO operation against the Black Panthers and the American Indian Movement. For statistics on the racist application of the death penalty we are indebted to defense attorney Stephen Bright and the Death Penalty Information Center. The Sentencing Project provided us with material on the disparity in federal and state sentencing guidelines between powder cocaine and crack. They also gave us statistics on incarceration rates over the past twenty years by offense, race, age and gender. There is no better guide to the recent cultural history of Los Angeles than Mike Davis's *City of Quartz*. Dan Baum's book, *Smoke and Mirrors*, is a funny and dire account of US drug policy since Nixon. *Cracked Coverage* by Jimmie Reeves and Richard Campbell is a detailed examination of how crack users came to be demonized, jailed and killed for the sake of politicians and ratings. But Clarence Lusane's *Pipe Dream Blues* remains the best critique of the racist nature of the drug war. It's a book that badly needs to be updated and republished to include the equally vile and racially motivated drug polices of the Clinton era.

Alder, Patricia. *Wheeling and Dealing: An Ethnography of the Upper Level Drug Dealing and Smuggling Community*. Columbia Univ. Press, 1985.

American Bar Association. *New Directions for National Substance Abuse Policy*. ABA, 1994.

Armstrong, Scott. "US Women's Prisons Overflow." *Christian Science Monitor*, July 24, 1990.

Associated Press. "Waters May Force Vote to Establish Probe." *San Jose Mercury News*, Sept. 18, 1996.

——. "South Central Residents Condemn CIA's Reputed Role." *San Jose Mercury News*, Sept. 29, 1996.

Baum, Dan. *Smoke and Mirrors: The War on Drugs and the Politics of Failure*. Little, Brown, 1996.

Blachman, Morris, and Kenneth E. Sharpe. "The War on Drugs: American Democracy Under Assault." *World Policy Journal*, Winter 1989–90.

Blackstock, Nelson. *COINTELPRO: The FBI's Secret War on Political Freedom*. Vintage, 1976.

Boyer, Peter. "Whip Cracker." *New Yorker*, Sept. 5, 1994.

Branch, Taylor. *Parting the Waters: America in the King Years, 1954–1963*. Simon and Schuster, 1988.

——. *Pillar of Fire: America in the King Years, 1963–1965*. Simon and Schuster, 1997,

Britt, Donna. "Finding the Truest Truth." *Washington Post*, Oct. 4, 1996.

Brown, Joseph. "Typecast for Genocide or Suicide?" *Tampa Tribune,* Sept. 29, 1996.

Chaiken, Jan, and Marcia Chaiken. "Drugs and Predatory Crime." In *Drugs and Crime*, edited by James Q. Wilson et al. Univ. of Chicago Press, 1990.

Chase, Allan. *The Legacy of Malthus: The Social Costs of the New Scientific Racism*. Knopf, 1975.

Churchill, Ward, and Jim Vander Wall. *Agents of Repression: The FBI's Secret Wars Against the Black Panther Party and the American Indian Movement.* South End Press, 1988.

——. *COINTELPRO Papers: Documents from the FBI's Secret Wars Against Dissent in the United States.* South End Press, 1989.

Cockburn, Alexander. "Clinton and Drugs: Drug War Without End." *Nation,* Nov. 15, 1993.

——. "Churchill, the Nazis and the US Sterilizers." In *The Golden Age Is in Us.* Verso, 1995.

Cohen, Richard. "A Racist Past and a Wary Present." *Washington Post,* Oct. 27, 1996.

Currie, Elliot. *Reckoning: Drugs, Cities and the American Future.* Hill and Wang, 1983.

Davis, Mike. *City of Quartz.* Verso, 1990.

De Benedicts, Don. "How Long Is Too Long?" *American Bar Association Journal,* vol. 79, 1993.

Dominick, Joe. "Police Power: Why No One Can Control the LAPD." *LA Weekly,* Feb. 16–22, 1990.

Duster, Troy. *The Legislation of Morality: Laws, Drugs and Moral Judgment.* Free Press, 1970.

Edsall, Thomas, and Mary Edsall. "Race." *Atlantic Monthly,* May 1991.

Epstein, Edward Jay. *The Agency of Fear.* Verso, 1990.

Farragher, Thomas. "Pair Arrested While Urging Probing of CIA." *San Jose Mercury News,* Sept. 12, 1996.

——. "Civil Rights Leader Calls Possible CIA–Drug Link 'Dastardly.'" *San Jose Mercury News,* Sept. 24, 1996.

Finkleman, Paul. "The Second Casualty of War: Civil Liberties and the War on Drugs." *Southern California Law Review,* vol. 66: 1389, 1993.

Fletcher, Michael. "Deutch Assures Black Caucus on Drug Charges." *Washington Post,* Sept. 20, 1996.

——. "Black Caucus Urges Probe of CIA Drug Charge." *Washington Post,* Sept. 13, 1996.

——. "History Lends Credence to Conspiracy Theories." *Washington Post,* Oct. 4, 1996.

Forman, James. *The Making of Black Revolutionaries.* Macmillan, 1972.

Gallman, Vanessa, and Lewis Kamb. "Congressional Black Caucus Demands Investigation." *San Jose Mercury News,* Sept. 13, 1996.

Garrow, David. *The FBI and Martin Luther King, Jr.* Norton, 1981.

Glick, Brian. *War at Home: Covert Action Against US Activists and What We Can Do About It.* South End Press, 1989.

Gregory, Dick. "White Press Doesn't Believe It? What Else Is New?" *Baltimore Sun,* Nov. 24, 1996.

Gordon, Diana. *The Return of the Dangerous Classes: Drug Prohibition and Policy Politics.* Norton, 1994.

Gorsney, E., and Paul Popenoe. *Sterilization for Human Betterment.* Macmillan, 1930.

Haldeman, H. R. *The Haldeman Diaries: Inside the Nixon White House.* Putnam, 1994.

Harris, Ron. "Blacks Feel Brunt of Drug War." *Los Angeles Times,* April 22, 1990.

Helmer, John. *Drugs and Minority Oppression.* Seabury Press, 1975.

Horne, Gerald. "Genes, Violence, Race and Genocide." *Covert Action Quarterly,* Winter 1992.

Inciardi, James. *The War on Drugs: Heroin, Cocaine, Crime and Public Policy,* Mayfield, 1986.

92

———. *Handbook of Drug Control in the United States*. Greenwood Press, 1990.
Isikoff, Michael. "From Justice Department to Drug Defendant." *Washington Post,* August 23, 1990.
———. "Bennett Exits Drug War with Potshots." *Washington Post,* Nov. 9, 1990.
———. "Drug Buy Set Up for Bush Speech; DEA Lured Seller to Lafayette Park." *Washington Post,* Sept. 22, 1987.
Jones, James. *Bad Blood: The Tuskegee Syphilis Experiments*. Simon and Schuster, 1993.
Keller, William. *The Liberals and J. Edgar Hoover*. Princeton Univ. Press. 1989.
Kelly, Jack and Sam Meddis. "Critics Say Bias Spurs Police Focus on Blacks." *USA Today*. Dec. 20, 1990.
Kinder, Douglas Clark. "Shutting Out the Evil: Nativism and Narcotics Control in the U.S." *Journal of Policy History* vol. 3, no. 4, 1991.
Kramer, Michael. "Clinton's Drug Policy Is a Bust." *Time*, Dec. 20, 1993.
LaCroix, Susan. "Jailing Mothers for Drug Abuse." *Nation,* May 1, 1989.
Lapham, Lewis. "A Political Opiate: The War on Drugs Is a Folly and a Menace." *Harper's*, Dec. 1989.
Larson, Carl. "US Army Decontamination of Water Containing Chemical Warfare Agents." *Military Review*, 1970.
Legon, Jordan. "Activist Vows to Continue Protests Over Alleged CIA-Crack Link." *San Jose Mercury News,* Sept. 27, 1996.
Lusane, Clarence. *Pipe Dream Blues: Racism and the War on Drugs*. South End Press, 1991.
———. "Cracking the CIA-Contra Drug Connection." *Covert Action Quarterly*, Fall 1996.
McWilliams, John. *The Protectors: Harry J. Anslinger and the Federal Bureau of Narcotics*. University of Delaware Press, 1990.
Maxwell, Evan. "Gold, Drugs and Clean Cash." *Los Angeles Times Magazine*, Feb. 18, 1990.
Meddis, Sam. "Whites, Not Blacks, at the Core of the Drug Crisis." *USA Today*, Dec. 20, 1989.
Meier, Kenneth. "Race and the War on Drugs: America's Dirty Little Secret." *Policy Currents* 2, no. 20. 1992.
Muller, Judy. "Crack and the CIA: Conspiracy or Myth?" *ABC News, Nightline*, Nov. 15, 1996.
Musto, David. *The American Disease*. Oxford Univ. Press, 1987.
National Center on Institutions and Alternatives. *Hobbling a Generation: Young African-American Males in the Criminal Justice System*. NCIA, 1992.
O'Reilly, Kenneth. *Racial Matters: The FBI's Secret File on Black America, 1960–1972*. Free Press, 1988.
Petras, James. "Drug War Rhetoric Conceals Cartel's Capital Ties." *In These Times,* Nov. 15, 1989.
Ram, David. "Overcommited." *Southern Exposure*, Fall 1989.
Reed, Ishmael. "Living at Ground Zero." *Image*, March 13, 1988.
Reinarman, Craig, and Harry Levine. "Crack in Context: Politics and the Media in the Making of a Drug Scare." *Contemporary Drug Problems*, Winter 1989.
Reeves, Jimmie, and Richard Campbell. *Cracked Coverage: Television News, the Anti-Cocaine Crusade and the Reagan Legacy*. Duke Univ. Press, 1994.
Ridgeway, James. "Prisons in Black." *Village Voice*, Sept. 19, 1988.
St. Clair, Jeffrey. "Germ War: The US Record." *CounterPunch*, Feb. 15–28, 1998.

———. "A Brazen Racial Animus." *CounterPunch*, Feb. 15–28, 1998.

Stark, Evan. "The Myth of Black Violence." *New York Times,* July 18, 1990.

Stevenson, John. "Norfolk Site of Germ War Tests." *Virginia Pilot,* Sept. 13, 1980.

Stober, Dan. "Jackson Calls for Investigation." *San Jose Mercury News,* Sept. 8, 1996.

Stone, Randolph. "The War on Drugs: The Wrong Enemy and the Wrong Battlefield." *National Bar Association Magazine,* Dec. 1989.

Sullivan, Joseph. "NJ Police Are Accused of Minority Arrest Campaign." *New York Times,* Feb. 19, 1990.

Tompkins, Stephen. "Spying on Martin Luther King." *Memphis Commercial Appeal,* March 1993.

Trocheck, Kathy. "Savannah Residents Angered by Army's '56 Mosquito Test." *Atlanta Journal,* Nov. 10, 1980.

Unger, Sanford. *FBI.* Little, Brown, 1976.

United Press International. "Army Used Mosquitoes in 1950s as a Test of Biological Warfare." *Bowling Green [Ohio] Sentinel-Tribune,* Oct. 29, 1980.

US Congress. Senate. Subcommittee on Constitutional Rights of the Committee on the Judiciary. *Individual Rights and the Federal Role in Behavior Modification.* Government Printing Office, 1974.

US Department of Justice. Bureau of Justice Statistics. *Federal Drug Case Processing, 1982–1991.* Government Printing Office. March 1994.

US Sentencing Commission. *Special Report to the Congress: Mandatory Minimum Penalties in the Federal Criminal Justice* System. Government Printing Office, August 1991.

Walker, William III. *Drug Control in the Americas.* Univ. of New Mexico Press, 1989.

Waters, Maxine. "Drugs, Democrats and Priorities." *Nation,* July 24, 1989.

———. "Cocaine in South-Central LA" (Special Orders Speech). *Congressional Record,* Sept. 20, 1996.

Webb, Gary. "Flawed Sentencing the Main Reason for Race Disparity." *San Jose Mercury News,* August 20, 1996.

Webb, Jim. "Ethnic Weapons Planned, May Be Developed." *Prairie Sun,* May, 1980.

Welsh, Patrick. "Young, Black, Male and Trapped." *Washington Post,* Sept. 1989.

Williams, Edward Hunting. "Negro Cocaine 'Fiends' Are New Southern Menace." *New York Times,* Feb. 8, 1914.

Wisotsky, Steven. *Beyond the War on Drugs: Overcoming a Failed Public Policy.* Prometheus, 1990.

4

Introducing the CIA

Even as John Deutch was flying back to CIA headquarters in Langley, Virginia from his town meeting in South Central Los Angeles, the US Department of Justice was preparing to file an indictment that shed a most unflattering light upon Deutch's protestations that, as he put it in an op-ed article in the *New York Times,* the CIA had never "directly or knowingly condoned drug smuggling into the United States."

On November 22, 1996, the US Justice Department indicted General Ramón Guillén Davila of Venezuela on charges of importing cocaine into the United States. The federal prosecutors alleged that while heading Venezuela's anti-drug unit, General Guillén smuggled more than 22 tons of cocaine into the US and Europe for the Calí and Bogotá cartels. Guillén responded to the indictment from the sanctuary of Caracas, whence his government refused to extradict him to Miami, while honoring him with a pardon for any possible crimes committed in the line of duty. He maintained that the cocaine shipments to the US had been approved by the CIA, and went on to say that "some drugs were lost and neither the CIA nor the DEA want to accept any responsibility for it."

The CIA had hired Guillén in 1988 to help it find out something about the Colombian drug cartels. The Agency and Guillén set up a drug-smuggling operation using agents of Guillén's in the Venezuelan

National Guard to buy cocaine from the Calí cartel and ship it to Venezuela, where it was stored in warehouses maintained by the Narcotics Intelligence Center, Caracas, which was run by Guillén and entirely funded by the CIA.

To avoid the Calí cartel asking inconvenient questions about the growing inventory of cocaine in the Narcotics Intelligence Center's warehouses and, as one CIA agent put it, "to keep our credibility with the traffickers," the CIA decided it was politic to let some of the cocaine proceed on to the cartel's network of dealers in the US. As another CIA agent put it, they wanted "to let the dope walk" – in other words, to allow it to be sold on the streets of Miami, New York and Los Angeles.

When it comes to what are called "controlled shipments" of drugs into the US, federal law requires that such imports have DEA approval, which the CIA duly sought. This was, however, denied by the DEA attaché in Caracas. The CIA then went to DEA headquarters in Washington, only to be met with a similar refusal, whereupon the CIA went ahead with the shipment anyway. One of the CIA men working with Guillén was Mark McFarlin. In 1989 McFarlin, so he later testified in federal court in Miami, told his CIA station chief in Caracas that the Guillén operation, already under way, had just seen 3,000 pounds of cocaine shipped to the US. When the station chief asked McFarlin if the DEA was aware of this, McFarlin answered no. "Let's keep it that way," the station chief instructed him.

Over the next three years, more than 22 tons of cocaine made its way through this pipeline into the US, with the shipments coming into Miami either in hollowed-out shipping pallets or in boxes of blue jeans. In 1990 DEA agents in Caracas learned what was going on, but security was lax since one female DEA agent in Venezuela was sleeping with a CIA man there, and another, reportedly with General Guillén himself. The CIA and Guillén duly changed their modes of operation, and the cocaine shipments from Caracas to Miami continued for another two years. Eventually, the US Customs Service brought down the curtain on the operation, and in 1992 seized an 800-pound shipment of cocaine in Miami.

One of Guillén's subordinates, Adolfo Romero, was arrested and ultimately convicted on drug conspiracy charges. None of the Colombian drug lords was ever inconvenienced by this project, despite the CIA's claim that it was after the Calí cartel. Guillén was indicted but remained safe in Caracas. McFarlin and his boss were ultimately edged out of the Agency. No other heads rolled after an operation that yielded nothing but the arrival, under CIA supervision, of 22 tons of cocaine in the United States. The CIA conducted an internal review of this debacle and asserted that there was "no evidence of criminal wrongdoing."

A DEA investigation reached a rather different conclusion, charging that the spy agency had engaged in "unauthorized controlled shipments" of narcotics into the US and that the CIA withheld "vital information" on the Calí cartel from the DEA and federal prosecutors.

Disingenuous denial has long been a specialty of the Central Intelligence Agency. Back in 1971, one of Deutch's better known predecessors as director of intelligence, Richard Helms, addressed the American Newspaper Editors Association at a moment when the Agency had been accused of infiltrating new organizations and of running a domestic spying operation for President Richard Nixon. The nation, Helms told the assembled editors, "should take on faith that we too are honorable men, devoted to her service." Helms was scarcely in hostile territory, any more than was Deutch in the *New York Times,* the venue for his article asserting the innocence of the CIA. More than any other director, Helms was part of the Georgetown circuit, on close terms with such journalists as Joseph Alsop, James Reston, Joseph Kraft, Chalmers Roberts and C. L. Sulzberger. Helms would often boast of his days as a reporter for United Press, during which he had gotten exclusive interviews with Adolf Hitler and the ice-skater Sonja Henie.

Less than two years after his denials to the Newspaper Editors Association, Helms went before the Senate Foreign Relations Committee and was grilled about the Agency's involvement in Watergate. In response, he lied brazenly about Howard Hunt and Gordon Liddy's ties to the CIA. Though the chairman of the committee, Sen. William Fulbright, was rightly incredulous, Helms was not formally put on the spot.

This wasn't the first time Helms, who led the Agency from 1966 through 1972, had lied, nor was it his most devious statement. Throughout the Vietnam War, Helms had withheld from Congress crucial information on the troop strength of the Vietnamese National Liberation Front (NLF, aka Viet Cong) developed by a young CIA analyst named Sam Adams. Adams's numbers showed that support for the NLF in South Vietnam was much greater than the military's estimates, so strong, indeed, that the war seemed to be unwinnable. Helms, however, sided with the military and sought unrelentingly to hound Adams out of the agency.

Later in 1973 the dapper spook again gave false testimony to Congress, this time about the CIA's part in overthrowing Salvador Allende's government in Chile. Of course, support for the coup against Allende was undertaken at the insistence of American corporations such as ITT and Anaconda Copper. The Agency is reported to have sent a drug smuggler to Santiago with a cash payment for a Chilean hitman endeavoring to assassinate Allende. In 1977 the Justice Department, headed by Carter appointee Griffin Bell, reluctantly charged Helms with perjury. The former CIA director took the advice of Washington superlawyer Edwin Bennett Williams and entered a plea of no contest. He was fined $2,000 and received a suspended sentence.

There were other historical counterpoints to Deutch's protestations. In 1976, at one of the most fraught moments in the Agency's relationship to Congress since its inception, Director William Colby (who had earlier blown the whistle on Helms's lies about Chile) went before the Select Committee on Intelligence being run by Senator Frank Church of Idaho. This time the mood of Congress was sharper, prompted by Seymour Hersh's exposés in the *New York Times* of domestic spying and also by charges that the CIA had been running an assassination program overseas.

Yes, Colby said, the possibility of using assassination had been entertained at the Agency, but at no time had it ever reached the level of successful practical application. As for domestic spying, there had been programs of mail surveillance and the like, but they were far from the "massive" operations alleged by Hersh, and they had long since been discontinued.

Colby was being typically modest. The CIA, through Operation CHAOS and similar programs, had compiled files on more than 10,000 Americans and kept a database with more than 300,000 names in it. It had wiretapped the phones of American reporters, infiltrated dissident groups and tried to disrupt anti-war protests. It spent $33,000 in support of a letter-writing campaign in support of the invasion of Cambodia.

As with the charges of complicity in drug running, the CIA's role in assassination is one of those topics gingerly handled by the press or Congress from time to time and then hastily put aside, with the habitual claim that the CIA may have dreamed of it, thought about it and maybe even dabbled in it, but had never actually gone successfully all the way. But in fact the Agency has gone all the way many times, and we should look at this history in some detail since the pattern of denial in these cases strongly parallels the CIA's relationship with the drug business.

There's no dispute that the CIA has used assassination as a weapon lower down the political and social pecking order, as no one knew better than William Colby. He had, by his own admission, supervised the Phoenix Program and other so-called "counter-terror" operations in Vietnam. Phoenix was aimed at "neutralizing" NLF political leaders and organizers in rural South Vietnam. In congressional testimony Colby boasted that 20,587 NLF activists had been killed between 1967 and 1971 alone. The South Vietnamese published a much higher estimate, declaring that nearly 41,000 had been killed. Barton Osborn, an intelligence officer in the Phoenix Program, spelled out in chilling terms the bureaucratic attitude of many of the agents toward their murderous assignments. "Quite often it was a matter of expediency just to eliminate a person in the field rather than deal with the paperwork."

Those killed outright in Phoenix operations may have been more fortunate than the 29,000 suspected NLF members arrested and interrogated with techniques that were horrible even by the standards of Pol Pot and Mobutu. In 1972 a parade of witnesses before Congress testified about the techniques of the Phoenix interrogators: how they interviewed suspects and then pushed them out of planes, how they cut off fingers, ears and testicles, how they used electro-shock, shoved wooden dowels into the brains of some prisoners, and rammed electric probes into the rectums of others.

For many of the Phoenix raids the agency employed the services of bandit tribes and ethnic groups, such as the Khmer Kampuchean Kram, the KKK. The KKK was comprised of anti-communist Cambodians and drug smugglers who, as one Phoenix veteran put it, "would kill anyone as long as there was something in it for them." The KKK even offered to knock off Prince Sihanouk for the Americans and frame the NLF for the killing.

These American death squads were a particular favorite of Richard Nixon. After the My Lai massacre, an operation with all the earmarks of a Phoenix-style extermination, there was a move to reduce the funding for these civilian killing programs. Nixon, according to an account by Seymour Hersh, objected vociferously. "No," Nixon demanded. "We've got to have more of this. Assassinations. Killings." The funds were promptly restored, and the death toll mounted.

Even at the senior level of executive action Colby was being bashful about the CIA's ambitions and achievements. In 1955 the CIA had very nearly managed to assassinate the Chinese Communist leader Chou En-lai. Bombs were put aboard Chou's plane as he flew from Hong Kong to Indonesia for the Bandung conference. At the last moment Chou changed planes, thus avoiding a terminal descent into the South China Sea, since the plane duly blew up. The role of the CIA was later described in detail by a British intelligence agent who defected to the Soviet Union, and evidence recovered by divers from portions of the plane, including the timing mechanisms for two bombs, confirmed his statements. The Hong Kong police called the crash a case of "carefully planned mass murder."

By 1960 Rafael Trujillo, president of the Dominican Republic, had become irksome to US foreign policy makers. His blatant corruption looked as though it might prompt a revolt akin to the upsurge that had brought Fidel Castro to power. The best way to head off this unwelcome contingency was to ensure that Trujillo's political career cease forthwith, which in early 1961 it did. Trujillo was gunned down in his car outside his own mansion in Ciudad Trujillo. It emerged that the CIA had provided guns and training to the assassins, though the Agency took care to point out that it was not absolutely 100 percent sure that these were the same weapons that ultimately deposed the tyrant (who had been originally installed in power by the CIA).

At about the same time, CIA director Allen Dulles decided that the leader of the Congo, Patrice Lumumba, was an unacceptable threat to the Free World and his removal was "an urgent and prime objective." For assistance in the task of banishing this threat the CIA turned to its own Technical Services Division (TSD), headed by that man of darkness, Sidney Gottlieb (whose career is detailed further in Chapter 8). Gottlieb's division housed a horror chamber of labs whose researches included brain-washing, chemical and biological warfare, the use of drugs and electro-shock as modes of interrogation, and the development of lethal toxins, along with the most efficient means of applying these to the victim, such as the notorious poison dart gun later displayed before the cameras by Senator Frank Church.

In Lumumba's case Gottlieb developed a bio-poison that would mime a disease endemic to the Congo. He personally delivered the deadly germs along with a special hypodermic syringe, gauze masks and rubber gloves to Lawrence Devlin, the CIA chief of station in the Congo. The lethal implements were carried into the country in a diplomatic pouch. Gottlieb instructed Devlin and his agents how to apply the toxin to Lumumba's toothpaste and food. However, the CIA's bio-assassins couldn't get close enough to Lumumba, so the "executive action" proceeded by a more traditional route. Lumumba was seized, tortured and murdered by soldiers of the CIA's selected replacement, Mobutu Sese Seko, and Lumumba's body ended up in the trunk of a CIA officer who drove around Lumumbashi trying to decide how to dispose of it.

When it came to Fidel Castro, the Agency has spared no effort across a quarter of a century. Colby admitted to the Church committee that the agency had tried and failed to kill Castro several times, but not nearly as often as its critics alleged. "It wasn't for lack of trying," Colby observed. "Castro gave McGovern in 1975 a list of the attempts made on his life – there were about thirty by that time – as he said, by the CIA. McGovern gave it to me and I looked through it and checked it off against our records and said we could account for about five or six. The others – I can understand Castro's feeling about them because they were all ex-Bay of Pigs people or something like that, so he thinks they're all CIA. Once you get into one of them, then bingo! – you get blamed for all the rest. We didn't have any connections with the rest of them, but we'd never convince Castro of that."

Five or six assassination plots is a sobering number, especially if you happen to be the intended target of these "executive actions." But even here Colby was dissembling. He certainly had the opportunity to consult a secret 1967 report on the plots against Castro by the CIA's Inspector General John S. Earman, and approved by Richard Helms. The CIA had in fact hatched attempts on the Cuban leader even prior to the revolution. One of the first occurred in 1958, when Eutimio Rojas, a member of the Cuban guerrillas, was hired to kill Castro as he slept at a camp in the Sierra Maestra.

On February 2, 1959, Cuban security guards arrested Allan Robert Nye, an American, in a hotel room facing the presidential palace. Nye had in his possession a high-powered rifle equipped with a telescopic scope, and had been contracted to shoot Castro as he arrived at the palace. A month later Rolando Masferrer, a former leader of Batista's death squads, turned up at a Miami meeting with American mobsters and a CIA officer. There this deadly conglomerate planned another scenario to kill Castro outside the presidential palace.

The agency tried to devise a way to saturate the radio studio where Castro broadcast his speeches with an aerosol form of LSD and other "psychic energizers." Another plan called for dousing Castro's favorite kind of cigars with psychoactive drugs. The doped cigars were kept in the safe of Jake Easterline, who headed the anti-Cuba task force in the pre–Bay of Pigs days, while he tried to find a way to deliver them to Castro without risking "serious blowback" to the Agency. The ingredients for both of these schemes were developed in the labs of Sydney Gottlieb. In 1967, Gottlieb told Inspector General Earman of another scheme in which he was asked to impregnate some cigars for Castro with lethal poisons.

During Castro's trip to New York for an appearance at the United Nations in 1960, CIA agents attempted to pull off what is referred to as the "depilatory action." The plan was to place thallium salts in Castro's shoes and on his night table in the hope that the poisons would make the leader's beard fall off. In high doses, thallium can cause paralysis or death. This scheme collapsed at the last minute.

By August 1960, the elimination of Castro had become a top priority for the leadership of the CIA. Allen Dulles and his deputy Richard Bissell paid Johnny Roselli, a Hollywood mobster and buddy of Frank Sinatra, $150,000 to arrange a hit on Castro. Roselli swiftly brought two more Mafia dons in on the plot: Sam Giancana, the Chicago gangster; and Santos Trafficante, the overseer of the Lansky/Luciano operations in Havana. Initially, the CIA recommended a gangland style hit in which Castro would be gunned down in a hail of machine-gun fire. But Giancana suggested a more subtle approach, a poison pill that could be slipped into Castro's food or drink. Six deadly botulinum pills – "the size of saccharin tablets" – were cooked up in the CIA's TSD labs, concealed in a hollow pencil and delivered to Roselli. On February 13, 1961, only a month after JFK's inauguration, Trafficante took the botulinum pills to Havana and gave them to his man inside the Cuban government, Jorgé Orta, who worked on Castro's executive staff and owed the mobsters large gambling debts.

Along with the pills, Trafficante also delivered a box of cigars soaked in botulinum toxin, which kills within hours. The cigars were prepared by Dr. Edward Gunn, chief of the CIA's medical division. Gunn kept one of the cigars in his safe as a souvenir. He tested it for the Inspector General in 1967 and found it to have retained 94 percent of its original level of toxicity. The cigar was so deadly, Gunn said, that it need only be touched, not smoked, in order to kill its victim.

Trafficante later reported back that the pills and cigars weren't given to Castro because "Orta got cold feet."

In April, Roselli approached his CIA handlers with a new plan, demands for $50,000, and a new batch of pills. This time the operation would be carried out by Trafficante's friend Dr. Manuel Antonio de Varona, leader of the anti-Castro Democratic Revolutionary Front. Verona and Trafficante had met through Edward K. Moss, the Washington, D.C. political fundraiser and influence peddler. Moss was pushing the cause of the Cuban exiles on the Hill, and he was sleeping with Julia Cellini, sister of the notorious Cellini brothers, Eddie and Dino, who were executives in Meyer Lansky's gambling operations in the Caribbean. Varona smuggled the botulinum pills to a waitress at a restaurant frequented by Castro. But, according to CIA man Sheffield Edwards, the scheme failed when the Cuban leader suddenly "ceased to visit that particular restaurant."

These mobsters are often referred to in CIA documents as the Havana gambling syndicate, after the casino hotels they ran there during the Batista regime. But the Mafia dons were also involved in a much more lucrative venture – drugs. Havana had become the key transfer point into the United States for much of the heroin produced by Lucky Luciano and by the Corsican syndicates in Marseilles. Lansky, who was Luciano's money man in the States, offered to put out a $1 million contract on Castro's head shortly after the revolution.

Over the next year, in the aftermath of the Bay of Pigs disaster, the CIA targeted Castro through its Executive Action Capability program, code-named ZR/RIFLE. This operation was headed by William "the Pear" Harvey, a former FBI man whom some suspected of being J. Edgar Hoover's mole inside the CIA. Harvey, one of the real characters of the Agency's formative years, was known for wearing his pistols to work at the office, slumbering through staff meetings and for his special animus toward Robert Kennedy, who he called "that little fucker."

It was in late 1961 that Sam Giancana approached his CIA contact, a D.C.-based private detective named Robert Maheu, with a personal problem – he suspected his girlfriend, Phyllis McGuire, one of the McGuire Sisters singing group, of having an affair in Las Vegas with comedian Dan Rowan, of Rowan and Martin. In return for his assistance in the Castro assassination plots, Giancana wanted the Agency to bug Rowan's Vegas hotel room. Rowan's phone was duly wiretapped, but the recording device was discovered by a hotel maid, who informed the police. The Vegas police turned the matter over to the FBI, which wanted to prosecute Giancana for wiretapping. Ultimately, Robert Kennedy had to be told of the affair in order to call off the FBI.

Years later, Richard Bissell, the CIA's deputy director for plans and architect of the Bay of Pigs disaster, said he regretted some of the Cuban ventures. Bissell told Bill Moyers, "I think we should not have involved ourselves with the Mafia. I think an organization that does so is losing control of its information. I think we should have been afraid that we would open ourselves to blackmail." Moyers asked Bissell if it was only the association with the mobsters that troubled him, not the capability of the CIA to assassinate foreign leaders. Bissell replied: "Correct."

Robert Kennedy, for one, didn't share Bissell's squeamishness. Kennedy, who was obsessed with the elimination of Castro, told Allen

Dulles that he didn't care if the Agency employed the Mob for the hit as long as they kept him fully briefed. Robert Kennedy would go to his grave defending the Agency. "What you're not aware of is what role the CIA plays in the government," RFK told Jack Newfield of the *Village Voice* shortly before his assassination. "During the 1950s, for example, many of the liberals who were forced out of other departments found a sanctuary, an enclave, in the CIA. So some of the best people in Washington, and around the country, began to collect there. One result of that was the CIA developed a very healthy view of Communism, especially compared to State and some other departments. They were very sympathetic, for example, to nationalist, and even socialist governments and movements. And I think now the CIA is becoming much more realistic, and critical, about the war, than other departments, or even the people in the White House. So it is not so black and white as you make."

By 1963, Robert Kennedy's friend Desmond Fitzgerald had taken over the Cuba operations from Harvey. Fitzgerald wasted little time in going after Castro. One of Fitzgerald's first schemes was to have James Donovan, then negotiating the release of the Bay of Pigs prisoners, unwittingly deliver as a gift to Castro expensive scuba-diving gear. Sid Gottlieb treated the lining of the suit with a Madura fungus and implanted tubercle bacilli – a lethal concoction. At the same time Fitzgerald had been reading up on deep sea clams and had asked Gottlieb's lab to rig some exceptionally attractive specimens with high explosives. The clams would then be dropped in an area were Castro frequently dived and rigged to explode when lifted.

In November 1963, the CIA's Desmond Fitzgerald was in Paris to meet Rolando Cubela, an anti-Castro Cuban who is referred to in CIA documents as AM-LASH. Fitzgerald portrayed himself as an emissary of Robert Kennedy and asked Cubela for help in killing Castro. On November 22, Cubela was given a ballpoint pen rigged as a syringe filled with deadly Blackleaf-40, a high-powered insecticide composed of 40 percent nicotine sulfate. As the Inspector General's report dryly notes, "It is likely that at the very moment President Kennedy was shot a CIA agent was meeting with a Cuban agent in Paris and giving him an assassination device for use against Castro."

Fidel Castro was not the only target. There were also repeated attempts to assassinate his brother Raúl and Che Guevara. The CIA's J. C. King pleaded with Allen Dulles to adopt a plan that would kill Fidel, Raúl and Che at the same time, "as a package." Ultimately, Che, whom the Agency chased around the globe, was tracked down in the jungles of Bolivia. Present at his execution in 1967 was the CIA's Félix Rodríguez, an old Cuba hand who would later become a central figure in the Contras' drugs-and-weapons operations at Ilopango air base in El Salvador.

Jimmy Carter's CIA director, Admiral Stansfield Turner, was reviled by many inside the Agency for purging some of the old guard. But Turner wasn't really much of a reformer, and he had his own problems with truth-telling. In 1977, as a result of a Freedom of Information Act lawsuit brought by investigative journalist John Marks, the CIA was forced to disclose the existence of seven boxes of information on the Agency's twenty-year research program into psycho-active drugs and behavior modification, known as MK/ULTRA.

The discovery of the records by the Agency's archivist came as a something of surprise to the CIA's leadership, since Richard Helms in his last days as director had ordered the destruction of all of the MK/ULTRA documents. When Turner briefed congressional committees and the press, he insisted that the program had been phased out in 1963 and had only involved drug experimentation. In fact, MK/ULTRA and a host of similar projects persisted until at least 1973 and involved a quest to develop techniques for mind control, including electro-shock and psychosurgery. The CIA wanted to create a kind of "Manchurian candidate," a roster of chemically and psychologically programmed assassins and spies.

Turner, who talked of bringing about a new openness at the Agency, quickly proved he was no friend of free speech when he attempted to suppress the publication of *Decent Interval*, a book by former CIA officer Frank Snepp. The CIA claimed Snepp had violated his employment agreement by not submitting the book to the Agency for approval prior to the publication. The CIA's lawyers subsequently won a suit requiring Snepp to hand over all of his royalties to the government.

For pure thuggishness and criminality, it's hard to find a better specimen than William Casey, the CIA's director during most of the Reagan years. Casey went straight from the management of Reagan's campaign into CIA headquarters at Langley, where he brought in some of the top public relations firms in the nation to advise him on how to sell his two pet projects, the Contras and the Afghani mujahedin, to a dubious American public. Casey called this work "perception management," but it was really a domestic propaganda campaign, a psy-ops for the home folks.

On December 4, 1981, Reagan signed Executive Order 12333 on assassinations. It reads, "No person employed by or acting on behalf of the U.S. government shall engage in, or conspire to engage in, assassinations." This legal restriction didn't deter the new CIA leader, who at that very moment was busy advocating the elimination of Desi Bouterse, the leader of Suriname, a South American country that had entered in "the Cuban orbit."

Likewise, Casey and his underlings were superintending the production of an assassination manual for the Nicaraguan Contras called *Psychological Operations in Guerrilla Warfare*. The manual, which reads like an update of the Phoenix Program, called for the use of violence "to neutralize carefully selected and planned targets such as court judges, police and state security officials, etc." It advised the Contras to develop "shock troops" to infiltrate Sandinista rallies. "These men should be equipped with weapons (knives, razors, chains, clubs, bludgeons) and should march slightly behind the innocent and gullible participants." In an echo of the Mafia operations against Castro, the manual also called for the Contras to hire organized crime figures to carry out many of these delicate operations. "If possible," the manual advised, "professional criminals will be hired to carry out selective 'jobs.'" *Psychological Operations in Guerrilla Warfare* wasn't just an academic exercise: it was put into action. Twice the agency sent teams to assassinate Nicaraguan Foreign Minister Miguel d'Escoto, a Catholic priest. On one occasion the would-be assassins tried to poison him with a bottle of Benedictine liqueur spiked with thallium, a favorite toxin of the agency. CIA agent Michael Tock was arrested by the Sandinistas for his role in one of the plots. When the *New York Times* finally got around to running a story on the murder manual, Reagan himself came to his old friend Casey's defense, dismissing the matter as "much ado about nothing."

Casey also put a $3 million bounty on the head of Sheikh Fadlallah, a

Lebanese Shi'ite. Casey paid for the Saudis and a British arms technician to put a bomb in a car outside the mosque where Fadlallah was overseeing religious observances. They detonated it on March 8, 1985, at a moment when the bombers assumed that the shiekh had emerged. In fact he had dallied to talk with some of his congregation inside the mosque. The bomb killed 80 people, many of them schoolchildren, and wounded 200. The CIA and Saudis later paid Fadlallah a $2 million bribe not to retaliate.

The following year Casey took personal control of an effort to kill Libya's Moammar Qaddafi, an obsession of the Reagan men. Casey's deputy, Robert Gates, developed a plan for a US/Egyptian military takeover of Libya, a bold move that would "redraw the map of North Africa." In the end, Casey went after Qaddafi himself. The Libyan leader's movements were closely tracked in early April 1986 with the assistance of the Israeli Mossad. A pretext for a move against Qaddafi was confected in alleging Libyan responsibility for a bomb set off in the La Belle nightclub in Berlin that killed an American soldier, Sergeant Kenneth Ford. On April 14, nine F-111s were sent to attack Qaddafi's compound with a payload of thirty-six laser-guided 2,000-pound bombs. The raid was timed to narrowly precede the evening news and a news release had been prepared to announce that Qaddafi's death had been an accidental byproduct of this "act of self-defense."

But the Libyan leader escaped, though two of his sons were maimed and his daughter and a hundred nearby residents were killed by the strikes. There were immediate denials that the Libyan ruler had been personally targeted. "There was no decision to kill Qaddafi," Casey mumbled. "There are dissident elements inside Libya. They might have seen their chances to rise and launch a coup. I'm sorry that didn't happen." Casey later said that the raid on Libya was meant to send a message. "Like Castro and Ortega got the message when we hit Grenada, this attack will scare the hell out of Qaddafi."

In subsequent years no CIA director has quite matched the appalling Casey. After Casey the job went to William Webster, who promptly certified Panamanian strongman Manuel Noriega as an ally in the drug war. Webster, who spent much of his time on the tennis court, looked on as the collapse of the Soviet Union confounded half a century of CIA intelligence analysis. Bush's choice to head the Agency was Casey's deputy Robert Gates, who barely survived a contentious confirmation hearing after senators were told by Iran/Contra prosecutor Lawrence Walsh's investigators that Gates probably lied to Congress about his knowledge of the Iran/Contra arms deals. Gates stood by as CIA-trained thugs overthrew the government of Haitian president Jean Baptiste Aristide and replaced him with a gang of military officers headed by Gen. Raoul Cédras. Gates's CIA called Cédras one of the most promising "Haitian leaders to emerge since the Duvalier family dictatorship was overthrown in 1986." Cédras and his colleagues proceeded to slaughter their political enemies and make millions from the drug trade.

With Clinton eventually came MIT academic and defense contractor John Deutch and his passionate defense of the Agency as the redoubt of honorable folk. Deutch was in more or less permanent denial during his tour at the Agency. Not only did he disclaim CIA involvement in the drug trade, but with equal heat he denied any Agency role in the murders in Guatemala of American Michael DeVine and rebel leader Efraín Bámaca. DeVine was kidnapped and beheaded in 1990. Bamaca was captured, tortured and killed in 1992. Both assassinations were ordered by Col. Julio Roberto Alpírez, who was on the CIA payroll. When State Department official Richard Nuccio attempted to investigate the matter, Deutch revoked his security clearance. Deutch also helped conceal information collected by his own analysts that more than 100,000 soldiers had been exposed to chemical weapons during the Gulf War and instead helped concoct the ruse that the Gulf War illnesses were merely the result of psychological stress.

In 1997 George Tenet assumed the helm of the Agency after Anthony Lake was forced to withdraw after failure to fully disclose his stock holdings in oil companies with a financial interest in Agency actions. Tenet is best known for his efforts to secure the assassination of Saddam Hussein. For this task Tenet employed a group known as the Iraqi National Accord. Failing to get anywhere near Saddam himself, this group took the easier road of leaving bombs in cinemas in Baghdad, killing a large number of people.

As such vignettes remind us, the Central Intelligence Agency is exactly what one would expect of an organization with a mandate stretching from the collection and analysis of intelligence data to the undertaking of subversion, manipulation of elections, assassination and the running of secret wars. Lying is part of the job description at the CIA, where falsehoods are regularly peddled to allies, the press, other federal agencies and Congress. "We'd go down and lie to them consistently," says former CIA officer Ralph McGehee. "In my 25 years, I have never seen the agency tell the truth to a congressional committee."

Agency officials have scant fear of being slapped on the wrist over their prevarications à la Helms. Joseph Fernández, CIA station chief in Costa Rica during the secret war against Nicaragua, lied about his role in channeling money and weapons to the Contras in violation of US law. So did Deputy CIA Director Clair George. Neither did time. "We've created a class of intelligence officers who can't be prosecuted," concluded Iran/Contra prosecutor Lawrence Walsh.

Organizations such as the CIA require immersion in criminal milieus, virtually unlimited supplies of "black" or laundered money and a long-term cadre of entirely ruthless executives (some of them not averse to making personal fortunes from their covert activities). The drug trade is an integral part of such a world. The zones of primary production of opium and coca have fallen in contested zones of the Cold War: Southeast Asia, Central Asia and the Andean countries. The drug distribution networks again passed through such contested territories as Afghanistan, Vietnam and Central America. The drug traders – from rural warlords in Laos to the Thai police and Honduran generals – were similarly of enormous interest to any intelligence agency. The drug money involved is both profuse and off the books.

The drug milieu is also, in its various stages of production and transmission, inevitably associated with organized violence, from enforcers to paramilitaries to guerrilla supervisors to military detachments to generals commanding their slice of the trade. All of these areas are once again central to the concerns of an organization such as the CIA. And the drug traders (unless they operate as an arm of government, as in Mexico) are often in opposition to the ruling power, a situation that is of paramount interest to a body such as the CIA.

From the perspective of the drug lords, an alliance with or employment by the CIA is equally fruitful. They can use CIA services to suppress their rivals and protect their turf. CIA proprietaries, such as Air America, can be used to provide access to international markets. And, despite Deutch's protestations to the contrary, the CIA has repeatedly suppressed criminal investigations of its operatives by the US Customs Service, the Drug Enforcement Agency and the FBI.

Given these areas of mutual interest it is not surprising that since its inception the Central Intelligence Agency has been in permanent collusion with narco-traffickers, assisting their safe passage, protecting their activities, rewarding drug lords, hiring them for covert missions and using money derived from these operations for other activities. The fact that these drugs end up in American veins has never deterred the Agency and, given the hue of the skin often covering those veins, has perhaps even been seen as a positive outcome.

Sources

The indictment of Gen. Ramón Guillén Davila, the CIA's man and anti-drug czar in Venezuela, was ably covered by Frank Davies at the *Miami Herald.* In digging through hundreds of books we did not come across a satisfactory history of the CIA. John Ranelagh's history, *The Agency*, is a bland, though detailed overview. John Prados's book, *The President's Secret Wars*, was also useful, though it steps lightly over the Agency's biggest war, the debacle in Afghanistan. William Blum's *Killing Hope* is an exquisitely documented and passionate assessment of the Agency's incessant and often violent interventions in the politics of other nations. Jonathan Kwitny's *Endless Enemies* is also a valuable account. Of the books written by former CIA officers four stand out: Ralph McGehee's *Deadly Deceits*, Victor Marchetti and John Mark's *The CIA and the Cult of Intelligence*, Frank Snepp's *Decent Interval* and John Stockwell's *In Search of Enemies.*

The CIA has recently announced plans once again to step up its activities in Africa. Stockwell's book presents a compelling case for why the Agency should be banned from the continent. Tim Weiner, a reporter at a newspaper that has too often tried to obscure the Agency's blood trails, provides the best account of how the CIA funds its operations in his book *Blank Check*. David Wise is one of the best writers about the CIA. His 1973 book, *The Politics of Lying*, remains a reliable road map to the mendacity of the Agency and its opposite numbers at the Pentagon. *Challenging the Secret Government*, Kathryn Olmsted's appraisal of Congress's investigations of the CIA in the 1970s, is excellent. Olmsted concludes that far from opening the Agency up to detailed scrutiny and meaningful oversight, the Pike and Church hearings backfired, permitting the CIA to become even more insulated from outside accountability. Even so, the hearing records and Final Report from the Church committee provided a trove of information on the Agency's covert actions, assassination plans and ongoing affiliation with criminal elements. The Inspector General's report on the CIA's ceaseless attempts to murder Fidel Castro is essential reading for anyone seeking to understand how the Agency operates.

Adams, Samuel. "Vietnam coverup: Playing War with Numbers." *Harper's*, May 1979.

Agee, Philip. *Inside the Company: CIA Diary*. Stonehill, 1975.

Alsop, Stuart, and Thomas Braden. *Sub Rosa: The OSS and American Espionage*. Reynal and Hitchcock, 1946.

Anderson, Jack. *Confessions of a Muckraker*. Random House, 1979.

Aronson, James. *The Press and the Cold War*. Monthly Review Press, 1990.

Aspin, Les. "Misreading Intelligence." *Foreign Policy*, 43, 1981.

Bamford, James. *The Puzzle Palace*. Houghton Miflin, 1984.

Bernstein, Carl."The CIA and the Media." *Rolling Stone*, Oct. 20, 1977.

Bissell, Richard. "Reflections on the Bay of Pigs: Operation ZAPATA." *Strategic Review* 8, Fall 1984.

Blum, William. *Killing Hope*. Common Courage Press, 1995.

Braden, Tom. "What's Wrong with the CIA?" *Saturday Review*, April 5, 1975.

Branch, Taylor. "The Trial of the CIA." *New York Times Magazine*, Sept. 12, 1976.

Church, Frank. "Do We Still Plot Murders? Who Will Believe We Don't?" *Los Angeles Times*, June 14, 1983.

Cline, Ray. *The CIA Under Reagan, Bush and Casey*. Acropolis, 1981.

Codevilla, Angelo. "The CIA: What Have Three Decades Wrought" *Strategic Review*, Winter 1980.

Colby, William, and Peter Forbath. *Honorable Men: My Life in the CIA*. Simon and Schuster, 1978.

Corson, William. *Armies of Ignorance: The Rise of the American Intelligence Establishment*. Dial Press, 1977.

Davies, Frank. "Drug Trial May Put CIA Actions in Spotlight." *Miami Herald*, Sept. 13, 1997.

——. "Agent Tells of CIA Defeat in Drug War."*Miami Herald*, Sept. 18, 1997.

——. "Deposed Venezuelan Drug Czar Denies He's a Dealer." *Miami Herald*, Nov. 25, 1996.

——. "CIA Operative Charged in Drug Smuggling Case." *Miami Herald*, Jan. 14, 1997.

Epstein, Edward Jay. "Disinformation: Or Why the CIA Cannot Verify an Arms Control Agreement." *Commentary* 74, July 1982.

Fallaci, Oriana. "Otis Pike and the CIA." *New Republic*, April 3, 1976.

Fisher, Roger. "The Fatal Flaw in Our Spy System." *Boston Globe*, Feb. 1, 1976.

Gelb, Leslie. "The CIA and the Press." *New Republic*, March 22, 1975.

Greene, John R. *The Limits of Power: The Nixon and Ford Administrations*. Indiana University Press, 1992.

Harbury, Jennifer. *Searching for Everado: A Story of Love, War and the CIA in Guatemala*. Warner Books, 1997.

Halperin, Morton. "Led Astray by the CIA." *New Republic*, June 28, 1975.

——. "The CIA's Distemper."*New Republic*, Feb. 9, 1980.

Halperin, Morton, Jerry Berman, Robert Borosage and Christine Marnick. *The Lawless State: The Crimes of the US Intelligence Agencies*. Penguin, 1981.

Hersh, Seymour. "Underground for the CIA in NY: An Ex-Agent Tells of Spying on Students." *New York Times*, Dec. 29, 1974.

———. "Hunt Tells of Early Work for CIA Unit."*New York Times*, Dec. 31, 1974.

———. "Target Qaddafi."*New York Times Magazine,* Feb. 22, 1987.

Hinckle, Warren. "CIA Reunion." *San Francisco Examiner*, Jan. 27, 1986.

Hougan, Jim. *Spooks: The Haunting of America: The Private Use of Secret Agents.* Morrow, 1978.

———. *Secret Agenda: Watergate, Deep Throat and the CIA.* Random House, 1984.

———. "A Surfeit of Spies." *Harper's*, Dec. 1974.

Ignatius, David. "Dan Schorr: The Secret Sharer." *Washington Monthly*, April 1976.

Immerman, Richard. *The CIA in Guatemala: The Foreign Policy of Intervention.* Univ. of Texas Press, 1982.

Jeffries-Jones, Rhodri. *American Espionage: From Secret Service to CIA.* Free Press, 1972.

Johnson, Loch. *America's Secret Power: The CIA in a Democratic Society.* Oxford Univ. Press, 1989.

Joselyn, Eric. "CIA Off Campus: Closing the Company Store." *Nation*, March 26, 1988.

Kessler, Ronald. *Inside the CIA.* Simon and Schuster, 1992.

Kirkpatrick, Lyman. *The Real CIA.* Macmillan, 1968.

Kwitny, Jonathan. *Endless Enemies: The Making of an Unfriendly World.* Congdon and Weed, 1984.

Le Moyne, James. "Testifying to Torture." *New York Times Magazine,* June 5, 1988.

Loory, Stuart. "The CIA's 'Man' in the White House." *Columbia Journalism Review,* Sept./Oct., 1975.

———. "The CIA's Use of the Press: A 'Mighty Wurlitzer.'"*Columbia Journalism Review,* Sept./Oct. 1974.

McGehee, Ralph. *Deadly Deceits: My 25 Years in the CIA.* Sheridan Square, 1983.

———. "The CIA and the White Paper on El Salvador." *Nation,* April 11, 1981.

Marchetti, Victor, and John Marks. *The CIA and the Cult of Intelligence.* Knopf, 1974.

Marks, John. "How to Spot a Spook." *Washington Monthly*, Nov. 1974.

———. "The CIA's Corporate Shell Game."*Washington Post, July 11, 1976.*

Melanson, Philip. "The CIA's Secret Ties to Local Police." *Nation,* March 26, 1983.

Miami Herald, editorial. "CIA Knifes Nuccio." *Miami Herald,* Dec. 16, 1996.

Morris, Roger. "William Casey's Secret Past." *Atlanta Constitution*, August 31, 1987.

Olmsted, Kathryn S. *Challenging the Secret Government: The Post Watergate Investigations of the CIA and FBI.* Univ. of North Carolina Press, 1996.

Persico, Joseph. *Casey: From the OSS to the CIA.* Viking Press, 1990

Peterzell, Jay. "Can Congress Really Check the CIA?" *Washington Post*, April 21, 1983.

Phillips, David Atlee. *The Night Watch.* Atheneum, 1977.

Pincus, Walter. "Covering Intelligence." *New Republic,* Feb. 1, 1975.

Powers, Thomas. *The Man Who Kept the Secrets: Richard Helms and the CIA.* Knopf, 1979.

Prados, John. *The President's Secret Wars: CIA and Pentagon Covert Operations.* Morrow, 1986.

Ransom, Harry Howe. *The Intelligence Establishment.* Harvard Univ. Press, 1970.

Roosevelt, Kermit. *Countercoup: The Struggle for Control of Iran.* McGraw-Hill, 1981.

Schlesinger, Stephen, and Stephen Kinzer. *Bitter Fruit: The Untold Story of the American Coup in Guatemala.* Doubleday, 1982.

Semas, Philip. "How the CIA Kept an Eye on Campus Dissent." *Chronicle of Higher Education,* Dec. 5, 1977.

Stockwell, John. *In Search of Enemies: A CIA Story.* Norton, 1978.

Turner, Stansfield. *Secrecy and Democracy: The CIA in Transition.* Houghton Miflin, 1985.

US Central Intelligence Agency, Office of Inspector General. *Report on Plots to Assassinate Fidel Castro.* CIA-IG, May 23, 1967.

US Congress. Senate. Select Committee (Church Committee) to Study Governmental Operations with Respect to Intelligence Activities. *Alleged Assassination Plots Involving Foreign Leaders: An Interim Report.* Government Printing Office, 1975.

———. Select Committee (Church Committee) to Study Governmental Operations with Respect to Intelligence Activities. Ninety-fourth Congress. *Final Report.* Government Printing Office, 1976.

US, Executive Office of the President, Commission on CIA Activities. *The Rockefeller Report to the President on CIA Activities.* Government Printing Office, 1975.

Valentine, Douglas. *The Phoenix Program.* Morrow, 1990.

Weissmann, Stephen. "CIA Covert Action in Zaire and Angola: Patterns and Consequences." *Political Science Quarterly*, Summer 1979.

Wills, Gary. "The CIA from Beginning to End." *New York Times Book Review,* Jan. 22, 1976.

Wise, David. *The American Police State.* Random House, 1976.

———. *The Politics of Lying.* Random House, 1973.

———. "Is Anybody Watching the CIA?" *Inquiry,* Nov. 1978.

Woodward, Bob. *Veil: The Secret Wars of the CIA, 1981–1987.* Simon and Schuster, 1987.

5

Lucky's Break

On July 14, 1943, five days after the Allied invasion of Sicily, a plane flew at low altitude over the villages in the mountains outside Palermo trailing a long banner made of yellow cloth. In the center of this pennant was a large black L. Above the town of Villalba the plane dropped a black nylon bag near the estate of Don Calogero Vizzini. Known as Don Calo, Vizzini was the most powerful Mafia baron in western Sicily. Inside the bag was a gold foulard handkerchief, also sporting the letter L. The handkerchief was a prearranged message for Don Calo indicating that it was time for him to meet with representatives of the Allied forces. The don immediately left Villalba with several of his underlings and made his way to a rendezvous with Allied tank commanders from General George Patton's Seventh Army. After further parleys, the Mafioso helped the Allied forces negotiate the difficult crossing of the San Vito mountains, a decisive maneuver that split the Axis forces. Don Calo received his reward for these services when the Allied command later permitted him and his Mafia colleagues to oversee the government of Sicily during the occupation.

The L on the pennant and handkerchief stood for one of Don Calo's old friends, Charles "Lucky" Luciano, who was at that very moment sitting in Great Meadows Prison outside Albany, New York. The story of how America's most notorious gangster after Al Capone came to a mutually profitable partnership with two of the CIA's progenitors, the Office of Strategic Services and the Office of Naval Intelligence, demonstrates with agreeable clarity the point made at the end of the preceding chapter, namely the existence of a perennial alliance between enterprises like the Central Intelligence Agency and the Mafia. In this case, the consequence of the relationship was an enormous increase in the global heroin trade.

In 1942 the so-called "secret intelligence office" of the OSS in Washington, D.C. was headed by Earl Brennan, a former State Department official and New Hampshire Republican who had spent his childhood in Italy. Brennan's task was to prepare for the invasion of Sicily and Italy. He had opened a channel to the Vatican, the so-called Vessel Operation. His Vatican contact, Monsignor Giovanni Battista Montini, an influential aide to Pope Pius XII, suggested that Brennan recruit the services of a range of Italian exiles, including Masons, business leaders and members of the Mafia. Twenty-one years later, in 1963, Giovanni Montini became Pope Paul VI.

Following Montini's advice, Brennan journeyed to Canada in 1942 to meet with exiled leaders of the Italian and Sicilian Mafias who had fled Benito Mussolini's vigorous campaign against them. Il Duce's attack on the Mafia began in 1924, after he had been publicly insulted by Don Ciccio Cuccia during a trip to Palermo. According to the detailed account by historian of the Mafia Michele Pantaleone, after the Cuccia affair Mussolini "started the real drive against the Mafia and resorted to methods that would have made the Holy Inquisition turn pale." Mafia leaders were rounded up, tortured and placed in large cages for public trials.

The man Mussolini placed in charge of eradicating the Mafia was Cesare Mori, whose favorite method of interrogation was the *casseta*. The suspect was tied to a wooden crate, whipped with a leather lash soaked in salt water, shocked with a cattle prod, his genitals squeezed in a vice, and the soles of his feet burned with a cigarette. Hundreds of Mafia leaders, or "reprobates" as Mori called them, were tracked down, tortured and then shot in the public square at Palermo. Mori, however, soon let his war on the *Società Onorata* go to his head. He began building triumphal arches to himself bearing the phrase *Ave Caesar*, and initiated trials of Mussolini's associates in Sicily. Mori was soon relieved of command and disposed of in the customary manner. But by 1942, as a result of Mori's purges, the Sicilian Mafia existed only in small mountain villages such as Villalba. Its other leaders were either dead or had fled to the sanctuary of the United States. Mussolini's triumph over the dons won him accolades from the *New York Times,* which exulted that "the Mafia is dead, a new Sicily is born."

Thus when Earl Brennan met with the dons in Montreal they were delighted to offer cooperation with the enemies of their persecutor, Mussolini, and smiled in agreement when the OSS man invited them to "take a shot at their relatives." The Mafia chieftains helped Brennan establish contacts with Sicilian Mafiosi and also with recent Italian immigrants to the United States. To further this work Brennan assembled a team of three intelligence officers, David Bruce, Max Corvo and Victor Anfuso. Bruce, the brother-in-law of Paul Mellon and one of arch-spy Allen Dulles's most hated rivals, went on to become commander of the OSS's European Operations, and later still US ambassador to London and also to Paris, and thereafter lead negotiator at the Vietnam peace talks in the early 1970s. Corvo was a Sicilian-born US Army private who recruited dozens of recent Italian immigrants to New York and Connecticut, infiltrating them back into Sicily in the weeks prior to the invasion. Anfuso was a Sicilian-born New York lawyer, part of the Democratic Party machine which had close ties to Frank Costello and other mobsters in the Luciano network. After helping to recruit Sicilian immigrants to the Allied cause, Anfuso resurfaced in Italy five years later, this time working as a CIA agent in the fixing of the 1948 elections, where Agency money and Mafia thugs helped turn back what had looked like certain victory for the Italian Communists.

Not everyone at the OSS was convinced of the usefulness of this alliance with the Mafia. Particularly hostile was Major George Hunter White, head of OSS counter-intelligence operations in the US. White was familiar with many of the Mafia gangs from his earlier work as an agent in the Bureau of Narcotics and Dangerous Drugs (BNDD). He had been looking for spies and potential turncoats in the Manhattan Project, America's program to produce an atomic bomb. He was also looking for subversives inside OSS, which had two derisive acronyms hanging around its neck, "Oh So Social" and "Oh So Socialist," referring both to its Georgetown timbre and to such of its leftist recruits as Norman O. Brown and Herbert Marcuse.

To these investigative ends White had been working with OSS scientists on a "truth serum" to be used in interrogations. At the time, the most effective drug developed in the OSS's labs at St. Elizabeth's Hospital in the early 1940s was a concentrated form of marijuana, which induced the subject "to be loquacious and free in his impartation of information." Briefed on the agency's agreement with the Mafia, White, who would later go on to manage some of the most nefarious schemes in the CIA's drug-testing program, saw in the OSS's new associates a fine chance to test the drug on a human guinea pig. At the end of May 1943, White arranged a meeting with Augusto Del Gracio, an enforcer for New York's crime lord, Lucky Luciano. White offered Del Gracio cigarettes of tobacco mixed with a THC concentrate from marijuana. To White's great interest Del Gracio babbled openly about the logistics of Luciano's heroin operation. At one point Del Gracio remarked to White, "Whatever you do, don't ever use any of the stuff I'm telling you." Having murdered many of them himself, the strongman was well aware of the fate of snitches and squealers.

In a second session White had increased the THC to such a degree that Del Gracio simply passed out for two hours. White left the sessions satisfied with the efficacy of his "truth serum" but even more unhappy about the OSS's partnership with the Mafia, having heard Del Gracio talk about the global reach of the Luciano drug networks. He strongly urged OSS head Bill Donovan to distance itself from the criminal gangs. Donovan concurred, and the OSS ceded most of its intelligence operations in Italy and Sicily to the Office of Naval Intelligence (ONI), which had been making its own overtures to the Mafia as part of its efforts to prevent sabotage in New York. The decision didn't set well with Max Corvo, who had been cut off from his Mafia contacts inside Sicily and was forced to stand by in North Africa as Patton's Seventh Army hit the beaches at Gela and Licata with the assistance of agents from the Office of Naval Intelligence.

There was good reason for the navy to be concerned. Between December 7, 1941 and February 28, 1942, the Allies had lost seventy-one merchant ships off the Atlantic coast to German submarines. The Allied intelligence services believed that many of the loses were the result of German espionage successes in monitoring ships as they left New York. There was also some evidence that the U-boats were being resupplied off the US coastline. The Office of Naval Intelligence set up a branch in New York headed by Captain Roscoe McFall, a forty-year veteran of the navy. McFall had been charged by Rear Admiral Arthur Train, head of ONI, to secure the New York City waterfront at all costs. "The entire waterfront situation was a matter of official concern," McFall said. "Information concerning possible sabotage by enemy agents in the Port of New York, and information concerning subversive activities among those who worked as longshoremen, stevedores and other similar workers was of great interest to Naval Intelligence. Furthermore, Naval Intelligence was greatly interested in obtaining information that enemy agents might be landed on the coast."

McFall's team in New York included Commander Charles Haffenden, who headed an investigations unit called the B-3, and Lieutenant Anthony Marzullo, a lawyer and a former aide to New York Governor Thomas Dewey, who was an expert on Sicily. In December 1941, McFall ordered Haffenden and Marzullo to develop a strategy for enlisting the aid of underworld figures in New York. McFall later said that "the use of underworld informers was a calculated risk that I assumed as District Intelligence Officer." Within a few months, more than 150 ONI officers were involved in the counter-espionage operation, which the group called the "ferret squad." "Intelligence as such is not a police agency," Marzullo later explained. "Its function is to prevent. In order to prevent, you must have a system and the system in its scope and latitude must encompass any and all means which will prevent the enemy from securing aid and comfort from others. By any and all means, I include the so-called underworld."

The task of the ONI became somewhat more urgent on February 9, 1942, when the USS *Normandie,* retooled to cruise at fast speeds to evade German U-boats, sank in flames at its dock on the Hudson River. Although it turned out that the sinking of the *Normandie* was most probably an accident, at the time sabotage was strongly suspected. After the *Normandie* disaster McFall instructed his officers to use the New York City police and district attorney's offices to help open contacts with the Mob.

On March 7, McFall and Haffenden held the first in a series of meetings with Manhattan District Attorney Frank Hogan and his deputy in charge of the rackets bureau, Murray Gurfein. Hogan assured the ONI officers of full cooperation and offered to turn over all of his files on the leading Mob figures in the city. (Hogan, a long-time associate of Thomas Dewey, had helped put Lucky Luciano behind bars in 1936 for compulsory prostitution.) Haffenden, now in charge of recruitment for ONI, said he was interested in more than mere development of sources on the waterfront. He asked Hogan if it might be possible to enlist Mob chieftains to act as overseers in the supervision of informants. Hogan said this shouldn't be a problem, particularly as the Mob leaders tended to be resolutely anti-Fascist on the grounds that Mussolini had been systematically wiping out their Italian cousins. The navy men also expressed concern about the reliability of intelligence generated by the Mafia. Hogan reassured them that the threat of selective prosecution and other punitive measures would keep them in line.

Hogan's deputy Murray Gurfein (as a federal judge he would rule for the *New York Times* thirty years later in the Pentagon Papers case) suggested an approach to Joey "Socks" Lanza, then under indictment for extortion. Lanza, a Luciano lieutenant, controlled the Fulton Fish Market and the United Seafood Workers Union. Lanza's indictment had stemmed from his habit of demanding kickbacks from workers in the fish market and from union members, and for beating those who failed to pay him. Lanza owned a long rap sheet, with arrests on charges of conspiracy, burglary, assault and murder. His parole officer considered him "a ruthless racketeer." This didn't deter the navy from seeking him out. On March 26 Gurfein and Haffenden arranged a meeting with Lanza at Haffenden's suite in the Astor Hotel, where they asked the gangster for help in rooting out spies and saboteurs on the Brooklyn docks. Lanza swiftly told the DA and the navy spy of his willingness to help. "I go along 100 percent," Lanza said. "I want to put an end to those sinkings."

But Lanza turned out to be mostly a big talker. After several weeks the thug had given Haffenden little in the way of useful information. His most significant contribution was to provide the navy spies with union cards so that they could prowl the docks under cover. He also suggested that the counter-espionage operation could be aided immensely if the support of the big boss were enlisted. And who would that be, Haffenden inquired. Lucky Luciano, Lanza replied. "He's the man who snaps the whip on the entire underworld."

Charles "Lucky" Luciano was born Salvatore Lucania in the village of Lecara Freddi, near the Sicilian capital of Palermo, on November 11, 1897. In 1907 the Luciano family moved to lower Manhattan, where his father, Anthony, found work in a brass bed factory. Charles quickly turned to a life of crime, and by 1916 he had been arrested on charges of peddling drugs, the first in a string of arrests over the next decade for offenses ranging from felonious assault to drug dealing and from weapons possession to bootlegging. Many of these encounters with the law stemmed from his violent struggle for control over the notorious Five Points gang.

In 1918 Luciano happened into an association that was to last half a century and make him the most powerful mobster in the world. In late October of that year he was engaged in the mundane task of beating one of his prostitutes while a nervous Bugsy Siegel, fourteen years old at the time, looked on, a pen knife in his hand. As the prostitute's screams drifted down to the street below they were heard by a young man named Meyer Lansky, who busted into the brownstone, ran upstairs, flung open the door, knocked Luciano on the back of the head and pulled the gangster off the woman. Hot on Lansky's heels were the New York cops, who duly arrested everyone. In the paddy wagon, Lansky and Luciano struck up a conversation and soon found they had large areas of mutual interest. Lansky was then the boy genius of the Lepke and Gurrah gang, which controlled much of the heroin trade in New York.

It was not long before Lansky convinced Luciano that heroin was the perfect black market commodity. It was easy to smuggle. There was an opportunity to monopolize the market, and the drug was enormously profitable. Luciano's entry into the drug racket alienated him from the older Sicilian Mafia dons, who had steered clear of the drug trade – not from any moral qualms but because they thought it might unnecessarily antagonize the police. On October 16, 1929, the old dons kidnapped Luciano, drove him to a New Jersey warehouse, hung him from a beam by his wrists, taped his mouth, beat him with a bat, slit his throat, stabbed him with an ice pick and left him for dead. The hoodlums didn't check for vital signs, which was a big mistake because Luciano managed to work himself free and soon began to exact a thoroughgoing revenge.

Over the next four years Luciano, Lansky and their associates in Murder, Inc. eliminated over seventy of the old-line capos and set up a crime syndicate that Lansky claimed to have modeled on John D. Rockefeller's Standard Oil Trust. The crime syndicate board directors included Lepke, Gurrah, Luciano, Lansky, Siegel, Abner "Longie" Zwillman, Vito Genovese, Dutch Schultz and Joe Adonis. Lansky once boasted that their underworld empire was "bigger than US Steel."

As befits empire builders, Lansky and Luciano wanted order and an absence of troublesome and bloody encounters with the law. To this end they established a wide-ranging system of political pay-offs and bribes. In New York City these were overseen by Frank Costello, whom Senator Estes Kefauver christened the "Prime Minister" of crime. The duo also sought to establish an off-shore entrepôt for their heroin operations, and Lansky traveled repeatedly to Cuba in the early 1930s to forge an arrangement with Fulgencio Batista, the US-backed dictator, which gave the syndicate a monopoly on gambling operations in Havana plus assurances that their shipments of heroin, manufactured in Sicily and eventually in Marseilles, could be landed and stored there pending distribution in the United States. In return, half the profits from the casinos went to Batista and his cronies.

The man whom Lansky and Luciano later picked to run the Cuban gambling and drug interests for the syndicate was Santos Trafficante, a Sicilian-born gangster who lived in Tampa. Trafficante and his son, Santos Jr., became intimate friends with Batista. In later years, the CIA asked for Santos Jr.'s help in killing Castro and returning Cuba to the Mahagonny ambience of the Batista era.

In New York, Luciano didn't relinquish his interest in the traditional enterprise of prostitution but simply added a new entrepreneurial twist.

Luciano made sure that the prostitutes were addicted to heroin and paid them with diluted doses of the opiate. The doped-up prostitutes were forced into a superexploitive work pace, so much so that when Manhattan DA Thomas E. Dewey began to train his sights on Luciano, the prostitutes were eager to testify against him. Fearing Dewey's crackdown, a Luciano lieutenant, the psychotic Dutch Schultz, recommended that the crusading prosecutor be assassinated. Luciano and Lansky correctly felt that this would be politically imprudent and instead ordered the assassins at Murder, Inc. to kill Schultz, thus ironically leaving Dewey to put Luciano away. The prostitutes opened up to Frank Hogan, whose engaging and priestly interrogation style earned him the nickname "Father Hogan."

Dewey's men finally arrested Luciano in Hot Springs, Arkansas in 1936. During the trial, Dewey, whose political ambitions were intense, made the front pages day after day and finally secured conviction of the crime boss on no less than sixty-two counts of racketeering. Luciano pulled a stiff thirty to fifty years and on the recommendation of a prison psychologist, who noted his violent temper and history of drug use, was sentenced to solitary confinement in New York's most brutal penitentiary, Dannemora, as inmate No. 92168.

Between 1936 and 1942, Lucky Luciano made three efforts to win clemency or parole. Each time he was rebuffed. Then, with Joey Lanza's suggestion to ONI's Haffenden, Luciano's fortunes changed abruptly. Naval Intelligence put out its first feeler to America's top gangster through Luciano's lawyer, Moses Polakoff, a former federal prosecutor and himself a veteran of Naval Intelligence in World War I, who had maintained close ties to the navy ever since. Polakoff had reportedly earned a fee of $100,000 for his work for Luciano in the 1936 trial, a gigantic sum at the time.

Polakoff told Haffenden and District Attorney Gurfein that he would be happy to help the navy in any way he could, and felt Luciano would as well. Polakoff added significantly that "if Luciano made an honest effort to be of service, they would have to bear that in mind at a later date." But, Polakoff said, there was a problem. He claimed he didn't know Luciano well enough on a personal level to convey this kind of offer to him. However, the lawyer intimated he knew the perfect intermediary, someone "whose patriotism, or affection for our country, irrespective of his reputation, was of the highest order." Polakoff was talking about Meyer Lansky.

Thus, on April 11, 1942, Haffenden, Gurfein and Polakoff met with Lansky for breakfast at Longchamps, a restaurant on West 58th Street in Manhattan. Lansky said he would be willing to advance the proposal to Luciano, but advised that the gangster might be more cooperative if moved from the rigors of Dannemora to less austere confinement. The Office of Naval Intelligence swiftly sent a letter to New York's prison commissioner, John A. Lyons, requesting that Luciano be transferred to a "better facility," where he could be interviewed by ONI officers and "others." An ONI memo records that "the Division Intelligence Office requested the transfer of Charles "Lucky" Luciano from Clinton Prison [that is, Dannemora] to Great Meadows prison so that he might be more readily accessible … We are advised that contacts were made with Luciano thereafter and that his influence on other criminal sources resulted in their cooperation with Naval Intelligence which was considered useful to the Navy."

On May 12, Luciano was moved to Great Meadows, a relatively new prison outside Albany. Lyons gave permission for Luciano to meet with Lansky and permitted the encounters to take place without the usual security procedures for visitors, such as fingerprinting and the presence of a guard. John Lyons, commissioner of prisons, said that he'd gladly made these concessions to Luciano "to save the life of one American soldier on a single American ship."

On May 17, Lansky and Polakoff traveled by train to Great Meadows and relayed to Luciano Naval Intelligence's request for cooperation. Lansky later testified that Luciano was at first reluctant to go along with the navy's proposal, agreeing only on the condition that the arrangement be kept secret. "He had a deportation warrant attached to his papers," Lansky said. "And he didn't want his cooperation with the US government to become known because whenever he would be deported and went back to Italy, he might get lynched. He was fearful of bodily harm." The intelligence officers had no problem with Luciano's request for secrecy, since they themselves had every incentive to keep things quiet.

In later meetings Lansky and Luciano plotted out the logistics of what the navy was so eager to get – namely, a Mob order to dockland to cooperate with the anti-sabotage effort. Luciano told Lansky to contact Johnny "Cockeyed" Dunn, the boss of the Hudson River docks and Luciano's strongman in the International Longshoremen's Association; the Camarda brothers, overlords of the Brooklyn waterfront; Mikey Lascari, Luciano's boyhood pal who handled the New Jersey operations; Frank "the Hands" Costello, Luciano's political henchman; and Albert Anastasia, the CEO of Murder, Inc., who would take care of anyone who got out of line. "You go up," Luciano told Lansky, "and mention my name and in the meantime I will have the word out and you won't have no difficulties."

Over the next few weeks there was a constant shuttle of Mafia commanders to Great Meadows Prison to receive personal instructions from Luciano. Visitors personally approved by Commissioner Lyons included Lanza, Costello, Joe Adonis and Bugsy Siegel. The phrase used by Commissioner Lyons to justify these visits was "so that the inmate might assist the war effort."

In the meantime Lansky was meeting with Haffenden and other Naval Intelligence officers at their headquarters in the Astor Hotel, orchestrating the infiltration of Naval Intelligence agents onto the docks and into the unions operating there. This was a time when special cargoes of war matériel for the planned invasion of Europe were being dispatched to Great Britain and to North Africa. The navy was worried not only about sabotage, but also about work stoppages and strikes – particularly the organizing efforts of Harry Bridges, the Australian-born union organizer with close ties to the Communist Party who had led the 1934 general strike on the docks in San Francisco. The Justice Department was busy trying to deport Bridges when he showed up on the East Coast in 1942, traveling between Boston and New York encouraging the dockworkers to abandon the mob-infested International Longshoremen's Association and join his International Longshoremen and Warehousemen's Union.

Not for the last time there was a confluence of interest between criminal and intelligence organizations to crush radical unions. We will see the same story repeated in Shanghai and in postwar Italy and France. In abetting crime/drug cartels and crushing independent political movements or unions, the CIA and its forebears never hesitated for a moment to make common cause with criminals. Take the congenial conversation between Haffenden and Joey "Socks" Lanza in 1942, as they worried about the organizing activities of Bridges, code-named Brooklyn Bridge. The phone conversation was tapped by Manhattan DA Frank Hogan, who was keeping his own eye on the partnership between Naval Intelligence and the Mob:

Haffenden: "How about that Brooklyn Bridge thing?"

Lanza: "Nothing on that."

Haffenden: "I don't want any trouble on the waterfront during the crucial times."

Lanza: "You won't have any. I'll see to that. I'll give you a ring. We'll get together."

Haffenden: "OK, Socks."

Bridges's planned strike was duly broken by Mob goons under the supervision of Lanza and Albert Anastasia, a man Luciano described as being "willing to kill anybody who came to mind that he got mad about." When Bridges showed up at an organizing rally in New York City a few weeks later, Lanza handled matters personally. "I had a fight with him," recalled Joey Lanza. "I belted him, and that was that." Between 1942 and 1946, there were twenty-six unsolved murders of labor organizers and dockworkers, presumed murdered and dumped in the river by the Mafia, working in collusion with Naval Intelligence.

If one had to draw a balance sheet on who benefited the most from the Naval Intelligence/Mob partnership, the answer would surely be the gangsters. In the first place, the partnership proved fatal to honest labor organizing and left union locals on the eastern seaboard, along with the ILA, ravaged by gangsterism and corruption. The intelligence triumphs were not always clearcut, however. The most successful operation concerned the visits of Senator David Walsh of Massachusetts to what was quaintly described as "a house of ill-fame." The establishment in question was a male brothel on the East River owned by a German-American with sympathies toward Hitler and the Third Reich. Lansky told Haffenden about Walsh's patronage and the senator's name immediately rang a bell. Haffenden recalled that Walsh sat on the Senate committee overseeing the navy, and Walsh was discreetly told to seek his pleasures at a more patriotic establishment (and the good senator no doubt felt it necessary to vote for larger naval budgets for the rest of his senatorial career). Shortly thereafter the brothel was raided. The owner and three Nazi agents were arrested, convicted of espionage and given twenty-year prison sentences.

The navy could claim a more substantial intelligence coup in Sicily. In January 1943 Winston Churchill and FDR met at Casablanca to plan the invasion of southern Europe. Sicily was chosen as the initial point of attack. But there were problems with this choice. The Allies lacked maps, tide tables, pier locations and kindred topographic intelligence. There were 400,000 Axis troops in Sicily and although there were pro-Allied partisans, information about them was cloudy. The Office of Naval Intelligence instructed Commander Haffenden to interview recent immigrants from Sicily, which he did – once again with the assistance of Luciano, who placed the matter in the hands of Joe Adonis. Adonis, whom Senator Estes Kefauver called "the most sinister gangster of them all," rounded up hundreds of Sicilians for interviews with ONI officers Paul Alfieri and Anthony Marzulla and with ONI cartographer George Tarbox. These interviews produced more than 5,000 files, copies of which were sent to invasion planners in Washington. Tarbox also produced dozens of large-scale maps showing roads, mountain passes, docks and locations of potential sympathizers.

It was at this point that Haffenden began to entertain the idea that Luciano should be dispatched to Sicily in advance of the invasion "to contact natives there and to win these natives over to the support of the US war effort." He drew up a detailed plan to get New York governor Thomas Dewey to pardon Luciano, have the gangster equipped with these papers and sent to Portugal and thence to Sicily. The proposal made it all the way up to the secretary of the navy, who promptly nixed the plan. Luciano would have to wait in Great Meadow Prison for another three years.

With the first wave of the invading Allied troops in 1943 went several officers primed by informants passed through the Haffenden/Luciano filter. They were led by Lt. Paul Alfieri. Soon after the landing, Alfieri made contacts with members of the Sicilian Mafia, who led him to the headquarters of the Italian Naval Command and assisted him in a nocturnal raid that yielded maps of minefields, codebooks and details of where Axis troops were deployed.

This was certainly a triumph. How much it contributed to the success of the invasion is hard to say. It can be said with certainty, however, that the Sicilian Mafia obtained enormous advantage from the partnership. Hundreds of Mafiosi were released from prison, and in setting up civil authority across Sicily the Allies installed dozens of Mafia capos as mayors, including Don Calogero Vizzini. The Allied commanders even went so far as to make Don Calo an honorary colonel; he returned the favor by using his power to eliminate his rivals and to destroy copies of his robust criminal record.

The Sicilian historian Francesco Renda writes in his thorough history of the invasion that "it was impossible that the Allies would not win, and people still in possession of their faculties, to think and decide with their own heads, drew the necessary conclusions ... the mechanism of Mafioso pollution of the island administration and the Allied Military Government was self-propelling in an altogether spontaneous way, also because it met no obstacle on the part of various Civil Affairs officers."

The key official overseeing this triumph of gangsterism, which would overshadow Sicily for the next two generations, was the head of the Allied Military Government (AMGOT) for southern Italy and Sicily, Colonel Charles Poletti, the former lieutenant governor of New York. Given his familiarity with New York's affairs, Poletti could scarcely have been in ignorance of the dark background of the man he chose to be his interpreter – Vito Genovese. The brutal Genovese had been the manager of Luciano's gambling and narcotics network in New York until 1936, when he fled New York to escape indictments lodged by Thomas Dewey for the murder of rival gangsters Willie Gallo and Ferdinand "The Shadow" Boccia. As Genovese left for Naples, Luciano instructed Meyer Lansky "to make sure Vito lands on his feet."

Knowing of Mussolini's enmity toward the Cosa Nostra, Genovese arrived in Italy bearing an appropriate gift for Il Duce, in the form of $200,000 in cash. Thus fertilized, the friendship between Mussolini and Genovese flourished to the point where they would dine together and Mussolini would probe Genovese for his knowledge of American culture, particularly films. By 1942, however, Genovese was an agent in the Luciano/Naval Intelligence partnership and was providing a link between navy spies and the Mafia capos of western Sicily, particularly Don Calo. When Poletti (who Luciano later described as "a good friend of ours") arrived in Naples to take up residence as head of AMGOT, Genovese welcomed him with a present: a 1939 Packard.

Genovese made full use of his position at Poletti's elbow to enhance his black market operations in Naples, using Allied military trucks in cooperation with Don Calo to smuggle olive oil, sugar and other commodities off the Allied docks in Sicily, thus perpetuating the very sabotage that ONI had turned to the Mob in New York to quell.

Orange Dickey, a former FBI agent working for the US Army investigating black market operations in Italy, probed the Genovese-Don Calo enterprise, arrested Genovese and had him sent back to New York for trial. Following the death – by "enough poison to kill eight horses" – of the prime witness against him, Genovese was acquitted, and prospered mightily thereafter, becoming once again head of Luciano's drug operations in New York and, ultimately, the city's chief and most bloodthirsty gangster.

On May 8, 1945 – VE Day – Moses Polakoff filed a petition with Governor Thomas Dewey, seeking clemency for Luciano by the reason of the mobster's "valuable, substantial and important aid to the US military authorities, which information and aid were conceded to have a contribution to the war." Polakoff's petition included a letter from Commander Haffenden of Naval Intelligence who wrote glowingly of Luciano's patriotic role: "I am confident that the greater part of the intelligence developed in the Sicilian campaign was directly responsible for the number of Sicilians that emanated from Charles "Lucky" Luciano's contacts."

Polakoff had also requested a letter of support from former DA Murray Gurfein, by now a colonel in the OSS. To Polakoff's disgust, the wily Gurfein would only send such a letter to District Attorney Hogan, requesting that it be publicly released only if Naval Intelligence approved. Of course, Naval Intelligence wanted the matter to remain deeply buried.

On December 3, 1945 the New York State Parole Board voted unanimously to grant clemency to Luciano, attaching the condition that he be deported to Italy. This move was possible because, unlike his father and brothers, Lucky had never acquired US citizenship. Dewey took the matter under advisement for a month, during which time he was quietly advised by three key figures and friends: Secretary of the Navy James Forrestal, John Foster Dulles and OSS man Allen Dulles. On January 3, 1946 Dewey agreed with the parole board and commuted Luciano's sentence, noting officially: "Upon the entry of the US into the war, Luciano's aid was sought by the armed services in inducing others to provide information concerning possible enemy attack. It appears that he cooperated in such effort, although the actual value of the information procured is not clear."

On February 9 a jolly crowd of mobsters converged on the cargo ship the SS *Laura Keene,* onto which Luciano had been led, after his release from Great Meadows. Hoisting champagne glasses and wolfing down lobster were Frank Costello, Joe Adonis, Mikey Lascari and Meyer Lansky, who had thoughtfully brought along two suitcases for Luciano, one containing clothes and the other $1 million in cash. When Luciano arrived in Italy, he was met by a band adorned in red, white and blue uniforms playing "The Stars and Stripes Forever."

Establishing himself in Naples, Luciano quickly picked up the black market operations abandoned by Vito Genovese. It was a lucrative enterprise. One of Luciano's subordinates later said that they "bought a quintal of grain from the Farm Board for 2,000 lire and sold it on the black market for more than 15,000 lire." He also established business ties with Don Calo in Sicily, setting up a number of front companies, including a candy factory, a hospital supply company and a fruit export enterprise. The gangsters even engaged in some real estate deals with Princess Anna of France. Luciano was not the only Mafioso deported. Over the next five years more than 500 Italian-born gangsters would follow him back to Italy. These felons would form the primary workforce for Luciano's most important venture: the reinvigoration of his global drug empire.

Heroin was still the name of the game. At first, Luciano was able to get a cheap and almost unlimited supply from a legal source, the Schiaparelli Company, a pharmaceutical giant based in Milan. Luciano bought 200 kilos – about a quarter of a ton – of Schiaparelli heroin a year, shipped it to Cuba, where it was adulterated and then smuggled into Miami and New York. The Cuban operations were overseen by Santos Trafficante and his son Santos Jr.

Luciano was so intrigued by Cuba that he visited the island in 1947, convening a meeting of his national crime board there. At this meeting, attended by Genovese, Lansky, Anastasia, Trafficante and Sam Giancana, the logistics of the new heroin network were worked out and the plans to hit Bugsy Siegel were finalized. Luciano made plans to settle in Havana. When this news reached Harry Anslinger, head of the Bureau of Narcotics and Dangerous Drugs, the drug czar convinced Fulgencio Batista that Luciano's presence in Havana would be a public embarrassment for the US-backed dictator. A BNDD report from the time noted that Luciano had made "Cuba the center of all international narcotics operations."

Anslinger also put pressure on the Italian government to eliminate the legal sales of Schiaparelli heroin, which finally came to a halt in 1950. Luciano was prepared for this eventuality, however, having made a connection with Sami El-Khoury, a Lebanese opium merchant. El-Khoury, who used Luciano's money to buy off Lebanese police and customs agents, imported raw opium grown on the Anatolian plateau of Turkey to Beirut, where it was manufactured into morphine base. From Lebanon, the morphine base was shipped to Luciano's heroin laboratories in Sicily and, later, Marseilles. The drug was then shipped to Cuba, often inside wax oranges, each capable of holding 120 grams of heroin.

The official indulgence shown toward Luciano's narcotics network persisted well into the 1950s. Even though Anslinger had sent several BNDD agents, notably Charles Siragusa, to haunt Luciano's every move in Italy, they could never make an arrest stick. In fact, until 1956 there was not one major arrest of a gangster in the heroin hierarchy, even though Siragusa once caught Luciano with nearly a half ton of smack being readied for shipment to Havana. Lucky Luciano was the original Teflon Don.

The navy watched the re-emergence of Luciano as the world's leading crime lord with trepidation. When word of the ONI's role in his release from prison began to leak out to the press (Walter Winchell actually suggested Luciano was in line for the Congressional Medal of Honor), the navy made haste to obscure its tracks. Archivists at the Office of Naval Intelligence were told "to collect and destroy by burning" all records and maps generated by the Luciano/Naval Intelligence relationship. Agents who had been involved in the affair were told to deny any relationship with the mobsters. Acting on these orders Captain McFall told the *New York Post* in 1948 that Luciano had contributed nothing to the war effort.

Then, in 1950, Thomas Dewey's opponent in the gubernatorial race, Representative Walter Lynch, accused Dewey of taking bribes from Luciano. This accusation was followed by a story in *True* magazine that purported to quote Luciano himself as bragging that he had given the New York Republican Party $75,000 to spring him from Dannemora. Both Luciano and Lansky later dismissed the story, with Lansky noting ominously that reporters would misquote Luciano at their peril. When Commander Haffenden was publicly quoted confirming Luciano's association with the navy agents, the navy began to smear Haffenden, suggesting to some that he was mentally unbalanced and to others that he had perhaps entered into an illicit partnership with the Mob during the 1940s and was now trying to cover his own ass.

In 1951, hearings on organized crime presided over by the Tennessee populist Estes Kefauver attempted to pursue the story. The Mafia wouldn't talk and officials from the CIA (speaking on behalf of their predecessors at OSS) and the Office of Naval Intelligence vigorously denied any wartime relationship with Luciano. This was followed by the outlandish charge made by State Senator Louis Cioffi, a Democrat, on the floor of the New York General Assembly in Albany that Luciano had bribed Dewey with $300,000.

There was ample reason to suspect that navy may have planted the stories against Dewey, both to cover their own tracks and to strike back at the governor for criticisms launched by Dewey at the intelligence community during his run against Truman in 1948. Ironically, Dewey's attacks on Truman's foreign policy were crafted by his secret advisers, John Foster Dulles and Secretary of the Navy James Forrestal. After Truman learned of Forrestal's covert dealings with Dewey, the navy secretary was told his days in the administration were numbered. On his last day as secretary of the navy, he sat at his desk in a trancelike state for hours, mumbling that commies, gangsters and Jews had done him in. Forrestal eventually ended up in Bethesda Naval Hospital. On May 22, 1949, as he was transcribing a translation of Sophocles' *Ajax,* Forrestal took a pajama cord and tried to hang himself from an open window. The cord snapped and he fell 120 feet to his death.

In 1954, as the allegations against Dewey reached a crescendo, New York Commissioner of Investigations William Herlands began a probe of the matter. Herlands subpoenaed the Mafia leaders, members of the Manhattan District Attorney's office and the New York Department of Corrections. He unearthed hundreds of hours of tapes of conversations between navy spies and Mafia leaders. Then Herlands hit a wall in the US Navy. The Office of Naval Intelligence said it would consent to co-operate under three conditions: no classified information would be turned over; the navy security officers could monitor all interviews with former agents; and Herlands's final report could not be released to the public.

The director of the Office of Naval Intelligence, Rear Admiral Carl Espe, feared, with considerable justification, that publication of the Herlands report "might bring harm to the Navy … [and] jeopardize operations of a similar nature in the future." In a letter to Herlands, Espe wrote: "It would seem inevitable that publication of this Report would inspire a rash of 'thriller' stories … Just where imaginative and irresponsible publicists would stop in the search for spicy bits for the public palate is hard to guess. That there is a potential for embarrassment of the Navy is apparent."

Herlands acceded to the navy's demands. He extracted damning testimony from McFall, Alfieri, Marzullo and other navy agents involved in the Luciano operation. He also tracked down the former head of the navy's counterintelligence program, then living in Portland, Oregon, who admitted that the deals with the Mob were approved at the highest levels of the US government. The Herlands report concluded that "the evidence demonstrates that Luciano's assistance and cooperation was secured by Naval Intelligence in the course of the evolving and expanding requirements of national security." The investigator kept his word. The report was given to the navy and to Dewey, but not to the public.

The Herlands report then lay dormant for twenty years. After the death of Dewey, Rodney Campbell, who had been picked to edit Dewey's papers, unearthed it and, with the approval of the Dewey estate, wrote a remarkable book on the subject called *The Luciano Project*.

But the thirty years of navy denials and aspersions against Dewey had solidified into the conventional wisdom of the press. That practitioner of fantasy Claire Sterling in her 1986 book on the Sicilian Mafia's heroin trade, *Octopus*, discounts the Luciano/navy collaboration as a kind of gangster legend. Even though *Octopus* came out ten years after the publication of *The Luciano Project*, Sterling did not mention the Herlands report, citing instead the official denials before the Kefauver committee

What cannot now be denied is that US intelligence agencies arranged for the release from prison of the world's preeminent drug lord, allowed him to rebuild his narcotics empire, watched the flow of drugs into the largely black ghettoes of New York and Washington, D.C. escalate, and then lied about what they had done. This founding saga of the relationship between American spies and gangsters set patterns that would be replicated from Laos and Burma to Marseilles and Panama.

Lucky Luciano died in 1962 of a heart attack at the airport in Naples. He was there to meet a Hollywood producer interested in making a film of his life. A few weeks before he died Luciano gave an interview to an Associated Press reporter, who asked him why he had been released from prison. "I got my pardon because of the great services I rendered the United States," Luciano said. Then the gangster grinned. "And, because, after all, they realized I was innocent."

From the moment of its inception the CIA held to the same policies of its progenitors in keeping gangster organizations in business. By 1947 the Agency was backing heroin producers in Marseilles, Burma, Lebanon and western Sicily.

The Agency gave its first yelp of bureaucratic life on July 26, 1947, after a gestation period of more than a year. OSS chieftain Bill Donovan had first proposed a postwar Central Intelligence Service to FDR in the fall of 1944. The president was keen on the idea but died without taking any action on the matter. As Harry Truman pondered Donovan's plan two influential figures lobbied vigorously against any such idea. FBI director J. Edgar Hoover saw any such postwar agency as a threat to his own organization and plunged into a deft propaganda campaign. Hoover's friends in the press, such as Walter Trowhan of the *Washington Times Herald*, ran stories to the effect that Donovan was "out to create an all-powerful intelligence service to spy on the postwar world and pry into the lives of citizens at home." At Hoover's instigation, Trowhan drew lurid and not entirely fictional pictures of luxury-loving intelligence officers living high on the hog, funding themselves through bribery.

As vehement as Hoover was Secretary of the Navy James Forrestal. Already gripped by paranoia, Forrestal mistrusted the OSS as a nest of crypto-Communists who had leaked information to French intelligence and demonstrated an unseemly liking for Chou En-lai and the Chinese Communist revolution. Forrestal urged Truman to finish off the OSS and give supervision of intelligence back to the Office of Naval Intelligence and the Army's G-2. Truman took the advice and shortly after VJ Day signed a curt order informing Donovan that OSS and indeed Donovan were permanently out of business.

With no congressional approval and financed out of the Pentagon's budget, supervision of America's multifarious intelligence organizations was in the hands of Admiral Sidney Souers, head of the Central Intelligence Group. Souers had served in Naval Intelligence during the war and was a Forrestal man. By this time US Army and Navy Intelligence officers were busy recruiting Nazi spies, SS men and scientists, and adding monsters like Klaus Barbie to the US government's payroll. A big supporter of such hiring was George Kennan of the State Department. Kennan was furiously opposed to the Nuremberg trials. In one memo to the State Department's Henry Leverich, who was planning postwar German economic reconstruction, Kennan wrote, "Whether we like it or not, nine-tenths of what is strong, able and respected in Germany has been poured into those very categories which we have in mind for purging from the German government – namely, those who had been more than nominal members of the Nazi Party."

In a letter from the same period Kennan urged John J. McCloy, the US High Commissioner in Germany, to release thousands of Nazi war criminals because "the degree of relative guilt which such inquiries may bring to light is something of which I, as an American, prefer to remain ignorant."

By 1947 it was becoming to clear to men like Forrestal and Kennan that a new permanent, well-financed intelligence agency was required, with the capacity not only for intelligence collection but for large-scale subversion. Concentrating the minds of these Cold War strategists were the upcoming 1948 elections in Italy, which could well produce a Communist majority through the ballot box. If Italy went, Kennan said, "our whole position in the Mediterranean and possibly in Europe as well would be undermined."

The National Security Act of 1947, written by a high-flying young Democrat, Clark Clifford, created both the Air Force and the National Security Council, changed the name of the Department of War to the Department of Defense and, almost as an afterthought, conjured the Central Intelligence Agency into being. Nobody paid much attention to the intelligence part of the bill, Clifford said later. Forrestal testified before Congress that the CIA's function would consist of intelligence analysis and that there would be no domestic component to its activities. Within months both these restraints had been breached, with Forrestal leading the charge.

The National Security Act was passed in July. By September Forrestal was ordering the CIA's new director, Admiral Roscoe Hillenkoetter, to begin covert operations in Europe, in Italy and Greece. Hillenkoetter believed that this would overstep the CIA's legal authority and sought an opinion from the Agency's legal counsel, Lawrence Houston. On September 25, 1947 Houston wrote a memo, saying that even in the deliberately vague language of the CIA's founding mandate he could not find any justification for Forrestal's instruction. An enraged Forrestal promptly instructed Houston to go back and give a better opinion. Houston duly complied, reasoning that "[i]f the president gave us the proper directive and Congress gave us the money for those purposes, then we had the administrative authority to undertake those covert operations."

Thus was set the modus operandi of the CIA for the next fifty years. Though Truman was pressing for the secret operations, his signature was on no compromising document. The authority for the operations was given by the National Security Council. There was no congressional appropriation, so funding came from private sources inside the US, through a network of proprietary front organizations, millionaires, and criminal enterprises.

The CIA's intervention in the Italian elections offers the paradigm. The Agency swiftly plunged in propaganda, bribery, and blackmail across Italy. "Whether such illegal action [that is, suborning the 1948 election] also is immoral raises another question," William Colby wrote in his own memoir, published in 1978. "The test involves both ends and means. The ends sought must be in the defense of the security of the state acting, not for aggression or aggrandizement, and the means used must be only those needed to accomplish that end, not excessive ones ... This framework cannot justify every act of political interference by CIA since 1947, but it certainly does in the case of Italy."

The alliance with the Mafia in Sicily continued to flourish as the election approached. Don Calogero and his thugs, including Vito Genovese's cousin Giovanni Genovese, burned down eleven Communist Party branch offices, made four assassination attempts on the Sicilian Communist leader Girolamo Li Causi and opened fire on a crowd of workers and their families peaceably celebrating May Day in Palermo, killing eleven and wounding fifty-seven. One of Sicily's leading labor organizers, Placido Rizzotto, was found at the bottom of a cliff, legs and arms chained and a bullet through his brain. His assassin was Luciana Leggio, a 23-year-old hitman for Lucky Luciano and Don Calo. During this period of CIA-backed terror and subversion the Sicilian Mafia alone was killing an average of five people a week.

Initially the Sicilian Mafia had been separatist in its political ambitions, seeking to render the island an independent state. The CIA counseled the advantages of dropping the formal separatist program while enjoying independent license for its operations under the patronage of an understanding government in Rome. The unattractive option would be a Communist central government entirely hostile to the Mafia.

As election day arrived, Don Calo convened a meeting of his lieutenants, who were instructed to stuff ballot boxes across Sicily and to dip into their drug accounts to distribute walking-around money with which to bribe voters. This precaution was prudent since the Communists were popular, pledging land reform and an end to corruption. Throughout Italy as a whole the Communists would probably have taken a majority of seats in the constituent assembly: Colby himself – who of course had reason to inflate – guessed at a Communist share of 60 percent without the CIA's sabotage.

CIA officer Miles Copeland wrote twenty-nine years later that had it not been for the Mafia the Communists would now be in control of Italy, so crucial had the criminal organization been in murdering labor organizers and terrorizing the political process.

The CIA was also closely in league with the Vatican, itself still embroiled in its wartime alliance with the Nazis. The Vatican was smuggling to the West war criminals such as Father Andrija Artukovic, the Franciscan who had helped exterminate hundreds of thousands of Serbs in Croatia. Hiding in the Vatican was one Walter Rauff, a German Nazi who had spent the last months of the war leading an extermination unit of SS men across Italy, gassing to death some 250,000 victims, mainly Jewish women and children. Rauff's protector was Allen Dulles's old friend Monsignor Don Giusseppe Bicchierai, who assembled a terror gang charged with the task of beating up left-wing candidates, smashing political gatherings and intimidating voters. Their money, guns and jeeps were furnished by the CIA.

Thus was set the covert American occupation of Italy amid a pattern of ultra-right gangsterism and Mafia dominance that corrupted Italian political life for the next half-century.

The CIA's financing mechanisms for these abuses of its charter came in the form of large subventions from American businessmen among whom Allen Dulles and Forrestal passed the hat at New York's Brook Club, getting contributions from fearful millionaires such as Arthur Amory Houghton, president of Steuben Glass; John Hay Whitney, owner of the *New York Herald Tribune;* and Oveta Culp Hobby, owner of the *Houston Post.* It was a technique that Oliver North, subverting the will of Congress forty years later, matched exactly. And American business contributions to the undermining of democracy in Italy were tax deductible.

Dulles also tapped into the crates of Nazi gold that he had heisted during his OSS days in Switzerland during the war, when he was running Project Safehaven. The money was laundered through private foundations, a practice that became standard operating procedure.

The partnership with gangster drug traffickers in Sicily was mirrored in the CIA's partnership with the Corsican underworld in Marseilles, a battleground in the Cold War. The labor unions, dominated by Communists, were strong and dockworkers were refusing to load military supplies on French ships headed to French Indochina, where Ho Chi Minh was leading the fight for independence. Also, Marseilles was a major entrepôt for supplies shipped into Europe under the Marshall Plan.

Politically, the Corsicans in Marseilles had been split during the war. Two of the leading gangsters in the city, François Spirito and Paul Carbone, had allied themselves with the mayor, Simon Sabiani, a Nazi collaborator. Spirito and Carbone headed up Sabiani's secret police and went to work tracking down and killing members of the Resistance, which in turn managed to kill Carbone in 1943. Spirito avoided this fate, and made his way to New York after the war, where he became a kingpin in the heroin trade.

Many of the Corsicans were strongly anti-fascist, in part because Mussolini's declared aim was to annex Corsica to Italy. These Corsicans worked in the French Resistance, where they were highly valued.

Among the leading Corsican gangsters at that time in Marseilles were the brothers Antoine and Barthelemy Guerini. They had apprenticed in their trade as enforcers for Paul Carbone but later went over to the Resistance. The Guerinis hid American and British intelligence agents in their nightclub and were rewarded for their services with arms and other supplies, which they were able to use to great advantage on the black market.

In 1945 a coalition of Communists and Socialists swept to power in Marseilles and made it an early order of business to declare war on the Corsican gangs. Such developments alarmed not only the Corsican gangsters but the United States and Charles de Gaulle as well. A counterattack was swiftly organized.

The aim was to divide and conquer by splitting the fragile left coalition. The CIA turned to American organized labor in the form of the AFL-CIO, which, from the end of the war to the early 1950s, funneled $1 million a year, to the Socialists, the price tag being severance of all political ties to the Communists. By 1947 De Gaulle's party had regained power, and Marseilles' new mayor was the right-wing Michele Carlini. He imposed an austerity regime that included hikes of bus fares that soon prompted strikes and boycotts, culminating in a large rally on November 12, 1947 after Guerini's thugs, acting on Carlini's orders, had attacked Communist members of the city council.

In response to these attacks, people poured into the streets, only to be met by a fusillade of bullets fired into them by the Guerinis and their men. Dozens were wounded and one man was killed. Although there were plenty of witnesses identifying the Guerinis, Carlini's prosecutors declined to press charges. A general strike broke out across France, with 3 million workers walking off their jobs. In Marseilles the docks fell silent.

The CIA sent a team to Marseilles with arms and cash for the Guerinis, which were duly delivered by CIA officer Edwin Wilson (who was to achieve notoriety many years later for his work for Moammar Qaddafi). The CIA's gangster agents embarked on a swift program of executive action, killing key strike organizers, paying legions of scab workers and stirring up riots on the docks. By early December the strike had been broken.

Three years later the pattern was repeated. Once again a strike closed down the Marseilles waterfront, aimed specifically at shipments of weapons and supplies destined for French forces in Indochina. Once again the CIA, working with the French Secret Service (SDECE), rallied the Guerinis to lead a terror campaign against the strikers. CIA funds sluiced into Marseilles, and into the Guerini bank accounts. Again the strike was beaten down, with many union organizers murdered, often by being pitched off the docks.

In this same year of 1950, Lucky Luciano, still based in Naples and with his supplies of heroin from the Schiaperelli pharmaceutical company cut off, was casting about for a new source of the drug. Meyer Lansky crossed the Atlantic to deal with the crisis. He went to Naples to confer with Luciano, to Marseilles to forge a partnership with the Guerinis and to Switzerland to set up the appropriate bank accounts, some of them in a Mob-owned bank called the Exchange and Investment Bank of Geneva.

Both Lansky and Luciano were eager to get out of the vulnerable business of heroin production and concentrate on drug sales. Production was assigned to the Guerinis and other Corsican syndicates based in Marseilles. The Corsicans already had a worldwide production network, with labs in Indochina, Latin America and the Middle East. They also enjoyed near perfect political protection. Not only did they have the gratitude of the French right (they had prudently never sold heroin in France) but also of the CIA, which had helped make them the most powerful force in Marseilles. Thus was forged the French Connection, whereby 80 percent of the heroin entering the United States via Cuba came from Marseilles with the compliance of US government agencies, primarily the CIA. Between 1950 and 1965 there were no arrests of any executive working in this French Connection. In 1965 a crackdown by the French government prompted a relocation of production to Indochina, where both the Corsican gangsters and the CIA were well entrenched.

The CIA's protection of the Corsican drug syndicate extended well into the 1970s, as is evident in the case of Frank Matthews. Matthews rose from an impoverished black neighborhood in Durham, North Carolina to become one of the biggest heroin dealers on the East Coast, pulling down more than $130 million a year. He got his start selling heroin for New York City mobster Louis Cirillo, but by 1967 he decided to cut out the Mob and buy directly from the Corsican syndicates. In a hugely profitable enterprise, Matthews sold the dope through a network of laundries, pool halls and dime stores in New York, Baltimore, Cleveland, Philadelphia and Detroit.

In 1973, Matthews was arrested for drug trafficking in Las Vegas. He was released on $325,000 bond. He returned to New York, picked up his girlfriend and $20 million in cash and disappeared. Charges against nine of Matthews's Corsican suppliers were dropped at the insistence of the CIA, according to a 1976 Justice Department report. The Corsicans had been moonlighting for the CIA and the Agency argued that prosecuting them would compromise national security interests.

Sources

The account of Lucky Luciano's handkerchief derives from Michele Pantaleone's book *The Mafia and Politics*. Luciano's deal with US Naval Intelligence is based largely on information disclosed in Rodney Campbell's book *The Luciano Project* and the documents from the Herlands Commission, now part of the collection at the University of Rochester's library. Al McCoy's *The Politics of Heroin* is the primary source for the growth of the Marseilles heroin syndicates. Tom Braden and William Colby's accounts of manipulating elections in Italy and France display a breathtaking hubris. A much more penetrating look at the Italian and French operations in the late 1940s and early 1950s can be found in William Blum's remarkable history of the Agency, *Killing Hope*. The account of Allen Dulles passing the hat at the Brook Club to fund CIA covert operations is from David Wise's early dissection of the CIA, *The Espionage Establishment*. Both Tim Weiner's *Blank Check* and William Corson's *Armies of Ignorance* were useful sources on how the CIA has used deceit, fearmongering and secrecy to build its $27 billion annual budget.

Aarons, Mark, and John Loftus. *Unholy Trinity: The Vatican, the Nazis and Soviet Intelligence*. St. Martin's Press, 1991.

Anslinger, Harry. *The Protectors*. Farrar, Strauss. 1964.

Aron, Robert. *France Reborn*. Scribners, 1964.

Bloch, Alan A. *East Side–West Side: Organizing Crime in New York, 1930–1950*. Transaction Books, 1983.

——. "European Drug Traffic and Traffickers Between the Wars: The Policy of Suppression and Its Consequences." *Journal of Social History*, vol. 23, no. 2, 1989.

Blum, William. *Killing Hope: US Military and CIA Interventions Since World War II*. Common Courage, 1995.

Braden, Tom. "I'm Glad the CIA Is Immoral." *Saturday Evening Post*, May 20, 1967.

Campbell, Rodney. *The Luciano Project: The Secret Wartime Collaboration Between the Mafia and the US Navy*. McGraw-Hill, 1977.

Colby, William, and Peter Forbath. *Honorable Men: My Life in the CIA*. Simon and Schuster, 1978.

Copeland, Miles. *The Game of Nations*. Simon and Schuster, 1969.

——. *Without Cloak or Dagger*. Simon and Schuster, 1974.

Corson, William. *Armies of Ignorance: The Rise of the American Intelligence Empire*. Dial Press, 1977.

Corvo, Max. *The OSS in Italy, 1942–1945*. Praeger, 1990.

Deacon, Richard. *The French Secret Service*. Grafton, 1990.

Demaris, Ovid. *Lucky Luciano*. Monarch Books, 1960.

Dolci, Danilo. *Report from Palermo*. Viking, 1970.

Domenico, Roy P. *Italian Fascism on Trial 1943–1948*. Univ. of North Carolina Press, 1991.

Duggan, Christopher. *Fascism and the Mafia*. Yale Univ. Press, 1989.

Feder, Sid, and Joachim Joesten. *The Luciano Story*. David McKay Co., 1954.

Filipelli, Ronald. *American Labor and Postwar Italy*. Stanford Univ. Press, 1989.

Gage, Nicholas. *The Mafia Is Not an Equal Opportunity Employer*. McGraw-Hill, 1971.

Ginsborg, Paul. *A History of Contemporary Italy*. Viking, 1990.

Goode, Stephen. *The CIA*. Franklin Watts, 1982.

Gosch, Martin, and Richard Hammer. *The Last Testament of Lucky Luciano*. Little, Brown, 1974.

Harper, John Lamberton. *America and the Reconstruction of Italy, 1945–1948*. Cambridge Univ. Press, 1986.

Herlands, William, Commissioner of Investigations. "Report." Thomas Dewey Papers, University of Rochester. Sept. 1954.

Holt, Robert, and Robert van de Velde. *Strategic Psychological Operations and American Foreign Policy*. Univ. of Chicago Press, 1960.

Hughes, Stuart. *The United States and Italy*. Harvard Univ. Press, 1965.

Johnson, Malcom. *Crime on the Labor Front*. McGraw-Hill, 1950.

Kolko, Gabriel. *The Politics of War*. Random House, 1968.

Lacey, Robert. *Little Man: Meyer Lansky and the Gangster Life*. Little, Brown, 1991.

Lewis, Norman. *The Honored Society*. Putnam, 1964.

Loftus, John. *The Belarus Secret*. Knopf, 1982.

Maas, Peter, *The Valachi Papers*. Putnam, 1968.

———. *Manhunt*. Random House, 1986.

Marchetti, Victor, and John Marks. *The CIA and the Cult of Intelligence*. Dell, 1980.

Martinez, E. Edda and Edward Suchman. "Letters from America and the 1948 Elections in Italy." *Public Opinion Quarterly*, Spring 1950.

MacKenzie, Norman, ed. *Secret Societies*. Collier, 1967.

Messick, Hank. *Lansky*. Putnam, 1971.

Nash, Jay Robert. *Bloodletters and Badmen*. M. Evans and Company, 1995.

Pantaleone, Michele. *The Mafia and Politics*. Chatto and Windus, 1966.

Pisan, Sallie. *The CIA and the Marshall Plan*. Univ. of Kansas Press, 1991.

Ranelagh, John. *The Agency: The Rise and Decline of the CIA*. Simon and Schuster, 1986.

Servadio, Gaia. *Mafioso: A History of the Mafia from Its Origins to the Present*. Dell Books, 1976.

Smith, R. Harris. *OSS: The Secret History of America's First Central Intelligence Agency*. Univ. of California Press, 1972.

Sterling, Claire. *Octopus*. Norton, 1990.

Tompkins, Peter. *A Spy in Rome*. Simon and Schuster, 1962.

Weber, Eugene. *Action Française*. Stanford Univ. Press, 1962.

Weiner, Tim. *Blank Check: The Pentagon's Black Budget*. Warner Books, 1990.

Wilhelm, Maria de Blasio. *The Other Italy*. Norton, 1988.

Wise, David. *The Espionage Establishment*. Random House, 1967.

Wise, David, and Thomas Ross. *The Invisible Government*. Random House, 1964.

Zuccotti, Susan. *The Italians and the Holocaust*. Basic Books, 1987.

6

Paperclip: Nazi Science
Heads West

In the wake of Gary Webb's articles, nothing more enraged the CIA's defenders than the charges that in its dealings with crack entrepreneurs the Agency might have deliberately targeted poor black and Latino communities in the inner cities as a covert attempt at social control. As we have seen, CIA director John Deutch traveled to South Central Los Angeles to face a furious black audience and deny in the strongest terms any such suggestion. Some of the most effective attacks on Webb were couched not in substantive challenges to his account, but in imputations that he was cynically fanning "black paranoia" and engaging in irresponsible conspiracy-mongering.

The bleak truth is that a careful review of the activities of the CIA and the organizations from which it sprang reveals an intense preoccupation with the development of techniques of behavior control, brainwashing, and covert medical and psychic experimentation on unwitting subjects including religious sects, ethnic minorities, prisoners, mental patients, soldiers and the terminally ill. The rationale for such activities, the techniques and indeed the human subjects chosen show an extraordinary and chilling similarity to Nazi experiments. This similarity becomes less surprising when we trace the determined and often successful efforts of US intelligence officers to acquire the records of Nazi experiments, and in many cases to recruit the Nazi researchers themselves and put them to work, transferring the laboratories from Dachau, the Kaiser Wilhelm Institute, Auschwitz and Buchenwald to Edgewood Arsenal, Fort Detrick, Huntsville Air Force Base, Ohio State, and the University of Washington.

As Allied forces crossed the English Channel during the D-Day invasion of June 1944, some 10,000 intelligence officers known as T-Forces were right behind the advance battalions. Their mission: seize munitions experts, technicians, German scientists and their research materials, along with French scientists who had collaborated with the Nazis. Soon a substantial number of such scientists had been picked up and placed in an internment camp known as the Dustbin. In the original planning for the mission a prime factor was the view that German military equipment – tanks, jets, rocketry and so forth – was technically superior and that captured scientists, technicians and engineers could be swiftly debriefed in an effort by the Allies to catch up.

Then, in December 1944, Bill Donovan, head of the OSS, and Allen Dulles, OSS head of intelligence operations in Europe operating out of Switzerland, strongly urged FDR to approve a plan allowing Nazi intelligence officers, scientists and industrialists to be "given permission for entry into the United States after the war and the placing of their earnings on deposit in an American bank and the like." FDR swiftly turned the proposal down, saying, "We expect that the number of Germans who are anxious to save their skins and property will rapidly increase. Among them may be some who should properly be tried for war crimes, or at least arrested for active participation in Nazi activities. Even with the necessary controls you mention, I am not prepared to authorize the giving of guarantees."

But this presidential veto was a dead letter even as it was being formulated. Operation Overcast was certainly under way by July 1945, approved by the Joint Chiefs of Staff to bring into the US 350 German scientists, including Werner Von Braun and his V2 rocket team, chemical weapons designers, and artillery and submarine engineers. There had been some theoretical ban on Nazis being imported, but this was as empty as FDR's edict. The Overcast shipment included such notorious Nazis and SS officers as Von Braun, Dr. Herbert Axster, Dr. Arthur

Rudolph and Georg Richkey.

Von Braun's team had used slave labor from the Dora concentration camp and had worked prisoners to death in the Mittelwerk complex: more than 20,000 had died from exhaustion and starvation. The supervising slavemaster was Richkey. In retaliation against sabotage in the missile plant – prisoners would urinate on electrical equipment, causing spectacular malfunctions – Richkey would hang them twelve at a time from factory cranes, with wooden sticks shoved into their mouths to muffle their cries. In the Dora camp itself he regarded children as useless mouths and instructed the SS guards to club them to death, which they did.

This record did not inhibit Richkey's speedy transfer to the United States, where he was deployed at Wright Field, an Army Air Corps base near Dayton, Ohio. Richkey went to work overseeing security for dozens of other Nazis now pursuing their researches for the United States. He was also assigned the task of translating all of the records from the Mittelwerk factory. He thus had the opportunity, which he used to the utmost, to destroy any material compromising to his colleagues and himself.

By 1947 there was enough public disquiet, stimulated by the columnist Drew Pearson, to require a pro forma war crimes trial for Richkey and a few others. Richkey was sent back to West Germany and put through a secret trial supervised by the US Army, which had every reason to clear Richkey since conviction would disclose that the entire Mittelwerk team now in the US had been accomplices in the use of slavery and the torture and killing of prisoners of war, and thus were also guilty of war crimes. The army therefore sabotaged Richkey's trial by withholding records now in the US and also by preventing any interrogation of Von Braun and others from Dayton: Richkey was acquitted. Because some of the trial materials implicated Rudolph, Von Braun and Walter Dornberger, however, the entire record was classified and held secret for forty years, thus burying evidence that could have sent the entire rocket team to the gallows.

Senior officers of the US Army knew the truth. Initially the recruitment of German war criminals was justified as necessary to the continuing war against Japan. Later, moral justification took the form of invoking "intellectual reparations" or as the Joint Chiefs of Staff put it, as "a form of exploitation of chosen rare minds whose continuing intellectual productivity we wish to use." Endorsement for this repellent posture came from a panel of the National Academy of Sciences, which adopted the collegial position that German scientists had somehow evaded the Nazi contagion by being "an island of nonconformity in the Nazified body politic," a statement that Von Braun, Richkey and the other slave drivers must have deeply appreciated.

By 1946 a rationale based on Cold War strategy was becoming more important. Nazis were needed in the struggle against Communism, and their capabilities certainly had to be withheld from the Soviets. In September 1946 President Harry Truman approved the Dulles-inspired Paperclip project, whose mission was to bring no less than 1,000 Nazi scientists to the United States. Among them were many of the vilest criminals of the war: there were doctors from Dachau concentration camp who had killed prisoners by putting them through high altitude tests, who had freezed their victims and given them massive doses of salt water to research the process of drowning. There were the chemical weapons engineers such as Kurt Blome, who had tested Sarin nerve gas on prisoners at Auschwitz. There were doctors who instigated battlefield traumas by taking women prisoners at Ravensbrück and filling their wounds with gangrene cultures, sawdust, mustard gas, and glass, then sewing them up and treating some with doses of sulfa drugs while timing others to see how long it took for them to develop lethal cases of gangrene.

Among the targets of the Paperclip recruitment program were Hermann Becker-Freyseng and Konrad Schaeffer, authors of the study "Thirst and Thirst Quenching in Emergency Situations at Sea." The study was designed to devise ways to prolong the survival of pilots downed over water. To this end the two scientists asked Heinrich Himmler for "forty healthy test subjects" from the SS chief's network of concentration camps, the only debate among the scientists being whether the research victims should be Jews, gypsies or Communists. The experiments took place at Dachau. These prisoners, most of them Jews, had salt water forced down their throats through tubes. Others had salt water injected directly into their veins. Half of the subjects were given a drug called berkatit, which was supposed to make salt water more palatable, though both scientists suspected that the berkatit itself would prove fatally toxic within two weeks. They were correct. During the tests the doctors used long needles to extract liver tissue. No anesthetic was given. All the research subjects died. Both Becker-Freyseng and Schaeffer received long-term contracts under Paperclip; Schaeffer ended up in Texas, where he continued his research into "thirst and desalinization of salt water."

Becker-Freyseng was given the responsibility of editing for the US Air Force the massive store of aviation research conducted by his fellow Nazis. By this time he had been tracked down and brought to trial at Nuremberg. The multivolume work, entitled *German Aviation Medicine: World War II,* was eventually published by the US Air Force, complete with an introduction written by Becker-Freyseng from his Nuremberg jail cell. The work neglected to mention the human victims of the research, and praised the Nazi scientists as sincere and honorable men "with a free and academic character" laboring under the constraints of the Third Reich.

One of their prominent colleagues was Dr. Sigmund Rascher, also assigned to Dachau. In 1941 Rascher informed Himmler of the vital need to conduct high-altitude experiments on human subjects. Rascher, who had developed a special low-pressure chamber during his tenure at the Kaiser Wilhelm Institute, asked Himmler for permission to have delivered into his custody "two or three professional criminals," a Nazi euphemism for Jews, Russian prisoners of war and members of the Polish underground resistance. Himmler quickly assented and Rascher's experiments were under way within a month.

Rascher's victims were locked inside his low-pressure chamber, which simulated altitudes of up to 68,000 feet. Eighty of the human guinea pigs died after being kept inside for half an hour without oxygen. Dozens of others were dragged semi-conscious from the chamber and immediately drowned in vats of ice water. Rascher quickly sliced open their heads to examine how many blood vessels in the brain had burst due to air embolisms. Rascher filmed these experiments and the autopsies, sending the footage along with his meticulous notes back to

Himmler. "Some experiments gave men such pressure in their heads that they would go mad and pull out their hair in an effort to relieve such pressure," Rascher wrote. "They would tear at their heads and faces with their hands and scream in an effort to relieve pressure on their eardrums." Rascher's records were scooped up by US intelligence agents and delivered to the Air Force.

The US intelligence officials viewed the criticism of people like Drew Pearson with disdain. Bosquet Wev, head of JOIA, dismissed the scientists' Nazi past as "a picayune detail"; continuing to condemn them for their work for Hitler and Himmler was simply "beating a dead horse." Playing on American fears about Stalin's intentions in Europe, Wev argued that leaving the Nazi scientists in Germany "presents a far greater security threat to this country than any former Nazi affiliation they may have had or even any Nazi sympathies which they may still have."

A similar pragmatism was expressed by one of Wev's colleagues, Colonel Montie Cone, head of G-2's exploitation division. "From a military point of view, we knew that these people were invaluable to us," Cone said. "Just think what we have from their research – all of our satellites, jet aircraft, rockets, almost everything else."

The US intelligence agents were so entranced with their mission that they went to extraordinary lengths to protect their recruits from criminal investigators at the US Department of Justice. One of the more despicable cases was that of Nazi aviation researcher Emil Salmon, who during the war had helped set fire to a synagogue filled with Jewish women and children. Salmon was sheltered by US officials at Wright Air Force Base in Ohio after being convicted of crimes by a denazification court in Germany.

Nazis were not the only scientists sought out by US intelligence agents after the end of World War II. In Japan the US Army put on its payroll Dr. Shiro Ishii, the head of the Japanese Imperial Army's bio-warfare unit. Dr. Ishii had deployed a wide range of biological and chemical agents against Chinese and Allied troops, and had also operated a large research center in Manchuria, where he conducted bio-weapons experiments on Chinese, Russian and American prisoners of war. Ishii infected prisoners with tetanus; gave them typhoid-laced tomatoes; developed plague-infected fleas; infected women with syphilis; and exploded germ bombs over dozens of POWs tied to stakes. Among other atrocities, Ishii's records show that he often performed "autopsies" on live victims. In a deal hatched by General Douglas MacArthur, Ishii turned over more than 10,000 pages of his "research findings" to the US Army, avoided prosecution for war crimes and was invited to lecture at Ft. Detrick, the US Army bio-weapons research center near Frederick, Maryland.

Under the terms of Paperclip there was fierce competition not only between the wartime allies but also between the various US services – always the most savage form of combat. Curtis LeMay saw his new-minted US Air Force as certain to prompt the navy's virtual extinction and thought this process would be speeded if he were able to acquire as many German scientists and engineers as possible. For its part, the US Navy was equally eager to snare its measure of war criminals. One of the first men picked up by the navy was a Nazi scientist named Theordore Benzinger. Benzinger was an expert on battlefield wounds, expertise he gained through explosive experiments conducted on human subjects during the waning stages of World War II. Benzinger ended up with a lucrative government contract working as a researcher at Bethesda Naval Hospital in Maryland.

Through its Technical Mission in Europe, the navy was also hot on the trail of state-of-the-art Nazi research into interrogation techniques. The Navy's intelligence officers soon came across Nazi research papers on truth serums, this research having been conducted at Dachau concentration camp by Dr. Kurt Plotner. Plotner had given Jewish and Russian prisoners high doses of mescalin and had watched them display schizophrenic behavior. The prisoners began to talk openly of their hatred of their German captors, and to make confessional statements about their psychological makeup.

American intelligence officers took a professional interest in Dr. Plotner's reports. OSS, Naval Intelligence and security personnel on the Manhattan Project had long been conducting their own investigations into what was known as TD, or "truth drug." As will be recalled from the description in Chapter 5 of OSS officer George Hunter White's use of THC on the Mafioso Augusto Del Gracio, they had been experimenting with TDs beginning in 1942. Some of the first subjects were people working on the Manhattan Project. The THC doses were administered to targets within the Manhattan Project in varied ways, with a liquid THC solution being injected into food and drinks, or saturated on a paper tissue. "TD appears to relax all inhibitions and to deaden the areas of the brain which govern the individual's discretion and caution" the Manhattan security team excitedly reported in an internal memo. "It accentuates the senses and makes manifest any strong characteristic of the individual."

But there was a problem. The doses of THC made the subjects throw up and the interrogators could never get the scientists to divulge any information, even with extra concentrations of the drug.

Reading Dr. Plotner's reports the US Naval Intelligence officers discovered he had experimented with some success with mescalin as a speech- and even truth-inducing drug, enabling interrogators to extract "even the most intimate secrets from the subject when questions were cleverly put." Plotner also reported researches into mescalin's potential as an agent of behavioral modification or mind control.

This information was of particular interest to Boris Pash, one of the more sinister figures in the CIA cast of characters in this early phase. Pash was a Russian émigré to the United States who had gone through the revolutionary years at the birth of the Soviet Union. In World War II he ended up working for OSS overseeing security for the Manhattan Project, where, among other activities, he supervised the investigation into Robert Oppenheimer and was the prime interrogator of the famous atomic scientist when the latter was under suspicion of helping leak secrets to the Soviet Union.

In his capacity as head of security Pash had supervised OSS officer George Hunter White's use of THC on Manhattan Project scientists. In 1944 Pash was picked by Donovan to head up what was called the Alsos Mission, designed to scoop up German scientists who had been involved in atomic, chemical and biological weapons research. Pash set up shop at the house of an old prewar friend, Dr. Eugene von Haagen, a professor at the University of Strasburg, where many Nazi scientists had been faculty members. Pash had met von Haagen when the doctor was on sabbatical at Rockefeller University in New York, researching tropical viruses. When von Haagen returned to Germany in the late 1930s he and Kurt Blome became joint heads of the Nazis' biological weapons unit. Von Haagen spent much of the war infecting Jewish inmates at the Natzweiler concentration camp with diseases including spotted fever. Undeterred by the wartime activities of his old friend, Pash immediately put von Haagen into the Paperclip program, where he worked for the US government for five years providing expertise in germ weapons research.

Von Haagen put Pash in touch with his former colleague Blome, who was also speedily enlisted in the Paperclip program. There was an inconvenient hiatus when Blome was arrested and tried at Nuremberg for medical war crimes, including the deliberate infecting of hundreds of prisoners from the Polish underground with TB and bubonic plague. But fortunately for the Nazi man of science, US Army Intelligence and the OSS withheld incriminating documents they had acquired through their interrogation. The evidence would not only have demonstrated Blome's guilt but also his supervising role in constructing a German CBW lab to test chemical and biological weapons for use on Allied troops. Blome got off.

In 1954, two months after Blome's acquittal, US intelligence officers journeyed to Germany to interview him. In a memo to his superiors, H. W. Batchelor described the purpose of this pilgrimage: "We have friends in Germany, scientific friends, and this is an opportunity to enjoy meeting them to discuss our various problems." At the session Blome gave Batchelor a list of the biological weapons researchers who had worked for him during the war and discussed promising new avenues of research into weapons of mass destruction. Blome was soon signed to a new Paperclip contract for $6,000 a year and flew to the United States, where he took up his duties at Camp King, an army base outside Washington, D.C. In 1951 von Haagen was picked up by the French authorities. Despite the tireless efforts of his protectors in US intelligence, the doctor was convicted of war crimes and sentenced to twenty years in prison.

From the Paperclip assignment, Pash, now in the new-born CIA, went on to become head of Program Branch/7, where his ongoing interest in techniques of interrogation was given ample employment. The mission of Program Branch/7, which came to light only in Senator Frank Church's 1976 hearings, was responsibility for CIA kidnappings, interrogations and killings of suspected CIA double agents. Pash pored over the work of the Nazi doctors at Dachau for useful leads in the most efficient methods of extracting information, including speech-inducing drugs, electro-shock, hypnosis and psycho-surgery. During the time Pash headed up PB/7 the CIA began pouring money into Project Bluebird, an effort to duplicate and extend the Dachau research. But instead of mescalin the CIA turned to LSD, which had been developed by the Swiss chemist Albert Hoffman.

The first CIA Bluebird test of LSD was administered to twelve subjects, the majority of whom were black, and, as the CIA psychiatrist-emulators of the Nazis doctors at Dachau noted, "of not too high mentality." The subjects were told they were being given a new drug. In the words of a CIA Bluebird memo, CIA doctors, well aware that LSD experiments had induced schizophrenia, assured them that "nothing serious or dangerous would happen to them." The CIA doctors gave the twelve 150 micrograms of LSD and then subjected them to hostile interrogation.

After these trial runs, the CIA and the US Army embarked on widespread testing at the Edgewood Chemical Arsenal in Maryland starting in 1949 and extending over the next decade. More than 7,000 US soldiers were the unwitting objects of this medical experimentation. The men would be ordered to ride exercise cycles with oxygen masks on their faces, into which a variety of hallucinogenic drugs had been sprayed, including LSD, mescalin, BZ (a hallucinogen) and SNA (sernyl, a relative of PCP, otherwise known on the street as angel dust). One of the aims of this research was to induce a state of total amnesia. This objective was attained in the case of several subjects. More than one thousand of the soldiers who enlisted in the experiments emerged with serious psychological afflictions and epilepsy: dozens attempted suicide.

One such was Lloyd Gamble, a black man who had enlisted in the air force. In 1957 Gamble was enticed to participate in a Department of Defense/CIA drug-testing program. Gamble was led to believe that he was testing new military clothing. As an inducement to participate in the program he was offered extended leave, private living quarters and more frequent conjugal visits. For three weeks Gamble put on and took off different types of uniform and each day in the midst of such exertions was given, on his recollection, two to three glasses of water-like liquid, which was in fact LSD. Gamble suffered terrible hallucinations and tried to kill himself. He learned the truth some nineteen years later when the Church hearings disclosed the existence of the program. Even then the Department of Defense denied that Gamble had been involved, and the coverup collapsed only when an old Department of Defense public relations photograph surfaced, proudly featuring Gamble and a dozen others as "volunteering for a program that was in the highest national security interest."

Few examples of the readiness of US intelligence agencies to experiment on unknowing subjects are more vivid than the foray of the national security establishment into researches on the effects of radiation exposure. There were three different types of experiments. One involved thousands of American military personnel and civilians who were directly exposed to radioactive fallout from US nuclear testing in the American Southwest and South Pacific. Many have heard of the black men who were the victims of four decades' worth of federally funded studies of syphilis in which some victims were given placebos so that doctors could monitor the progress of the disease. In the case of the Marshall Islanders, US scientists first devised the H-test – a thousand times the strength of the Hiroshima bomb – then failed to warn the inhabitants of the nearby atoll of Rongelap of the dangers of the radiation and then, with precisely the equanimity of the Nazi scientists (not surprising, since Nazi veterans of the German radiation experiments rescued by CIA officer Boris Pash were now on the US team), observed how they fared.

Initially the Marshall Islanders were allowed to remain on their atoll for two days, exposed to radiation. Then they were evacuated. Two years later Dr. G. Faill, chair of the Atomic Energy Commission's committee on biology and medicine, requested that the Rongelap Islanders be returned to their atoll "for a useful genetic study of the effects on these people." His request was granted. In 1953 the Central Intelligence

Agency and the Department of Defense signed a directive bringing the US government into compliance with the Nuremberg code on medical research. But that directive was classified as top secret, and its existence was kept secret from researchers, subjects and policy makers for twenty-two years. The policy was succinctly summed up by the Atomic Energy Commission's Colonel O. G. Haywood, who formalized his directive thus: "It is desired that no document be released which refers to experiments with humans. This might have adverse effects on the public or result in legal suits. Documents covering such fieldwork should be classified secret."

Among such fieldwork thus classified as secret were five different experiments overseen by the CIA, the Atomic Energy Commission and the Department of Defense involving the injection of plutonium into at least eighteen people, mainly black and poor, without informed consent. There were thirteen deliberate releases of radioactive material over US and Canadian cities between 1948 and 1952 to study fallout patterns and the decay of radioactive particles. There were dozens of experiments funded by the CIA and Atomic Energy Commission, often conducted by scientists at UC Berkeley, the University of Chicago, Vanderbilt and MIT, which exposed more than 2,000 unknowing people to radiation scans.

The case of Elmer Allen is typical. In 1947 this 36-year-old black railroad worker went to a hospital in Chicago with pains in his legs. The doctors diagnosed his illness as apparently a case of bone cancer. They injected his left leg with huge doses of plutonium over the next two days. On the third day, the doctors amputated his leg and sent it to the Atomic Energy Commission's physiologist to research how the plutonium had dispersed through the tissue. Twenty-six years later, in 1973, they brought Allen back to the Argonne National Laboratory outside Chicago, where they gave him a full body radiation scan, then took urine, fecal and blood samples to assess the plutonium residue in his body from the 1947 experiment.

In 1994 Patricia Durbin, who worked at the Lawrence Livermore labs on plutonium experiments, recalled, "We were always on the lookout for somebody who had some kind of terminal disease who was going to undergo an amputation. These things were not done to plague people or make them sick or miserable. They were not done to kill people. They were done to gain potentially valuable information. The fact that they were injected and provided this valuable data should almost be a sort of memorial rather than something to be ashamed of. It doesn't bother me to talk about the plutonium injectees because of the value of the information they provided." The only problem with this misty-eyed account is that Elmer Allen seems to have had nothing seriously wrong with him when he went to the hospital with leg pain and was never told of the researches conducted on his body.

In 1949 parents of mentally retarded boys at the Fernald School in Massachusetts were asked to give consent for their children to join the school's "science club." Those boys who did join the club were unwitting objects of experiments in which the Atomic Energy Commission in partnership with the Quaker Oats company gave them radioactive oatmeal. The researchers wanted to see if the chemical preservatives in cereal prevented the body from absorbing vitamins and minerals, with the radioactive materials acting as tracers. They also wanted to assess the effects of radioactive materials on the kids.

Aping the Nazis' methods, the covert medical experiments of the US government sought out the most vulnerable and captive of subjects: the mentally retarded, terminally ill, and, unsurprisingly, prisoners. In 1963 133 prisoners in Oregon and Washington had their scrotums and testicles exposed to 600 roentgens of radiation. One of the subjects was Harold Bibeau. These days he's a 55-year-old draftsman who lives in Troutdale, Oregon. Since 1994 Bibeau has been waging a one-man battle against the US Department of Energy, the Oregon Department of Corrections, the Battelle Pacific Northwest Labs and the Oregon Health Sciences University. Because he's an ex-con he has not, thus far, obtained much satisfaction.

In 1963 Bibeau was convicted of killing a man who had tried to molest him sexually. Bibeau got twelve years for voluntary manslaughter. While in prison another inmate told him of a way he might get some time knocked off his sentence and make a small amount of money. Bibeau could do this by joining a medical research project supposedly managed by the Oregon Health Sciences University, the state's medical school. Bibeau says that though he did sign an agreement to be part of the research project, he was never told that there might be dangerous consequences for his health. The experiments on Bibeau and other inmates (all told, 133 prisoners in Oregon and Washington) proved damaging in the extreme. The research involved the study of the effects of radiation on human sperm and gonadal cell development.

Bibeau and his fellows were doused with 650 rads of radiation. This is a very hefty dose. One chest X-ray today involves about 1 rad. But this wasn't all. Over the next few years in prison Bibeau says he was subjected to numerous injections of other drugs, of a nature unknown to him. He had biopsies and other surgeries. He claims that after he was released from prison he was never contacted again for monitoring.

The Oregon experiments were done for the Atomic Energy Commission, with the CIA as a cooperating agency. In charge of the Oregon tests was Dr. Carl Heller. But the actual X-rays on Bibeau and the other prisoners were done by entirely unqualified people, in the form of other prison inmates. Bibeau got no time off his sentence and was paid $5 a month and $25 for each biopsy performed on his testicles. Many of the prisoners in the experiments in the Oregon and Washington state prisons were given vasectomies or were surgically castrated. The doctor who performed the sterilization operations told the prisoners the sterilizations were necessary to "keep from contaminating the general population with radiation-induced mutants."

In defending the sterilization experiments, Dr. Victor Bond, a physician at the Brookhaven nuclear lab, said, "It's useful to know what dose of radiation sterilizes. It's useful to know what different doses of radiation will do to human beings." One of Bond's colleagues, Dr. Joseph Hamilton of the University of California Medical School in San Francisco, said more candidly that the radiation experiments (which he had helped oversee) "had a little of the Buchenwald touch."

From 1960 to 1971 Dr. Eugene Sanger and his colleagues at the University of Cincinnati performed "whole body radiation experiments" on 88 subjects who were black, poor and suffering from cancer and other diseases. The subjects were exposed to 100 rads of radiation – the equivalent of 7,500 chest X-rays. The experiments often caused intense pain, vomiting and bleeding from the nose and ears. All but one of the patients died. In the mid-1970s a congressional committee discovered that Sanger had forged consent forms for these experiments.

Between 1946 and 1963 more than 200,000 US soldiers were forced to observe, at dangerously close range, atmospheric nuclear bomb tests in the Pacific and Nevada. One such participant, a US Army private named Jim O'Connor, recalled in 1994, "There was a guy with a mannikin look, who had apparently crawled behind a bunker. Something like wires were attached to his arms, and his face was bloody. I smelled an odor like burning flesh. The rotary camera I'd seen was going zoom zoom zoom and the guy kept trying to get up." O'Connor himself fled the blast area but was picked up by the Atomic Energy Commission patrols and given prolonged tests to measure his exposure. O'Connor said in 1994 that ever since the test he had experienced many health problems.

Up in the state of Washington, at the nuclear reservation at Hanford, the Atomic Energy Commission engaged in the largest intentional release of radioactive chemicals to date in December 1949. The test did not involve a nuclear explosion but the emission of thousands of curies of radioactive iodine in a plume that extended hundreds of miles south and west as far as Seattle, Portland and the California–Oregon border, irradiating hundreds of thousands of people. So far from being alerted to the test at the time, the civilian population learned of it only in the late 1970s, although there had been persistent suspicions because of the clusters of thyroid cancers occurring among the communities downwind.

In 1997 the National Cancer Institute found that millions of American children had been exposed to high-levels of radioactive iodine known to cause thyroid cancer. Most of this exposure was due to drinking milk contaminated with fallout from above-ground nuclear testing carried out between 1951 and 1962. The institute conservatively estimated that this was enough radiation to cause 50,000 thyroid cancers. The total releases of radiation were estimated to be ten times larger than those released by the explosion in the Soviet Chernobyl reactor in 1986.

A presidential commission in 1995 began looking into radiation experiments on humans and requested the CIA to turn over all of its records. The Agency responded with a terse claim that "it had no records or other information on such experiments." One reason the CIA may have felt confidence in this brusque stonewalling was that in 1973, CIA director Richard Helms had used the last moments before he retired to order that all records of CIA experiments on humans be destroyed. A 1963 report from the CIA's Inspector General indicates that for more than a decade previously the Agency had been engaged in "research and development of chemical, biological and radiological materials capable of employment in clandestine operations to control human behavior. The 1963 report went on to say that CIA director Allen Dulles had approved various forms of human experimentation as "avenues to the control of human behavior" including "radiation, electroshock, various fields of psychology, sociology and anthropology, graphology, harassment studies and paramilitary devices and materials."

The Inspector General's report emerged in congressional hearings in 1975 in a highly edited form. It remains classified to this day. In 1976 the CIA told the Church committee that it had never used radiation. But this claim was undercut in 1991 when documents were unearthed on the Agency's ARTICHOKE program. A CIA summary of ARTICHOKE says that "in addition to hypnosis, chemical and psychiatric research, the following fields have been explored ... Other physical manifestations including heat, cold, atmospheric pressure, radiation."

The 1994 presidential commission, set up by Department of Energy secretary Hazel O'Leary, followed this trail of evidence and reached the conclusion that the CIA did explore radiation as a possibility for the defensive and offensive use of brainwashing and other interrogation techniques. The commission's final report cites CIA records showing that the Agency secretly funded the construction of a wing of Georgetown University Hospital in the 1950s. This was to become a haven for CIA-sponsored research on chemical and biological programs. The CIA's money for this went via a pass-through to Dr. Charles F. Geschickter, who ran the Geschickter Fund for Medical Research. The doctor was a Georgetown cancer researcher who made his name experimenting with high doses of radiation. In 1977 Dr. Geschickter testified that the CIA paid for his radio-isotope lab and equipment and closely monitored his research.

The CIA was a major player in a whole series of inter-agency government panels on human experimentation. For example, three CIA officers served on the Defense Department's committee on medical sciences and these same officers were also key members on the joint panel on medical aspects of atomic warfare. This is the government committee that planned, funded and reviewed most human radiation experiments, including the placement of US troops in proximity to nuclear tests conducted in the 1940s and 1950s.

The CIA was also part of the armed forces' medical intelligence organization, created in 1948, where the Agency was put in charge of "foreign, atomic, biological, and chemical intelligence, from medical science's point of view." Among the more bizarre chapters in this mission was the dispatch of a team of agents to engage in a form of body-snatching, as they tried to collect tissue and bone samples from corpses to determine levels of fallout after nuclear tests. To this end they sliced tissue from some 1,500 bodies – without the knowledge or consent of the relatives of the deceased. Further evidence of the Agency's central role was its lead part in the Joint Atomic Energy Intelligence Committee, the clearing house for intelligence on foreign nuclear programs. The CIA chaired the Scientific Intelligence Committee and its subsidiary, the Joint Medical Science Intelligence Committee. Both these bodies planned the radiation and human experimentation research for the Department of Defense.

This was by no means the full extent of the Agency's role in experimenting on living people. As noted, in 1973 Richard Helms officially discontinued such work by the Agency and ordered all records destroyed, saying that he did not want the Agency's associates in such work to be "embarrassed." Thus officially ended the prolongation by the US Central Intelligence Agency of the labors of such Nazi "scientists" as Becker-Freyseng and Blome.

Sources

The story of the recruitment of Nazi scientists and warfare technicians by the Pentagon and the Central Intelligence Agency is told in two excellent but unjustly neglected books: Tom Bower's *The Paperclip Conspiracy* and Linda Hunt's *Secret Agenda*. Hunt's reporting, in particular, is first rate. Using the Freedom of Information Act, she has opened up thousands of pages of documents from the Pentagon, State Department and CIA that should keep researchers occupied for years to come. The history of the experiments of the Nazi doctors comes largely from the trial record of the medical cases at the Nuremberg tribunal, Alexander Mitscherlich and Fred Mielke's *Doctors of Infamy,* and Robert Proctor's frightening account in *Racial Hygiene.* The US government's research into biological warfare is admirably profiled in Jeanne McDermott's book, *The Killing Winds.*

The best account of the US government's role in developing and deploying chemical warfare agents remains Seymour Hersh's book *Chemical and Biological Warfare* from the late 1960s. In an attempt to track down the cause of Gulf War Syndrome, Senator Jay Rockefeller held a series of remarkable hearings on human experimentation by the US government. The hearing record provided much of the information for the sections of this chapter dealing with unwitting experimentation on US citizens by the CIA and the US Army. Information on human radiation testing by the Atomic Energy Commission and cooperating agencies (including the CIA) comes largely from several GAO studies, from the massive report compiled by the Department of Energy in 1994 and from author interviews with four of the victims of the plutonium and sterilization experiments.

Allen, Charles. "Hubertus Strughold, Nazi in USA." *Jewish Currents,* Dec. 1974.

Annas, G. J., and M. A. Grodin. *Human Rights in Human Experimentation.* Oxford Univ. Press, 1992.

Bar-Zohar, M. *The Hunt for the German Scientists.* Barker, 1967.

Bellant, Russ. *Old Nazis, the New Right and the Reagan Administration.* Political Research Associates, 1988.

Bernstein, Victor. "I Saw the Bodies of 3,000 Slaves Murdered by Nazis." *PM,* April 17, 1945.

Beyerchen, A.D. *Scientists Under Hitler.* Yale Univ. Press, 1977.

Borkin, Joseph. *The Crime and Punishment of I.G. Farben.* Andre Deutsch, 1979.

Bower, Tom. *Blind Eye to Murder.* Andre Deutsch, 1981.

———. *The Paperclip Conspiracy.* Michael Joseph Ltd., 1987.

Clay, Lucius. *Decisions in Germany.* Doubleday, 1950.

Cole, Leonard. "Risk and Biological Defense Program." *Physicians for Social Responsibility Quarterly,* March 1992.

———. *Clouds of Secrecy: The Army's Germ Warfare Tests over Populated Areas.* Rowman and Littlefield, 1988.

Corn, David. *Blond Ghost: Ted Shackley and the CIA's Crusaders.* Simon and Schuster, 1994.

D'Antonio, Michael. *Atomic Harvest: Hanford and the Lethal Toll of America's Nuclear Arsenal.* Crown, 1993.

Dornberger, Walter. *V-2.* Viking, 1958.

DuBois, Josiah. *The Devil's Chemists.* Beacon Press, 1952.

Ensign, Tod, and Glenn Alcalay. "Duck and Cover(up): US Radiation Testing on Humans." *Covert Action Quarterly,* Summer 1994.

Ferenscz, Benjamin. *Less Than Slaves.* Harvard Univ. Press, 1979.

Gallagher, Carole. *American Ground Zero: The Secret Nuclear War.* Random House,

1993.

Gimble, John. *The American Occupation of Germany*, Stanford Univ. Press, 1968.

——. "US on Policy German Scientists: The Early Cold War." *Political Science Quarterly*, 101, 1986.

Goudsmit, Samuel. *Alsos*. Henry Schuman, 1947.

Herken, Gregg, and James David. "Doctors of Death." *New York Times*, Jan. 13, 1994.

Hersh, Seymour. *Chemical and Biological Warfare*. Doubleday, 1969.

Hilts, Philip. "Medical Experts Testify on Tests Done Without Consent." *New York Times*, June 3, 1991.

Hubner, . "The Americanization of Nazi Scientist." *West*, Sept. 25, 1985.

——. "The Unmaking of a Hero." *West*, Oct. 6, 1985.

Hunt, Linda. "US Coverup of Nazi Scientists." *Bulletin of Atomic Scientists*, April, 1985.

——. "Arthur Rudolf, NASA and Dora." *Moment*, April 1987.

——. "NASA's Nazis." *Nation*, May 23, 1987.

——. *Secret Agenda: The United States Government, Nazi Scientists and Project Paperclip, 1945–1990*. St. Martin's Press, 1991.

Irving, David. *The Virus House*. Kimber, 1967.

——. *The Mare's Nest*. Panther, 1985.

Kolata, Gina. "In Debate on Radiation Tests, Rush to Judgement Is Resisted." *New York Times*, Jan. 1, 1994.

Lasby, Clarence. *Project Paperclip*. Atheneum, 1971.

Lifton, Robert Jay. *The Nazi Doctors: Medical Killing and the Psychology of Genocide*. Basic Books, 1986.

McDermott, Jeanne. *The Killing Winds: The Menace of Biological Warfare*. Arbor House, 1987.

Michel, Jean. *Dora*. Weidenfeld and Nicolson, 1979.

Middlebrook, J. L. "Contributions of the US Army to Botulinum Toxin Research." *Botulinum and Tetanus Neurotoxins*. B. R. Das Gupta, ed. Plenum Press, 1993.

Miller, Richard. *Under the Cloud*. The Free Press, 1986.

Mitscherlich, Alexander, and Fred Mielke. *Doctors of Infamy*. Schuman, 1949.

Nishimi, Robyn. *Research Involving Human Subjects*. US Office of Technology Assessment, 1994.

Nuremberg Military Tribunals. *United States of America v. Karl Brandt et al. (The Medical Case)*. Government Printing Office, 1947.

Pash, Boris. *The Alsos Mission*. Award House, 1969.

Pechura, C. M. and D. P. Rall, eds. *Veterans at Risk: The Health Effects of Mustard Gas and Lewisite*. National Academy Press, 1993.

Piller, C., and K. R. Yamamoto. *Military Control over the New Genetic Technologies*. Beech Tree Books, 1988.

Proctor, Robert. *Racial Hygiene: Medicine Under the Nazis*. Harvard Univ. Press, 1988.

Rhodes, Richard. *The Making of the Atomic Bomb*. Simon and Schuster, 1986.

——. *Dark Sun: The Making of the Hydrogen Bomb*. Simon and Schuster, 1995.

Rodal, Alti. *Nazi War Criminals in Canada*. Canadian Government Commission of Inquiry on War Criminals, 1986.

St. Clair, Jeffrey. "Germ War: The US Record." *CounterPunch*, April 1–15, 1998.

St. Clair, Jeffrey, and Alexander Cockburn. "Meet Harold Bibeau: Human Guinea Pig." *CounterPunch*, Dec. 1–15, 1997.

Schneider, Keith. "Cold War Tests on Humans to Undergo a Congressional Review." *New York Times*, April 11, 1994.

Schoemaker, Lloyd. *The Escape Factory*. St. Martin's Press, 1990.

Simon, Leslie. *German Research in World War II*. Wiley, 1947.

Simpson, Christopher. *Blowback*. Weidenfeld and Nicolson, 1988.

Somani, S.M. *Chemical Warfare Agents*. Academic Press, 1992.

Speer, Albert. *Inside the Third Reich*. Weidenfeld and Nicolson, 1970.

Uhl, Michael, and Tod Ensign. *G.I. Guinea Pigs*. Playboy Press, 1980.

US Army Intelligence Center. *History of the Counter-Intelligence Corps*. USAIC, 1959.

US Chief Counsel for Prosecution of Axis Criminality. *Nazi Conspiracy and Aggression*. Government Printing Office, 1948.

US Congress. House. Committee on Armed Services. *Military Hallucinogenic Experiments*. Goverment Printing Office, 1976.

——. Committee on the Judiciary. *Alleged Nazi War Criminals*. Government Printing Office, 1977.

——. Subcommittee on Energy of the Committee on Science, Space and Technology. *Human Radiation Experimentation and Gene Therapy*. Government Printing Office, 1994.

——. Subcommittee on Conservation and Natural Resources of the Committee on Government Operations. *Environmental Dangers of Open-Air Testing of Lethal Chemicals*. Government Printing Office, 1969.

——. Subcommittee on Administrative Law and Governmental Relations of the Committee on the Judiciary. "Statement of David Gries, Director, Center for the Study of Human Intelligence, CIA." *Government-Sponsored Tests on Humans and Possible Compensation for People Harmed in the Tests*. Washington: Government Printing Office, 1994.

US Congress. Senate. Committee on Veterans Affairs (Rockefeller Committee). *Is Military Research Hazardous to Veterans' Health? Lessons Spanning Half a Century*. Committee Print, Dec. 8, 1994.

——. Subcommittee on Health and Scientific Research of the Committee on Human Resources. *Human Drug Testing by the CIA: Testimony of Sidney Gottlieb*. Government Printing Office, 1977.

US Department of the Air Force. *German Aviation Medicine: World War II*. Government Printing Office, 1950.

——. *History of AAF Participation in Project Paperclip, May 1945–March 1947*. Air Materiel Command, Wright Air Force Base, 1948.

US Department of Defense. Research and Development Board, Committee on Medical Sciences. *Medical Aspects of Atomic Warfare*. Committee Report, 1951.

US Department of Energy. Health and Environmental Research Advisory Committee. *Summary of Findings and Recommendations, Review of the Office of Health and Environmental Research Program, Protection of Human Research Subjects*. Government Printing Office, 1994.

US Office of the Comptroller General, General Accounting Office. *Nazis and Axis Collaborators Were Used to Further US Anti-Communist Objectives in Europe—Some Immigrated to the United States*. Government Printing Office, 1985.

——. *Widespread Conspiracy to Obstruct Probes of Alleged Nazi War Criminals Not Supported by Available Evidence—Controversy May Continue*. Government Printing Office, 1978.

——. *Nuclear Health and Safety: Examples of Post–World War II Radiation Releases at US Nuclear Sites*. Government Printing Office, 1993.

——. *Human Experimentation: An Overview on Cold War Era Programs*. Government Printing Office, 1994.

Weiner, Tim. "CIA Seeks Documents from Its Radiation Tests." *New York Times*, Jan. 5, 1994.

Welcome, Eileen. "The Plutonium Experiment: Even in Death, Albert's Still Their Guinea Pig." *Albuquerque Tribune*, Nov. 16, 1993.

Wilkenson, Isabel. "Medical Experiment Still Haunts Blacks." *New York Times*, June 3, 1991.

Winterbotham, F. W. *The Nazi Connection*. Weidenfeld and Nicolson, 1979.

7

Klaus Barbie and the
Cocaine Coup

By the time he went on the payroll of an American intelligence organization in 1947, Klaus Barbie had lived several lifetimes of human vileness. He sought out opponents of the Nazis in Holland, chasing them down with dogs. He had worked for the Nazi mobile death squads on the Eastern Front, massacring Slavs and Jews. He'd put in two years heading the Gestapo office in Lyons, torturing to death Jews and French Resistance fighters (among them the head of the Resistance, Jean Moulin). After the liberation of France, Barbie participated in the final Nazi killing frenzy before the Allies moved into Germany.

Yet the career of this frightful war criminal scarcely missed a beat before he was securely on the US payroll in postwar Germany, then was shipped out by his new paymasters along the ratline to Bolivia. There he began a new life remarkably like his old one, working for the secret police and for drug lords and engaging in arms trafficking. His old skills as a torturer were frequently in demand. By the early 1960s he was once again working with the CIA to put a US-backed thug in power. In the years that followed he became a major player in the US-inspired Condor Program to suppress popular insurgencies and keep US-backed dictators in power throughout Latin America. He helped orchestrate the so-called "cocaine coup" of 1980, when a junta of Bolivian generals seized power, slaughtering their leftist opponents and reaping billions in the cocaine boom, in which Bolivia was a prime supplier.

All this time Klaus Barbie was one of the most wanted men on the planet. But he flourished until 1983, when he was finally returned to France to face trial for his crimes. In the whole sordid history of collusion between US intelligence agencies, fascists and criminals, no one more vividly represents the evils of such partnerships than Klaus Barbie.

On August 18, 1947, three men sat over drinks in a cafe in Memmingen in American-occupied Germany. One was Kurt Merck, a former officer in Nazi Germany's military intelligence agency, the Abwehr. Merck had worked in France during the war and was now on the payroll of American intelligence. The second man was Lieutenant Robert Taylor, an American officer in the Army's Counter-Intelligence Corps (CIC). The third man was Klaus Barbie, at that time on the run and number three on a US/British list of wanted SS men. Barbie had already been interrogated by the British and had not cared for the experience.

Merck was an old friend of Barbie's. Despite interservice rivalries between the Gestapo and the Abwehr, the two had worked together in France and had gotten along well. Merck was more than willing to vouch to the American officer that Barbie would be a good hire. Merck had been recruited by the Counter-Intelligence Corps in 1946, at a time when several US intelligence agencies were trying to pick up Nazi talent. CIC's cover story for this unwholesome head-hunting was the need to root out and suppress a supposed network of Hitler Youth, whose fanatical detachments were pledged to fight on, no matter what official terms of surrender had been signed. But CIC's interest in Barbie had nothing to do with the so-called Werewolves of the Hitler Youth. His hiring as an agent of the CIC was contingent on Barbie's willingness to impart information about British techniques of interrogation and about the identity of SS men the British might have tried to recruit. Barbie was only too happy to comply, particularly as this enthusiastic torturer had been slightly roughed up when he was questioned by the British.

For the next four years, the third most wanted SS man in Germany worked for the Army's Counter-Intelligence Corps. The Americans set Barbie up in a hotel in Memmingen, brought his family from Kassel and partly paid him in commodities – cigarettes, medicines, sugar and gasoline – that he could trade for a handsome price on the black market.

After initial debriefings about the intentions and techniques of the British, Barbie's main assignment, as described in a CIC memo, was to file reports on "French intelligence activities in the French zone and their agents operating in the US zone."

By 1948, the French government had information that Barbie was living under the protection of the US somewhere in Germany. They were more eager than ever to get their hands on Barbie, who had already been sentenced to death in absentia for his war crimes. Barbie was needed to testify in the upcoming trial of René Hardy, the Resistance man who saved himself from Barbie's torture by turning in Jean Moulin. But the CIC had no intention of giving its catch to the French, even on loan for the Hardy trial. Barbie's handlers at CIC, who saw the French as allies of Stalin, had nightmares about Barbie spilling the beans about his American employers. Eugene Kolb, the US Army Intelligence officer who had worked with Barbie for a year, said that the Gestapo man couldn't be given to the French because he "knew too much about our agents in Europe and the French intelligence agency was saturated with communists." Kolb's opinion is backed up by CIC memos which suggest that the French Sûreté's intention was to "kidnap Barbie, reveal his CIC connections and embarrass the US."

So, in December 1950, the US decided to trundle Barbie and his family down the ratline, an escape hatch for Nazi agents created by CIC officers Lt. Colonel James Milano and Paul Lyon. Lyon and Milano had been shuttling Nazis out of Germany, Austria and eastern Europe since 1946, sending them to Argentina, Chile, Peru, Brazil and Bolivia. The tour guide for this operation was himself a war criminal, Father Krunoslav Draganovic, a Croatian who oversaw the relocation of several hundred thousand Jews from Yugoslavia to their deaths in Nazi concentration camps. As the fascist government in Croatia began to crumble at the end of the war, the priest made his way to the safety of the Vatican. Then Draganovic, using the cover of his position in the Red Cross and with the Vatican, shuttled hundreds of war criminals out of Europe.

Many of Draganovic's first recruits were members of the Ustashi regime, the death squads under the control of the Croatian dictator Ante Pavelic, who supervised one of the great killing sprees of the war. Hundreds of thousands of Serbs – on some estimates more than 2 million –

were killed by Pavelic's forces in an insane desire to make Croatia "a 100 percent Catholic state." Pavelic would show his favorite trophy to visitors at his office: a forty-pound jar of human eyeballs extracted from his Serbian victims. After the war Draganovic helped Pavelic secure safe passage to Argentina, where he became a frequent dining companion of Juan and Eva Peron.

Other Nazis whom Draganovic helped escape Europe for South America included Colonel Hans Rudel, who went to Argentina, where he headed Peron's air force and became a leader of the international neo-Nazi movement; Dr. Willi Tank, a chief designer for the Luftwaffe; and Dr. Carl Vaernet, who had overseen surgical experiments on homosexuals at Buchenwald, castrating gay men and replacing their testicles with metal balls. Vaernet was adored by the Perons, who made the Nazi doctor head of Buenos Aires's public health department.

In 1947, the Counter-Intelligence Corps contracted with Father Draganovic to help them dispose of some of their problematic agents and recruits, namely Nazi scientists, doctors, intelligence officers and engineers. The deal was made in Rome by CIC officer Paul Lyon, who noted that Draganovic had established "several clandestine evacuation channels to the various South American countries for various types of European refugees."

The priest Draganovic was not an altruist, even on behalf of his Nazi colleagues. He demanded from the American intelligence agencies $1,400 for each war criminal who passed through his doors, and the US intelligence agencies were glad to pay his price.

A memo from an intelligence officer working at the US State Department explained that "the Vatican justifies its participation by its desire to infiltrate not only European countries, but Latin American countries as well, [with] people of all political beliefs as long as they are anti-communists and pro-catholic church."

Fearing that Barbie might slip through their fingers, the French protested directly to John J. McCloy, the US High Commissioner in Germany. McCloy icily replied that the US would not hand over Barbie to the French for possible execution, "because the allegations of the citizens of Lyons can be disregarded as being hearsay only." McCloy knew this not to be true. In 1944 Barbie's name was prominently displayed in

McCloy's office on a list called CROWCASS (the Central Registry of War Criminals and Security Suspects), where Barbie was identified as being wanted for "the murder of civilians and the torture and murder of military personnel."

Barbie was hardly the only SS man whom McCloy and his cohorts endeavored to protect from justice. Another was Adolf Eichmann's right-hand man, Baron Otto von Bolschwing. This SS officer was hired by the CIC in 1945, where he became one of the agency's most productive assets, recruiting, interrogating and hiring former SS officers. Von Bolschwing was later traded to the CIA and did work in East Germany. Like Barbie, von Bolschwingwas a top-rank war criminal, having been one of Eichmann's ideological gurus on Jewish matters, helping to script the plan to "purge Germany of the Jews" and rob of them of their wealth. It was von Bolschwing who had directed one of the most brutal slaughters of the war, the murder of hundreds of Jews in Bucharest. The Bucharest pogrom is described in detail by historian Christopher Simpson in his remarkable book *Blowback*. "Hundreds of innocent people were rounded up for execution," Simpson writes. "Some victims were actually butchered in a municipal meat-packing plant, hung on meathooks, and branded as 'kosher meat' with red-hot irons. Their throats were cut in an intentional desecration of kosher laws. Some were beheaded. 'Sixty Jewish corpses [were discovered] on the hooks used for carcasses,' US ambassador to Romania Franklin Mott Gunther wired back to Washington after the pogrom. 'They were all skinned ... [and] the quantity of blood about [was evidence] that they had been skinned alive.' Among the victims, according to eyewitnesses, was a girl no more than five years old, who was left hanging by her feet like a slaughtered calf, her body bathed in blood."

In 1954, von Bolschwing was brought to the United States. Richard Helms, who had helped recruit many of these criminals, defended the use of people like von Bolschwing, saying, "We're not in the Boy Scouts. If we'd wanted to be in the Boy Scouts we would have joined the Boy Scouts," a flippant way of dealing with his recruiting practices.

Barbie's Counter-Intelligence Corps handlers went to extraordinary lengths to protect their recruit. Eugene Kolb rejected the idea that Barbie might have physically tortured people on the grounds that he "was such a skilled interrogator, Barbie did not need to torture anyone." In fact, Barbie was a sadistic monster whose vocational priorities were the infliction of pain and ultimately death, rather than the extraction of information. His upward career in the SS, heralded by games of volleyball with Heinrich Himmler in Berlin in 1940, came abruptly to an end when he beat Jean Moulin to death without getting any information out of him. Barbie's expertise as a torturer relied on the use of bullwhips, needles pushed under fingernails, drugs, and, most uniquely, electricity sent by nodes attached to the nipples and testicles. A generation later, Barbie and CIA operatives would happily cooperate in applying these techniques to left oppositionists in Bolivia and elsewhere.

When it came to Barbie's anti-Semitism, his American intelligence patrons once again sprang to his defense. Lieutenant Taylor said that Barbie "was not an anti-Semite. He was just a loyal Nazi." Another CIC memo held that Barbie "showed no particular enthusiasm towards the idea of killing Jews." In fact, Klaus Barbie got his start as an officer for the SD, a subunit of the SS charged by Reinhard Heydrich with solving the Jewish problem as rapidly as possible. In an early purge in Holland, Barbie led the infamous raid on the Jewish farm village of Wieringer-meer, where he and his men used German shepherd dogs to round up 420 Jews, who were sent to their deaths in the stone quarries and experimental gas chambers of Mauthausen.

From the training grounds of Holland, Barbie was transferred in July 1941 to the Eastern Front, where he joined one of the SS's so-called "special task forces," the Einsatzgruppen. These mobile killing units were assigned the task of murdering every Communist and Jew they could find in Russia and the Ukraine without regard – in Heydrich's phrase – "to age or sex." In less than a year, these mobile death squads under the command of men such as Barbie killed more than a million people. Here was the model for the CIA's death squads in Vietnam – William Colby's Phoenix Program and cognate operations – and in Latin America, where CIA-sponsored teams in Guatemala, El Salvador, Chile, Colombia and Argentina applied similar methods of brutal terror, killing hundreds of thousands. There's nothing, in terms of ferocity, to separate a Barbie-supervised killing in Russia from later operations such as My Lai or El Mozote.

Rewarded with a new promotion for his work on the Eastern Front, Barbie headed to Lyons in 1942. One of his tasks was to help fulfill Himmler's recent order that the SS in France deport at least 22,000 Jews to concentration camps in the east. Barbie and his henchman Erich Bartlemus took up the task with enthusiasm. Barbie and Bartlemus raided the offices of the Union Générale des Israelites de France in Lyons, seizing records showing the addresses of Jewish orphans and other children hidden in the countryside. Later that day, Barbie arrested a hundred Jews, sending them off to their deaths at Auschwitz and Sobibor. Next Barbie descended upon the Jewish orphans home at Izieu, rounding up forty-one children aged three to thirteen along with ten of their teachers. All were trucked off to the Nazi death camps. Reporting on this raid of the schoolhouse to his supervisor, Barbie noted, "Unfortunately in this operation it was not possible to secure any money or valuables."

During his time in Lyons, Barbie was delightedly alert to the suffering of the prisoners he held in Montluc prison. He apparently derived a sadistic pleasure from locking his prisoners in cells for days at a time with the mutilated corpses of their friends. He would assemble captured members of the French Resistance before mock firing squads, apply hot irons to the soles of their feet and palms of their hands, repeatedly plunge their heads into toilets filled with piss and shit and entice his black Alsatian dog, Wolf, to bite their genitals. Barbie's torture of Lise Leserve was particularly horrific. He shackled her naked body to a beam and beat her with a spiked chain. But despite his "great skill" as an interrogator, Barbie never got Leserve to talk. She survived his torture and a year in a Ravensbrück work camp to testify against him at his trial in 1984.

In 1944, with the Allies advancing on Lyons, Barbie prepared to flee France. But before he left, he ordered the remaining 109 Jewish inmates of Montluc machine-gunned to death and had their bodies dumped in a bomb crater near the Lyons airport. Barbie also tried to wipe out the last of the French Resistance leaders under his control. On August 20, 1944, Barbie's men loaded 120 suspected members of the Resistance on trucks and drove them to an abandoned warehouse near St. Genis Laval. The prisoners were led into the building, where they were machine-gunned. The mound of corpses was drenched in gasoline and the building was destroyed by phosphorus grenades and dynamite. The explosion sent body parts flying into the town 1,000 feet away.

Such were the highlights in the career of the man who was dispatched in 1951 along with his family by US military intelligence to a Counter-Intelligence Corps safehouse in Austria. There the Barbie family was given a crash course in Spanish and was furnished with $8,000 cash; Barbie was provided, courtesy of in-house forgers, with his new identity: Klaus Altmann, mechanic. In a grim jest, Barbie picked the name Altmann himself, after the name of the chief rabbi in Barbie's hometown of Trier. The Rabbi Altmann had been one of the luminaries of the anti-Nazi resistance until 1938, when he had gone into exile in Holland, where he was tracked down in 1942 and sent to his death at Auschwitz.

From Vienna the Barbies were passed via Draganovic's ratline to Argentina and then to Bolivia. A CIC memo triumphantly noted, in this rescue of a war criminal, that "the final disposal of an extremely sensitive individual has been handled."

On April 23, 1951, Klaus Barbie and his family arrived in La Paz, Bolivia, a city the young Che Guevara would later call "the Shanghai of the Americas." Che, who visited La Paz in the summer of 1953, described it as inhabited by "a rich gamut of adventurers of all the nationalities." Some of those adventurers, including Klaus Barbie, whom Che may have unwittingly passed on the streets or in the bars of La Paz, would, with the aid of the CIA, help track down and kill the revolutionary fifteen years later in the jungles outside Vallegrande.

Upon arrival in Bolivia, the Barbies were warmly embraced by Father Rogue Romac, another of Father Draganovic's exiles. Romac's real name was Father Osvaldo Toth, a Croatian priest wanted for war crimes. Toth helped Barbie establish a lucrative business destroying the Bolivian rain forest. The Nazi made a small fortune operating sawmills in the Bolivian jungles near Santa Cruz and lumber yards in La Paz. But Barbie soon became restless and could not long conceal his political ambitions. He was quickly drawn into the service of the proto-fascist government of Victor Paz Estensorro, where he consulted on internal security matters with the Nazi exiles Heinz Wolf and a certain Herr Müller. Müller was a former Nazi prosecutor who had condemned to death the young leaders of the White Rose Resistance. Their crime: handing out anti-Nazi pamphlets at Munich University in 1943.

Barbie proved so useful to the Bolivian ruler that on October 7, 1957 he and his family were rewarded a highly sought prize: Bolivian citizenship, a status that would frustrate attempts to extradite him back to Europe. Barbie's citizenship papers were personally signed by Bolivian vice president Hernán Siles Zuazo, who, many coups later, would be forced to relinquish Barbie to the French Nazi hunters. Barbie, however, had no particular loyalty to Paz Estensorro. Indeed, he soon found himself griping at a man whose bizarre political ideology merged leftist populism with fascist notions of social order. Barbie's uneasiness with Paz Estenssoro was mirrored by similar grumblings in Washington. Paz Estenssoro had disappointed his American patrons on two touchstone issues: he maintained cordial relations with Castro's government in Cuba and he refused to send the Bolivian military to crush striking tin miners. The CIA sent Colonel Edward Fox to La Paz to search for a candidate to replace Paz.

The man who won the CIA's favor was General René Barrientos Ortuño. Barrientos was no stranger to Klaus Barbie. Indeed, they had been secretly plotting the overthrow of Paz for some time. The moment came in 1964 when the presidential palace was stormed and Paz was presented with a simple choice: he could "take a ride either to the cemetery or to the airport." Paz packed his bags and caught a plane to Argentina. The Barrientos coup returned Bolivia once more into the clutches of a military dictatorship. But this time the US government was taking no chances. It took firm control of the Bolivian army, sending dozens of US advisers to La Paz and bringing 1,600 of Bolivia's military officers back to the United States for training at American military bases. The group sent to the United States included twenty of Bolivia's top twenty-three generals.

It was during this time that the French renewed their hunt for Barbie. They began to look for him in South America and sent repeated cables to the American government regarding Barbie's whereabouts. The US denied any knowledge of its former agent, even though the CIA and other intelligence agencies were well aware that he had gone to work for the Barrientos regime.

Barbie secured a position in Barrientos's internal security force, known as Department 4, where he planned counterinsurgency operations and instructed his underlings on Nazi techniques of interrogation and state terror. Barbie also used this position to put into play once more his ideology of political eugenics. This time his victims were Bolivian Indian tribes, whom he considered genetically and culturally inferior.

Barrientos and Barbie lost no time in going after the tin miners, executing a series of bloody raids by the army and Barbie's secret police. Hundreds of miners and labor organizers were killed. Leaders of the union and of the opposition political party were forced into exile, dooming the tin mines, which were then the principal source of revenue for the Bolivian economy. Barrientos attempted to replace the lost revenue from the mines with oil profits, handing out huge concessions around the town of Santa Cruz to Gulf Oil. In return, Barrientos received what the company chastely termed "campaign contributions." Gulf also presented Barrientos with a helicopter, a gift the company said was made at the instruction of the CIA. As we shall see, it was a present that would come back to haunt the general.

Revolutionary movements were multiplying across Central and South America and the CIA correctly feared that Bolivia, with its mixture of Indian peasants and radical labor groups, was ripe terrain for revolt. The CIA poured several million dollars into Bolivia during 1966 and 1967. Some of the cash, about $800,000, went directly into the pockets of Barrientos, no doubt making it easier for the general to tolerate the American takeover of his government. The CIA justified its presence in Bolivia in a 1967 memo: "Violence in the mining areas and in the cities of Bolivia has continued to occur intermittently, and we are assisting this country to improve its training and equipment."

With a more stable and authoritarian regime in power, Barbie took the opportunity to expand his financial empire. He started an enterprise called the Estrella Company, which sold quinine bark, coca paste and assault weapons. He also hooked up with Frederich Schwend, the SS's financial whiz, who had ended up in Lima, Peru. Schwend had been sent to Latin America through the Nazi underground by the OSS after telling Allen Dulles where the SS had cached millions in cash, gold and jewels looted from its victims. Schwend claimed to be a chicken farmer, but in reality he was a high-paid consultant to generals in Peru, Colombia,

Bolivia and Argentina.

The two Nazis also joined forces to create Transmaritania, a shipping company that was to generate millions in profits. Barbie shared the wealth by inviting onto the board of his company some of the heavy hitters of the Bolivian government, including the head of the Bolivian navy, the head of the joint chiefs of staff; and the head of the Bolivian secret police, General Alfredo Ovando Candía. This shipping company began by handling flour, cotton, tin and coffee, but soon turned to much more profitable cargo: guns and drugs. The source for most of the weapons, including attack boats, tanks and fighter planes, marketed by Barbie and Schwend to regimes across South America was a Bonn-based company called Merex. Merex was controlled by another ex-Nazi taken on by the US: Colonel Otto Skorzeny, Hitler's favorite stormtrooper and the man who had rescued Mussolini from prison. During the height of the Contra War, Oliver North's operation would turn to Merex to consummate a $2 million weapons deal, thus underlining the essential continuity of Nazi alliances in US agencies from Army Intelligence to the OSS to the CIA to Reagan's National Security Council.

At least one of the people associated with Transmaritania was a CIA agent: Antonio Arguedas Mendieta, who served as minister of interior during the Barrientos regime and had been on the CIA's payroll for many years when he entered into business with Klaus Barbie.

A year after Barrientos took power, Che Guevara vanished from the radar of the CIA. CIA director Richard Helms believed that the revolutionary had been killed after a supposed rupture with Fidel Castro following Che's fiery public advocacy of a revolutionary line at a moment when Fidel was moderating his rhetoric. Helms was wrong. Che spent more than a year in the jungles of the Congo, helping orchestrate a revolutionary movement to oust the CIA-installed dictator Mobutu. Then in 1967 CIA agents in Bolivia had learned that Che was leading a revolution among the peasants in the Bolivian Andes. A detail squad of CIA officers and Green Berets were sent to La Paz. Four of the new advisers were Cuban veterans of the CIA's previous plots against Che and Castro, including Aurelio Hernández and Félix Rodríguez.

At this critical hour, the CIA once again sought out Barbie's help. Acting through intermediaries in the Barrientos government such as

Ovando Candía and Arguedas, the Agency opened a conduit that would last through the 1970s with Barbie sending back a steady stream of information to his handlers at Langley. Barbie, given his close association with General Ovando Candía, almost certainly played a role in the tracking down and murder of Che Guevara.

In true Nazi fashion, General Ovando Candía demanded proof of Che's identity after he had been shot on Barrientos's orders. The general originally ordered that Che's head be cut off and sent back to La Paz. Félix Rodríguez, the CIA man who had looted Che's watch and a pouch of his pipe tobacco from his body, claims he pursuaded the general that this might be counterproductive. Ovando relented, commanding instead that Che's hands be amputated and embalmed. His body was buried near the airstrip at Vallegrande, and exhumed and returned to Cuba in 1997.

Ultimately, Che's preserved hands and his diary ended up in the possession of Interior Minister (and CIA asset) Antonio Arguedas. But in 1968 Arguedas turned on the Barrientos regime, secretly released Che's diary of his Bolivian campaign to the public and fled to Cuba with the guerrilla leader's embalmed hands.

In 1969, Barrientos died when his Gulf Oil helicopter crashed under suspicious circumstances. His death paved the way for General Ovando Candía's short-lived presidency. Ovando's government lasted less than a year before he was ousted in an election by the nationalist General Juan José Torres. Torres released Che's comrades Regis Debray and Ciro Bustos from prison and made dangerous overtures to the Chilean government of Salvador Allende and to Castro's Cuba. His government also seized lands owned by foreign corporations, including the lucrative mineral rights controlled by Gulf Oil.

This turn of events did not come as welcome news for the CIA, which had invested so heavily in Bolivia. Another coup was plotted. This time the general of choice was Hugo Banzer Suárez, a man trained by the US military at Fort Hunt and at the Escuela de Golpes (the School of the Americas) in Panama. Banzer proved to be such a prize student that he earned the Order of Military Merit from the US military; he was also a longtime friend of Klaus Barbie, who was to play a crucial role in the coup.

The coup against President Torres culminated in August 1970, a week before President Torres was scheduled to journey to Santiago, Chile for a meeting with Salvador Allende. Even in Bolivia, the overthrow of the Torres government became known for its extreme violence and the lengths the new regime took to eradicate leftist elements in the country. Universities were shut down as "hotbeds" of radicalism, tin miners were once again violently suppressed, more than 3,000 leftists and union organizers were hauled in for interrogations and "disappeared." The Soviet embassy was shut down, and relations with Cuba and Chile cooled. Gulf Oil was swiftly compensated for its seized properties.

Barbie defended the violent nature of the Banzer coup to Brazilian journalist Dantex Ferreira by saying that Torres's leftist sympathies posed a threat to all of South America. "What Bolivia did in '67 to defend herself against a coup by Che Guevara was also condemned in many parts of the world," Barbie said.

For his role in helping to plot Banzer's bloody takeover of Bolivia, Klaus Barbie was made an honorary colonel, and he became a paid consultant to both the Ministry of the Interior and the notorious Department 7, the counterinsurgency wing of the Bolivian army. Both institutions were thoroughly penetrated and funded by the CIA. Indeed, records from the CIA and the Bolivian government show that Barbie passed information to the CIA on suspected Soviet and Cuban agents in South America. He also sent back to Langley copies of documents he stole from the Peruvian embassy and information on the operations of the Chilean intelligence agency, DINA.

A Bolivian report on Barbie speaks glowingly of his service to the Banzer government: "One of the most important aspects of Barbie's work was advising Banzer on how to adapt the military effectively for internal repression rather than external aggression. Many of the features of the Army which were later to become standard were first developed by Barbie in the early 1970s. The system of concentration camps ... became standard for important military and political prisoners."

The Nazi also continued to advise the military's secret police on methods of interrogating prisoners, which seem not have to evolved much since his days in Lyons. "Under Barbie, they [the Bolivian military] learned to use the techniques of electricity and the use of medical supervision to keep the suspect alive till they had finished with him."

The Bolivian government paid Barbie $2,000 a month for his consulting services. But this was just a small portion of his take. He was also earning enormous profits from arms sales to the Bolivian military. Many of these purchases were paid for using funds provided by the US government, which was underwriting the cost of the Bolivian military.

The 1970s were a heady time for Barbie. He lectured widely on the new South American fascism, often at candlelight vigils in so-called Thule halls adorned with Nazi flags and other iconography from the Third Reich. The war criminal also traveled freely. During the late 1960s and 1970s Barbie visited the US at least seven times. Incredibly, he also journeyed back to France, where he claims to have laid a wreath on the tomb of Jean Moulin.

Catholic missionaries and priests were one of the groups that Barbie and Banzer went after with particular zeal, since Banzer believed that they had "become infiltrated with Marxists." Priests were hauled in for interrogation, harassed, tortured and killed. One who was murdered was an American missionary from Iowa named Raymond Herman. This repression campaign against liberationist clergy became known as the Banzer Plan, and it was enthusiastically adopted in 1977 by his fellow dictators in the Latin America Anti-Communist Confederation. This crackdown was also backed by the CIA, which provided information to Barbie's men on the addresses, backgrounds, writings and friends of the priests. Barbie also was at the heart of the US-sponsored Condor Operation, a kind of trade association of South American dictators, who merged their forces in an effort to stamp out insurgencies wherever they broke out on the continent.

Banzer's startling consolidation of power was backed by millions from two friends, the German-born industrialist Eduardo Gasser and the cattle rancher Roberto Suárez Gómez. But Suárez also had another business. He oversaw one of the world's most profitable drug empires. Gasser's son, José, would later join Suárez in this billion-dollar enterprise, as would Hugo Banzer's cousin, Guillermo Banzer Ojopi, two of Bolivia's top generals, the head of the customs office at Santa Cruz and Klaus Barbie.

Suárez's drug syndicate became known as La Mafia Cruzeña. He enjoyed a near monopoly on the most productive coca-growing fields in the world: 80 percent of the world's cocaine originated from his fields in the Alto Beni. He was the primary supplier of raw coca and cocaine paste to Medellín cartel. Suárez maintained one of the largest private fleets of aircraft in world, which he used to fly much of his coca paste to Colombian cocaine labs. The cocaine planes were launched from one of Suárez's network of private airstrips. Other coca paste was shipped to Colombia via Barbie's firm, Transmaritania.

As Suárez's operation grew into a multibillion dollar empire, he turned to Barbie for help with his burgeoning security needs. Barbie duly assembled his band of narco-mercenaries, which the Nazi christened Los Novios de la Muerte, the fiancés of death. Their ranks included two former SS officers, a white Rhodesian terrorist, and Joachim Fiebelkorn, a neo-fascist madman from Frankfurt.

Barbie assigned fifteen bodyguards to follow Suárez's every footstep. He ensured that Colombian buyers made their payments and sent armed bands of Novios on forays into the jungle to destroy the operations of rival drug lords. The weapons for Barbie's men were provided gratis by the Banzer government, which in turn had bought them from Barbie's arms company.

By the mid-1970s the Bolivian economy was in ruins. Banzer, following the advice of his close friend from Santa Cruz, Roberto Suárez, concocted a bold plan to save Bolivia: he ordered the nation's ailing cotton fields to be planted with coca trees. Between 1974 and 1980 land in coca production tripled, prompting one DEA agent to note, "Someone out there planted a heck of a lot of trees." This tremendous upsurge in supply sharply drove down the price of cocaine, fueling a huge new market and the rise of the Colombian cartels. The street price of cocaine in 1975 was $1,500 per gram. By 1986 the price had fallen to about $200 per gram.

"The Bolivian military leaders began to export cocaine and cocaine base as though it were a legal product, without any pretense of narcotics control," recounted former DEA agent Michael Levine. "At the same time there was a tremendous upswing in demand from the United States. The Bolivian dictatorship quickly became the primary source of supply for the Colombian cartels, which formed during this period. And the cartels, in turn, became the main distributors of cocaine throughout the

US. It was truly the beginning of the cocaine explosion of the 1980s."

Banzer's take from the drug trade reportedly tallied at several million dollars a year. It was an enterprise he shared with his family and friends. By 1978, Banzer's private secretary, his son-in-law, his nephew and his wife had been arrested for cocaine trafficking in the US and Canada. Embarrassed by these revelations, Banzer stood down in 1978 and promised free elections in 1979. Despite widespread fraud and voter intimidation, the right-wing parties unexpectedly lost the elections, an event that prompted the infamous cocaine coup of 1980.

This time the coup plotters were led by General Luis Arce Gómez, Roberto Suárez's cousin, and his partner General Luis García-Meza. Arce Gómez, then head of Bolivia's military intelligence agency, had been using the military to assist Suárez's drug running since early 1970s. In plotting the coup, Arce Gómez called on the services of his close friend, the man he called "my teacher," Klaus Barbie. The CIA was posted on the events leading up to the coup and, in fact, had been given a tape recording of a planning session involving Arce Gómez, Roberto Suárez and Klaus Barbie.

To aid the cause, Barbie recruited the help of the Italian terrorist Stefano "Alfa" Delle Chiaie. At the time, Delle Chiaie was on the move, following the murder in Washington, D.C. of the Chilean Orlando Letelier by the Italian's associate Michael Townley, the American agent in the employ of Pinochet's secret police. Delle Chiaie brought with him to Bolivia a group of 200 Argentine terrorists, veterans of the "dirty war." In a nod to William Colby's Vietnam assassins, Delle Chiaie called his band of murderers "the Phoenix Commandos."

Delle Chiaie had his own ties to the CIA that stretched back to the close of World War II. The young Italian, who battled his way up through street gangs in Rome and Naples, became the protégé of Count Junio Valerio Borghese, the Italian fascist known as the Black Prince. Borghese headed up Mussolini's intelligence apparatus and hunted down and killed thousands of Italian resistance fighters. At the close of the war, Borghese was captured by Italian Communists, who were intent on seeing the butcher put to death for his crimes. But when the CIA's legendary James Jesus Angleton, then with the OSS, learned of the Black Prince's impending fate, he rushed to Milan and saved Borghese from the firing squad. The Black Prince spent a few months in prison and then went to work in the CIA's campaign to suppress the Italian left.

Delle Chiaie was recruited from his street gang into the neo-fascist group the P-2, where he intimidated Italian Communists, initiated a string of bombings and, in 1969, plotted a coup against the Italian government. When that coup failed, Delle Chiaie and Borghese fled to Franco's Spain, where they supervised covert attacks on Basque separatists. From Madrid, Delle Chiaie launched his career as an international consultant on right-wing terrorism, lending his services to Jonas Savimbi, leader of the CIA-backed UNITA forces in Angola; José Lopez Rega, architect of Argentina's death squads; and the Chilean dictator helped to power by the CIA, Augusto Pinochet.

On July 17, 1980 the Bolivian cocaine coup unfolded. Liberal newspapers and radio stations were bombed. The universities were shut down. Barbie and Delle Chiaie's hooded troops, armed with machine guns, swept through the streets of La Paz in ambulances. They converged on the center of resistance, the COB building, the headquarters of the Bolivian national union. Inside was Marcelo Quiroga, a labor leader recently elected to parliament, who had called a general strike. The doors were blasted down, and Los Novios de la Muerte entered, guns blazing. Quiroga was quickly found and shot. Severely wounded, he and a dozen other leaders were taken to army headquarters, where they were beaten and treated to Barbie's electro-shock machines. The women prisoners were raped. Quiroga's body was found three days later on the outskirts of La Paz. He had been shot, beaten, burned and castrated.

The following day General García-Meza was sworn in as Bolivia's new president. He duly appointed General Arce Gómez as minister of interior. Barbie was selected as the head of Bolivia's internal security forces and Stephano Delle Chiaie was assigned the task of securing international support for the regime, which quickly came from Argentina, Chile, South Africa and El Salvador.

Over the next few weeks, thousands of opposition leaders were rounded up and herded into the large soccer stadium in La Paz. In true Argentine style, they were shot en masse, their bodies dumped in rivers and deep canyons outside the capital. The Novios de la Muerte began dressing in SS-style uniforms and were called upon by Arce Gómez and

Barbie to suppress "organized delinquency."

In a show of support for the international drug war, the new Bolivian regime quickly began a drug suppression campaign. Klaus Barbie was appointed its supervisor. The operation had three objectives: soften criticism from the US and the United Nations of Bolivia's role in the drug trade; eliminate 140 rivals to the Suárez monopoly; and ruthlessly suppress the regime's political opponents. Over the next year, the cocaine generals made an estimated $2 billion in the drug trade.

Ultimately, the situation in Bolivia became so flagrant that the regime's backers in the United States decided to pull the plug. García-Meza was forced to resign in August 1981: he left Bolivia a wealthy man after securing his country's position as world's leading supplier of cocaine.

Barbie and Delle Chiaie would remain in Bolivia another year and half. The Italian police and the US DEA planned a raid to capture Delle Chiaie in 1982, but he fled Bolivia after being tipped off by a CIA contact. On January 25, 1983, Klaus Barbie was arrested and later handed over to the French. He was brought back to Lyons and imprisoned at Montluc, the scene of so many of his crimes. After his arrest in Bolivia, Barbie was asked by a French journalist if he any regrets about his life. "No, personally, no," Barbie said. "If there were mistakes, there were mistakes. But a man has to have a line of work, no?"

But while Barbie languished in prison, the cocaine empire he helped to build flourished. Indeed, after the masterminds of the cocaine coup fled, the situation actually deteriorated. The amount of cocaine produced in Bolivia rocketed from 35,000 metric tons in 1980 to 60,000 metric tons a year by the late 1980s. Nearly all of it was marked for sale in the US. The drug accounted for 30 percent of the country's gross domestic product. By 1987, Bolivia was racking up $3 billion a year in cocaine sales, more than six times the value of all other Bolivian exports. In 1998 estimated 70,000 Bolivian families remain dependent on the cultivation of coca, though they earn less than $1,000 a year for their arduous work. "If narcotics were to disappear overnight, we would have rampant unemployment," commented Flavio Machicado, the former finance minister of Bolivia. "There would be protest and open violence."

In the 1980s, the DEA and CIA went to Bolivia to train and arm the

Bolivian police's anti-drug shock troops, the Leopards. It soon turned out that many of the Leopards had begun a fruitful partnership with the coca growers and drug traffickers. A congressional review in 1985 found that "not one hectare of coca leaf has been eradicated since the US established the narcotics assistance program in 1971." But the CIA didn't mind much, because the Leopards turned their guns on Indian insurgents.

The level of official corruption also hardly abated after the exile of Barbie, Arce Gómez and García-Meza. A 1988 report by the GAO described "an unprecedented level of corruption which extends to virtually every level of Bolivian govt. and Bolivian society." Cocaine lord Roberto Suárez himself announced in 1989 that "since the 1985 elections, all the country's politicians have been involved in cocaine." This point was driven home in 1997 when Suárez's old partner Hugo Banzer once again assumed power as president of Bolivia.

As we have already noted, the career of Klaus Barbie – perhaps more strikingly than any other – illuminates the monstrosities of CIA conduct, and the drug empires it has helped spawn and protect. Such conduct, it should again be emphasized, springs not from a "rogue" Agency. but always as the expression of US government policy.

Sources

Many of the documents relating to Klaus Barbie's relationship to American intelligence agencies come from Allan Ryan's thick report for the US Justice Department. Even so, Ryan's conclusions are a tremendous whitewash. Incredibly, Ryan claims Barbie was the only wanted Nazi war criminal the US intelligence agencies helped to escape Europe, and he asserts that the US had no contact with Barbie after he arrived in South America. Both claims are ludicrous. Three books on Barbie's career as a Nazi and US intelligence recruit were indispensable: Tom Bower's *Klaus Barbie,* Magnus Linklater and Neal Ascherson's *The Nazi Legacy* and Erhard Dabringhaus's (one of Barbie's US intelligence handlers) *Klaus Barbie.* Marcel Ophuls's epic documentary film *Hotel Terminus: The Life and Times of Klaus Barbie* was also an important source. The Bolivian cocaine trade is graphically detailed in Paul Eddy's book *Cocaine Wars.* Michael Levine gives a gripping account of the 1980 "cocaine coup" in his book, *The Big White Lie. Drug War Politics* by Eve Bertram, et al., is the best account we've come across of the failures of the US drug policy since Reagan for Latin American countries and in the United States itself.

Aarons, Mark, and John Loftus. *Unholy Trinity*. St. Martin's Press, 1992.

Agee, Philip. *Inside the Company: CIA Diary*. Stonehill, 1975.

Agee, Philip, and Louis Wolf, eds. *Dirty Work: The CIA in Western Europe*. Lyle Stuart, 1978.

Allen, Charles. *Nazi War Criminals in America: Facts ... Action*. Charles Allen Productions, 1981.

Andreas, Peter. "Drug War Zone." *Nation*, Dec. 11, 1989.

Andreas, Peter, Eve Bertram, Morris Blachman, and Kenneth Sharpe. "Dead End Drug Wars." *Foreign Policy*, no. 85, 1991–1992.

Anderson, Jon Lee. *Che Guevara: A Revolutionary Life*. Grove Press, 1997.

Anderson, Scott, and Jon Lee Anderson. *Inside the League*. Dodd & Mead, 1986.

Ashman, Charles, and Robert J. Wagman. *The Nazi Hunters*. Pharos Books, 1988.

Bertram, Eve, Morris Blachman, Kenneth Sharpe and Peter Andreas. *Drug War Politics: The Price of Denial*. Univ. of California Press, 1996.

Bird, Kai. "Klaus Barbie: A Killer's Career." *Covert Action Information Bulletin*. Winter, 1986.

Black, George. "Delle Chiaie: From Bologna to Bolivia." *Nation*, April 25, 1987.

Blum, Howard. *Wanted: The Search for Nazis in America*. Fawcett, 1977.

Blum, William. *Killing Hope: US Military and CIA Intervention Since World War II*. Common Courage, 1995.

Blumenthal, Ralph. "Canadian Says Barbie Boasted of Visiting the US." *New York Times*, Feb. 28, 1983.

Bower, Tom. *Klaus Barbie*. Pantheon, 1984.

Brill, William. *Military Intervention in Bolivia: From the MNR to Military Rule*. Washington, 1967.

Burke, Melvin. "Bolivia: The Politics of Cocaine." *Current History*, 90, 1991.

Christie, Stuart. *Stefano delle Chiaie*. Refract, 1984.

Colby, Gerard, and Charlotte Dennett. *Thy Will Be Done: The Conquest of the Amazon*. HarperCollins, 1995.

Corn, David. "The CIA and the Cocaine Coup." *Nation*, Oct. 7, 1991.

Dabringhaus, Erhard. *Klaus Barbie*. Acropolis Books, 1984.

Dulles, Allen. *The Craft of Intelligence*. Harper and Row, 1963.

Dunkerly, James. *Rebellion in the Veins: Political Struggle in Bolivia, 1952–1982*. Verso, 1984.

James, Daniel, ed. *The Complete Diaries of Che Guevara and Other Captured Documents*. Stein and Day, 1968.

Gilbert, Martin. *The Holocaust*. Holt, Rinehart and Winston, 1985.

Goldhagen, Daniel Jonah. *Hitler's Willing Executioners*. Vintage, 1997.

Hargreaves, Clare. *Snow Fields: The War on Cocaine in the Andes*. Holmes and Meier, 1992.

Healy, Kevin. "Coca, the State, and the Peasantry in Bolivia." *Journal of InterAmerican Studies and World Affairs*, 30, 1988.

Higham, Charles. *Trading with the Enemy*. Delacorte, 1983.

——. *American Swastika*. Doubleday, 1985.

Höhne, Heinz. *The Order of the Death's Head*. Ballantine, 1971.

Gott, Richard. *Rural Guerillas in Latin America*. Penguin, 1973.

Kahn, David. *Hitler's Spies: German Military Intelligence in World War II*. Macmillan, 1978.

Klare, Michael. *War Without End*. Random House, 1972.

Lee, Martin A. *The Beast Reawakens*. Little, Brown, 1997.

Lernoux, Penny. *Cry of the People: The Struggle for Human Rights in Latin America – The Catholic Church in Conflict with US Policy*. Penguin, 1982.

——. "The US in Bolivia: Playing Golf While the Drugs Flow." *Nation*, Feb. 13, 1989.

Levine, Michael. *The Big White Lie*. Thunder's Mouth, 1993.

——. *Deep Cover*. Delacorte Press, 1990.

Linklater, Magnus, Isabel Hinton and Neal Ascherson. *The Nazi Legacy: Klaus Barbie and the Rise of International Fascism*. Holt, Rinehart and Winston, 1984.

Loftus, John. *The Belarus Secret*. Knopf, 1982.

Loftus, John, and Mark Aarons. *The Secret War Against the Jews*. St. Martin's Press, 1994.

Marchetti, Victor, and John Marks. *The CIA and the Cult of Intelligence*. Dell, 1980.

Molloy, James and Richard Thorn, eds. *Beyond the Revolution: Bolivia Since 1952*. Univ. of Pittsburgh Press, 1971.

Murphy, Brendan. *The Butcher of Lyons*. Empire Books, 1983.

Posner, Gerald, and John Ware. *Mengele*. Dell, 1987.

Ray, Michele. "In Cold Blood: How the CIA Executed Che." *Ramparts,* May 1969.

Rempel, William. "CIA's Purchase of Smuggled Arms from North Aides Probed by Panels." *Los Angeles Times,* March 31, 1987.

Rodríguez, Félix, and John Weisman. *Shadow Warrior*. Simon and Schuster, 1989.

Ryan, Allan. *Klaus Barbie and the United States Government*. Government Printing Office, 1983.

——. *Klaus Barbie and the United States Government: Exhibits to the Report*. Government Printing Office, 1983.

St. George, Andrew. "How the US Got Che." *True*, April, 1969.

Shafer, D. Michael. *Deadly Paradigms: The Failure of US Counter-Insurgency Policy*. Princeton University Press, 1988.

Simpson, Christopher. *Blowback*. Weidenfeld and Nicolson, 1988.

——. *The Splendid Blond Beast*. Grove, 1993.

US. Office of the Comptroller, General Accounting Office. *Nazis and Axis Collaborators Were Used to Further US Anti-Communist Objectives in Europe–Some Immigrated to the United States*. Government Printing Office, 1985.

——. *Widespread Conspiracy to Obstruct Probes of Alleged Nazi War Criminals Not Supported by Available Evidence – Controversy May Continue*. Government Printing Office, 1978.

Wiesenthal, Simon. *The Murderers Among Us*. McGraw-Hill, 1967.

8

Dr. Gottlieb's House of Horrors

By the early 1950s the CIA's relationship with drugs stretched from alliances with criminal smugglers of heroin to research in, and application of, lethal or mind-altering chemical agents. On November 18, 1953 a group of seven men gathered for a meeting at the Deer Creek Lodge, in the mountains of western Maryland. Three were from the US Army's biological weapons center at Fort Detrick; the other four were CIA officers from the Agency's Technical Services Division. This encounter was one in a regular series of working sessions on Project MK-NAOMI, with MK being the prefix for work by Technical Services and NAOMI referring to a project to develop poisons for operational use by the CIA and its clients. The men at Fort Detrick had, at the CIA's request, already stockpiled a lethal arsenal of shellfish toxins, botulinum, anthrax and equine encephalitis.

A day later, during the evening of November 19, the scientists shared an after-dinner glass of Cointreau. Unknown to those round the convivial table, the CIA's Dr. Sidney Gottlieb had decided to spike the Cointreau with a heavy dose of LSD. Gottlieb didn't tell the officers they had been drugged and indeed had violated CIA rules by failing to get prior approval for the experiment. About thirty minutes after they had tossed back their liqueurs Gottlieb asked if anyone had noticed anything unusual. The doctor found that most of men round the table experienced a little buzz, but nothing significant. Then Gottlieb fessed up and disclosed the covert LSD dosage.

At some point soon thereafter, one member of the group, Dr. Frank Olson from Fort Detrick, began to embark on what would enter sixties argot as "a bad trip." One of Olson's companions said that later that evening Olson became "psychotic." Olson was the army's foremost expert on biological warfare, his specialty being the development of techniques of airborne dispersal for lethal agents. The next morning Olson was still disturbed, and as a consequence the meeting broke up early. Olson went home and, according to his wife, displayed irrational behavior. He seemed to be obsessed with the notion that he had somehow "made a terrible mistake" at the lodge, that he had humiliated himself and that his colleagues had laughed at him. The Olsons spent a somber weekend, capped by a possibly unwise outing to see the movie *Luther*.

On Monday Olson arrived early in the morning for work at Fort Detrick. He went directly to the office of his supervisor, Lieutenant Colonel Vincent Ruwet, and demanded to be fired, repeating his belief that he had discredited himself. Ruwet told Olson that his behavior at the retreat had apparently been beyond reproach. Olson was appeased, but not for long. The next day he was back in Ruwet's office, saying he was "all mixed up." Ruwet concluded that Olson was having a mental breakdown and blamed the CIA. He placed a call to Sidney Gottlieb's deputy, Richard Lashbrook, who had also been at the lodge. Ruwet told the CIA officer that Olson needed immediate psychiatric counseling. Lashbrook conferred with Gottlieb and they agreed to pick up Olson and send him off to be examined by Dr. Harold Abramson in New York City, who ran the allergy clinic at Mount Sinai Hospital. Abramson was no psychiatrist, but far as Gottlieb was concerned, he had two important credentials: a top-secret security clearance and absolute loyalty to Gottlieb, as one of his most enthusiastic CIA-funded LSD researchers.

As the CIA's Inspector General, Lyman Kirkpatrick, later concluded, Gottlieb's paramount concerns were keeping the CIA's LSD program a secret and self-protection against possible charges that he had bypassed regular procedures. Olson was taken to New York by Lashbrook and Ruwet. Abramson came to see Olson at their room at the Statler Hilton, and promptly administered the stricken army man a brew of bourbon and Nembutal. After a cursory interview Abramson decided that Olson was well enough to go home for Thanksgiving. Despite this optimistic assessment, Olson continued to deteriorate. He now believed that the CIA men were out to get him and were spiking his drinks with benzedrine. The night before they were scheduled to fly home, Olson became delusional: he staggered around the streets of New York, with Ruwet's voice ringing in his head, ordering him to tear up all his money and throw away his wallet, which the poor man promptly did.

At 5:30 a.m. Olson was found crouching in the lobby of the Statler-Hilton. Lashbrook and Ruwet got him to his room, cleaned him up and headed for the plane to Washington. Back in D.C., Olson begged Lashbrook and Ruwet not to take him home because he feared that he might become violent and hurt his wife and children. Gottlieb's was called to Lashbrook's apartment to examine Olson; he quickly concluded that Olson had to go back to Abramson.

Lashbrook took Olson back to New York, where Abramson spent a few hours with him before determining that Olson was still in a psychotic condition and well beyond his own capabilities as an allergist who dabbled in the covert administration of hallucinogens. He recommended that Olson be confined at Chestnut Lodge, a Rockville, Maryland asylum on the CIA's list of trustworthy institutions.

Olson agreed to this plan, but his handlers couldn't book a flight till the next day. Late that night, Lashbrook claimed, he awoke to see Olson run across the room and jump through a curtained and closed window. The glass broke and Olson crashed down to the street from the tenth-floor room.

Lashbrook immediately began to cover the CIA's tracks.. His first phone call was not to a hospital or the police, but to Gottlieb. When the police arrived, Lashbrook told them that he was with the Defense Department and implied that Olson might have killed himself because of job-related stress. He told the officers that Olson "suffered from ulcers," but said little else. Surveying the circumstances, New York City's finest made the assessment, which they entered in police files, that Olson had killed himself because of a homosexual lovers' quarrel with Lashbrook.

Gottlieb's men all closed ranks, even lying to the CIA's internal investigators. Lashbrook and Abramson said that Olson had been beleaguered by depression for some time. They claimed that his wife, Alice, had told them that some months earlier she'd tried to get Olson to visit a psychiatrist. Years later, when the cover-up began to unravel, Olson's wife testified that this was an outright lie. For his part, Abramson told the CIA investigators that the LSD given to Olson at the Deer Creek Lodge was essentially harmless and was indeed a therapeutic dosage.

Ruwet had been close to Olson and might have been able to hold his friend together if Gottlieb had allowed him to accompany Olson on that last visit to New York. Instead, Gottlieb instructed Ruwet to make a call on Olson's family and inform them that Olson wouldn't be back for a few days. Later Ruwet told the CIA that unless the Agency made sure that Olson's wife received a pension valued at two-thirds of Olson's pay, he'd go public with what had happened. The CIA agreed to his terms and Ruwet duly kept quiet about the true circumstances surrounding Olson's death, noting in his own report that Olson had died from "a classified illness."

After the CIA's internal investigation into Olson's death, Inspector General Kirkpatrick wanted to give Sidney Gottlieb a harsh censure. But the doctor had at least two powerful protectors, Director of Central Intelligence Allen Dulles and Deputy Director for Plans Richard Helms. All they would allow was a mild rebuke to their favorite scientist, saying that Gottlieb had exercised "poor judgement." The CIA never told the Olson family that Frank had been an unwitting human guinea pig in an Agency drug experiment that went horribly awry. The Olsons weren't even allowed to examine Frank's body before his burial. They were told it was in "too bad a condition."

For twenty-two years Alice Olson and her children resisted the conclusion that Frank Olson had intentionally killed himself. Then, in 1975, Frank and Alice Olson's son, Eric, by now a 31-year-old clinical psychologist, read a *Washington Post* story describing the findings of the Rockefeller Commission, which had been set up by President Gerald Ford to report on charges relating to the CIA's domestic activities. The story described the death of a man who had jumped from a hotel window after having been secretly given LSD by the CIA. A few days later the Olson family contacted Frank Olson's old colleague, Vincent Ruwet, who finally admitted what had really happened at Deer Creek Lodge and in Manhattan. Ever the government man, Ruwet persisted in urging descretion. But by this time, the Olsons had had enough and Ruwet's counsel was unavailing. A furious Alice Olson and her children went public on national television, demanding that justice be done.

"In telling our story," read the Olson families' joint statement, "we are concerned that neither the personal pain this family has experienced nor the moral and political outrage we feel should be slighted. Only in this way can Frank Olson's death become part of the American memory and serve the purpose of political and ethical reform so needed in our society."

In the face of mounting outrage, President Ford publicly apologized to the Olsons. But it would be another fifteen years before the family finally received a full settlement from the Agency.

The more the Olson family learned about Frank Olson's death, the more questions they began to ask. Ultimately, Alice Olson forgave the actions of Vincent Ruwet. But she had only one word for Gottlieb: "despicable."

The two sons, Eric and Nils, nurture deep suspicions about their father's death. Olson was one of the army's top experts on biological warfare and could have exposed the work he and other army scientists had done on developing lethal toxins for the CIA to use in covert operations and political assassinations. "The implications of this kind of frightened me," said Eric Olson. "But the story has just never checked out. I felt like I was back where I was at nine years old, scratching my head."

So long as their mother was still alive, the sons took no major initiative. Alice Olson died in 1993, and soon thereafter Eric and Nils decided to move their father's body from a cemetary near Fort Detrick in Frederick, Maryland to one where their mother was buried. They took advantage of the removal to have a forensic team examine Frank Olson's remains.

Eric Olson was present when his father's body was exhumed. Despite the government's earlier contention that Frank's body had been horribly mangled in the fall, Eric found the body in fairly good condition. "I was surprised at how good he looked. He was embalmed and I still recognized him forty years later."

The forensic pathologist, Dr. James Starrs of George Washington University, found a deep bruise on Olson's forehead. The bruise was severe enough to have rendered Olson unconscious, but probably didn't result from the fall. Starrs also discovered no evidence of cuts from broken glass that should have been present had Olson leaped out a closed window. Starrs concluded that the evidence was starkly suggestive. At a press conference in 1995, Starrs spoke of the "desperate need for subpoena authority."

Federal prosecutors refused to pursue the inquiry. The CIA's spokesman, Dave Christian, said there was no need for further investigation since Congress had thoroughly scrutinized the Olson case in 1977 during hearings chaired by Senator Edward Kennedy. Kennedy himself declared that his probe "had closed the book on this sorry chapter." In order to reach this conclusion, Kennedy had contrived to give Dr. Gottlieb immunity from prosecution in exchange for his (exceedingly obscure) testimony. In November 1997, however, Manhattan District Attorney Robert Morgenthau announced his intention to reopen the case.

Introducing Dr. Gottlieb

Frank Olson's fate was but a hint of the enormous secret CIA program of research into techniques of mind alteration and control. The whole enterprise was assigned the code-name MK-ULTRA and was run out of the CIA's Technical Services Division, headed in the 1950s by Willis Gibbons, a former executive of the US Rubber Company. In the division's laboratories and workshops researchers labored on poisons, gadgets designed to maim and kill, techniques of torture and implements to carry such techniques to agonizing fruition. Here also were developed surveillance equipment and kindred tools of the espionage trade. All of these activities made the Technical Services Division a vital partner of the covert operations wing of the Agency.

Within Technical Services MK-ULTRA projects came under the control of the Chemical Division, headed from 1951 to 1956 by Dr. Sidney Gottlieb, a New York Jew who received his doctorate in chemistry from California Tech. Born with a clubfoot and afflicted with a severe stammer, Gottlieb pushed himself with unremitting intensity. Despite his physical affliction he was an ardent square dancer and exponent of the polka, capering across many a dance floor and dragging visiting psychiatrists and chemists on terpsichorean trysts where appalling plans of mind control were ruminated amidst the blare of the bands.

Gottlieb and his wife, a fundamentalist Christian, lived on a farm in the Shenandoah Mountains in northern Virginia. Their house was a former slave quarters, and Gottlieb rose every morning before sunrise to milk his herd of goats.

As was demonstrated in the Olson affair, Gottlieb had powerful friends inside the Agency, notably Richard Helms, at that time deputy director for covert operations. MK-ULTRA was created on April 13, 1953, when CIA director Allen Dulles approved Helms's proposal to develop the "covert use" of biological and chemical materials. The code-name ULTRA may have been an echo from Helms's and Dulles's OSS days, when ULTRA (the breaking of the primary German code) represented one of the biggest secrets of World War II.

Gottlieb himself said that the creation of MK-ULTRA was inspired by reports of mind-control work in the Soviet Union and China. He defined the mission as "an investigation into how individual behavior could be altered through covert means." He gave this description in 1977 during the Kennedy hearings, testifying via remote speaker from another room. "It was felt to be mandatory," Gottlieb went on, "and of the utmost urgency for our intelligence organization to establish what was possible in this field."

The CIA had followed the trial of the Hungarian Roman Catholic Cardinal Josef Mindszenty in Budapest in 1949 and concluded that the Cardinal's ultimate confession had been manipulated through "some unknown force." Initially the belief was that Mindszenty had been hypnotized, and intrigued CIA officers conjectured that they might use the same techniques on people they were interrogating. The CIA's Office of Security, headed at the time by Sheffield Edwards, developed a hypnosis project called Bluebird, whose object was to get an individual "to do our bidding against his will and even against such fundamental laws of nature as self-preservation."

The first Bluebird operations were conducted in Japan in October

1950 and were reportedly witnessed by Richard Helms. Twenty-five North Korean prisoners of war were given alternating doses of depressants and stimulants. The POWs were shot up with barbiturates, allowing them to go to sleep, then abruptly awoken with injections of amphetamines, hypnotized, then questioned. This operation was in total contravention of international protocols on the treatment of POWs. These Bluebird interrogations continued throughout the Korean War.

Simultaneously, US POWs held in North Korea were being paraded by their captors, alleging that the US was using chemical and biological agents against the Koreans and the Chinese. An international commission in 1952 concluded that the charges had merit. But the CIA's response was to leak to favored reporters at *Time,* the *Chicago Tribune,* and the *Miami Herald* stories to the effect that the American POWs had been brainwashed by their Communist captors. This had the double utility of squelching the charges of germ warfare and also of justifying the Bluebird program.

In fact, US military and intelligence agencies had been dabbling in mind control research for more than forty years. One of the early experimenters was George H. Estabrooks, a research psychologist who taught for years at Colgate College in upstate New York. Estabrooks was a Rhodes scholar who had trained in psychology at Harvard with Gardner Murphy. The psychologist, whose specialty was the use of hypnosis in intelligence operations, worked as a contractor for Naval Intelligence and was later to advise CIA researchers such as Martin Orne and Milton Erickson.

In 1971, Estabrooks gave a chilling portrait of his career in an article in *Science Digest* titled "Hypnosis Comes of Age." "One of the most fascinating but dangerous applications of hypnosis is its use in military intelligence," Estabrooks wrote. "This is a field with which I am familiar through formulating guidelines for the technique used by the US in two world wars. Communication in war is always a headache. Codes can be broken. A professional spy may or may not stay bought. Your own man may have unquestionable loyalty but his judgement is always open to question. The hypnotic courier, on the other hand, provides a unique solution." Estabrooks related in matter-of-fact detail his role in hypnotizing intelligence officers for dangerous missions inside occupied Japan, describing how through hypnosis he had "locked" information inside the mind of unwitting soldiers, information that could only be retrieved by Estabrooks and other designated military psychologists.

Then Estabrooks described how he and other government doctors developed techniques to split personalities, using a combination of hypnosis and drugs. "The potential for military intelligence has been nightmarish," Estabrooks wrote. In one case, he claimed that he had created a new personality in a "normal" Marine. The new personality "talked Communist doctrine and meant it." Estabrooks and the army contrived to have the Marine given a dishonorable discharge and encouraged him to penetrate the Communist Party. All along, Estabrooks said, the "deeper personality" was that of the Marine, which had been programmed to operate as a kind of "subconscious spy." "I had a pipeline straight into the Communist camp. It worked beautifully for months with this subject, but the technique backfired. While there was no way for an enemy to expose Jones's dual personality, they suspected it, and played the same trick on us later."

The CIA's Bluebird project, which investigated hypnosis and other techniques in the early 1950s, was headed by Morse Allen, a veteran of Naval Intelligence and a specialist in techniques of interrogation. Criminologists revere Allen as a pioneer in the use of the polygraph. Allen eventually became disappointed with the research into hypnosis, and developed a keen interest in the more robust fields of electro-shock therapy and psycho-surgery.

One of the CIA's first grants to an outside contractor was to a psychiatrist who claimed that he could use electro-shock therapy to produce a state of total amnesia "or excruciating pain." Another $100,000 CIA grant went to a neurologist who vouched for lobotomies and other types of brain surgery as useful tools in the art of interrogation. Both of these techniques would later become staples of the operations of one of MK-ULTRA's most infamous contractors, Dr. D. Ewen Cameron.

In 1952, the codeword Bluebird was changed to Artichoke. A CIA report on the project says that, among other things, Artichoke was meant to investigate the theory that "agents might be given cover stories under hypnosis and not only learn them faultlessly, but actually believe them. Every detail could be made to sink in. The conviction and apparent sincerity with which an individual will defend a false given under post-hypnotic suggestion is almost unbelievable."

In one experiment, a female CIA security officer was hypnotized and provided with a new identity. When she was later interrogated, the agent "defended it hotly, denying her true name and rationalizing with conviction the possession of identity cards made out to her real self." Artichoke also explored using hypnosis to recruit high-level political agents and unmask spies and double agents, a particular obsession of James Jesus Angleton, the CIA's counterintelligence chief.

The CIA memos of the time are filled with complaints about the difficulties of finding suitable human subjects for experimental research. "Human subjects" were evoked in the tactful phrase "unique research material." At first the CIA experimented mostly on prisoners, drug addicts and terminally sick destitutes. Details are scanty because Helms ordered all CIA records on the programs destroyed, but much of the "unique research material" came in the form of prisoners at California's Vacaville prison, the Georgia state penitentiary and the Tennessee state prison system. There was a problem, however. In these instances a certain modicum of informed consent was often required. Prisoners could get reduced sentences for agreeing to participate in the experiments. Drug addicts would get cash, drugs or treatment. Informed consent was often a condition in any treatment of the terminally ill poor. For the CIA researchers any type of informed consent was antithetical to their research task, which was to make unwilling subjects talk and covertly elicit cooperation.

By 1952 the CIA's scientists began to test their techniques on what a CIA memo described as "individuals of dubious loyalty, suspected agents or plants, subjects having known reasons for deception." As one CIA psychologist told John Marks, author of *The Search for the Manchurian Candidate*, a pioneering investigation into these activities in the late 1970s, "one did not put a high premium on the civil rights of a person who was treasonable to his own country." One suspected double agent was taken to a "thoroughly isolated" CIA safehouse in rural Germany, "far removed from surrounding neighbors." The man was told that he was to undergo a series of routine medical and psychological tests as condition of his employment. According to detailed account in the Artichoke files, the entire operation was conducted on the second floor of the safehouse, so as not to arouse the curiosity of "the household staff and security detail."

The session was recorded with "a special device that is easily concealable" and was monitored by the CIA medical division and investigators from Angleton's counterintelligence division. The subject was brought to the safehouse at about 10:30 p.m. and was given a casual interview that lasted about an hour. Then he was offered a glass of whiskey, which had been spiked with Nembutal. Over the next three days, the subject underwent intense interrogation, while CIA doctors gave him "intravenous infusions" of hallucinogens and placed him under hypnosis. The subject was also attached to a polygraph machine. The Artichoke scientists deemed the interrogation "profitable and successful." They noted that post-hypnotic suggestion had left the subject "completely confused" with a "severe headache" and a "vague and faulty" memory of the interrogation.

Though Bluebird had begun in the CIA's Security division, a contretemps at the CIA station in Frankfurt, Germany caused the transfer of these CIA researchers to the Covert Operations sector of the agency. In Frankfurt, where the CIA was ensconced in the former offices of IG Farben, a CIA civilian contractor – an American psychologist named Richard Wendt – was assigned the task of testing a cocktail of THC, Dexedrine and Seconal on five people under interrogation who were suspected of being double agents or bogus defectors. Wendt brought along his mistress to the Frankfurt sessions and was partying hard when his wife arrived. Amid the ensuing fracas, the CIA's man fled up a cathedral tower and threatened to throw himself off it. Amid these security lapses, the Security branch lost control of research, which now passed to Covert Operations, and eventually into the hands of Dr. Gottlieb.

Furnished with $300,000 from Allen Dulles, Gottlieb started farming out research to characters such as Harold Abramson, Olson's nemesis. In 1953, Dr. Abramson was given $85,000. His grant proposal listed six areas of investigation: disturbance of memory, discrediting by aberrant behavior, alteration of sex patterns, eliciting of information, suggestibility and creation of dependency.

Another early recipient of Gottlieb's money was Dr. Harris Isbell, who ran the Center for Addiction Research in Lexington, Kentucky. Passing through Isbell's center was a captive group of human guinea pigs in the shape of a steady stream of black heroin addicts. Isbell developed a "points system" to secure their cooperation in his research. These people, supposedly being delivered from their drug habits, were awarded heroin and morphine in amounts relative to the nature of a particular research task. It was the normal habit of Gottlieb and his CIA colleagues back in Virginia to test all materials on themselves, but more than 800 different compounds were sent over to Isbell's shop for the addicts to try first.

Perhaps the most infamous experiment in Louisville came when Isbell gave LSD to seven black male heroin addicts for seventy-seven straight days. Isbell's research notes indicate "double," "triple" and "quadruple" as he hiked the doses. Noting the apparent tolerance of the subjects to this incredible regimen of lysergic acid, Isbell explained in chilling tones that "this type of behavior is to be expected in patients of this type." In another eerie reprise of the Nazi doctors' Dachau experiments, Isbell had nine black males strapped to tables, injected with psilocybin, rectal thermometers inserted, lights shown in their eyes to measure pupil dilation and joints whacked to test neural reactions. The money for Isbell's research was being funneled by the CIA through the National Institutes of Health.

Isbell also played a key role as the middleman for the CIA in getting supplies of narcotics and hallucinogens from drug companies. The Agency had two main concerns: the acquisition of supplies and new compounds, and veto power over sales of such materials to the Eastern bloc. To take one example, in 1953 the CIA became concerned that Sandoz, the Swiss pharmaceutical firm for which Albert Hoffman had developed LSD, was planning to put the drug on the open market. So the Agency offered to buy Sandoz's entire production run of LSD for $250,000. Ultimately, Sandoz agreed to supply the Agency with 100 grams a week, deny requests from the Soviet Union and China, and also to furnish the Agency with a regular list of its LSD customers.

In the meantime, the CIA helped underwrite Eli Lilly's efforts to produce synthetic LSD. Lilly, the Indianapolis-based drug company, succeeded in this endeavor in 1954. Gottlieb hailed this triumph as a key breakthrough that would enable the CIA to buy the drug "in tonnage quantities." Such large amounts were not of course required for interrogation: Gottlieb's aim was instead to have the ability to incapacitate large populations and armies.

The MK-ULTRA projects were not limited to research on adults. The CIA funded a project at the Children's International Summer Village. The objective was to research how children who spoke different languages were able to communicate. But CIA documents reveal that an ulterior motive was the identification of promising young foreign agents. The well-known psychiatrist Loretta Bender was also a recipient of MK-ULTRA funds. The author of the Bender-Gestalt used her CIA money to pump hallucinogens, including LSD, into children between the ages of seven and eleven. Many of the children were kept on the drugs for weeks at a time. In two cases, Dr. Bender's "treatments" lasted, on and off, more than a year.

The CIA funneled large grants to the University of Oklahoma, home to Dr. Louis "Jolly" West. West would later go on to head the Violence Project at UCLA, where he and Dr. James Hamilton, an OSS colleague of George White and a recipient of CIA largesse, performed psychological research involving behavior modifications on inmates at Vacaville state prison in northern California. The MK-ULTRA funds pouring into the University of Oklahoma in the 1950s had a similar purpose: the study of the structure and dynamics of urban youth gangs. These studies indicate that from the CIA's earliest days it has had a keen interest in developing methods of social control over potentially disruptive elements in American society.

Certainly one of the most nefarious of the MK-ULTRA projects was the "depatterning" research conducted by Scottish-born psychiatrist Dr. D. Ewen Cameron. Cameron was not hidden away in a dark closet: he was one of the most esteemed psychiatrists of his time. He headed both the American Psychiatric Association and the World Psychiatry Association. He sat on numerous boards and was a contributing editor to dozens of journals. He also enjoyed a long relationship with US intelligence agencies dating back to World War II, having been brought to Nuremberg by Allen Dulles to help evaluate Nazi war criminals, most notably Rudolf Hess. While in Germany Cameron also lent his hand to the crafting of the Nuremberg Code on medical research.

After the war Cameron developed a near obsession with schizophrenia. He believed that he could cure the condition by first inducing a state of total amnesia in his patients and then reprogramming their consciousness through a process he termed "psychic driving." Cameron's base of operations was the Allan Memorial Institute at McGill University in Montreal. Through the early 1950s, Cameron's work received the lavish support of the Rockefeller Foundation. Then in 1957 Cameron found a new stream of money, Gottlieb's MK-ULTRA accounts. Over the next four years, the CIA gave Cameron more than $60,000 for his work in consciousness-alteration and mind control.

Using CIA and Rockefeller funds, Cameron pioneered research into the use of sensory deprivation techniques. He once locked a woman in a small white "box" for thirty-five days, where she was deprived of all light, smells and sounds. The CIA doctors back at Langley looked on with some amazement at this research, since its own experiments with a similar sensory deprivation tank in 1955 had induced severe psychological reactions in subjects locked up for less than forty hours.

Cameron used a variety of exotic drugs on his patients, once slipping LSD to an unsuspecting woman fourteen times over a two-month period. He also investigated the practical benefits of inducing paralysis in some of his patients by giving them injections of curare. Lobotomies were another area of intense interest for Dr. Cameron, who instructed his psycho-surgeons to perform their operations using only mild local anesthetics. He wanted the patients awake so that he could chart the minute changes in their consciousness the deeper the scalpel blade sliced into the frontal lobe.

Nothing satisfied Cameron quite like the use of electro-shock therapy, which he believed could "wipe the mind clean," allowing him to purge his patients of their disease. To this end Cameron developed a dire treatment. First, he put his patients into a prolonged sleep by injecting them with a daily mixture of Thorazine, Nembutal and Seconal. Using injections of amphetamines he brought patients out of their sleep three times a day when they would be forced to endure severe electro-shock treatments involving voltages forty times more intense than those con-

sidered safe and therapeutic at the time. This treatment would sometimes last two and half to three months. Then Cameron would begin his
"psychic driving" experiment. This bizarre foray in behavioral condi-
tioning consisted of the patients being assaulted by verbal messages
played on a loop-feed tape player for sixteen hours a day; the speaker
was often hidden under a pillow and was designed to deliver the messages subliminally while the patient slept.

These experiments were conducted on more than 150 patients, one of
whom was Robert Loguey. Loguey was sent to Cameron by his family
doctor, who believed that a persistent pain Loguey complained about in
his leg was psychosomatic. Loguey was duly diagnosed as a schizophrenic by Cameron, which rendered him immediately available as a
guinea pig for Cameron's CIA project. Loguey recalls that one of the
negative messages Cameron piped into his room for twenty-three
straight days was, "You killed your mother. You killed your mother."
When Loguey went home, he was shocked to discover that his mother
was alive and apparently well.

Linda McDonald was typical of Cameron's victims, who tended to be
women. McDonald was a 25-year-old mother of five young children.
She was suffering from a modest case of post-partem depression and
chronic back pains. Her physician advised her husband that he should
take Linda to see Dr. Cameron at his clinic in Montreal. The doctor
assured her husband that Cameron was "the best there was" and would
have her back home and healthy in no time. "So we went," Linda
McDonald recalled in 1994 on the Canadian Broadcasting Company
program, *The Fifth Estate*. "My medical file even says I took my guitar
with me. And that was the end of my life."

After a few days of observation, Cameron had diagnosed McDonald
as an acute schizophrenic and had her transferred to the medical torture
chamber he called "the Sleep Room." For the next eighty-six days,
McDonald was kept in a near comatose state by the use of powerful
narcotics, and awakened only for massive jolts from Cameron's electro-
shock machine. Over that period, McDonald received 102 electro-shock
treatments.

"The aim was to wipe out the patterns of thought and behavior which
were detrimental to the patient and replace them with healthy patterns of

thought and behavior," said Dr. Peter Roper, a colleague of Cameron's who still defends the experiments. "I think this was stimulated by the effects on the American troops of the war in Korea, how they seemed to have been brainwashed."

Linda McDonald emerged from Cameron's care in a near infantile condition. "I had to be toilet trained," McDonald said. "I was a vegetable. I had no identity, no memory. I had never existed in the world before. Like a baby."

Cameron was eased out of his post at Allan Memorial in 1964 and died of a heart attack while mountain climbing in 1967 at the age of sixty-six. But that didn't end the matter. After the MK-ULTRA program was exposed, McDonald, Loguey and six other Cameron victims filed suit against the CIA. The Agency eventually agreed to a settlement, paying out $750,000 – but the CIA still maintains it was not culpable for Cameron's actions.

Anthropologists also got into the MK-ULTRA act. Richard Prince was given CIA money for research on "folk medicine and faith healing" among the Yoruba people in Nigeria. Gottlieb was interested in finding possible new drugs in Nigeria and in the mind-control techniques of Yoruba shamans. Margaret Mead sat with Ewen Cameron on the editorial board of a CIA-funded publication called the *Research in Mental Health Newsletter,* which discussed the use of psychedelic drugs to induce and treat schizophrenia. Mead's former husband, medical anthropologist Gregory Bateson, was given CIA-procured LSD by Harold Abramson. Bateson, in turn, gave some to his friend, the beat poet Allen Ginsberg. It was also Bateson's stash of LSD that eventually found its way to experiments being conducted on student volunteers by Dr. Leo Hollister. One of his subjects was a young creative writing student at Stanford, Ken Kesey, who would become the drug's chief proponent in the sixties counterculture.

In the early 1960s, the CIA even helped set up a company to scour the Amazon for potential new drugs, the Amazon Natural Drug Company. This nominally private enterprise was run by an old CIA hand named J. C. King, who had headed the CIA's Western Hemisphere Division during the Bay of Pigs and was officially moved out of the Agency shortly thereafter. Operating from his houseboat, King supervised a network of

Amazon tribespeople, anthropologists and botanists to bring back new toxic compounds, including yage, the powerful hallucinogen used by the Yanomamo.

In 1954, Gottlieb and his colleagues in the Technical Services Division concocted a plan to spike punchbowls with LSD at the Agency's Christmas party, an amazing idea considering that only a year earlier a similar stunt had resulted in the death of Frank Olson. A more ambitious project was described in a CIA memo as follows: "We thought about the possibility of putting some [LSD] in a city water supply and having citizens wander around in a more or less happy state, not terribly interested in defending themselves."

This was certainly a hazardous time to be at any public function attended by Dr. Sidney Gottlieb and his associates. In the midst of their MK-ULTRA researches, the CIA had concluded that since prisoners had lawyers who might turn ugly, it was probably not a good idea to use them as human guinea pigs. Initially they cut down the risk margin by administering the various hallucinogens to themselves, tripping regularly at CIA safehouses and institutions such as the CIA's wing at Georgetown and at Dr. Abramson's floor at Mount Sinai Hospital. The trips lacked the consciousness-heightening ambitions of the Leary generation, however. As John Marks put it, "the CIA experimenters did not trip for the experience itself, or to get high, or to sample new realities. They were testing a weapon; for their purposes, they might as well have been in a ballistics lab." But the Olson disaster reduced their enthusiasm for self-testing, and so did another mishap that occurred when an unwitting CIA officer had a dose of LSD slipped into his coffee at the Agency's offices on the Mall in Washington, D.C. The man dashed out the building, across the street, past the Washington Monument and the Lincoln Memorial, hallucinating that he was beset by monsters with huge eyes. Hotly pursued by CIA colleagues, he fled across a bridge over the Potomac and was finally cornered, crouching in a fetal position near Arlington National Cemetary.

After these mishaps, Gottlieb became persuaded that the best course was simply to test the hallucinogens on a random basis at public gatherings, or to pick out street people and induce them to swallow a dram of whatever potion was under review that day.

In late 1953, Gottlieb took his black bag to Europe, where at a political rally he primed the water glass of a speaker whom the CIA wanted to render ridiculous. The psycho-sabotage was apparently a rousing success, and greatly encouraged Gottlieb with the potential for similar dosing of charismatic left figures around the world. Gottlieb then gave the green light for CIA station officers in Manila and Atsugi, Japan, to begin the operational use of LSD.

For continued experimentation, Gottlieb now decided to begin widespread testing on the urban poor: street people, prostitutes and other undesirables. He had two reasons: they were unlikely to complain, and there was, he believed, a higher potential that these people could handle untoward side-effects. To oversee this operation, Gottlieb turned to George Hunter White, whom we last encountered testing the marijuana truth drug on Mafia muscle man Augusto Del Gracio. White had now gone back to work at the Narcotics Bureau in New York. He was a somewhat bizarre-looking figure, 200 pounds, 5-feet-7-inches tall and bald. White claimed he was such an expert in physical combat that he had killed a Japanese agent in a hand-to-hand encounter. He was also a lusty drinker with a preference for straight gin.

Gottlieb asked White to establish a CIA safehouse in New York, invite suitable subjects to party there, drug them covertly and then review their behavior. White rented two adjoining apartments at 81 Bedford Street in Greenwich Village. The cooperation of the Narcotics Bureau was secured by a deal whereby the bureau could use the apartments for drug stings during CIA downtime. White was guaranteed an unceasing flow of drink, all of it paid for by Gottlieb. The safehouse became a working lab for the CIA's Technical Services Division, fitted out with two-way mirrors, listening devices and concealed cameras. Indeed, the house became a model for subsequent CIA interrogation facilities.

From the fall of 1953 to the late spring of the following year, White hosted a string of parties, inviting a stream of unsuspecting CIA subjects to Bedford Street, spiking their food and drink with chemicals such as sodium pentothal, Nembutal, THC and, of course, what White referred to as "the LSD surprise." White's immediate supervisor in New York was Richard Lashbrook, the man who shared Frank Olson's room on the latter's last night on earth.

White's diary records that Lashbrook visited the apartment on numerous occasions, delivering drugs and watching the human guinea pigs through the two-way mirror. Connoisseurs of CIA denials should study Lashbrook's performance in 1977, when he was questioned during Ted Kennedy's senatorial probe. Despite the fact that Kennedy's subcommittee had White's records, which documented Lashbrook's visits to Bedford Street, Lashbrook received no challenge from the subcommittee when he insisted that he had never gone anywhere near the CIA safehouse. And not only did the subcommittee have White's diary, it also had Lashbrook's signature on receipts for White's substantial expenses in New York.

In 1955 the Narcotics Bureau transferred White to San Francisco. This didn't end his role as an agent for MK-ULTRA. He simply continued his researches in Baghdad-by-the-Bay. He rented a new safehouse on Telegraph Hill and had it wired with state-of-the-art equipment from Technical Services. This time White's surveillance post was a small bathroom, with a two-way mirror allowing him to peer into the main room. White would sit on the lavatory, martini in hand, watching prostitutes give CIA designer drugs to their unsuspecting clients. White called this enterprise Operation Midnight Climax. He assembled a string of whores, many of them black heroin addicts whom he paid in drugs, to lure their clients to the CIA-sponsored drug and sex sessions. The women, who were known by the San Francisco police as George's Girls, were protected from arrest.

To further the scientific work, Gottlieb sent out the Agency's chief psychologist, John Gittinger, to evaluate the prostitutes through personality tests and, since part of the research was to evaluate the use of sex as a means of eliciting information, to instruct the women in interviewing techniques. Unsurprisingly, it was soon discovered that the clients were more likely to talk after sexual activity. The content of their conversations often centered on family and work problems – something the prostitutes probably could have told the CIA without any investment of taxpayer money.

All of these San Francisco sessions were filmed and tape-recorded, in another eerie parallel with Nazi research: Himmler had recommended to the doctors conducting the Dachau experiments in cold water immersion that perhaps the subjects be revived by "animal warmth," meaning sex with prostitutes held in a special building at Dachau. The therapeutic sessions were filmed and passed along for viewing by Himmler.

It wasn't long before the CIA researchers carried their investigations beyond the safehouse on Telegraph Hill. CIA men would often go down to the Tenderloin district, visit bars and slip hallucinogens into patrons' drinks. They would also hand out doctored cigarettes. Hundreds of people were thus unknowingly dosed, and there is no way of knowing how many psychological and physical traumas the CIA was responsible for. The CIA did know of several test victims who took themselves or were taken to hospitals in the San Francisco area. But it never assisted in diagnosis or paid any hospital bills, or in any other way took the slightest responsibility for what it had done. In fact it was in the Agency's self-interest that these people be diagnosed as drug addicts or as psychotics. Some of the drugs being thus furtively administered were extremely dangerous. One of the men in the CIA's Technical Services Division later told Marks, "If we were scared enough of a drug not to try it on ourselves we sent it to San Francisco."

The CIA men organized a weekend party at another Agency safehouse in Marin County, north of San Francisco. The plan was to invite a crowd of party-goers and then spray the rooms with an aerosol formulation of LSD concocted in Gottlieb's shop. But it turned out to be an exceedingly hot day and the party-goers kept the windows open, allowing breezes off the Pacific to swirl through the room, thus dispersing the LSD. In frustration, Gittinger, the CIA psychologist, locked himself in the bathroom, sprayed furiously and inhaled as deeply as possible.

The LSD safehouse program continued in both New York and San Francisco until 1963, when the CIA's new Inspector General, John Earman, stumbled across the enterprise. Earman was particularly galled by the itemized list of expenses, including $44 for a telescope, $1,000 for a few days of White's liquor bill and $31 to pay off a local lady whose car White had rammed. Earman probed deeper, unearthing what he swiftly concluded was an illegal, indeed criminal, venture. He gathered his findings and confronted Gottlieb and Helms.

Helms knew he was in a spot of trouble. He had not told new agency director John McCone about the program, and he double-crossed Earman on a promise to do so. Eventually Earman wrote a 24-page report for McCone in which he harshly denounced the drug-testing program, which he said "put the rights and interests of all Americans in jeopardy." Helms and Gottlieb fiercely defended MK-ULTRA to McCone, with Helms raising the spectre of a Soviet chemical gap, claiming that widespread testing was necessary to keep pace with Soviet advances. Helms told McCone that "positive operational capacity to use drugs is diminishing owing to a lack of realistic testing."

McCone put a freeze on CIA-sponsored testing at the safe-houses, but they remained open for George White's use – with the CIA paying the bills – until 1966, when White retired. As he headed off toward eventual death from cirrhosis of the liver, White wrote an envoi to his old sponsor Sidney Gottlieb: "I toiled wholeheartedly in the vineyards because it was fun, fun, fun. Where else could a red-blooded American boy lie, kill, cheat, steal, rape and pillage with the sanction and bidding of the All-Highest."

Gottlieb's colleagues at Army Intelligence were conducting their own experiments with LSD, called Operation Third Chance. In 1961, James Thornwell, a black US Army sergeant who worked at a NATO office in Orleans, France, came under suspicion of stealing classified documents. He was interrogated, hypnotized, and given a polygraph and truth serum. All these attempts to coerce a confession from him failed, but the Army Intelligence men remained convinced of his guilt. They even concocted a bizarre scenario involving the French police, who pulled over Thornwell's car, drew their guns and opened fire as he sped away.

The officers also told colleagues of Thornwell that the black man had been sleeping with their wives and girlfriends: several of these men beat up Thornwell in a jealous rage. Eventually Thornwell turned to the intelligence officers for help in escaping this harassment. They duly offered to put the sergeant in protective custody in an abandoned millhouse. There Thornwell was secretly given LSD over a period of several days by army and CIA interrogators, during which he was forced to undergo extremely aggressive questioning, replete with racial slurs. At one point his interrogators threatened "to extend the state indefinitely, even to a permanent condition of insanity." They consummated this promise. Thornwell experienced a major mental crisis from which he never recovered. In 1982 he was found drowned in his swimming pool in Maryland. There was never any evidence that Thornwell had anything to do with the missing NATO papers.

MK-ULTRA was never designed to be pure research. It was always intended as an operational program, and by the early 1960s these techniques were being fully deployed in the field, sometimes in situations so vile that they rivaled in evil the efforts of the Nazi scientists in German concentration camps. Well-known is the journey of Dr. Sidney Gottlieb to the Congo, where his little black bag held an Agency-developed biotoxin scheduled for Patrice Lumumba's toothbrush. Less well-known is the handkerchief laced with botulinum that was to sent to an Iraqi colonel. Then there are the endless potions directed at Fidel Castro, from the LSD the Agency wanted to spray in his radio booth to the poisonous fountain pen intended for Castro that was handed by a CIA man to Rolando Cubela in Paris on November 22, 1963.

And even less well remembered is one mission in the Agency's Phoenix operation in Vietnam in the late 1960s. In July 1968 a team of CIA psychologists set up shop at Bien Hoa Prison outside Saigon, where NLF suspects were being held after Phoenix Program round-ups. The CIA had become increasingly frustrated with its inability to break down suspected NLF leaders by using traditional means of interrogation and torture. They had doped up NLF officers with LSD, hoping that by inducing irrational behavior, the seemingly unbreakable solidarity of their captives could be broken and that the other inmates would then begin to talk. These experiments ended in failure, leaving the prisoners to became little more than lab material for experiments.

In one such experiment, three prisoners were anaesthetized; their skulls were then opened and electrodes were implanted by CIA doctors into different parts of their brains. The prisoners were revived, placed in a room with knives and the electrodes in the brains activated by the CIA psychiatrists who were covertly observing them. The hope was that they could be prompted in this manner to attack each other. The experiment failed. The electrodes were removed, the patients were shot and their bodies burned. This rivaled anything in Dachau.

The CIA's drug testing and adventures into mind control became the subject of four ground-breaking book-length investigations: John

Marks's *The Search for the Manchurian Candidate* (1979), Walter Bowart's *Operation Mind Control* (1978), Alan Scheflin's *The Mind Manipulators* (1978) and Martin Lee and Bruce Schlain's *Acid Dreams* (1985). But aside from these pioneering works, how did the American press and historians of the CIA deal with this astonishing saga, in which a man such as Olson lost his life, thousands of people were involuntarily and unknowingly dosed with drugs so dangerous or untested that the CIA's own chemists dared not try them? A story in which for more than twenty years the CIA paid for such illegal activities, protected criminals from arrest, let others suffer without intervention and tried to destroy all evidence of its crimes? When the saga did unfold before the Kennedy hearings in 1977, the *Washington Post* offered this laconic and dismissive headline, "The Gang that Couldn't Spray Straight," accompanied by a trivial story designed to downplay the whole MK-ULTRA scandal. Tom Powers, the biographer of MK-ULTRA's patron and protector, Richard Helms, skips over the program in his 350-page book *The Man Who Kept the Secrets*.

"I thought in 1978 when our books were appearing, when we were doing media work all over the world, that we would finally get the story out, the vaults would be cleansed, the victims would learn their identities, the story would become part of history, and the people who had been injured could seek recompense," recalled Alan Scheflin. "Instead, what happened was the great void. As soon as the story hit the paper it was yesterday's news, and we waited and waited for real congressional hearings and we waited for the lists of people who were victims to be notified. And none of that happened."

Sources

Nearly twenty years after its publication, John Marks's book *The Search for the Manchurian Candidate* remains the most important and provocative work on the CIA's development and use of methods to control human behavior. It provided much of the background for this chapter. Martin Lee and Bruce Shlain's *Acid Dreams* was also an important source, particularly in placing the CIA's experiments with hallucinogens in a cultural context. Much of the primary source material is contained in the reports and testimony from the Church hearings and the rather superficial hearings on CIA medical abuse and drug testing chaired by Senator Edward Kennedy. Richard Helms and Sidney Gottlieb destroyed most of the MK-ULTRA files. What remain are brief project descriptions, contracts, memos and receipts. And these are only available because of a Freedom of Information Act lawsuit brought by John Marks. Marks's files are available to researchers at the National Security Archives. The persistent digging by the family of Frank Olson has also helped to illuminate some of the darker corners in this wing of the CIA. The horrible account of medical torture of Vietnamese prisoners comes from Gordon Thomas's chilling book, *Journey into Madness*.

Abramson, Harold. *The Use of LSD in Psychotherapy*. Bobbs-Merrill, 1967.
Alexander, John. "The New Military Battlefield." *Military Review*, Dec. 1980.
Alexander, Leo. "Sociopsychologic Structures of the SS." *Archives of Neurology and Psychiatry*, May 1948.
Anderson, Jack. "'Voodoo Gap' Looms as Latest Weapons Crisis." *Washington Post*, April 24, 1984.
——. "US Still in Psychic Research." *Washington Post*, Feb. 15, 1985.
——. "CIA Secrets and Customs Agent Firing." *Washington Post*, Nov. 2, 1995.
Biderman, Albert, and Herbert Zimmer, eds. *The Manipulation of Human Behavior*. John Wiley and Sons, 1961.
Bowart, Walter. *Operation Mind Control*. Dell, 1978.
Broad, William. "Pentagon Is Said to Focus on ESP for Wartime Use." *New York Times*, Jan. 10, 1984.
Brennan, Patricia. "Solving Mysteries, Finding Felons." *Washington Post*, Oct. 16, 1994.
Chavkin, Samuel. *The Mind Stealers*. Houghton Miflin, 1978.
Cohen, Sidney. *The Beyond Within: The LSD Story*. Atheneum, 1972.
Collins, Larry. "Mind Control." *Playboy*, Jan. 1990.
Cookson, John, and Judith Nottingham. *A Survey of Chemical and Biological Warfare*. Monthly Review Press, 1969.
Corson, William. *Armies of Ignorance: The Rise of the American Intelligence Empire*. Dial Press, 1977.
Cox, Bob. "Brainwash Victims to Receive $100,000." Canadian Press Wire Service. Nov. 18, 1992.
Ebon, Martin. *Psychic Warfare: Threat or Illusion?* McGraw-Hill, 1983.
Estabrooks, George. *Hypnotism*. EP Dutton & Company, 1945.
Estabrooks, George, and Richard Lockridge. *Death in the Mind*. EP Dutton & Company, 1946.
Hersh, Seymour M. *Chemical and Biological Warfare: America's Hidden Arsenal*. Doubleday, 1969.
Hockstader, Lee. "Victims of 1950s Mind-Control Experiments Settle with CIA." *Washington Post*, Oct. 5, 1988.
Lasby, Charles. *Project Paperclip: German Scientists and the Cold War*. Atheneum, 1971.
Lee, Martin A., and Bruce Schlain. *Acid Dreams: The Complete Social History of LSD*. Grove Press, 1992.
Levine, Art, Steven Emerson and Charles Fenyvesi. "The Twilight Zone in Washington." *US News and World Report*, Dec. 5, 1988.

Lilly, John. *The Scientist: A Novel Autobiography*. Lippincott, 1978.
London, Perry. *Behavior Control*. New American Library, 1977.
Lovell, Stanley. *Of Spies and Strategems*. Prentice Hall, 1963.
Marks, John. *The Search for the Manchurian Candidate*. Times Books, 1979.
——. "The CIA Won't Quite Go Public." *Rolling Stone,* July 18, 1974.
McIntyre, Linden. "MK-ULTRA's Dr. Ewen Cameron: Psychiatrist and Torturer." Transcript. *Fifth Estate*. Canadian Broadcasting Company, Jan. 6, 1998.
McRae, Ronald. *Mind Wars: The True Story of Government Research into the Military Potential of Psychic Weapons*. St. Martin's Press, 1984.
Mitscherlich, Alexander, and Fred Mielke. *Doctors of Infamy*. Schuman, 1949.
Mooar, Brian. "1953 CIA Death Draws Scrutiny." *Washington Post,* Sept. 8, 1997.
Morris, Wayne, interviewer. "Mind Control Series: Interviews with Walter Bowart, Alan Scheflin and Randy Noblitt." Transcript. CKLN-FM Radio. 1995.
Orth, Maureen. "Memoirs of a CIA Psychiatrist." *New Times,* June 23, 1975.
Reuters. "Carter Says Psychic Found Lost Plane for CIA." *The Oregonian,* Sept. 20, 1995.
Roth, Melissa. "Frank Olson File: The CIA's Bad Trip." *George,* Oct. 1997.
Ross, Colin. *Multiple Personality Disorder*. Wiley, 1989.
——. "The CIA and Military Mind Control Research." Lecture at 9th Annual Western Clinical Conference on Trauma and Dissociation, April 18, 1996.
Scheflin, Alan W., and Edward M. Opton, Jr. *The Mind Manipulators*. Paddington Press, 1978.
Schnable, Jim. *Remote Viewers: The Secret History of America's Psychic Spies*. Dell Publishing, 1997.
Schrag, Peter. *Mind Control*. Pantheon, 1978.
Schwartz, Stephen. "Deep Quest." *Omni*, March 1979.
Squires, Sally. "The Pentagon's Twilight Zone." *Washington Post,* April 17, 1988.
Thomas, Gordon. *Journey into Madness: The True Story of Secret CIA Mind Control and Medical Abuse*. Bantam, 1989.
US Congress. House. Committee on Un-American Activities. *Communist Psychological Warfare (Thought Control)*. Government Printing Office, 1958.
——. Subcommittee on Oversight of the Permanent Select Committee on Intelligence. *The CIA and the Media*. Government Printing Office, 1978.
US Congress. Senate. Select Committee (Church Committee) to Study Governmental Operations with Respect to Intelligence Activities. *Alleged Assassination Plots Involving Foreign Leaders: An Interim Report*. Government Printing Office, 1975.
——. Select Committee (Church Committee) to Study Governmental Operations with Respect to Intelligence Activities. Ninety-fourth Congress. *Final Report*. Government Printing Office, 1976.
——. Joint Hearing Before the Subcommittee on Health of the Committee on Labor and Public Welfare and the Subcommittee on Administrative Practice and Procedure of the Committee on the Judiciary. *Biomedical and Behavioral Research*. Government Printing Office, 1975.
——. Subcommittee on Health and Scientific Research of the Committee on Human Resources. *Human Drug Testing by the CIA*. Government Printing Office, 1977.
——. Select Committee on Intelligence and the Subcommittee on Health and Scientific Research of the Committee on Human Resources. *Project MK-ULTRA: The CIA's Research in Behavior Modification*. Government Printing Office, 1977.
——. Select Committee to Study Governmental Operations with Respect to Intelligence Activities (Church Committee). *Unauthorized Storage of Toxic Agents*. Government

Printing Office, 1975.
US, Executive Office of the President, Commission on CIA Activities. *The Rockefeller Report to the President on CIA Activities.* Government Printing Office, 1975.
West, Louis Jolyon. "Dissociative Reaction." Chapter in *Comprehensive Textbook of Psychiatry.* Williams and Wilkins, 1967.
Wilhelm, John. "Psychic Spying." *Washington Post,* August 2, 1977.

9

The US Opium Wars: China, Burma and the CIA

You won't find a star of remembrance for him on the wall of fallen heroes at CIA HQ in Langley, but one of the Agency's first casualties in its covert war against Mao's China was a man named Jack Killam. He was a pilot for the CIA's proprietary airline, Civil Air Transport, forerunner to the notorious Air America which figured so largely in the Agency's activities in Vietnam, Laos and Cambodia. Killam's job was to fly weapons and supplies from the CIA's base in Bangkok, Thailand, to the mountain camps of General Li Mi in the Shan States of Burma. Li Mi, Chinese in origin, was the leader of 10,000 Chinese troops still loyal to Generalissimo Chiang Kai-shek, who had been driven off the Chinese mainland by Mao's forces and was now ensconced on Taiwan.

Under the direction of the CIA, Li Mi's army was plotting a strike across Burma's northern border into China's Hunan province. But Li Mi's troops were not just warriors in Chiang's cause: they had also taken control of the largest opium poppy fields in Asia. The CAT pilots working for the CIA carried loads of Li Mi's opium on their return flights to Bangkok, where it was delivered to General Phao Siyanan, head of the Thai secret police and a long-time CIA asset.

Jack Killam was murdered in 1951 when one of these arms-and-drugs round trips went bad. His body was buried in an unmarked grave by Sherman Joost, the CIA's station chief in Bangkok.

The exiled Kuomintang (KMT) army of Li Mi was as much a proprietary of the Central Intelligence Agency as Civil Air Transport. Installed in Burma, this army was armed by the CIA, fed by the CIA, and paid by the CIA. In later operations in Laos, Cambodia and Vietnam the CIA used it as a labor pool. Under this patronage and protection the KMT was able to build up its opium operations in the area of Southeast Asia known as the Golden Triangle.

As a result, the KMT became a pivotal force in the Asian opium trade. Using the infrastructure of remote airstrips and airplanes set in place by the CIA, the KMT was able to export its opium crop from the Shan States of Burma and the mountains of Laos to international wholesalers. For its part, the CIA was more than pleased to see the KMT forces sustained by a stable flow of opium revenue impervious to the whims of Congress or new arrivals in the White House. By the mid-1970s the KMT controlled more than 80 percent of the Golden Triangle opium market. It was a situation that put the newly created Drug Enforcement Agency at odds with the CIA's opium warlords. Invariably, the DEA emerged defeated from these conflicts.

In 1988, a newspaper reporter named Elaine Shannon interviewed dozens of DEA agents for a book, *Desperados,* on the international narcotics trade. The agents told her that the drug smugglers of Southeast Asia and the CIA were "natural allies." Shannon wrote that "DEA agents who served in south east Asia in the late 1970s and 1980s said they frequently discovered that they were tracking heroin smugglers who were on the CIA payroll."

By the 1970s Nixon was staking more political capital on his War on Drugs and the CIA had to adjust to the new situation. Rather than allow the KMT to use its planes to ship opium out, the Agency bought 26 tons of opium at a cost of $1 million and destroyed it. This was a mere fraction of the KMT's total output, but the purchase had the advantage of deflecting criticism from other agencies and putting US taxpayers' money into the pockets of its mercenaries. In the mid-1970s the DEA suggested that the US government could buy Burma's entire opium crop for $12 million. This time the US State Department and the CIA intervened, claiming that such a buy-out program might put money into the hands of "Communist insurgencies against the friendly governments of

Burma and Thailand" and successfully opposed the plan. Later the CIA and State Department used the War on Drugs as a rationale for funneling even more weapons into the hands of Burma's military dictatorship. These weapons were used to quell internal opposition, and the herbicides supposedly destined for the poppy fields were instead employed by Burma's dictatorship against rural opponents, along with their food crops. By 1997 Burma reigned supreme as the world's top producer of raw opium and high-grade heroin.

The opium poppy was not native to Southeast Asia but was introduced by Arab traders in the seventh century AD. The habit of opium smoking didn't take hold till the seventeenth century, when it was spread by the Spanish and Dutch, who used opium as a treatment for malaria. The Portuguese became the first to profit from the importing of opium into China from the poppy fields in its colonies in India. After the Battle of Plassey in 1757, the British East India Company took over the opium monopoly and soon found it to be an irresistible source of profit. By 1772 the new British governor, Warren Hastings, was auctioning off opium-trading concessions and encouraging opium exports to China. Such exports were already generating £500,000 a year despite the strenuous objections of the Chinese imperial government. As early as 1729 the Chinese emperor Yung Cheng had issued an edict outlawing opium smoking. The sanctions for repeat offenders were stern: many had their lips slit. In 1789 the Chinese outlawed both the import and domestic cultivation of opium, and invoked the death penalty for violators. It did little good.

Inside China these prohibitions merely drove the opium trade underground, making it a target of opportunity for Chinese secret societies such as the powerful Green Circles Gang, from whose ranks Chiang Kai-shek was later to emerge. These bans did not deter the British, who continued shipping opium by the ton into the ports of Canton and Shanghai, using what was to become a well-worn rationale: "It is evident that the Chinese could not exist without the use of opium, and if we do not supply their necessary wants, foreigners will."

Between 1800 and 1840 British opium exports to China increased from 350 tons to more than 2,000 tons a year. In 1839 the Chinese Emperor Tao Kwang sent his trade commissioner Lin Tze-su to Canton to close the port to British opium ships. Lin took his assignment seriously, destroying tons of British opium on the docks in Canton, thus igniting the Opium Wars of 1839–42 and 1856. In these bloody campaigns the British forced China open to the opium trade, meanwhile slaughtering hundreds of thousands of Chinese, a slaughter assisted by the fact by 1840 there were 15 million opium addicts in China, 27 percent of the adult male population, including much of the Chinese military. After the first Opium War, as part of the treaty of Nanking China had to pay the British government £6 million in compensation for the opium destroyed by Lin in Canton. In all essential respects Shanghai thereafter became a western colony. In 1858 China officially legalized sales and consumption of opium. The British hiked their Indian opium exports to China, which by 1880 reached 6,500 tons, an immensely profitable business that established the fortunes of such famous Hong Kong trading houses as Jardine, Matheson.

Meanwhile, the Chinese gangs embarked on a program of import substitution, growing their poppy crops particularly in Szechwan and Hunan provinces. Labor was plentiful and the poppies were easy to grow and cheap to transport – and the flowers were also three times more valuable as a cash crop than rice or wheat. The British did not take kindly to this homegrown challenge to their Indian shipments, and after the crushing of the Boxer Rebellion in 1900 they forced the Chinese government to start a program to eradicate the domestic crop, a program that by 1906 had finished off opium cultivation in the whole of Hunan province.

It was at this point that the Chinese gangs shifted their opium cultivation southward into the Shan States of Burma and into Indochina, making the necessary arrangements with the French colonial administration, which held the monopoly on opium growing there. Hill tribes in Indochina and Burma were conscripted to the task of cultivation, with the gangs handling trafficking and distribution.

The suppression campaign run by the Chinese government had the effect of increasing the demand for processed opium products such as morphine and heroin. Morphine had recently been introduced to the Chinese mainland by Christian missionaries, who used the drug to win converts and gratefully referred to their morphine as Jesus opium. There was also a distinct economic advantage to be realized from the sale of heroin and morphine, which were cheap to produce and thus had much higher profit margins than opium.

Despite mounting international outrage, the British government continued to dump opium into China well into the first two decades of the twentieth century. Defenders of the traffic argued that opium smoking was "less deleterious" to the health of Chinese addicts than morphine, which was being pressed on China, the officials noted pointedly, by German and Japanese drug firms. The British opium magnates also recruited scientific studies to back up their claims. One paper, written by Dr. H. Moissan and Dr. F. Browne, purported to show that opium smoking produced "only a trifling amount of morphia" and was no more injurious than the inhalation of tobacco smoke.

After the opium wars reached their bloody conclusion and China was pried fully open to European trade, the coastal city of Shanghai rapidly became the import/export capital of China and its most westernized city. A municipal opium monopoly had been established in 1842, allowing the city's dozens of opium-smoking dens to be leased out to British merchants. This situation prevailed until 1918, when the British finally bowed to pressure from the government of Sun Yat-sen and relinquished their leases.

This concession did little to quell the Shanghai drug market, which duly fell into the hands of Chinese secret societies such as the notorious Green Circles Gang, which, under the leadership of Tu Yueh-shing, came to dominate the narcotics trade in Shanghai for the next thirty years, earning the gang lord the title of King of Opium. Tu acquired a taste for the appurtenances of American gangsters, eventually purchasing Al Capone's limousine, which he proudly drove around the streets of Nanking and Hong Kong.

Tu was extraordinarily skilled both as a muscle man and an entrepreneur. When the authorities made one of their periodic crackdowns on opium smoking in Shanghai, Tu responded by mass-marketing "anti-opium pills," red tablets laced with heroin. When the government took action to restrict the import of heroin, Tu seized the opportunity to build his own heroin factories. By 1934, heroin use in Shanghai had outpaced opium smoking as the most popular form of narcotics use. Tu's labs were so efficient and so productive that he began exporting his Green Circles Gang heroin to Chinese users in San Francisco and Seattle.

Tu's climb to the top of the Chinese underworld was closely linked to the rise to political power of the Chinese nationalist warlord General Chiang Kai-shek. Indeed, both men were initiates into the so-called "21st Generation" of the Green Circles Gang. These ties proved useful in 1926, when Chiang's northern expeditionary forces were attempting to sweep across central and northern China. As Chiang's troops approached Shanghai, the city's labor unions and Communist organizers rose up in a series of strikes and demonstrations designed to make it easier for Chiang to take control of the city. But Chiang stopped his march outside Shanghai, where he conferred with envoys from the city's business leaders and from Tu's gang. This coalition asked the Generalissimo to keep his forces stationed outside Shanghai until the city's criminal gangs, acting in concert with the police force maintained by foreign businesses, could crush the left.

When Chiang finally entered Shanghai, he stepped over the bodies of Communist workers. He soon solemnized his alliance with Tu by making him a general in the KMT. As the Chinese historian Y. C. Wang concludes, Tu's promotion to general was testimony to the gangsterism endemic to Chiang Kai-shek and his KMT: "Perhaps for the first time in Chinese history, the underworld gained formal recognition in national politics." The Green Circles Gang became the KMT's internal security force, known officially as the Statistical and Investigation Office. This unit was headed by one of Tu's sidekicks, Tai Li.

Under the guidance of Tu and Tai Li, opium sales soon became a major source of revenue for the KMT. In that same year of 1926 Chiang Kai-shek legalized the opium trade for a period of twelve months; taxes on the trade netted the KMT enormous sums of money. After the year was over Chiang pretended to acknowledge the protests against legalization and set up the Opium Suppression Bureau, which duly went about the business of shutting down all competitors to the KMT in the drug trade.

In 1933 the Japanese invaded China's northern provinces and soon forged an accord with the KMT, buying large amounts of opium from

Generals Tu and Tai Li, refining it into heroin and dispensing it to the Chinese through 2,000 pharmacies across northern China, exercising imperial supervision by the addiction of the Chinese population. General Tu's opium partnership with the occupying Japanese enjoyed the official sanction of Chiang Kai-shek, according to a contemporary report by US Army Intelligence, which also noted that it had the backing of five major Chinese banks "to the tune of $150 million Chinese dollars." The leadership of the KMT justified this relationship as an excellent opportunity for espionage, since Tu's men were able to move freely through the northern provinces on their opium runs.

In 1937 the Generalissimo's wife, Madam Chiang, went to Washington, where she recruited a US Army Air Corps general named Claire Chennault to assume control of the KMT's makeshift air force, then overseen by a group of Italian pilots on loan from Mussolini. Chennault was a Louisiana Cajun with unconventional ideas about air combat that had been soundly rejected by the top army brass, but his fanatic anti-Communism had won him friends among the far right in Congress and in US intelligence circles.

Chennault resigned his commission, went on the KMT payroll, and set up operations in Nanking, where he worked side by side with Chiang Kai-shek and Tai Li. For nearly four years Chennault's tiny air force lurked discreetly, ceding the air space of China to the Japanese imperial air force. Then came Pearl Harbor, December 7, 1941. Chennault made haste to Washington and pushed the idea that wise use of air power in China against the Japanese would be an excellent contribution to the war effort. He was duly furnished with 100 P-40 fighters and was allowed to recruit army and navy pilots and ground troops. Chennault called his operation the American Volunteer Group, but they soon became hallowed as the Flying Tigers.

The recruits to Chennault's force were told that theirs was a covert mission and that under no circumstances should they reveal that they were in China with the knowledge of the US government. When the Flying Tigers were allowed to engage the Japanese they quickly established a formidable combat record, knocking down nearly 500 Japanese fighters. But for most of the war, because of the unofficial detente between Chiang and the Japanese occupiers, the pilots found themselves shuttling personal contraband for the KMT leaders – opium, gold, and other valuable commodities.

Chiang's reluctance to fight the Japanese infuriated General Joseph "Vinegar Joe" Stilwell. Stilwell had no respect for Chiang, calling him "a peanut dictator" and describing the KMT nationalist regime as being based "on fear and favor, in the hands of an ignorant, arbitrary stubborn man." Stilwell was also highly critical of Chennault's strategy. The latter had convinced US commanders in Washington that the battle in China could be won by the strength of air power and by covert action alone. Stilwell correctly deemed this absurd, but he lost the battle for influence in Washington and became increasingly sidelined as Chennault rallied support for his position.

In the fall of 1942 the OSS made US Navy Captain Milton "Mary" Miles the head of its intelligence operations in China. Miles lost no time in forming an alliance with Tai Li, referring to this career gangster and opium lord as a "kindly labor union leader." In his services as head of Chiang's internal security force Tai was notably brutal, running dozens of concentration camps in which were held hundreds of thousands of Chiang Kai-shek's political opponents. Tai was notorious for his use of poison, having a stockpile of arsenic made up to look like Bayer aspirin and Carter's Little Liver Pills. In 1941 Tai had been arrested by the British in Hong Kong, who accused him of running "an intelligence organization modeled on the German Gestapo." He was released only after the personal intervention of Chiang Kai-shek.

Tai Li bragged about maintaining an army of undercover agents spread not only across China, but in every major city in the world that had Chinese residents who might be supporting Mao Tse-tung, China's Communist leader. Stilwell urged Washington to end its association with Tai Li, calling him the "Heinrich Himmler of China," but once again his advice was ignored and with the approval of the OSS the United States and Tai Li entered into an officially sanctioned relationship, which Tai Li called the "Friendship Plan," though it was formally known as the Sino-American Cooperative Organization, or SACO. Tai Li was put in charge of the new network and Captain Miles served as his deputy, the overall mission being espionage and sabotage against the Japanese in China. The Chinese were to supply the manpower, with the

US furnishing training, money and weapons. The OSS even established an FBI school in Nanking to train Tai's secret police in the use of police dogs, lie detectors and truth serums. Among the more remarkable instructors was a law enforcement delegation from Mississippi in the form of district attorneys and eight state troopers to impart their own indigenous knowledge of the use of police dogs.

Stilwell always believed that Chiang had no interest in fighting the Japanese and that the SACO operation was being used to assist in the KMT's criminal enterprises: "The Chinese had a great nose for money," Stilwell wrote in his diary, adding that the OSS man Miles "looked like he had lots of it." Stilwell favored a US alliance with Mao, for whose troops he had great admiration, describing them as being "battle-hardened, disciplined, well trained in guerrilla war and fired by a bitter hatred of the Japanese."

In 1944 Stilwell, based at the time in Nanking, sent a delegation of his staff officers to meet the Communist leaders, Mao Tse-tung and Chou En-lai. The Americans were warmly received and the Chinese Communists shared intelligence with them, taking them on a tour of their redoubt in the Yenan caves and allowing them to interrogate 150 Japanese prisoners.

Stilwell's view that China would be better off under the leadership of the Communists did not survive a furious counterattack by Tai Li and the OSS officer Miles. Tai Li had placed SACO agents in Stilwell's house and was well-informed about the general's views. In fairly short order Chiang demanded that FDR remove Stilwell from his command for "working with the Communists." FDR complied and the general abruptly departed. The KMT criminals, with a US intelligence organization at their disposal, had prevailed, with fateful consequences.

As the war edged to a close the US delayed making assaults on the Japanese in northern China as part of a plan to damage the Communists. Harry Truman described this strategy in his memoirs: "It was perfectly clear to us that if we told the Japanese to lay down their arms immediately and march to seaboard, the entire country would be taken over by the Communists. We therefore had to take the unusual step of using the enemy as a garrison until we could airlift Chinese national troops to south China and send Marines to guard the sea ports."

After the war, Chiang and Tai Li welcomed into their ranks dozens of warlords who had collaborated with the Japanese. These men now worked side by side with the OSS and the US Marines in the war against Mao. The US military didn't leave China until 1947, after channeling $3 billion in weapons and military aid to Chiang. This aid now gave way to covert US support for Claire Chennault's newly named Civil Air Transport, or CAT. Chennault's partner in this enterprise was a man with long-standing ties to US spy agencies, William Willauer. (He later showed up in 1954 in Central America as US ambassador to Honduras, when the CIA, using CAT planes and pilots, was readying the coup against Jacobo Arbenz's moderate left government in Guatemala.)

The US government gave Chennault and Willauer cut-rate prices on a fleet of surplus C-46 and C-47 transport planes, and as pilots Chennault hired many of the veterans of the Flying Tigers operation. In Nanking these pilots lived in a blue house known as the Opium Den. At this point CAT was at least nominally a private enterprise, though underpinned by US government subsidies in the form of cheap planes and US contracts to fly supplies to Chiang's forces, who were still fighting Mao. But by the summer of 1949 the Communists were on victory's threshold. Chennault went to Washington and met with Colonel Richard Stilwell, who was chief of covert operations in the CIA's Far East division. Chennault said that his airline was in dire financial straits, but nonetheless could fulfill a vital role in covert operations against Mao. Stilwell and his deputy, Desmond FitzGerald, thereupon approved what was in practical terms a CIA buyout of Civil Air Transport. They gave Chennault $500,000 in cash and began using the airline as a front for CIA operations throughout the Far East.

One of the first of these CIA-controlled CAT operations in China was to aid the ill-fated campaign against Mao by General Ma Pu-fang, whose army of 250,000 Muslims in northwest China had been crushed by the People's Liberation Army. The CAT planes rescued General Ma and his fortune, estimated at $1.5 million in gold bars, much of it garnered through his control of the region's opium trade. In 1950 the CAT planes began dropping food and guns to KMT general Li Tsun-yen's forces in southern China. The aid did not turn the tide, and the general's forces began to flee south into Burma. Li himself was airlifted by CAT to Taiwan, where Chiang Kai-shek had now installed his government.

Voyaging to Washington, General Li began promoting the notion that his forces in Burma could – with suitable US backing – return to China, wage war on the Communists and recapture the province of Hunan. Truman soon signed orders authorizing the CIA, with a budget of $300 million, to undertake covert actions on the Chinese mainland. As Mao threw the People's Liberation Army behind the North Koreans and hurled General MacArthur's forces southward down the peninsula Truman became obsessed with the opening of a so-called southern front to harry southwest China from Burma. So, in February 1951 planning for Operation Paper began: the invasion of China by KMT troops from the Shan States, all supposedly taking place without the knowledge of the Burmese government, the US State Department, the US ambassador to Burma, and the CIA's own deputy director of intelligence, Robert Armory, who was less than enthusiastic about any relationship with Chiang or the KMT.

Although General Li Tsun-yen had told Truman that there were as many as 175,000 KMT troops ready to be thrown into the fray, the actual KMT forces in Burma amounted to no more than about 5,000, and they were under the command of General Li Mi, whom we encountered at the start of this chapter. His forces had been chased out of China a year earlier, in January 1950, and had exerted themselves since then in waging war on the Karen hill tribes in the Shan States, soon obtaining the upper hand and using this victory to tax the opium farmers.

The makings of a classic CIA/drug paradigm were now in place. Starting on February 7, 1951, CIA planes began to shuttle arms and supplies from Bangkok to Li Mi's forces in north Burma, at first in the form of air drops five times a week and then with landings at Mong Hsat, an airfield constructed by the CIA fifteen miles from the Thai border. For the return journey the CIA planes were often reloaded with raw opium, which was flown back to Bangkok or Chiang Mai in northern Thailand and sold to General Phao Siyanan, head of the Thai police. General Phao had been made director of Thailand's national police after the CIA-backed coup in 1948 led by Major General Phin Choohannan. Phao's 40,000-member police force, the Police Knights, immediately engaged in a campaign of assassinations of Phin and Phao's political enemies. These troops also assumed control of Thailand's lucrative opium trade. In Phao's able hands the supply of cheap opium from the Shan States made Bangkok the hub of the Southeast Asia opium trade, according to the British Customs Office. Phao's control of the opium trade was directly abetted by the CIA, which had funnelled him $35 million in aid. Thailand would thereafter become the CIA's main base of operations in the region.

In the 1950s the CIA backed General Phao in a struggle with another Thai general for monopoly of control of Thailand's opium and heroin trade. Using artillery and aircraft supplied by the CIA's Overseas Supply Company, based in Bangkok, Phao easily outgunned his rival and duly imposed near total control over the government of Thailand and the country's criminal enterprises. Backed by squads of CIA advisers, Phao set about the task of turning Thailand into a police state. The country's leading dissidents and academics were jailed and CIA-trained police reconnaissance units patrolled the countryside, among other activities levying a protection fee on the opium caravans. In addition to controlling the opium and heroin trade, Phao also cornered the country's gold market, played a leading role on the top twenty corporate boards in the country, charged leading executives and businessmen protection fees and ran prostitution houses and gambling dens. Phao became great friends with Bill Donovan, at that time US ambassador to Thailand. Donovan was so enamored of Phao that he put him up for a Legion of Merit award. This for a man described by one Thai diplomat as "the worst man in the whole history of modern Thailand."

The military aspect of the venture was less efficiently executed. Li Mi's troops managed three forays into China. The first, in June 1951, lasted only a week. The next, in July, ended in disaster within a month, with 900 dead, including several CIA advisers. The final bid came in August 1952 and went equally badly.

The weapons going to the KMT were supplied by a CIA front company called Overseas Supply, run by a CIA lawyer called Paul Helliwell, an old Asia hand who had worked in China and Burma with the OSS. Helliwell later bragged about paying his Asian informants with "sticky brown bars of opium."

The CIA's operation in Burma had been deliberately kept from the

US ambassador in Rangoon, William Sebald, who had faced a barrage of complaints from the Burmese government. Sebald confronted Secretary of State John Foster Dulles over persistent accusations that the CIA had been assisting KMT troops in northern Burma, and was assured unequivocally that there was no involvement. Armed with such reassurances Sebald relayed this to General Ne Win, the Burmese army's chief of staff. Ne Win interrupted the diplomat, saying "Ambassador, I have it cold. If I were you, I'd just keep quiet."

Burma took its grievance to the UN, bringing along captured caches of CIA-supplied weaponry. The American response to these charges was that the KMT had been buying its weapons on the open market with money generated from the opium trade. Finally, under mounting international pressure, the US agreed in 1953 to evacuate the KMT. The operation was supervised by Bill Donovan and Thailand's General Phao. General Phao would not allow any representatives of the Burmese government to witness the evacuation, and in fact the majority of those who departed were women, children and injured soldiers, leaving behind more than 5,000 well-armed KMT troops who continued to assert control over poppy cultivation and the opium trade. They also joined forces with rebel hill tribes in a war against the Burmese army.

One of the CIA's strategic objectives had been to provoke an attack by China across the Burmese border in retaliation for forays by the KMT. This plan misfired, however. In 1961 the Chinese did indeed launch a drive into the Shan States, but at the request of the Burmese government to deal, once and for all, with the KMT. The People's Liberation Army drove the KMT remnant into Thailand, where it settled outside Chiang Mai. After this operation the Burmese army discovered a fresh cache of weapons and supplies at the former KMT base, still in boxes with US markings, and containing more than five tons of ammunition and hundreds of rifles and machine guns. They also discovered more than a dozen opium-processing labs.

The CIA's liaison to the KMT at its new quarters in Thailand was William Young, the son of a Baptist missionary. Young had joined the CIA in 1958 and quickly proved himself to be one of the Agency's most capable hands, and one of the few CIA men respected by the tribal leaders. Young had been born in the Shan States and used his intimate knowledge of the culture and his fluency in the difficult languages of the hill country to recruit the local tribesmen as surrogate warriors in the CIA's operations across Southeast Asia. Young was more than willing to indulge his hill tribe mercenaries in the opium trade with the excuse that "[a]s long as there is opium in Burma somebody will market it."

In 1963 Young recruited KMT soldiers into a raiding force that led attacks on villages in northern Laos believed to be sympathetic to the Communist Pathet Lao. From 1962 to 1971 Young's mercenaries carried out more than fifty cross-border ventures into China, where they monitored truck traffic and tapped phone lines. These expeditions were propelled by the CIA's fear that China might intervene in Laos and Vietnam. His recruits were trained by the Thai secret police, taken to Mong Hkan, a CIA base near the Burma–China border, then from Mong Hkan into China using the Shan opium caravans as cover. The mules that carried bags of opium also packed radios and surveillance equipment.

One of the CIA-backed guerrilla groups was called the Sixteen Musketeers. This force was run by U Ba Thein, a leading Shan States revolutionary who for many years had funded his war against the Burmese government with opium sales. He had worked for British intelligence during World War II. In 1958 he joined forces with Gnar Kham to form the Shan Nationalist Army. To fund their operations U Ba Thein struck an opium deal with General Ouane Rattikone, the CIA asset who headed the Laotian army. Ouane also had another line of business. He oversaw the Laotian government's secret Opium Administration, which was generating millions of dollars a year for the Laotian junta. Ouane had an enormous stockpile of weapons generously supplied by the CIA, which he traded for U Ba Thein's opium shipments.

The Shan bought automatic weapons, machine guns, rockets and radios and within a year or two had amassed enough supplies to equip a 5,000-man army and gain control over more than 120 square miles of territory. U Ba Thein told historian Al McCoy in the early 1970s that the CIA's William Young "knew about the arrangement, saw the arms and opium being exchanged and never made any move to stop it." In a familiar pattern the CIA was to use General Ouane as the intermediary in the project of arming the Shan nationalists, thus slightly minimizing the risk of being directly denounced by the Burmese government.

In 1964 the Shan nationalist army and the CIA were dealt a serious blow when Gnar Kham, the popular leader of the Shan army who had managed by force of personality to weld together the fractious coalition, got in a dispute over an opium deal and was shot in the head and killed at Huei Krai, a small outpost on the opium trail connecting the poppy fields of Burma to General Ouane's heroin labs in Laos.

The CIA's covert activities in Burma also fueled the operations of one of the world's most notorious heroin lords, Khun Sa, born in a small mountain hamlet in the Shan States near the Chinese border. His father was a KMT soldier and his mother a Shan. He had received military training by the KMT and in 1963 was tapped by the Burmese government to head up a local defense force, the KYYY, against the Shan rebels. Instead of paying Khun Sa in money or provisions, the Burmese government granted him a concession to use state roads and facilities for drug trafficking. With the backing of the Burmese government Khun Sa's opium trading soon posed a threat to the KMT's monopoly, giving rise to an opium war of 1967. Khun Sa had sent 500 men and 300 mules carrying 16 tons of raw opium across 200 miles of mountain trails for delivery to General Ouane Rattikone's heroin factory in the small lumber town of Ban Khwan on the Mekong River. Khun Sa's caravan was shadowed most of the way by KMT forces, who launched an ambush about fifty miles outside Ban Khwan. The Shan traders fended off the attack, escaped across the Mekong and set up a defensive position in the town. The KMT forces regrouped and launched another attack. At this point General Ouane relayed word that both the Shan and the KMT should leave Laos or face attack by his men. The KMT forces demanded a payment of $250,000 to retreat. Khun Sa told his forces to remain in place till they received a $500,000 payment for the opium shipment. The next morning six bombers from the Laotian air force, then under the control of the CIA, flew over the village and dropped 500-pound bombs on both the KMT and Khun Sa's troops. The bombing continued for two days. The KMT forces eventually fled north, deeper into Laos, while the Shan headed across the river, leaving behind most of the opium – which General Ouane promptly dispatched his men to retrieve.

The drug war left Ouane richer than ever, Khun Sa in a weakened state from which it took him a decade to recover, and the KMT in control of 80 percent of the opium market in Burma, according to a survey of opium trading the CIA requested William Young to prepare in 1968. As General Tuan Shi-wen told a reporter for the *London Weekend Telegraph,* "Necessity knows no law. We have to continue to fight the evil of communism, and to fight you must have an army and an army must have guns and to buy guns you must have money. In these mountains the only money is opium." In late 1960 Burmese opium was selling for $60 a kilo in Chiang Mai, where the going price for an M-16 was $250.

Khun Sa made his comeback in the early 1980s after he forged an alliance with the Shan rebels whom he had once been paid in drugs by the Burmese government to put down. He ran his new opium empire from the small mountain village of Wan Ho Mong, ten miles from the Thai border. By the late 1980s he had built a 20,000-man rebel force called the Mong Tai Army, and had amassed a prodigious amount of money from his control of almost 300,000 acres of land in the Shan States given over to the opium poppy. There were twenty heroin factories under his control, and his gross revenues were reckoned by *Newsweek* to amount to $1.5 billion a year, which – even at the $500,000 a month he claimed it cost to supply and feed his army – left him with plenty in savings.

In 1988 the Burmese government was taken over by the State Law and Order Restoration Council, or SLORC. To fund its new regime the SLORC set a goal of doubling opium exports, and by 1990 Burma was producing more than 60 percent of the world's heroin supply, valued at more than $40 billion a year. The SLORC used the proceeds of this trade to bought $1.2 billion worth of military hardware, according to the International Monetary Fund. The US Embassy in Rangoon noted flatly that "exports of opium appear to be worth about as much as all legal exports." Banks in Rangoon were, and at the time of writing still are, offering money laundering services at a 40 percent commission. The profits of Khun Sa and other opium lords were cleansed by comingling them with the huge revenue stream from the SLORC's favored oil companies, UNOCAL (from the US) and Total (from France).

In 1992 U Saw Lu, a leader of a Wa tribe in the Shan States, began a campaign to try to shift his region's agriculture out of opium production. He told agents from the US Drug Enforcement Agency about the opium-running practices of Major Than Aye, an intelligence officer with the SLORC. News of this exchange soon made its way to SLORC agents, who arrested U Saw Lu, and began fifty-six days of appalling tortures, during which he was hung upside down, beaten with chains, and had electric wires attached to his genitals while buckets of urine were dashed in his face. Lu's torture was overseen by Major Than Aye, the very man he had informed on to the DEA. Than had every intention of killing the Wa leader, whose life was spared only after other Wa leaders threatened to take up arms against the SLORC regime.

When U Saw Lu recovered, he didn't back down. Instead, he prepared a detailed plan to substitute other crops for opium in the Wa region. The report was titled "The Bondage of Opium – The Agony of the Wa People, a Proposal and Plan."

In 1993 Wa gave his plan to the new DEA agent in Rangoon, Richard Horn. Horn was a 23-year veteran of the DEA who saw his appointment as head of the Agency's bureau in Rangoon as his "dream job." He seized on U Saw Lu's ideas as an exciting opportunity and began to support him and his Wa comrades. But the CIA station chief in Rangoon, Arthur Brown, got a copy of Lu's report and leaked it to his friends in SLORC intelligence. The SLORC tried to arrest Lu again, and were only dissuaded after Horn's intervention. Horn himself now paid the price for sticking his nose into such affairs of state. According to a suit he later filed against the CIA, the first intimation he had of the Agency's hostility was what he construed as an attempt to set him up for assassination. He also discovered that his phone lines were being tapped and that his own conversations with his superiors at DEA HQ back in Washington were being quoted verbatim by Franklin Huddle, the number two at the US Embassy in the latter's communications to the State Department. Horn was angered not only by this personal harassment but by the fact that the CIA was continuing to provide intelligence and training to SLORC's internal security force, even as the Agency sabotaged his attempts to back U Saw Lu's anti-opium plans. Finally, the DEA recalled Horn and he was reassigned to New Orleans. He filed suit against the CIA in 1994 as an individual and again in 1996 as part of a class action suit by a number of DEA agents, charging that they had been harassed, intimidated and secretly spied on by the CIA. The court documents related to this lawsuit are sealed.

In 1996 the SLORC made a deal with Khun Sa. The warlord had been indicted by the US Justice Department in 1990, but the SLORC announced that he would neither be sent to the US nor brought up on any charges in his own country. Instead, he was given the Burma-to-Thailand taxi concession and a 44-acre site outside Rangoon where his son has plans to build a gambling and shopping complex. Khun Sa predicted that his deal with the SLORC wouldn't end the opium trade in the Shan States. "On the contrary, there will be more. My people need to grow opium to make a living. If Americans and Europeans didn't come here there would be no drug trade."

Sources

Our description of the British opium trade is based largely on three less than satisfactory books, Michael Greenberg's *British Trade and the Opening of China*, David Owen's 65-year-old *British Opium Policy in China and India* and Arthur Waley's *The Opium War Through Chinese Eyes*. Joseph Stilwell's own writings provide the best guide to his frustrating experience in China. Harris Smith's book on the OSS is excellent on the disastrous decision-making by American anti-Communists in the waning days of the war in Asia. Smith's history of the OSS far surpasses any similar work on the CIA. Our profile of Tu Yueh-sheng draws heavily on essays by Y. C. Wang and Jonathan Marshall. William Corson and David Wise give useful accounts of the CIA's much overlooked early misadventures in Burma. Al McCoy's *Politics of Heroin*, as always, was an indispensable map to the confusing terrain of Southeast Asia's narcotics trade. Over the past two years, Dennis Bernstein and Leslie Kean have written fine articles on the horrors of contemporary Burma. Equally informative was the *Frontline* series on the Burma opium trade written by Adrian Cowell. Bertel Lintner has reported on Burma and the Shan States with consistent brilliance in the *Far Eastern Economic Review*.

Anderson, Martin Edwin. "Spy Agency Rivalries." *Washington Times,* Dec. 19, 1994.

Associated Press. "DEA Agent Sues CIA over Mission." *Washington Times,* Oct. 28, 1994.

Bernstein, Dennis, and Leslie Kean. "People of the Opiate: Burma's Dictatorship Touches Everything, Even the CIA." *Nation,* Dec. 16, 1996.

Berrigan, Darrell. "They Smuggle Dope by the Ton." *Saturday Evening Post,* May 5, 1956.

Boyle, John Hunter. *China and Japan at War, 1937–1945.* Stanford Univ. Press, 1972.

Brown, Richard Harvey. "Drug Policies and Politics in Comparative Perspective: The Case of Opium in India, China, Britain and the United States." Paper presented at Drug Policy seminar at Columbia University, Feb. 1993.

Chennault, Claire. *Way of a Fighter: The Memoirs of Claire Chennault.* Putnam, 1949.

Colby, Gerard, and Charlotte Dennett. *Thy Will Be Done.* HarperCollins, 1996.

Corson, William. *The Armies of Ignorance.* Dial, 1977.

Cowell, Adrian. "The Opium Kings." (Transcript) *Frontline*/WGBH, May 20, 1997.

Faligot, Roger. *Invisible Empire: The Overseas Chinese.* Putnam, 1995.

Gravel, Mike, ed. *The Pentagon Papers: The Defense Department History of US Decision-making on Vietnam.* Beacon, 1971.

Greenberg, Michael. *British Trade and the Opening of China, 1800–42.* Cambridge Univ. Press, 1951.

Isikoff, Michael. "International Opium Crop Production up 8 Percent Last Year; Despite US Efforts Against Poppy Crop, Concern Grows About Expanding Heroin Market." *Washington Post,* March 1, 1992.

Kean, Leslie, and Dennis Bernstein. "Burma–Singapore Axis: Globalizing the Heroin Trade." *Covert Action Quarterly,* Spring 1998.

Kerry, John. *The New War: The Web of Crime that Threatens America's Security.* Simon and Schuster, 1996.

Kleinknecht, William. *The New Ethnic Mobs: The Changing Face of Organized Crime in America.* Free Press, 1996.

Kohn, Marek. *Narcomania: On Heroin.* Faber and Faber, 1987.

Kwitny, Jonathan. *The Crimes of Patriots: A True Tale of Dope, Dirty Money and the CIA.* Norton, 1987.

Lamour, Catherine, and Michel Lamberti. *The International Connection: Opium from Growers to Pushers.* Pantheon, 1974.

Latimer, Dean, and Jeff Goldberg. *Flowers in the Blood: The Story of Opium.* Franklin Watts, 1981.

LaGesse, David and George Rodriguez. "Drug War Often Finds CIA at Odds with DEA." *Dallas Morning News,* Feb. 16, 1997.

Liu, Melinda. "Burma's Money Tree." *Newsweek,* May 15, 1989.

McAllister, J. F. "Getting in the Way of Good Policy." *Time,* Nov. 7, 1994.

Marshall, Jonathan. "Opium and the Politics of Gangsterism in Nationalist China, 1927–1945." *Bulletin of Concerned Asian Scholars.* July/Sept. 1976.

——. *Drug Wars.* Cohan and Cohen, 1991.

Miles, Milton. *A Different Kind of War.* Doubleday, 1967.

Morley, Jefferson, and Malcolm Byrne. "The Drug War and 'National Security.'" *Dissent, Winter 1989.*

Musto, David. *The American Disease: The Origins of Narcotics Control.* Yale Univ. Press, 1973.

Owen, David. *British Opium Policy in China and India.* Yale Univ. Press, 1934.

Robinson, Jeffrey. *The Laundrymen.* Arcade, 1996.

Rush, James. *Opium to Java.* Cornell, 1990.

Shannon, Eileen. *Desperados: Latin Drug Lords, US Lawmen, and the War America Can't Win.* Viking, 1988.

Smith, R. Harris. *OSS: The Secret History of America's First Central Intelligence Agency.* Univ. of California Press, 1972.

Stares, Paul. *Global Habit: The Drug Problem in a Borderless World.* Brookings Institute, 1997.

Stilwell, Joseph. *The Stilwell Papers.* Sloane, 1948.

Tuchman, Barbara. *Stilwell and the American Experience in China.* Macmillan, 1971.
US Congress. House. Committee on Foreign Affairs. *Justice Department Treatment of Criminal Cases Involving CIA Personnel and Claims of National Security.* Government Printing Office, 1975.
——. Select Committee on Narcotics Abuse and Control. *Opium Production, Narcotics Financing, and Trafficking in Southeast Asia.* Government Printing Office, 1977.
——. Committee on International Relations. *Proposal to Control Opium from the Golden Triangle and Terminate the Shan Opium Trade.* Government Printing Office, 1975.
US Office of the Comptroller General, General Accounting Office. *Drug Control: US Support Efforts in Burma, Pakistan and Thailand.* Government Printing Office, Feb. 1988.
US State Department. *International Narcotics Strategy.* Government Printing Office, 1996.
Vest, Jason. "Drug Official Cites Burma Problem." *Washington Post,* June 17, 1994.
Waley, Arthur. *The Opium War Through Chinese Eyes.* Macmillan, 1958.
Wang, Y. C. "Tu Yueh-sheng (1888–1951) A Tentative Political Biography." *Journal of Asian Scholars.* May 1967.
Washington Post, editorial. "Burma's Drug Lords." *Washington Post,* March 18, 1988.
White, Peter. "The Poppy." *National Geographic,* Feb. 1985.
Wise, David, and Thomas Ross. *The Invisible Government.* Random House, 1964.

10

Armies and Addicts:
Vietnam and Laos

At 7:30 a.m., on March 16, 1968, Task Force Barker descended on the small hamlet of My Lai in the Quang Nai province of South Vietnam. Two squads cordoned off the village and one, led by Lieutenant William Calley, moved in and, accompanied by US Army Intelligence officers, began to slaughter all the inhabitants. Over the next eight hours US soldiers methodically killed 504 men, women and children. As the late Ron Ridenhour, who first exposed the massacre, said years later to one of the present authors, "Above My Lai were helicopters filled with the entire command staff of the brigade, division and task force. All three tiers in the chain of command were literally flying overhead while it was going on. It takes a long time to kill 600 people. It's a dirty job, you might say. These guys were flying overhead from 7:30 in the morning, when the unit first landed and began to move into those hamlets. They were there at least two hours, at 500 feet, 1000 feet and 1500 feet."

The cover-up of this operation began almost from the start. The problem wasn't the massacre itself: polls right after the event showed 65 percent of Americans approved of the US action. The cover-up was instead to disguise the fact that My Lai was part of the CIA killing program called Operation Phoenix. As Douglas Valentine writes in his brilliant book, *The Phoenix Program,* "the My Lai massacre was a result of Phoenix, the 'jerry-built' counter-terror program that provided an outlet for the repressed fears and anger of the psyched-up men of Task Force Barker. Under the aegis of neutralizing the infrastructure, old men, women and children became the enemy. Phoenix made it as easy to shoot a Vietnamese child as it was to shoot a sparrow in a tree. The ammunition was faulty intelligence provided by secret agents harboring grudges – in violation of the agreement that Census Grievance intelligence would not be provided to the police. The trigger was the blacklist."

The My Lai operation was principally developed by two men, the CIA's Paul Ramsdell and a Colonel Khien, the Quang Nai province chief. Operating under cover of the US Agency for International Development, Ramsdell headed the Phoenix program in Quang Nai province, where it was his task to prepare lists of suspected NLF (called by the Americans "Viet Cong") leaders, organizers and sympathizers. Ramsdell would then pass these lists on to the US Army units that were carrying out the killings. In the case of My Lai, Ramsdell told Task Force Barker's intelligence officer, Captain Koutac, that "anyone in that area was considered a VC sympathizer because they couldn't survive in that area unless they were sympathizers."

Ramsdell had acquired this estimate from Col. Khien, who had his own agenda. For one thing, his family had been hit hard by the Tet offensive launched by the NLF earlier in the year. In addition, the NLF had seriously disrupted his business enterprises. Khien was notorious for being one of South Vietnam's most corrupt chieftains, an officer who had his hand in everything from payroll fraud to prostitution. But Khien apparently made his really big money from heroin sales to US soldiers.

For the CIA, the need to cover its involvement in the My Lai massacre became acute in August 1970, when Sergeant David Mitchell, a member of Task Force Barker, was put on trial for killing dozens of Vietnamese civilians at My Lai. Mitchell claimed that the My Lai operation had been conducted under the supervision of the CIA. The Agency's lawyer, John Greaney, successfully prevented Mitchell's lawyers from lodging subpoenas against any Agency personnel. But despite such maneuvers, high CIA and army brass were worried that the truth might trickle out, and so General William Peers of US Army Intelligence was given the task - so to speak - of straightening out the furniture. Peers was a former CIA man whose ties to Agency operations in Southeast Asia dated back to World War II, when he supervised the OSS's Detachment 101, the Burma campaign that often operated under the cover of Shan opium trafficking. Peers had also served as CIA station chief in Taiwan in the early 1950s, when the Agency was backing the exiled KMT supremo, Chiang Kai-shek and his henchman Li Mi.

Peers had helped design the pacification strategy for South Vietnam and was a good friend of Evan Parker, the CIA officer who headed ICEX (Intelligence Coordination and Exploitation), the command structure that oversaw Phoenix and other covert killing operations. It's not surprising, then, that the Peers investigation found no CIA fingerprints on the massacre and instead placed the blame on the crazed actions of the enlisted men and junior officers of Task Force Barker.

In the immediate aftermath of My Lai the polls may have shown 65 percent approval by Americans, but it's doubtful whether such momentary enthusiasm would have survived the brute facts of what Operation Phoenix involved. As Bart Osborn, a US Army Intelligence officer collecting names of suspects in the Phoenix Program testified before Congress in 1972, "I never knew in the course of all of these operations any detainee to live through his interrogation. They all died. There was never any reasonable establishment of the fact that any one of those individuals was, in fact, cooperating with the VC, but they all died and the majority were either tortured to death or things like thrown out of helicopters."

One of the more outlandish efforts to protect the true instigators of My Lai came during the 1970 congressional hearings run by Senator Thomas Dodd (father of the present US senator from Connecticut). Dodd was trying to pin the blame for My Lai on drug use by US soldiers. He had seized on this idea after seeing a CBS news item showing a US soldier smoking marijuana in the jungle after a fire-fight. The senator forthwith convened hearings of his subcommittee on juvenile deliquency, and his staff contacted Ron Ridenhour, the man who had first brought the massacre to light prior to Seymour Hersh's journalistic exposé. Ridenhour had long made it his quest to show that My Lai was planned from the top, so he agreed to testify on the condition that he would not have to deal with any foolishness about blaming the murder of over 500 people on dope.

But no sooner had Ridenhour presented himself in the hearing chamber than Dodd began to issue pronouncements about the properties of marijuana so outlandish that Harry Anslinger himself would have approved. Ridenhour got nowhere, denounced the proceedings and expostulated outside the hearing room that "Dodd is stacking the evidence. Nobody mentioned drugs at My Lai after it happened and they would have been looking for any excuse. Many, many Americans are looking for any reason other than a command decision."

Although Dodd had simply wanted to blame My Lai on drugs and move on, the press now began to take an interest in the whole question of drug use in Vietnam by US forces. The attention prompted a congressional delegation to travel to Vietnam headed by Rep. Robert Steele, a Connecticut Republican, and Rep. Morgan Murphy, a Democrat from Illinois. They spent a month in Vietnam talking to soldiers and medics and returned with a startling conclusion. "The soldier going to Vietnam," Steele said, "runs a far greater risk of becoming a heroin addict than a combat casualty." They estimated that as many as 40,000 soldiers in Vietnam were addicted to heroin. A follow-up investigation by the *New York Times* reckoned that the count might be even higher – perhaps as many as 80,000.

The Pentagon naturally preferred a lower figure, putting the total number of heroin addicts at between 100 and 200. But by this time President Nixon had begun to mistrust the flow of numbers out of the Defense Department and dispatched his White House domestic policy council chief, Egil Krogh Jr., to Vietnam for another look. Krogh didn't spend time with the generals, but headed out into the field where he watched soldiers openly light up joints and Thai sticks and brag about the purity of the grades of heroin they were taking. Krogh came back with the news that as many as 20 percent of the US troops were heroin users. The figure made a big impression on Richard Nixon, who readily appreciated that although Americans might be prepared to see their sons die on the front lines battling communism, they would be far less enthusiastic at the news that hundreds of thousands of these same sons would be returning home as heroin addicts.

Partially in response to these findings Nixon recruited the CIA into his drug war. The man the Agency chose to put forward as coordinator with the White House was Lucien Conein, a veteran of the CIA's station in Saigon, where he had been involved in the coup in 1963 that saw South Vietnam's President Ngo Dinh Diem, assassinated along with his brother Ngo Dhin Nhu. (The Diems were regarded by President Kennedy and his advisers as insufficiently robust in pursuing the war. What the CIA proposed, local South Vietnamese generals disposed, and the Diems died in a hail of machine-gun bullets.) At the time of his death Nhu was one of the largest heroin brokers in South Vietnam. His supplier was a Corsican living in Laos named Bonaventure Francisi.

Lucien Conein himself was of Corsican origin, and as part of his intelligence work had maintained ties to Corsican gangsters in Southeast Asia and in Marseilles. His role in the White House drug war team appears to have been not so much one of advancing an effective interdiction of drug supplies as in protecting CIA assets who were tied to the drug trade. For example, one of the CIA's first recommendations – an instinctive reflex, really – was a "campaign of assassination" against global drug lords. The CIA argued that there were only a handful of heroin kingpins and that it would be easy to eliminate all of them. A White House policy memo from 1971 records this piece of Agency advice: "With 150 key assassinations the entire heroin-refining industry can be thrown into chaos." On that list were relatively small-time players and those without any links to the CIA-backed KMT forces that controlled the crucial supply lines out of the Shan States. This discretion was nothing new, since there had been an agreement between Anslinger's Bureau of Narcotics and Dangerous Drugs (the forerunner of the DEA) and the CIA not to run any of Anslinger's agents in Southeast Asia, lest it discommode the CIA's complex living arrangements in the region.

Another tactic advanced by Conein was to contaminate US cocaine supplies with methedrine, the theory being that users would react violently when dosing themselves with this potion and turn violently on their suppliers. There's no evidence that either of these schemes – assassination or methedrine adulteration – was ever put into play. But the Agency was able to convince the Nixon administration that its eradication effort should be directed at Turkey rather than Southeast Asia, said effort culminating in an attempt at export substitution, with opium growers in Anatolia being helped to set up a factory to produce bicycles.

The CIA was well aware that Turkey provided only between 3 and 5 percent of the world's supplies of raw opium at that time. In fact, the Agency had prepared an internal survey that estimated that 60 percent of the opium on the world market was coming from Southeast Asia and noted the precise whereabouts of the four largest heroin labs in the region, in villages in Laos, Burma and Thailand. This report was leaked to the *New York Times,* whose reporter relayed the main conclusions, without realizing that these villages were all next to CIA stations with the labs being run by people on the CIA's payroll.

In April 1971, the CIA's ties to the opium kings of Southeast Asia nearly sparked a major international confrontation. Crown Prince Sopsaisana had been appointed Laotian ambassador to France. On arrival in Paris, the prince angrily announced that some of his copious luggage was missing. He berated French airport officials, who meekly promised they would restore his property. In fact the prince's bags had been intercepted by French customs after a tip that Sopsaisana was carrying high-grade heroin; indeed, his luggage contained 60 kilos of heroin, worth $13.5 million, then the largest drug seizure in French history. The prince had planned to ship his drug cargo on to New York. The CIA station in Paris convinced the French to cover up the affair, although the prince was not given back his dope. It hardly mattered. Sopsaisana returned two weeks later to Vientiane to nearly inexhaustible supplies of the drug.

Why the CIA interest in protecting the largest trafficker nabbed on the French soil? The opium used to manufacture the prince's drugs had been grown in the highlands of Laos. It was purchased by a Hmong general, Vang Pao, who commanded the CIA's secret air base in Laos, where it was processed into high-grade Number 4 heroin in labs just down the block from CIA quarters. The heroin was then flown to Vientiane on Vang Pao's private airline, which consisted of two C-47s given to him by the CIA.

Vang Pao was the leader of a CIA-sponsored 30,000-man force of Hmong, which by 1971 consisted mostly of teenagers, fighting the Pathet Lao Communist forces. The Hmong had a reputation for fierceness, in part due to a century of conflict with the Chinese, who had, back in the nineteenth century, driven them into Laos after taking over their opium fields in Hunan. As one Hmong put it to Christopher Robbins, author of *Air America*, "They say we are a people who like to fight, a cruel people, enemy of everybody, always changing our region and being happy nowhere. If you want to know the truth about our people, ask the bear who is hurt why he defends himself, ask the dog who is kicked why he barks, ask the deer who is chased why he changes mountains." The Hmong practiced slash-and-burn agriculture, with two crops – rice and opium, the first for sustenance and the latter for medicinal and trading purposes.

Vang Pao was born in 1932 in a Laotian hamlet called Nong Het. At the age of thirteen he served as an interpreter for the French forces then fighting the Japanese. Two years later he was battling Viet Minh incursions into Laos in the First Indochina War. He underwent officer training at the French military academy near Saigon, becoming the highest-ranking Hmong in the Royal Laotian Air Force. In 1954 Vang Pao led a group of 850 Hmong soldiers on a fruitless mission to relieve the beleaguered French during their debacle at Dien Bien Phu in Vietnam.

The Hmong were first marshaled into a surrogate army by a French colonel called Roger Trinquier, who confronted a crisis in the French budget for local covert operations and intelligence in a fashion that covered more than one objective. "The money from the opium," he wrote later, "financed the maquis [that is, the Hmong mercenaries] in Laos. It was flown to Cp. St. Jacques [a French military base sixty miles south of Saigon] in Vietnam in a DC-3 and sold. The money was put into an account and used to feed and arm the guerrillas. Trinquier cynically added than the trade "was strictly controlled even though it was outlawed." Overseeing the marketing in Saigon was the local French director of the Deuxiéme Bureau, Colonel Antoine Savani. A Corsican with ties to the Marseilles drug syndicates, Savani organized the Bin Xuyen River gang on the lower Mekong to run the heroin labs, manage the opium dens and sell the surplus to the Corsican drug syndicate. This enterprise, called Operation X, ran from 1946 through 1954.

Ho Chi Minh made opposition to the opium trade a key feature of his campaign to run the French out of Vietnam. The Viet Minh leader said, quite accurately, that the French were pushing opium on the people of Vietnam as a means of social control. A drugged people, Ho said, is less likely to rise up and throw off the oppressor.

During World War II, OSS officers working to oust the Japanese from Southeast Asia developed a cordial relationship with Ho Chi Minh, finding that the Viet Minh leader spoke fluent English and was well versed in American history. Ho quoted from memory lengthy passages from the Declaration of Independence, and chided the intelligence agents, noting that Vietnamese nationalists had been asking American presidents since Lincoln for help in booting out the French colonialists. As with Mao's forces in China, the OSS operatives in Vietnam realized that Ho's well-trained troops were a vital ally, more capable and less corrupt than Chiang Kai-shek's Kuomintang army and the pro-French forces in Indochina. When Ho was stricken with malaria, the OSS sent one of its agents, Paul Helliwell, who would later head up the CIA's Overseas Supply Company, to treat the ailing Communist. Similar to Joe Stilwell's view of Mao, many military and OSS men recommended that the US should back Ho after the eviction of the Japanese.

After arriving in Vietnam in 1945, US Army General Phillip Gallagher asked the OSS to compile a detailed background on Ho. An OSS operative named Le Xuan, who would later work for the CIA during the Vietnam War, acquired a dossier on Ho from a disaffected Vietnamese nationalist: Le Xuan paid the man off with a bag of opium. The dossier disclosed to US intelligence agencies that Ho had had extended stays in the Soviet Union, a revelation that doomed any future aid from the Americans for his cause. Le Xuan would later turn on the CIA, showing up in Paris in 1968 to reveal his services to the Agency and denounce its murderous policies in Vietnam.

In 1953, Trinquier's Operation X opium network was discovered by Colonel Edwin Lansdale, at the time the CIA's military adviser in Southeast Asia. Lansdale later claimed that he protested about this French role in opium trafficking, but was admonished to hold his tongue because, in his words, exposure of "the operation would prove a major embarrassment to a friendly government." In fact, the CIA's director, Allen Dulles, was mightily impressed by Trinquier's operation and, looking ahead to the time when the US would take over from the French in the region, began funneling money, guns and CIA advisers to Trinquier's Hmong army.

The post–Dien Bien Phu accords, signed in Geneva in 1954, decreed that Laos was to be neutral, off-limits to all foreign military forces. This had the effect of opening Laos to the CIA, which did not consider itself a military force. The CIA became the unchallenged principal in all US actions inside Laos. Once in this position of dominance the CIA brooked no interference from the Pentagon. This point was driven home by the military attaché to Laos, Colonel Paul Pettigrew, who advised his replacement in Vientiane in 1961, "For God's sake, don't buck the CIA or you'll find yourself floating face down on that Mekong River."

From the moment the Geneva Accords were signed, the US government was determined to undermine them and do everything in its power to prevent the installation of Ho Chi Minh as president of all Vietnam, even though elections would have clearly showed he was the choice of most Vietnamese, as President Dwight D. Eisenhower famously admitted. Eisenhower and his advisers decreed that Laos's neutral status should be subverted. On the ground this meant that the neutralist government of Prime Minister Souvanna Phouma, which had amicable relations with the Pathet Lao, should be subverted by the CIA, whose preferred client was General Nosavan Phoumi. The Agency fixed elections in 1960 in an attempt to legitimize his rule. Also in 1960 the CIA began a more sustained effort to build up Vang Pao and his army, furnishing him with rifles, mortars, rockets and grenades.

After John Kennedy's victory in 1960, Eisenhower advised him that the next big battleground in Southeast Asia would not be Vietnam but Laos. His counsel found its mark, even though Kennedy initially snooted Laos as "a country not worthy of engaging the attention of great powers." In public Kennedy pronounced the country's name as L-A-Y-o-s, thinking that Americans would not rally to the cause of a place pronounced "louse." In 1960 there were but a thousand men in Vang Pao's army. By 1961 "L'Armée Clandestine" had grown to 9,000. By the time of Kennedy's assassination in late 1963, Vang Pao was at the head of some 30,000 troops. This army and its air force were entirely funded by the United States to the tune of $300 million, administered and overseen by the CIA.

Vang Pao's original CIA case officer was William Young, the Baptist missionary-become-CIA-officer we met in the preceding chapter. Young never had any problem with the opium trafficking of the Hmong tribes. After Young was transferred out of the area in 1962, the CIA asked the Frenchman Trinquier to return as military adviser to the Hmong. Trinquier had just completed his tour of duty in the French Congo and consented to perform that function for a few months before the arrival of one of the most notorious characters in this saga, an American named Anthony Posephny, always known as Tony Poe.

Poe was a CIA officer, a former US Marine who had been wounded at Iwo Jima. By the early 1950s he was working for the Agency in Asia, starting with the training of Tibetan Khamba tribesmen in Colorado (thus breaching the law against CIA activities inside the US), prior to leading them back to retrieve the Dalai Lama. In 1958 Poe showed up in Indonesia in an early effort to topple Sukarno. In 1960 he was training KMT forces for raids into China; his right hand was by now mangled after ill-advised contact with a car's fanbelt. In 1963 Poe became Vang Pao's case officer and forthwith instituted new incentives to fire up the Hmong's dedication to freedom's cause, announcing that he would pay a cash bounty for every pair of Pathet Lao ears delivered to him. He kept a plastic bag on his front porch where the ears were deposited and strung his collection along the verandah. To convince skeptical CIA superiors, in this case Ted Shackley in Vientiane, that his body counts were accurate, Poe once stapled a pair of ears to a report and sent it to HQ.

This souvenir of early methods of computing the slaughter of native Americans was not as foolproof as Poe imagined. He himself later described going up country and finding a small boy with no ears, then was told that the boy's father had sliced them off "to get money from the Americans." Poe shifted his incentive to the entire heads of Pathet Lao, claiming that he preserved them in formaldehyde in his bedroom.

This man, described by an associate as an "amiable psychopath," was running Phoenix-type operations into Lao villages near the Vietnam border. The teams were officially termed "home defense units," though Poe more frankly described them as "hunter-killer teams." Poe later claimed that he was booted out of Long Tieng because he had objected to CIA tolerance of Vang Pao's drug trading, but his description suggests more an envy for the French style of direct supervision of the opium trade. In a filmed TV interview at his home in Northern Thailand Poe said in 1987, "You don't let 'em run loose without a chain on 'em. They're like any kind of animals, or a baby. You have to control 'em. Vang Pao was the only guy with a pair of shoes when I met him. Why does he need Mercedes and hotels and homes when he never had them before? Why are you going to give him them? He was making millions. He had his own avenue for selling heroin. He put his money in US bank accounts and Swiss banks, and we all knew it. We tried to monitor it. We controlled all the pilots. We were giving him free rides into Thailand. They were flying it [that is, the opium cargoes] into Danang, where it was picked up by the number two man to Thieu [at the time South Vietnam's president]. It was all a contractual relationship, just like bankers and businessmen. A wonderful relationship. Just a Mafia. A big organized Mafia."

By the time Poe left this area of Laos in 1965, the situation was just as he described it twenty years later. The CIA's client army was collecting and shipping the opium on CIA planes, which by now were flying under the American flag.

"Yes, I've seen the sticky bricks come on board, and no one challenged it," Neal Hanson, an Air America pilot, said in a filmed interview in the late 1980s. "It was as if it was their personal property. We were a freebie air line. Whoever was put on our plane we flew. Primarily it was the smaller aircraft that would visit outlying villages and bring it [the opium] back to Long Tieng. If they put something on the airplane and told you not to look at it, you didn't look at it."

The Air America operation played a key role in expanding the opium market. CIA and US Agency for International Development funds went to the construction of more than 150 short, so-called LIMA landing strips in the mountains near the opium fields, thus opening these remote spots to the export trade – and also ensuring that such exports went to Vang Pao. The head of AID in that area at the time, Ron Rickenbach, said later, "I was on the air strips. My people were in charge of supplying the aircraft. I was in the areas where the opium was grown. I personally witnessed it being placed on Air America planes. We didn't create the opium product. But our presence accelerated it dramatically." In

1959 Laos was producing about 150 tons. By 1971 production had risen to 300 tons. Another boost to opium production, much of which was ultimately destined for the veins of Americans then fighting in Vietnam, was enabled by the USAID's supplying rice to the Hmong, thus allowing them to stop growing this staple and use the land to cultivate opium poppies.

Vang Pao controlled the opium trade in the Plain of Jars region of Laos. By buying up the one salable crop the general could garner the allegiance of the hill tribes as well as stuff his own bank account. He would pay $60 a kilo, $10 over the prevailing rate, and would purchase a village's crop if, in return, the village would supply recruits for his army. As a village leader described it, "Meo [that is, Hmong] officers with three or four stripes came from Long Tieng to buy their opium. They came in American helicopters, perhaps two or three men at one time. The helicopter leaves them here for a few days and they walk to the villages, then come back here and radio Long Tieng to send another helicopter for them and take the opium back."

John Everingham, an Australian war photographer, was at that time based in Laos and visited the Hmong village of Long Pot; he recalled in the late 1980s that "I was given the guest bed in a district village leader's house. I ended up sharing it with a military guy, who I later discovered was a leader in Vang Pao's army. I was wakened by a great confusion of people and noise at the bottom of the bed, where there was a packet of black sticky stuff on bamboo leaves. And the village leader was weighing it out and paying quite a considerable amount of money. This went on several mornings. I found out it was raw opium. They all wore American uniforms. The opium went to Long Tieng by helicopters, Air America helicopters on contract to the CIA. I know as a fact that shortly after Vang Pao's army was formed, the military officers gained control of the opium trade. It not only helped make them a lot of money. It also helped the villagers who needed their opium carried out, a difficult task in wartime. The officers were obviously paying a very good price because the villagers were very anxious to sell it to them."

In the early 1960s the trading chain from Long Tieng was as follows: the opium would be shipped into Vietnam on Laos Commercial Air, an airline run jointly by Ngo Dinh Nhu and the Corsican Bonaventure

Francisi. Nhu, brother of South Vietnam's President Diem, had presided over a huge expansion in Saigon's opium parlors in order to fund his own security operation. But after the Diem brothers' assassination, Marshall Nguyen Cao Ky, the man selected by the CIA as South Vietnam's new leader, began bringing the opium in from Long Tieng on Vietnamese air force planes. (Ky had previously been head of South Vietnam's air force.) A CIA man, Sam Mustard, testified to this arrangement in congressional hearings in 1968.

At the Laotian end, General Phoumi had placed Ouane Rattikone in charge of overall opium operations, and his dealings resulted in about a ton of opium a month being landed in Saigon. For his services, however, Rattikone was getting only about $200 a month from the parsimonious Phoumi. With the backing of the CIA, Rattikone rebelled and launched a coup in 1965 against Phoumi, driving his former boss into exile in Thailand.

Rattikone now wanted to drop the contract with the Corsican's Air Laos, which, despite Marshall Ky's switch, was still doing business. Rattikone's plan was to use the Royal Lao Air Force, entirely funded by the CIA. He referred to the opium shipments on the national air force as "requisitions militaires." But CIA air commander Jack Drummond objected to what he deemed a logistically inefficient use of the Royal Lao Air Force's T-28s and instead decreed that the CIA would furnish a C-47 for the dope runs "if they'd leave the T-28s alone."

That's precisely what happened. Two years later, in 1967, the CIA and USAID purchased two C-47s for Vang Pao, who opened up his own air transport company, which he called Xieng Khouang Air, known by one and all as Air Opium.

At the time the CIA decided to give Vang Pao his own airline, the CIA station chief in Vientiane was Ted Shackley, a man who had gotten his start in the CIA's Paperclip project, recruiting Nazi scientists. Before he came to Laos Shackley had headed the Agency's Miami station, where he orchestrated the repeated terror raids and assassination bids against Cuba and consorted with the local Cuban émigrés, themselves deeply involved in the drug trade. Shackley was an ardent exponent of the idea of purchasing the loyalty of CIA clients by a policy of economic assistance, calling this "the third option." Tolerance – indeed active support –

of the opium trade was therefore a proper military and diplomatic strategy. He also had a reputation for preferring to work with a team of long-term associates whom he would deploy in appropriate posts. Thus one can follow, through the decades, the Shackley team from Miami, to Laos, to Vietnam (where he later became CIA station chief in Saigon) to his private business operations in Central America. When Shackley was in Vientiane, his associate, Thomas Clines, was handling business at Long Tieng. Another CIA man, Edwin Wilson, was delivering espionage equipment to Shackley in Laos. Richard Secord was supervising CIA operations, thus participating in a bombing program depositing more high explosive on peasants and guerrillas in the Plain of Jars than did the US on Germany and Japan during the whole of World War II. Shackley, Clines, Secord and Air America cargo kicker Eugene Hasenfus show up later in our story, in Central America, once again amid the CIA's active complicity in the drug trade.

By the time Shackley moved to Saigon in 1968, the war had turned against Vang Pao. The Pathet Lao now had the upper hand. Over the next three years the story of the Hmong was one of forced marches and military defeats, and as the ground war went badly the CIA took to bombing campaigns that killed yet more Hmong. As Edgar "Pop" Buell, a missionary working in the hills, wrote in a memo to the CIA in 1968, "A short time ago we rounded up 300 fresh recruits [from the Hmong], 30 percent were 14 years old. Another 30 percent were 15 or 16. The remaining 40 percent were 45 or over. Where were the ages between? I'll tell you – they're all dead."

By the end of the war in Laos a third of the entire population of the country had become refugees. In their forced marches the Hmong experienced 30 percent casualty rates, with young children often having to put their exhausted parents, prostrated along the trail, out of their misery. By 1971 the CIA was practicing a scorched-earth policy in Hmong territory against the incoming Pathet Lao. The land was drenched with herbicides, which killed the opium crop and also poisoned the Hmong. Later, when Hmong refugees in Thai refugee camps reported this "yellow rain," CIA-patronized journalists spread the story that this was a Communist essay in biological warfare. The *Wall Street Journal* editorial page ran an extensive propaganda campaign on the issue in the early

Reagan years. Vang Pao ended up in Missoula, Montana. General Ouane Rattikone went into exile in Thailand.

This CIA-transported opium engendered an addiction rate among US servicemen in Vietnam of up to 30 percent, with the soldiers spending some $80 million a year in Vietnam on heroin. In the early 1970s some of this same heroin was being smuggled back to the US in the body bags of dead servicemen, and when DEA agent Michael Levine attempted to bust the operation, he was warned off by his superiors because it might have led to exposure of the supply line from Long Tieng.

In 1971 a second-year grad student at Yale named Alfred McCoy met the poet Allen Ginsberg at a demonstration for Bobby Seale in New Haven. Ginsberg found out that McCoy had studied up on the drug trade and also knew several Southeast Asian languages as well as the political history of the region. He encouraged McCoy to research allegations about CIA involvement in the drug trade. McCoy finished his term papers and traveled to Southeast Asia in the summer of 1971, where he embarked on a courageous and far-reaching investigation that yielded brilliant results. He interviewed troops and officers in Saigon, and there also met John Everingham, the photographer who had witnessed the opium dealings in Laos. Everingham took him back into Laos to that same village. McCoy interviewed Hmong, both villagers and chiefs. He tracked down General Ouane Rattikone in Thailand. He interviewed Pop Buell and the CIA agent William Young.

Back in the United States by the spring of 1972, McCoy had finished the first draft of what was to be the path-breaking *The Politics of Heroin in Southeast Asia.* In June of that year he was invited to testify before the US Senate by Senator William Proxmire of Wisconsin. Following that testimony, he was called by his publisher Harper & Row, demanding that he come to New York and meet with the company's president, Winthrop Knowlton. Knowlton told McCoy that Cord Meyer, a top-ranking CIA officer, had paid a visit to the owner of Harper & Row, Cass Canfield, and had told Canfield that McCoy's book posed a national security threat. Meyer demanded that Harper & Row cancel the contract. Canfield refused, but did agree to let the CIA review McCoy's book before publication.

While McCoy was deliberating what to do, the CIA's approach to

Canfield leaked out to Seymour Hersh, then working at the *New York Times*. Hersh promptly published the story. As McCoy wrote in the preface to a new edition of his book published in 1990, "Humiliated in the public arena, the CIA turned to covert harassment. Over the coming months, my federal education grant was investigated. My phones were tapped. My income tax was audited and my sources were intimidated." Some of his interpreters were threatened with assassination.

The book was duly published by Harper & Row in 1972. Amid Congressional disquiet, the CIA told the Joint Committee on Intelligence that it was pressing forward with an internal review by the CIA's Inspector General. The Agency sent twelve investigators into the field, where they spent two brief weeks in interviews. The report has never been released in its entirety, but this is its conclusion:

> No evidence that the Agency or any senior officer of the Agency has ever sanctioned, or supported drug trafficking, as a matter of policy. Also we found not the slightest suspicion, much less evidence, that any Agency officer, staff or contact, has ever been involved with the drug business. With respect to Air America, we found that it has always forbidden, as a matter of policy, the transportation of contraband goods. We believe that its Security Inspection Service which is used by the cooperating air transport company as well, is now serving as an added deterrent to drug traffickers.
>
> The one area of our activities in South East Asia that gives us some concern has to do with the agents and local officials with whom we are in contact and who have been or may still be involved in one way or another in the drug business. We are not referring here to those agents who are run as penetrations of the narcotics industry for collection of intelligence on the industry but, rather, to those with whom we are in touch in our other operations. What to do about these people is particularly troublesome in view of its implications for some of our operations, particularly in Laos. Yet their good will, if not mutual cooperation, considerably facilitates the military activities of the Agency-supported irregulars.

The report admitted that "the war has clearly been our over-riding priority in Southeast Asia and all other issues have taken second place in the scheme of things." The report also suggested that there was no financial incentive for the pilots in Air America to be involved in smuggling, since they were "making good money."

Reviews of McCoy's book were hostile, suggesting that his hundreds of pages of well-sourced interviews and reporting amounted to conspiratorial rumor-mongering by a radical opponent of the war. McCoy's charges were dismissed out of hand in the Church hearings of 1975, which concluded that allegations of drug smuggling by CIA assets and proprietaries "lacked substance."

As McCoy himself summed it up in 1990, in words which no doubt strike a chord in the heart of Gary Webb, "Although I had scored in the first engagement with a media blitz, the CIA won the longer bureaucratic battle. By silencing my sources and publicly announcing its abhorrence of drugs, the Agency convinced Congress that it had been innocent of any complicity in the Southeast Asian opium trade."

Sources

Two books served as important sources for the origins of Nixon's drug war, Edward Jay Epstein's *The Agency of Fear* and Dan Baum's *Smoke and Mirrors*. The account of the My Lai massacre was given to us by Ron Ridenhour a few months before his death. Information on the CIA's Vietnam assassination project comes from talks with Douglas Valentine and his book *The Phoenix Program*, which is one of the best histories of what really happened in Vietnam. Christopher Robbins's *Air America* remains the classic account of the CIA's airlines and his follow-up book, *Ravens*, is a useful guide to the CIA's air war in Laos. Not enough can be said about Alfred McCoy's *The Politics of Heroin in Southeast Asia*. This is a marvelously documented account of how the CIA tolerated and encouraged opium production by the Hmong, allowed it to be converted into heroin, and helped transport it to Vietnam were it was consumed by American soldiers. Andrew and Leslie Cockburn's interview with the legendary CIA operative Tony Poe is an astounding portrait of the kind of people who were running the show in Southeast Asia.

Adams, Nina S., and Alfred McCoy, eds. *Laos: War and Revolution*. Random House, 1970.
Adams, Sam. "Vietnam Cover-up: Playing War with Numbers." *Harper's*, May 1975.
——. *War of Numbers: An Intelligence Memoir*. Steerforth Press, 1994.
Andrade, Dale. *Ashes to Ashes: The Phoenix Program and the Vietnam War*. Lexington Books, 1990.
Ashley, Richard. *Heroin: The Myth and Facts*. St. Martin's Press, 1972.
Brecher, Edward. *Licit and Illicit Drugs*. Little, Brown, 1972.
Branfman, Fred, ed. *Voices from the Plain of Jars: Life Under an Air War*. Harper & Row, 1972.
Breckinridge, Scott. *CIA and the Cold War: A Memoir*. Praeger, 1993.
Brun, Dan. *Smoke and Mirrors*. Little, Brown, 1996.

Castle, Timothy. *At War in the Shadow of Vietnam: United States Military Aid to the Royal Lao Government.* Columbia Univ. Press, 1993.

Cockburn, Andrew, and Leslie Cockburn. "Guns, Drugs and the CIA." Transcript. *Frontline,* WGBH-Boston, 1988.

Corn, David. *Blond Ghost: Ted Shackley and the CIA's Crusades.* Simon and Schuster, 1994.

Dai, Bingham. *Opium Addiction in Chicago.* Patterson Smith, 1970.

DeSilva, Peer. *Sub Rosa: The CIA and the Uses of Intelligence.* Times Books, 1978.

Dommen, Arthur J. *Conflict in Laos: The Politics of Neutralization.* Praeger, 1971.

——. *Laos: Keystone of Indochina.* Westview, 1985.

Drury, Richard. *My Secret War.* St. Martin's Press, 1986.

Epstein, Edward Jay. "Against the Poppies." *Esquire,* Dec. 1974.

——. *Agency of Fear.* Verso, 1990.

Everingham, John. "Let Them Eat Bombs." *Washington Monthly,* Sept. 1972.

Haldeman, H. R. *The Haldeman Diaries: Inside the Nixon White House.* Putnam, 1994.

Hamilton-Merritt, Jane. *Tragic Mountains: The Hmong, the Americans and the Secret Wars for Laos, 1942–1992.* Indiana Univ. Press, 1993.

Hannah, Norman. *The Key to Failure: Laos and the Vietnam War.* Madison Books, 1987.

Harris, David. "Ex-Narc Tells Tales." *Rolling Stone,* Dec. 5, 1974.

Hersh, Seymour. *Cover-Up.* Random House, 1972.

——. *The Price of Power: Kissinger in the Nixon White House.* Summit Books, 1983.

Hood, Charles. "Vang Pao Guerilla General." *The Missoulian,* Nov. 21, 1976.

Isaacs, Arnold. *Without Honor: Defeat in Vietnam and Cambodia.* Johns Hopkins Univ. Press, 1983.

Johnson, Lloyd. *Drugs and American Youth.* Institute for Social Research, 1973.

Johnson, Ralph. *Phoenix/Phung Hoang: Planned Assassination or Legitimate Conflict Management?* American Univ. Press, 1982.

Lamour, Catherine, and Michel Lamberti. *The International Connection: Opium from Growers to Pushers.* Pantheon, 1974.

Lansdale, Edward. *In the Midst of Wars: An American's Mission to Southeast Asia.* Harper & Row, 1972.

Leary, William. *Perilous Missions: Civil Air Transport and CIA Covert Operations in Asia.* University of Alabama, 1986.

McCoy, Alfred with Catherine Read and Leonard Adams II. *The Politics of Heroin in Southeast Asia.* Harper and Row, 1972.

McCoy, Alfred. *The Politics of Heroin: The Complicity of the CIA in the Global Drug Trade.* Lawrence Hill, 1991.

——. "A Correspondence with the CIA." *New York Review of Books,* Sept. 21, 1972.

McGehee, Ralph. *Deadly Deceits: My 25 Years in the CIA.* Sheridan Square Publications, 1983.

Musto, David. *The American Disease.* Yale Univ. Press, 1973.

Nighswonger, William A. *Rural Pacification in Vietnam.* Praeger, 1966.

Rantala, Judy. *Laos: A Personal Portrait from the Mid-1970s.* McFarland, 1993.

Robbins, Christopher. *Air America.* Putnam, 1979.

——. *The Ravens.* Crown, 1987.

Secord, Richard and Jay Wurtz. *Honored and Betrayed.* Wiley, 1992.

Smith, Joseph. *Portrait of a Cold Warrior.* Putnam, 1976.

Snepp, Frank. *Decent Interval.* Random House, 1987.

Stieglitz, Perry. *In a Little Kingdom.* M. E. Sharpe, 1990.

Stein, Jeffrey, and Michael Klare, "From the Ashes: Phoenix." *Commonweal,* April 20, 1975.

Thee, Marek. *Notes of a Witness: Laos and the Second Indochina War.* Random House, 1973.

Valentine, Douglas. *The Phoenix Program.* Morrow, 1990.

Warner, Roger. *Backfire: The CIA's Secret War in Laos and Its Link to the War in Vietnam.* HarperCollins, 1995.

Welch, David. "Pacification in Vietnam." *Ramparts,* Oct. 1967.

Yang Dao. *Hmong at the Turning Point.* Worldbridge, 1993.

US Congress. House. Committee on International Relations. *The Narcotics Situation in Southeast Asia: The Asian Connection.* Government Printing Office, 1975.

——. Select Committee on Alcoholism and Narcotics. *Staff Report on Drug Abuse in the Military.* Government Printing Office, 1971.

US Executive Office of the President. Office for Drug Abuse Prevention. *The Vietnam Drug User Returns: Final Report.* Government Printing Office, 1974.

US Office of the Comptroller, General Accounting Office. *Federal Efforts to Combat Drug Abuse.* Government Printing Office, 1972.

11

Making Afghanistan Safe
for Opium

The first indelible image of the war in Afghanistan for many Americans was probably that of CBS anchorman Dan Rather, wrapped in the voluminous drapery of a mujahedin fighter, looking like a healthy relative of Lawrence of Arabia (albeit with hair that seemed freshly blow-dried, as some viewers were quick to point out). From his secret mountainside "somewhere in the Hindu Kush" Rather unloaded on his audience a barrowload of nonsense about the conflict. The Soviets, Rather confided portentiously, had put a bounty on his head "of many thousands of dollars." He went on, "It was the best compliment they could have given me. And having a price put on my head was a small price to pay for the truths we told about Afghanistan."

Every one of these observations turned out to be entirely false. Rather described the government of Hafizullah Amin as a "Moscow-installed puppet regime in Kabul." But Amin had closer ties to the CIA than he did to the KGB. Rather called the mujahedin the "Afghan freedom fighters ... who were engaged in a deeply patriotic fight to the death for home and hearth." The mujahedin were scarcely fighting for freedom, in any sense Rather would have been comfortable with, but instead to impose one of the most repressive brands of Islamic fundamentalism known to the world, barbarous, ignorant and notably cruel to women.

It was a "fact," Rather announced, that the Soviets had used chemical weapons against Afghan villagers. This was a claim promoted by the Reagan administration, which charged that the extraordinarily precise number of 3,042 Afghans had been killed by this yellow chemical rain, a substance that had won glorious propaganda victories in its manifestation in Laos a few years earlier, when the yellow rain turned out to be bee feces heavily loaded with pollen. As Frank Brodhead put it in the London *Guardian*, "Its composition: one part bee feces, plus many parts State Department disinformation mixed with media gullibility."

Rather claimed that the mujahedin were severely underequipped, doing their best with Kalashnikov rifles taken from dead Soviet soldiers. In fact the mujahedin were extremely well-equipped, being the recipients of CIA-furnished weapons in the most expensive covert war the Agency had ever mounted. They did carry Soviet weapons, but they came courtesy of the CIA. Rather also showed news footage that he claimed was of Soviet bombers strafing defenseless Afghan villages. This footage was staged, with the "Soviet bomber" actually a Pakistani air force plane on a training mission over northwest Pakistan.

CBS claimed to have discovered in Soviet-bombed areas stuffed animals filled with Soviet explosives, designed to blow Afghan children to bits. These booby-trapped toys had in fact been manufactured by the mujahedin for the exclusive purpose of gulling CBS News, as an entertaining article in the *New York Post* later made clear.

Rather made his heroically filmed way to Yunas Khalis, described as the leader of the Afghan warriors. In tones of awe he normally reserves for hurricanes in the Gulf of Mexico, Rather recalls in his book, *The Camera Never Blinks Twice,* "Belief in 'right' makes 'might' may have been fading in other parts of the world. In Afghanistan it was alive and well, and beating the Soviets." Khalis was a ruthless butcher, with his troops fondly boasting of their slaughter of 700 prisoners of war. He spent most of his time fighting, but the wars were not primarily with the Soviets. Instead, Khalis battled other Afghan rebel groups, the object of the conflicts being control of poppy fields and the roads and trails from them to his seven heroin labs near his headquarters in the town of Ribat al Ali. Sixty percent of Afghanistan's opium crop was cultivated in the Helmand Valley, with an irrigation infrastructure underwritten by USAID.

In his dispatches from the front Rather did mention the local opium trade, but in a remarkably disingenuous fashion. "Afghans," he said, "had turned Darra into a boom town, selling their home-grown opium for the best available weapons, then going back into Afghanistan to fight."

Now Darra is a town in northwest Pakistan where the CIA had set up a factory to manufacture Soviet-style weapons that it was giving away to all Afghan comers. The weapons factory was run under contract to Pakistani Inter-Service Intelligence (ISI). Much of the opium trucked into Darra from Afghanistan by the mujahedin was sold to the Pakistani governor of the northwest territory, Lieutenant General Fazle Huq. From this opium the heroin was refined in labs in Darra, placed on Pakistani army trucks and transported to Karachi, then shipped to Europe and the United States.

Rather belittled the Carter administration's reaction to the Soviet-backed coup in 1979, charging that Carter's response had been tepid and slow in coming. In fact, President Carter had reacted with a range of moves that should have been the envy of the Reagan hawks who, a couple of years later, were belaboring him for being a Cold War wimp. Not only did Carter withdraw the United States from the 1980 Olympics, he slashed grain sales to the Soviet Union, to the great distress of Midwestern farmers; put the SALT II treaty hold; pledged to increase the US defense budget by 5 percent a year until the Soviets pulled out of Afghanistan; and unveiled the Carter doctrine of containment in southern Asia, which CIA historian John Ranelagh says led Carter to approve "more secret CIA operations than Reagan later did."

Carter later confessed in his memoirs that he was more shaken by the invasion of Afghanistan than any other event of his presidency, including the Iranian revolution. Carter was convinced by the CIA that it could be the start of a push by the Soviets toward the Persian Gulf, a scenario that led the president to seriously consider the use of tactical nuclear weapons.

Three weeks after Soviet tanks rolled into Kabul, Carter's secretary of defense, Harold Brown, was in Beijing, arranging for a weapons transfer from the Chinese to the CIA-backed Afghani troops mustered in Pakistan. The Chinese, who were generously compensated for the deal, agreed and even consented to send military advisers. Brown worked out a similar arrangement with Egypt to buy $15 million worth of weapons. "The US contacted me," Anwar Sadat recalled shortly before his assassination. "They told me, 'Please open your stores for us so that we can give the Afghans the armaments they need to fight.' And I gave them the armaments. The transport of arms to the Afghans started from Cairo on US planes."

But few in the Carter administration believed the rebels had any chance of toppling the Soviets. Under most scenarios, the war seemed destined to be a slaughter, with civilians and the rebels paying a heavy price. The objective of the Carter doctrine was more cynical. It was to bleed the Soviets, hoping to entrap them in a Vietnam-style quagmire. The high level of civilian casualties didn't faze the architects of covert American intervention. "I decided I could live with that," recalled Carter's CIA director Stansfield Turner.

Prior to the Soviet invasion, Afghanistan barely registered as a topic of interest for the national press, surfacing in only a handful of annual newspaper stories. In December 1973, when détente was near its zenith, the *Wall Street Journal* ran a rare front-page story on the country, titled "Do the Russians Covet Afghanistan? If so, It's Hard to Figure Why." Reporter Peter Kann, later to become the *Journal*'s chairman and publisher, wrote that "great power strategists tend to think of Afghanistan as a kind of fulcrum upon which the world balance of power tips. But from close up, Afghanistan tends to look less like a fulcrum or a domino or a stepping stone than like a vast expanse of desert waste with a few fly-ridden bazaars, a fair number of feuding tribes and a lot of miserably poor people."

After the Soviet Union invaded, this wasteland swiftly acquired the status of a precious geopolitical prize. A *Journal* editorial following the Soviet takeover said Afghanistan was "more serious than a mere stepping-stone" and, in response, called for stationing of US troops in the Middle East, increased military outlays, expanded covert operations and reinstatement of draft registration. Drew Middleton, then a *New York*

Times Defense Department correspondent, filed a tremulous postinvasion analysis in January 1980: "The conventional wisdom in the Pentagon," he wrote. "is that in purely military terms, the Russians are in a far better position vis-à-vis the United States than Hitler was against Britain and France in 1939."

The Pentagon and CIA agitprop machine went into high gear: on January 3, 1980, George Wilson of the *Washington Post* reported that military leaders hoped the invasion would "help cure the Vietnam 'never again' hangover of the American public." *Newsweek* said the "Soviet thrust" represented "a severe threat" to US interests: "Control of Afghanistan would put the Russians within 350 miles of the Arabian Sea, the oil lifeline of the West and Japan. Soviet warplanes based in Afghanistan could cut the lifeline at will." The *New York Times* endorsed Carter's call for increased military spending and supported the Cruise and Trident missile programs, "faster research on the MX or some other mobile land missile," and the creation of a rapid deployment force for Third World intervention, calling the latter an "investment in diplomacy."

In sum, Afghanistan proved to be a glorious campaign for both the CIA and Defense Department, a dazzling offensive in which waves of credulous and compliant journalists were dispatched to promulgate the ludicrous proposition that the United States was under military threat. By the time Reagan assumed office, he and his CIA director William Casey saw support for their own stepped-up Afghan plan from an unlikely source, the Democrat-controlled Congress, which was pushing to double spending on the war. "It was a windfall [for the Reagan administration]," a congressional staffer told the *Washington Post*. "They'd faced so much opposition to covert action in Central America and here comes the Congress helping and throwing money at them, putting money their way and they say, 'Who are we to say no?'"

As the CIA increased its backing of the mujahedin (the CIA budget for Afghanistan finally reached $3.2 billion, the most expensive secret operation in its history) a White House member of the president's Strategic Council on Drug Abuse, David Musto, informed the administration that the decision to arm the mujahedin would misfire: "I told the Council that we were going into Afghanistan to support the opium growers in their rebellion against the Soviets. Shouldn't we try to avoid what we'd done in Laos? Shouldn't we try to pay the growers if they will eradicate their opium production? There was silence."

After issuing this warning, Musto and a colleague on the council, Joyce Lowinson, continued to question US policy, but found their queries blocked by the CIA and the State Department. Frustrated, they then turned to the *New York Times* op-ed page and wrote, on May 22, 1980: "We worry about the growing of opium in Afghanistan or Pakistan by rebel tribesmen who apparently are the chief adversaries of the Soviet troops in Afghanistan. Are we erring in befriending these tribes as we did in Laos when Air America (chartered by the Central Intelligence Agency) helped transport crude opium from certain tribal areas?" But Musto and Lowinson met with silence once again, not only from the administration but from the press. It was heresy to question covert intervention in Afghanistan.

Later in 1980, Hoag Levins, a writer for *Philadelphia Magazine,* interviewed a man he identified as a "high level" law enforcement official in the Carter administration's Justice Department and quoted him thus: "You have the administration tiptoeing around this like it's a land mine. The issue of opium and heroin in Afghanistan is explosive ... In the State of the Union speech, the president mentioned drug abuse but he was very careful to avoid mentioning Afghanistan, even though Afghanistan is where things are really happening right now ... Why aren't we taking a more critical look at the arms we are now shipping into gangs of drug runners who are obviously going to use them to increase the efficiency of their drug-smuggling operation?"

The DEA was well aware that the mujahedin rebels were deeply involved in the opium trade. The drug agency's reports in 1980 showed that Afghan rebel incursions from their Pakistan bases into Soviet-held positions were "determined in part by opium planting and harvest seasons." The numbers were stark and forbidding. Afghan opium production tripled between 1979 and 1982. There was evidence that by 1981 the Afghan heroin producers had captured 60 percent of the heroin market in Western Europe and the United States (these are UN and DEA figures).

In 1971, during the height of the CIA's involvement in Laos, there were about 500,000 heroin addicts in the United States. By the mid- to late 1970s this total had fallen to 200,000. But in 1981 with the new flood of Afghan heroin and consequent low prices, the heroin addict population rose to 450,000. In New York City in 1979 alone (the year that the flow of arms to the mujahedin began), heroin-related drug deaths increased by 77 percent. The only publicly acknowledged US casualties on the Afghan battlefields were some Black Muslims who journeyed to the Hindu Kush from the United States to fight on the Prophet's behalf. But the drug casualties inside the US from the secret CIA war, particularly in the inner cities, numbered in the thousands, plus untold social blight and suffering.

Since the seventeenth century opium poppies have been grown in the so-called Golden Crescent, where the highlands of Afghanistan, Pakistan and Iran all converge. For nearly four centuries this was an internal market. By the 1950s very little opium was produced in either Afghanistan or Pakistan, with perhaps 2,500 acres in these two countries under cultivation. The fertile growing fields of Afghanistan's Helmand Valley, by the 1980s under intensive opium poppy cultivation, were covered with vineyards, wheat fields and cotton plantations.

In Iran, the situation was markedly different in the early 1950s. The country, dominated by British and US oil companies and intelligence agencies, was producing 600 tons of opium a year and had 1.3 million opium addicts, second only to China where, at the same moment, the western opium imperialists still held sway. Then, in 1953, Mohammed Mossadegh, Iran's nationalist equivalent of China's Sun Yat-sen, won elections and immediately moved to suppress the opium trade. Within a few weeks, US Secretary of State John Foster Dulles was calling Mossadegh a madman, and Dulles's brother Allen, head of the CIA, dispatched Kermit Roosevelt to organize a coup against him. In August 1953 Mossadegh was overthrown, the Shah was installed by the CIA, and the oil and opium fields of Iran were once again in friendly hands. Production continued unabated until the assumption of power in 1979 of the Ayatollah Khomeini, at which point Iran had a very serious opium problem in terms of the addiction of its own population. Unlike the mujahedin chieftains, the Ayatollah was a strict constructionist of Islamic law on the matter of intoxicants: addicts and dealers faced the death penalty. Opium production in Iran dropped drastically.

In Afghanistan in the 1950s and 1960s, the relatively sparse opium trade was controlled by the royal family, headed by King Mohammed Zahir, The large feudal estates all had their opium fields, primarily to feed domestic consumption of the drug. In April 1978 a populist coup overthrew the regime of Mohammed Daoud, who had formed an alliance with the Shah of Iran. The Shah had shoveled money in Daoud's direction – $2 billion on one report – and the Iranian secret police; the Savak, were imported to train Daoud's internal security force. The new Afghan government was led by Noor Mohammed Taraki. The Taraki administration moved toward land reform, hence an attack on the opium-growing feudal estates. Taraki went to the UN, where he requested and received loans for crop substitution for the poppy fields.

Taraki also pressed hard against opium production in the border areas held by fundamentalists, since the latter were using opium revenues to finance attacks on the Afghan central government, which they regarded as an unwholesome incarnation of modernity that allowed women to go to school and outlawed arranged marriages and the bride price.

By the spring of 1979 the character of Dan Rather's heroes, the mujahedin, was also beginning to emerge. The *Washington Post* reported that the mujahedin liked to "torture their victims by first cutting off their noses, ears and genitals, then removing one slice of skin after another." Over that year the mujahedin evinced particular animosity toward westerners, killing six West Germans and a Canadian tourist and severely beating a US military attaché. It's also ironic that in that year the mujahedin were getting money not only from the CIA but from Libya's Moammar Qaddaffi, who sent $250,000 in their direction.

In the summer of 1979, over six months before the Soviets moved in, the US State Department produced a memorandum making clear how it saw the stakes, no matter how modern-minded Taraki might be, or how feudal the mujahedin: "The United States' larger interest ... would be served by the demise of the Taraki-Amin regime, despite whatever setbacks this might mean for future social and economic reforms in Afghanistan." The report continued, "The overthrow of the DRA [Democratic Republic of Afghanistan] would show the rest of the world, particularly the Third World, that the Soviets' view of the socialist course of history as being inevitable is not accurate."

Hard pressed by conservative forces in Afghanistan, Taraki appealed to the Soviets for help, which they declined to furnish on the grounds that this was exactly what their mutual enemies were waiting for.

In September 1979 Taraki was killed in a coup organized by Afghan military officers. Hafizullah Amin was installed as president. He had impeccable western credentials, having been to Columbia University in New York and the University of Wisconsin. Amin had served as the president of the Afghan Students Association, which had been funded by the Asia Foundation, a CIA pass-through group, or front. After the coup Amin began meeting regularly with US Embassy officials at a time when the US was arming Islamic rebels in Pakistan. Fearing a fundamentalist, US-backed regime pressing against its own border, the Soviet Union invaded Afghanistan in force on December 27, 1979.

Then began the Carter-initiated CIA buildup that so worried White House drug expert David Musto. In a replication of what happened following the CIA-backed coup in Iran, the feudal estates were soon back in opium production and the crop-substitution program ended.

Because Pakistan had a nuclear program, the US had a foreign aid ban on the country. This was soon lifted it as the waging of a proxy war in Afghanistan became prime policy. In fairly short order, without any discernible slowdown in its nuclear program, Pakistan became the third largest recipient of US aid worldwide, right behind Israel and Egypt. Arms poured into Karachi from the US and were shipped up to Peshawar by the National Logistics Cell, a military unit controlled by Pakistan's secret police, the ISI. From Peshawar those guns that weren't simply sold to any and all customers (the Iranians got 16 Stinger missiles, one of which was used against a US helicopter in the Gulf) were divvied out by the ISI to the Afghan factions.

Though the US press, Dan Rather to the fore, portrayed the mujahedin as a unified force of freedom fighters, the fact (unsurprising to anyone with an inkling of Afghan history) was that the mujahedin consisted of at least seven warring factions, all battling for territory and control of the opium trade. The ISI gave the bulk of the arms – at one count 60 percent – to a particularly fanatical fundamentalist and woman-hater Gulbuddin Hekmatyar, who made his public debut at the

University of Kabul by killing a leftist student. In 1972 Hekmatyar fled to Pakistan, where he became an agent of the ISI. He urged his followers to throw acid in the faces of women not wearing the veil, kidnapped rival leaders, and built up his CIA-furnished arsenal against the day the Soviets would leave and the war for the mastery of Afghanistan would truly break out.

Using his weapons to get control of the opium fields, Hekmatyar and his men would urge the peasants, at gun point, to increase production. They would collect the raw opium and bring it back to Hekmatyar's six heroin factories in the town of Koh-i-Soltan. One of Hekmatyar's chief rivals in the mujahedin, Mullah Nassim, controlled the opium poppy fields in the Helmand Valley, producing 260 tons of opium a year. His brother, Mohammed Rasul, defended this agricultural enterprise by stating, "We must grow and sell opium to fight our holy war against the Russian nonbelievers." Despite this well-calculated pronouncement, they spent almost all their time fighting their fellow-believers, using the weapons sent them by the CIA to try to win the advantage in these internecine struggles. In 1989 Hekmatyar launched an assault against Nassim, attempting to take control of the Helmand Valley. Nassim fought him off, but a few months later Hekmatyar successfully engineered Nassim's assassination when he was holding the post of deputy defense minister in the provisional post-Soviet Afghan government. Hekmatyar now controlled opium growing in the Helmand Valley.

American DEA agents were fully apprised of the drug running of the mujahedin in concert with Pakistani intelligence and military leaders. In 1983 the DEA's congressional liaison, David Melocik, told a congressional committee, "You can say the rebels make their money off the sale of opium. There's no doubt about it. These rebels keep their cause going through the sale of opium." But talk about "the cause" depending on drug sales was nonsense at that particular moment. The CIA was paying for everything regardless. The opium revenues were ending up in offshore accounts in the Habib Bank, one of Pakistan's largest, and in the accounts of BCCI, founded by Agha Hasan Abedi, who began his banking career at Habib. The CIA was simultaneously using BCCI for its own secret transactions.

The DEA had evidence of over forty heroin syndicates operating in

Pakistan in the mid-1980s during the Afghan war, and there was evidence of more than 200 heroin labs operating in northwest Pakistan. Even though Islamabad houses one of the largest DEA offices in Asia, no action was ever taken by the DEA agents against any of these operations. An Interpol officer told the journalist Lawrence Lifschultz, "It is very strange that the Americans, with the size of their resources, and political power they possess in Pakistan, have failed to break a single case. The explanation cannot be found in a lack of adequate police work. They have had some excellent men working in Pakistan." But working in the same offices as those DEA agents were five CIA officers who, so one of the DEA agents later told the *Washington Post,* ordered them to pull back their operations in Afghanistan and Pakistan for the duration of the war.

Those DEA agents were well aware of the drug-tainted profile of a firm the CIA was using to funnel cash to the mujahedin, namely Shakarchi Trading Company. This Lebanese-owned company had been the subject of a long-running DEA investigation into money laundering. One of Shakarchi's chief clients was Yasir Musullulu, who had once been nabbed attempting to deliver an 8.5-ton shipment of Afghan opium to members of the Gambino crime syndicate in New York City. A DEA memo noted that Shakarchi mingled "the currency of heroin, morphine base, and hashish traffickers with that of jewelers buying gold on the black market and Middle Eastern arms traffickers."

In May 1984 Vice President George Bush journeyed to Pakistan to confer with General Zia al Huq and other ranking members of the Pakistani regime. At the time, Bush was the head of President Reagan's National Narcotics Border Interdiction System. In this latter function, one of Bush's first moves was to expand the role of the CIA in drug operations. He gave the Agency primary responsibility in the use of, and control over, drug informants. The operational head of this task force was retired Admiral Daniel J. Murphy. Murphy pushed for access to intelligence on drug syndicates but complained that the CIA was forever dragging its feet. "I didn't win," he said later to the *New York Times*. "I didn't get as much effective participation from the CIA as I wanted." Another member of the task force put it more bluntly, "The CIA could be of value, but you need a change of values and attitude. I don't know of a single thing they've ever given us that was useful."

Bush certainly knew well that Pakistan had become the source for most of the high-grade heroin entering Western Europe and the United States and that the generals with whom he was consorting were deeply involved in the drug trade. But the vice president, who proclaimed later that "I will never bargain with drug dealers on US or foreign soil," used his journey to Pakistan to praise the Zia regime for its unflinching support for the War on Drugs. (Amid such rhetorical excursions he did find time, it has to be said, to extract from Zia a contract to buy $40 million worth of gas turbines made by the General Electric Co.)

Predictably, through the 1980s the Reagan and Bush administrations went to great lengths to pin the blame for the upswing in Pakistani heroin production on the Soviet generals in Kabul. "The regime maintains an absolute indifference to any measures to control poppy," Reagan's attorney general Edwin Meese declared during a visit to Islamabad in March 1986. "We strongly believe that there is actually encouragement, at least tacitly, over growing opium poppy."

Meese knew better. His own Justice Department had been tracking the import of drugs from Pakistan since at least 1982 and was well aware that the trade was controlled by Afghan rebels and the Pakistani military. A few months after Meese's speech in Pakistan, the US Customs Office nabbed a Pakistani man named Abdul Wali as he tried to unload more than a ton of hash and a smaller amount of heroin into the United States at Port Newark, New Jersey. The Justice Department informed the press that Wali headed a 50,000-member organization in northwest Pakistan – but Deputy Attorney General Claudia Flynn refused to reveal the group's identity. Another federal official told the Associated Press that Wali was a top leader of the mujahedin.

It was also known to US officials that people on intimate terms with President Zia were making fortunes in the opium trade. The word "fortune" here is no exaggeration, since one such Zia associate had $3 billion in his BCCI accounts. In 1983, a year before George Bush's visit to Pakistan, one of President Zia's doctors, a Japanese herbalist named Hisayoshi Maruyama was arrested in Amsterdam packing 17.5 kilos of high-grade heroin manufactured in Pakistan out of Afghan opium. At the time of his arrest he was disguised as a boy scout.

Interrogated by DEA agents after his arrest, Maruyama said that he was just a courier for Mirza Iqbal Baig, a man whom Pakistani customs agents described as "the most active dope dealer in the country." Baig was on close terms with the Zia family and other ranking officials in the government. He had twice been a target of the DEA, whose agents were told not to pursue investigations of him because of his ties to the Zia government. A top Pakistani lawyer, Said Sani Ahmed, told the BBC that this was standard procedure in Pakistan: "We may have evidence against a particular individual, but still our law-enforcing agencies cannot lay hands on such people, because they are forbidden to act by their superiors. The real culprits have enough money and resources. Frankly, they are enjoying some sort of immunity."

Baig was one of the tycoons of the Pakistani city of Lahore, owning cinemas, shopping centers, factories and a textile mill. He wasn't indicted on drug charges until 1992, after the fall of the Zia regime, when a US federal court in Brooklyn indicted him for heroin trafficking. The US finally exerted enough pressure on Pakistan to have him arrested in 1993; as of the spring of 1998 he was in prison in Pakistan.

One of Baig's partners (as described in *Newsweek*) in his drug business was Haji Ayub Afridi, a close ally of President Zia, who had served in the Pakistani General Assembly. Afridi lives thirty-five miles outside Peshawar in a large compound sealed off by 20-foot-high walls topped with concertina-wire and with defenses including an anti-aircraft battery and a private army of tribesmen. Afridi was said to be in charge of purchasing raw opium from the Afghan drug lords, while Baig looked after logistics and shipping to Europe and the United States. In 1993 Afridi was alleged to have put out a contract on the life of a DEA agent working in Pakistan.

Another case close to the Zia government involved the arrest on drug charges of Hamid Hasnain, the vice president of Pakistan's largest financial house, the Habib Bank. Hasnain's arrest became the centerpiece of a scandal known as the "Pakistani League affair." The drug ring was investigated by a dogged Norwegian investigator named Olyvind Olsen. On December 13, 1983 Norwegian police seized 3.5 kilos of heroin at Oslo airport in the luggage of a Pakistani named Raza Qureishi. In exchange for a reduced sentence Qureishi agreed to name his suppliers to

Olsen, the narcotics investigator. Shortly after his interview with Qureishi, Olsen flew to Islamabad to ferret out the other members of the heroin syndicate. For more than a year Olsen pressured Pakistan's Federal Investigate Agency (FIA) to arrest the three men Qureishi had fingered: Tahir Butt, Munawaar Hussain, and Hasnain. All were associates of Baig and Zia. It wasn't until Olsen threatened to publicly condemn the FIA's conduct that the Agency took any action: finally, on October 25, 1985 the FIA arrested the three men. When the Pakistani agents picked up Hasnain they were assailed with a barrage of threats. Hasnain spoke of "dire consequences" and claimed to be "like a son" to President Zia. Inside Hasnain's suitcase FIA agents discovered records of the ample bank accounts of President Zia plus those of Zia's wife and daughter.

Immediately after learning of Hasnain's arrest, Zia's wife, who was in Egypt at the time, telephoned the head of the FIA. The president's wife imperiously demanded the release of her family's "personal banker." It turned out that Hasnain not only attended to the secret financial affairs of the presidential family, but also of the senior Pakistani generals, who were skimming money off the arms imports from the CIA and making millions from the opium traffic. A few days after his wife's call, President Zia himself was on the phone to the FIA, demanding that the investigators explain the circumstances surrounding Hasnain's arrest. Zia soon arranged for Hasnain to be released on bail pending trial. When Qureishi, the courier, took the stand to testify against Hasnain, the banker and his co-defendant hurled death threats against the witness in open court, prompting a protest from the Norwegian investigator, who threatened to withdraw from the proceedings.

Eventually the judge in the case clamped down, revoking Hasnain's bail and handing him a stiff prison term after his conviction. But Hasnain was just a relatively small fish who went to prison while guilty generals went free. "He's been made a scapegoat," Munir Bhatti told journalist Lawrence Lifschultz, "The CIA spoiled the case. The evidence was distorted. There was no justification in letting off the actual culprits who include senior personalities in this country. There was evidence in this case identifying such people."

Such were the men to whom the CIA was paying $3.2 billion to run the Afghan war, and no person better epitomizes this relationship than Lieutenant General Fazle Huq, who oversaw military operations in northwest Pakistan for General Zia, including the arming of the muja-hedin who were using the region as a staging area for their raids. It was Huq who ensured that his ally Hekmatyar received the bulk of the CIA arms shipments, and it was also Huq who oversaw and protected the operations of the 200 heroin labs within his jurisdiction. Huq had been identified in 1982 by Interpol as a key player in the Afghan–Pakistani opium trade. The Pakistani opposition leaders referred to Huq as Paki-stan's Noriega. He had been protected from drug investigations by Zia and the CIA and later boasted that with these connections he could get away "with blue murder."

Like other narco-generals in the Zia regime, Huq was also on close terms with Agha Hassan Abedi, the head of the BCCI. Abedi, Huq and Zia would dine together nearly every month, and conferred several times with Reagan's CIA director William Casey. Huq had a BCCI ac-count worth $3 million. After Zia was assassinated in 1988 by a bomb planted (probably by senior military officers) in his presidential plane, Huq lost some of his official protection, and he was soon arrested for ordering the murder of a Shi'ite cleric.

After Prime Minister Benazir Bhutto was deposed, her replacement Ishaq Khan swiftly released Huq from prison. In 1991 Huq was shot to death, probably in revenge for the cleric's death. The opium general was given a state funeral, where he was eulogized by Ishaq Khan as "a great soldier and competent administrator who played a commendable role in Pakistan's national progress."

Benazir Bhutto had swept to power in 1988 amid fierce vows to clean up Pakistan's drug-sodden corruption, but it wasn't long before her own regime became the focus of serious charges. In 1989 the US Drug En-forcement Agency came across information that Benazir's husband, Asif Ali Zardari, may have been financing large shipments of heroin from Pakistan to Great Britain and the United States. The DEA assigned one of its agents, a man named John Banks, to work undercover in Paki-stan. Banks was a former British mercenary who had worked under-cover for Scotland Yard in big international drug cases.

While in Pakistan, Banks claims he posed as a member of the Mafia and that he had met with Bhutto and her husband at their home in Sind. Banks further claims that he traveled with Zadari to Islamabad, where he secretly recorded five hours of conversation between Zadari, a Pakistani air force general and a Pakistani banker. The men discussed the logistics of transporting heroin to the US and to Britain: "We talked about how they were going to ship the drugs to America in a metal cutter," Banks said in 1996. "They told me that the United Kingdom was another area where they had shipped heroin and hashish on a regular basis." The British Customs Office had also been monitoring Zadari for dope running: "We received intelligence from about three or four sources, about his alleged involvement as a financier," a retired British customs officer told the *Financial Times*. "This was all reported to British intelligence." The customs official says his government failed to act on this report. Similarly, Banks asserts that the CIA halted the DEA's investigation of Zardari. All this emerged when Bhutto's government fell for the second time, in 1996, on charges of corruption lodged primarily against Zardari, who is now in prison for his role in the murder of his brother-in-law Murtaza. Zardari also stands accused of embezzling more than $1 billion in government funds.

In 1991 Nawz Sharif says that while he served as prime minister he was approached by two Pakistani generals – Aslam Beg, chief of staff for the army, and Asad Durrani, head of the ISI – with a plan to fund dozens of covert operations through the sale of heroin. "General Durrani told me, 'We have a blueprint ready for your approval,' Sharif explained to *Washington Post* reporter John Ward Anderson in 1994. "I was totally flabbergasted. Both Beg and Durrani insisted that Pakistan's name would not be cited at any place because the whole operation would be carried out by trustworthy third parties. Durrani then went on to list a series of covert military operations in desperate need of money." Sharif said that he rejected the plan, but believes it was put in place when Bhutto resumed power.

The impact of the Afghan war on Pakistan's addiction rates was even more drastic than the surge in heroin addiction in the US and Europe. Before the CIA program began, there were fewer than 5,000 heroin addicts in Pakistan. By 1996, according to the United Nations, there were more than 1.6 million. The Pakistani representative to the UN Commission on Narcotics, Raoolf Ali Khan, said in 1993 that "there is no branch of government where drug corruption doesn't pervade." As an example he pointed to the fact that Pakistan spends only $1.8 million a year on anti-drug efforts, with an allotment of $1,000 to purchase gasoline for its seven trucks.

By 1994 the value of the heroin trade in Pakistan was twice the amount of the government's budget. A Western diplomat told the *Washington Post* in that year that "when you get to the stage where narco-traffickers have more money than the government it's going to take remarkable efforts and remarkable people to turn it around." The magnitude of commitment required is illustrated by two episodes. In 1991 the largest drug bust in world history occurred on the road from Peshawar to Kharachi. Pakistani customs officers seized 3.5 tons of heroin and 44 tons of hashish. Several days later half the hashish and heroin had vanished along with the witnesses. The suspects, four men with ties to Pakistani intelligence, had "mysteriously escaped," to use the words of a Pakistani customs officer. In 1993 Pakistani border guards seized 8 tons of hashish and 1.7 tons of heroin. When the case was turned over to the Pakistani narcotics control board, the entire staff went on vacation to avoid being involved in the investigation. No one was disciplined or otherwise inconvenienced and the narco-traffickers got off scot free. Even the CIA was eventually forced to admit in a 1994 report to Congress that heroin had become the "life blood of the Pakistani economy and political system."

In February 1989 Mikhail Gorbachev pulled the Soviet troops out of Afghanistan, and asked the US to agree to an embargo on the provision of weapons to any of the Afghan mujahedin factions, who were preparing for another phase of internecine war for control of the country. President Bush refused, thus ensuring a period of continued misery and horror for most Afghans. The war had already turned half the population into refugees, and seen 3 million wounded and more than a million killed. The proclivities of the mujahedin at this point are illustrated by a couple of anecdotes. The Kabul correspondent of the *Far Eastern Economic Review* reported in 1989 the mujahedin's treatment of Soviet prisoners: "One group was killed, skinned and hung up in a butcher's shop. One captive found himself the center of attraction in a game of buzkashi, that rough-and-tumble form of Afghan polo in which a headless goat is usually the ball. The captive was used instead. Alive. He was literally torn to pieces." The CIA also had evidence that its freedom fighters had doped up more than 200 Soviet soldiers with heroin and locked them in animal cages where, the *Washington Post* reported in 1990, they led "lives of indescribable horror."

In September 1996 the Taliban, fundamentalists nurtured originally in Pakistan as creatures of both the ISI and the CIA, seized power in Kabul, whereupon Mullah Omar, their leader, announced that all laws inconsistent with the Muslim Sharia would be changed. Women would be forced to assume the *chador* and remain at home, with total segregation of the sexes and women kept out of hospitals, schools and public bathrooms. The CIA continued to support these medieval fanatics who, according to Emma Bonino, the European Union's commissioner for humanitarian affairs, were committing "gender genocide."

One law at odds with the Sharia that the Taliban had no apparent interest in changing was the prophet's injunction against intoxicants. In fact, the Taliban urged its Afghan farmers to increase their production of opium. One of the Taliban leaders, the "drug czar" Abdul Rashid, noted, "If we try to stop this [opium farming] the people will be against us." By the end 1996, according to the UN, Afghan opium production had reached 2,000 metric tons. There were an estimated 200,000 families in Afghanistan working in the opium trade. The Taliban were in control of the 96 percent of all Afghan land in opium cultivation and imposed a tax on opium production and a road toll on trucks carrying the crop.

In 1997 an Afghan opium farmer gave an ironic reply to Jimmy Carter's brooding on whether to use nuclear weapons as part of a response to the Soviet invasion of Afghanistan in 1979. Amhud Gul told a reporter from the *Washington Post,* "We are cultivating this [that is, opium] and exporting this as an atom bomb." CIA intervention had worked its magic once again. By 1994, Afghanistan, according to the UN drug control program had surpassed Burma as the world's number one supplier of raw opium.

Sources

To date, the war in Afghanistan has been the CIA's most expensive covert action. But it has received a paltry degree of critical scrutiny. This is hardly shocking. From the beginning, Afghanistan was a bipartisan adventure. Nobody in the US press wrote much of anything about Afghanistan until the Soviet invasion. Then suddenly Afghanistan looked like it might become the Soviets' Vietnam and everyone jumped on board. Today newspapers occasionally run a story about some repressive new decree or crackdown by the Taliban. But these stories hardly ever mention where the Taliban came from and how they got their guns. In the spring of 1998, the US press was filled with reports on the renegade nature of the government in Pakistan, which had recently conducted a round of underground nuclear tests in response to similar testing by the Pakistanis' neighbor, India. Again few stories looked behind the official text to disclose the true nature of the US relationship with the Pakistani military and secret police.

Dan Rather certainly wasn't the only media pawn of the CIA, but he took their Afghan project to prime time. Rather published an account of his ridiculous venture to the Hindu Kush in 1994. Though more than a decade had passed, Rather seems not to have read a thing about Afghanistan in the interim. After the massacres, the dope- and gun-running and the abuse of women, Rather still viewed his friends in the mujahedin as the ascetic and moral freedom fighters of old. Rather's cheerleading is almost matched in the print media by *New York Times* reporter John Burns, author of an article strangely devoid of any sense of historical irony, in *New York Times Magazine* titled "Afghans: Now They Blame America." There was some excellent reporting on Afghanistan and the real context of the war, notably by Tim Weiner and Lawrence Lifschultz. The reference to drug policy expert David Musto's protest against Carter's Afghan policy derives from Al McCoy, whose book has a brief, though information-packed, section on opium trafficking in the Golden Crescent. Bob Woodward's *Veil* describes William Casey's Afghan strategy. Martin Lee and Norman Solomon deconstruct the biased newspaper reporting during the early stages of the war in their book *Unreliable Sources*. We also turned frequently to Peter Truell and Larry Gurwin's *False Profits*, the best account of the BCCI scandal.

Adams, James Ring, and Douglas Frantz. *A Full Service Bank*. Pocket Books, 1992.

Ali, Tariq. *Can Pakistan Survive?* Penguin, 1983.

Anderson, John Ward and Kamran Khan. "Heroin Plan by Top Pakistanis Alleged; Former Prime Minister Says Drug Deals Were to Pay for Covert Military Operations." *Washington Post,* Sept. 12, 1994.

Associated Press. "Taliban Religious Police Jail Seven Singers." *Washington Post,* Nov. 30, 1997.

——. "Evidence Found of Mass Killings in Afghanistan." *Washington Post,* Dec. 14, 1997.

Bhutto, Benazir. *Daughter of the East*. Hamish Hamilton, 1988.

Blum, William. *Killing Hope*. Common Courage, 1995.

Boustany, Nora. "A Visit from the Men (Only) Who Now Rule Afghanistan." *Washington Post,* Feb. 26, 1997.

Bradsher, Henry. *Afghanistan and the Soviet Invasion*. Duke Univ. Press, 1985.

Brister, Robert. "Afghanistan in Perspective." *Churchman,* March 1980.

Burns, John. "Afghans: Now They Blame America." *New York Times Magazine,* Feb. 4, 1990.

Carter, Jimmy. *Keeping Faith: Memoirs of a President*. Bantam, 1982.

Cooper, Kenneth. "Afghanistan's Neighbors Wary of Taliban Militia." *Washington Post,* May 31, 1997.

——. "For Afghan Rivals, Warrior Traditions Complicate Unity." *Washington Post,* June 4, 1997.

——. "Afghans Cultivate Islamic State, But Ignore Illicit Harvest." *Washington Post,* May 11, 1997.

Evans, Kathy. "The Tribal Trail." *Newsline,* Dec. 1989.

Galster, Steven. "Biography: Hekmatyar, Gulbuddin." National Security Archives, 1990.

Hammond, Thomas. *Red Flag over Afghanistan*. Westview, 1984.

Hammer, Joshua. "Poppy Fight." *Newsweek*, Sept. 18, 1989.

Harrison, Selig. "The Shah, Not the Kremlin, Touched Off the Afghan Coup." *Washington Post,* May 13, 1979.

——. "Did Moscow Fear an Afghan Tito?" *New York Times,* Jan. 13, 1980.

Hirst, David, and Irene Bacon. *Sadat*. Faber and Faber, 1981.

Hussain, Zahid. "Narcopower: Pakistan's Parallel Government." *Newsline,* Dec. 1989.

Isikoff, Michael. "International Opium Crop Production up 8 Percent Last Year; Despite US Efforts Against Poppy Crop, Concern Grows About Expanding Heroin Market." *Washington Post,* March 1, 1992.

Kamm, Henry. "Afghan Guerrillas Hijack Convoy of UN Aid for Rival Rebel Area." *New York Times,* Dec. 1, 1988.

Khan, Afzal. "Afghanistan's Holy War." *National Review,* Feb. 1980.

LaGesse, David and George Rodriguez. "Drug War Often Finds CIA at Odds with DEA." *Dallas Morning News,* Feb. 16, 1997.

Lee, Martin A., and Norman Solomon. *Unreliable Sources: A Guide to Detecting Bias in the Media*. Lyle Stuart, 1990.

Levins, Hoag. "The Kabul Connection." *Philadelphia Magazine*. March 1980.

Lifschultz, Lawrence. "Dangerous Liaison: The CIA–ISI Connection." *Newsline,* Nov. 1989.

McCoy, Alfred. *The Politics of Heroin: CIA Complicity in the Global Drug Trade*. Lawrence Hill, 1991.

Morgan, Dan, and David Ottaway. "Women's Fury Toward Taliban Stalls Pipeline; Afghan Plan Snagged in US Political Issues." *Washington Post,* Jan. 11, 1998.

Naylor, R. T. *Hot Money*. Simon and Schuster, 1987.

Pear, Robert. "Thirty Afghan Rebels Slain by Rival Band." *New York Times,* July 18, 1989.

Prados, John. *The Presidents' Secret Wars*. Ivan R. Dee, 1996.

Rather, Dan and Mickey Hershkowitz. *The Camera Never Blinks Twice*. Morrow, 1994.

Roy, Oliver. *Islam and Resistance in Afghanistan*. Cambridge Univ. Press, 1989.

Reuters. "Afghans' Executions Described by UN Official." *Washington Post,* Dec. 17, 1997.

Rupert, James, and Steve Coll. "US Declines to Probe Afghan Drug Trade; Rebels, Pakistani Officers Implicated." *Washington Post,* May 13, 1990.

Shawcross, William. "Where the Music has Died and the Women Walk Softly." *Washington Post,* Nov. 23, 1997.

Thornton, Mary. "Sales of Opium Reportedly Fund Afghan Rebels." *Washington Post,* Dec. 17, 1983.

Timmerman, Kenneth. *The Death Lobby.* Houghton Miflin, 1991.

Witkin, Gordon, and Jennifer Griffin. "The New Opium Wars." *US News and World Report.* Oct. 10, 1994.

US Congress. Senate. Committee on Foreign Affairs. *The BCCI Affair: Final Report.* Government Printing Office, 1992.

US Department of State. *International Narcotics Control Strategy Report.* Government Printing Office, 1984.

———. *International Narcotics Control Strategy Report.* Government Printing Office, 1986.

———. *International Narcotics Control Strategy Report.* Government Printing Office, 1990.

———. *International Narcotics Control Strategy Report.* Government Printing Office, 1995.

US Office of the Comptroller General, General Accounting Office. *Drug Control: US Support Efforts in Burma, Pakistan and Thailand.* Government Printing Office. Feb. 1988.

Vornberger, William. "Afghan Rebels and Drugs." *Covert Action Information Bulletin.* Summer 1987.

Weiner, Tim. *Blank Check.* Warner Books, 1990.

Woolridge, Mike. "Afghanistan's Opium Harvest." (Transcript) *BBC News,* May 9, 1998.

Yousai, Mohammed, and M. Adkin. *The Beartrap: Afghanistan's Untold Story.* Cooper, 1992.

12

The CIA, Drugs and
Central America

Oliver North, Drugs and the Great Senate Race

The longest story the *Washington Post* ever ran on allegations of drugs-for-arms shipments involving the Contras (aside from its attacks on Gary Webb) came in the final moments of Oliver North's 1994 Senate bid in Virginia. The *Post* disliked North as much as, probably even more than, Webb, and since the best way to put the boot into Candidate North was to say that he had turned a blind eye to drug smuggling by the Contras, the *Post* endorsed the story of Contra drug running, exactly the reverse of what it did when it was putting the boot into Gary Webb two years later. One can almost feel sorry for North amid these whimsical changes in direction on the part of the *Post,* were it not for the central lack of likeability in the cocky Colonel. But all the same, North was obeying not only the directives of his president to flout the will of Congress, but also the urgings of major papers like the *Post,* which wanted to see the Sandinistas "pressured," harried, sabotaged and ultimately driven to the wall – with all due discretion.

For a large portion of the 1980s there was a pretense on the part of the establishment press that there were somehow legitimate means of bearing down on Nicaragua without instructing CIA-trained teams of killers to murder schoolteachers and rural organizers. But when it turned out that the effective means of pressure were illegal under national and international laws, the establishment press by and large simply turned a blind eye to what was going on.

This chapter mostly concerns itself with the CIA-supervised efforts of the Contras to raise money by running drugs into the United States. The story was there to be found, and some enterprising journalists duly dug it up and managed to get it out into the light of day. But there were scores of other stories of the US war on Nicaragua much easier to find but also ignored by most newspapers: the consistent flouting by the US government of the World Court rulings against it on the trade embargo – a particularly deadly weapon against Nicaragua; or the ludicrous campaign by the Reagan administration to suggest that the Sandinistas were set to invade Honduras.

The lesson of this history is one kindred to our observation in the first paragraph of the preface of this book. Just as one should reject the idea of a "rogue CIA," perverting or betraying the intentions of an honorable government, so one should banish illusions of a "rogue press" fulfilling its watchdog role by barking furiously at the crimes of government. Loyal and obedient in its function, just as the CIA has been, the US corporate papers behave, in the main and with a few exceptions, like most well-fed and prosperous watchdogs, fast asleep in their kennels, eyes firmly closed.

Now back to the cocky Colonel.

It was the end of October 1994, the race was down to the wire, and North was thought to have a pretty good shot at taking out incumbent Chuck Robb. Then, on Saturday, October 22, the *Post* ran a story of around 3,700 words under the headline "North Didn't Relay Drug Tips." The *Post*'s reporter, Lorraine Adams, described entries from North's diaries in the year 1985, when he had been working at the National Security Council in Ronald Reagan's White House. Some of the diaries had become public during his trial, and other important sections had been disinterred by the National Security Archive through the Freedom of Information Act. The *Post* also used memos to North from Robert Owen, North's contact in Central America with the Contras. On April 15, 1985, for example, Owen wrote a lengthy memo to North expressing his concern that several of the men Adolfo Calero, the lead the main

Contra organization, the FDN, had tapped to head up a new Contra division in Costa Rica were "involved with drug running." Of José Robelo, Owen wrote: "Potential involvement with drug running and the sale of goods provided by the USG [US government]." Of the other, Sebastian González, Owen warned: "Now involved in drug running out of Panama." "These are just some of the people Sparkplug [Owen's code name for Adolfo Calero] and others should be worried about." González was an associate of Norwin Meneses.

On July 12, 1985, North's notebook records a conversation with Richard Secord, who had been recruited by North to run the Contra weapons supply operation (recall that Secord was a veteran of the CIA's Southeast Asia operation run by Ted Shackley). The conversation was about an arms warehouse in Honduras from which the Contras were buying weapons. Secord tells North that "14 Million to finance [the arms] came from drugs."

On August 9, 1985, North notes a conversation with Robert Owen about an airplane being used by Mario Calero, brother of Adolfo, and also chief of logistics for the Contras. Owen had told North that Calero was using a plane based in New Orleans to ship supplies to Contra camps in Honduras. North's diary entry says, "Honduran DC-6 which is being used for runs out of New Orleans is probably being used for drug runs into US."

On February 10, 1986, Robert Owen sends North a memo stating that a plane being used for humanitarian aid to the Contras had also been used to run drugs. The plane was owned by a company called Vortex, controlled by Michael Palmer, one of the largest marijuana smugglers in the United States.

Having cited these passages, the *Post* story recounted North's testimony before Congress during the Iran/Contra investigation, in which he claimed that he had turned over to the DEA all evidence about Contra drug running. The *Post*'s Adams described how she contacted the DEA and had been told that there was absolutely no record that North had ever made any such contacts: "There's no evidence he talked to anyone," the DEA stated in an unusual response to the *Post*. "We can't find the person he talked to, if he did talk to them. There's no record of the person he talked to."

The *Post* also contacted Jack Lawn, head of the DEA at the time, who said that, yes, he had talked to North several times in 1985 and 1986, but "Ollie did not provide any intelligence to me" about Contra drug running. Similar statements came from the new DEA chief, Robert Bryden; and from North's former boss at the NSC, Robert McFarlane. Robert Duemling, an old State Department hand who had been put in charge of the Nicaraguan Humanitarian Assistance Organization contracting with airlines and pilots to deliver aid to the Contras, said that North urged him to do business with people who known to be involved with drugs. "He wanted me to work with Mario [Calero]," Duemling said.

The *Post* also quoted former head of US Customs William Von Robb, who claimed that he was "absolutely stunned" by the revelations in North's diaries. CIA man Robert Gates spoke to the *Post* in like terms. Gates said North should have turned over his information to the DEA. "A normal person would have reacted strongly," Gates said. To round out these somewhat theatrical expressions of astonishment, the *Post* wheeled on former State Department official Elliott Abrams, who had been indicted for perjury by Iran/Contra prosecutor Lawrence Walsh. Abrams said carefully that "legally speaking that [drug running by Contras and their suppliers] was none of our business."

Of course, all these expostulations at North's supposed deceptiveness were as self-serving as the *Post*'s sudden eagerness to publish allegations of Contra drug running. Gates, for example, said that he would have expected that North, on coming across evidence of drug running by the Contras, would immediately go ballistic and pass on the evidence to Von Robb or the DEA. But as a senior CIA officer, Gates had headed a 1988 investigation into charges of Contra drug running in the wake of the Kerry hearings. Back then he had as much information on the Contras and their contractors as North did. So did Von Robb. But neither said anything at the time.

Now the game was to pin everything on North, and the *Post,* eager to trash him as a senatorial candidate, played along. The story probably did contribute to North's narrow defeat in the Virginia Senate race a couple of weeks later. But though North was most certainly culpable – indeed far more that the *Post* alleged – the CIA had been years ahead of the cocky young colonel in conniving at Contra drug running.

Take the case of SETCO, a Honduran airline company that from 1983 to 1985 was the principal firm used to transport supplies and weapons from the US to Contra camps in Honduras. In those years SETCO planes alone carried more than a million rounds of ammunition. The company was controlled by Juan Matta Ballesteros, one of the largest drug dealers in Latin America and a man with useful contacts in the CIA and the Pentagon. Ballesteros had been arrested in 1970 for bringing 26 kilos of cocaine into Dulles International Airport, outside Washington, D.C. This misfortune did not earn a life sentence in the US for the friend of the CIA, but merely deportation to Honduras, where in 1975 he formed a partnership with the Mexican drug kingpin Félix Gallardo. In 1978 Matta used his drug profits to finance the overthrow of Honduran president Juan Alberto Melgar Castro, thus ushering into power General Policarpo Paz García. The CIA took a close and friendly interest in this transfer of power because, unlike the man he ousted, Paz was a keen supporter of Nicaragua's Somoza.

Under the Paz regime the Honduran army and intelligence service began to get a cut of Matta's drug trafficking in exchange for protecting his burgeoning operations. Honduras was now becoming a major point of transit for cocaine and marijuana coming north from Colombia.

At the nexus between the Contras and their mutual patron, the CIA, was a man named Leonides Torres Arias, the head of Honduran military intelligence. Since the 1978 coup by Paz García, Torres, according to a US Senate investigation, had been getting cocaine money kickbacks from Matta. When the Argentinian military officers training the Contras pulled out at the onset of the Falklands/Malvinas War, the CIA's top man in Latin America, Dewey Clarridge, began to depend more and more on Torres and Juan Matta Ballesteros's company to prop up the Contras until money appropriated by Congress began to flow south.

In 1983 SETCO got one of the first supply contracts to haul arms from the US to the Contras. The contract was awarded even though US law enforcement and the CIA knew the firm was owned by the notorious drug smuggler Matta and that his airline company had been flagged in DEA and US Customs records for its history of drug running. A 1983 Customs Service report declared that "SETCO stands for Services Ejec-tutizox Touristas Comander [sic] and is headed by Juan Ramon Matta

Ballesteros, a Class I DEA violator."

The Customs Service also made reference to a DEA profile of the company, noting that SETCO was being used by Matta to smuggle cocaine into the US. One of Matta's partners in SETCO was an American pilot named Frank Moss. Moss flew more than a dozen Contra supply missions for SETCO, and in 1985 set up his own Contra supply company called Hondu-Caribe. Moss himself had been tagged as a drug smuggler by the DEA as far back as 1979. Under the terms of the Boland amendment, passed in the fall of 1984, the only aid allowed to the Contras was so-called "humanitarian" supplies. SETCO got one of the contracts to haul these supplies, and Moss got his cut of the action, all under the CIA's protective umbrella.

The Hondu-Caribe planes were used to carry weapons bought from a US firm called R&M Equipment, which maintained a large warehouse in Tegucigalpa, Honduras filled with weapons. Oliver North called it "the supermarket." R&M was partly owned by Ron Martin, a former CIA operative. His partner was James McCoy, who had served as the US military attaché to the Somoza regime. R&M became an arms vending rival to Richard Secord's Enterprise venture. It was R&M's warehouse that Secord was discussing with North in that July 1985 notebook entry recording that $14 million worth of weapons was paid for with drug money. Martin claims that the allegation of drug money was a smear planted by rivals.

Moss's firm owned two DC-4 cargo planes, one of which was known to the DEA as a drug plane. A Customs officer spotted another Hondu-Caribe DC-4 dumping its cargo in the waters off the west coast of Florida. When the plane finally landed at Port Charlotte airport, the Customs Service impounded it. On board agents discovered an address book containing telephone numbers for Contra leaders and for Oliver North's man Robert Owen. Among other documents retrieved by US Customs was evidence of Mario Calero's partial ownership of Hondu-Caribe.

Alan Fiers, the CIA man picked to replace Dewey Clarridge as head of the CIA's Latin America task force in 1983, testified to Congress the following year that "[e]veryone around Pastora was involved in cocaine." Eden Pastora was a wild card in the Contra alliance, and by this time the CIA, wearying of his intractability, was eager to discredit him (at the very least). Fiers was implying in his testimony that its creature, the FDN, was not similarly encumbered with cocaine smugglers. Yet here was a drug-smuggling airline part-owned by the brother of the FDN's civilian leader, Adolfo Calero, and Mario himself was in charge of the FDN's logistical operations.

Nor could the DEA claim ignorance of what was going on. In 1981 the DEA set up its first office in Tegucigalpa, the Honduran capital, and assigned Thomas Zepeda as the resident agent. Zepeda rapidly came to the accurate conclusion that the entire Honduran government was deeply involved in the drug trade. His attempts to investigate top Honduran officials whom he believed were on Matta's drug payroll were thwarted by the CIA. We know this because Zepeda was quoted as saying as much in a good story in the *Los Angeles Times* on February 13, 1988, apparently overlooked by the authors of the newspaper's later attacks on Gary Webb. In May 1983 Zepeda opened an investigation into SETCO. A month later the probe was cut off, Zepeda was pulled out of Honduras, and the DEA's Honduran station was shut down. The man responsible for this retreat was Ed Heath, the DEA's head of Latin American operations, resident in Mexico City and suspected by many DEA agents of being too cozy with the CIA. Former DEA agent Michael Levine described Heath as being "a man so mistrusted by the street agents working for him in Mexico that they conducted enforcement operations without informing him."

In 1985 the GAO was requested to explore the reasons why the DEA shut down the Honduran office. This investigation was also quashed by the NSC and CIA.

The Subcontractors

In 1985, Congress authorized the creation of the Nicaraguan Humanitarian Assistance Organization, known as NHAO, to provide $27 million worth of "humanitarian assistance to the Contras." Oliver North and Elliott Abrams secured the appointment of Robert Duemling, a career State Department officer the two deemed capable of handling the delicate business of furnishing military assistance under the flag of humanitarian aid. NHAO operated under the aegis of the State Department, and was overseen by the triumvirs North, Abrams and the CIA's Alan Fiers. In addition, North placed Robert Owen inside the NHAO.

At least four of the companies that received State Department grants to transport "humanitarian aid" had been, or were, involved in drug trafficking: DIACSA, a Miami-based airline that pulled in $41,120 in these State Department contracts; SETCO/Hondu-Caribe; Frigorificos de Puntarenas/Ocean Hunter, a Costa Rican seafood company; and Vortex Air International, a Miami-based airline that received $317,425 from NHAO.

Leslie Cockburn interviewed Duemling when she was preparing her ground-breaking CBS documentary about drug running by companies given contracts by NHAO. He told her that he was unaware of the backgrounds of these companies and that they had all been selected by the CIA. Duemling's contention is backed up by a memo written by Robert Owen to Oliver North on February 10, 1986: "No doubt you know the DC-4 Foley got was used at one time to run drugs, and part of the crew had criminal records. Nice group THE BOYS chose. The company is also one that Mario [Calero] has been involved in using in the past, only they had a quick name change. Incompetence reigns." Foley was later identified as Pat Foley of Summit Aviation from Middletown, Delaware. "THE BOYS" was Robert Owen's code name for the CIA.

Foley's company, Summit Aviation, was believed by congressional investigators to be a CIA proprietary. The DC-4 acquired by Foley for his contract work for NHAO was provided by Vortex, run by Michael Palmer. At the time Vortex received its NHAO contract the DEA reckoned Palmer to be one of the largest marijuana smugglers in the US. Throughout the 1980s Palmer received extraordinarily forgiving treatment at the hands of US law enforcement. For example, one of Palmer's planes on an NHAO flight developed engine trouble and was forced to land on San Andreas Island off the coast of Colombia, a favored transfer point for drug shipments. Colombian police detained the plane and soon discovered that it was identified in their files as having been involved in drug-running operations. They also discovered that the flight crew had criminal records. But the crew complained that they were on a US government mission and demanded to be released, together with their plane.

The Colombian police called the US State Department to ask what should be done about the situation. Frank McNeil, who worked in the State Department's intelligence section, called the CIA, whose officials told him that the Vortex plane was indeed on a government mission and to release it along with its crew. A CIA official told McNeil, "It's unfortunate, but it's pretty hard to find folks to do this kind of work."

Palmer had been flying marijuana from Colombia since 1977. His associate, Leigh Ritch, testified before Congress that their business "grossed billions." Palmer himself had been arrested in Colombia in the early 1980s but was released under mysterious circumstances. A *Boston Globe* story in February 1988 reported that one of the Vortex planes was stopped in Miami for a Customs inspection. When Palmer arrived at the airport to get his plane released, Customs ran his name through its computers, and records came up showing that he was currently under indictment for smuggling marijuana. Palmer maintained that both he and his planes were working for the CIA. Customs officials called the CIA and once again was told that Palmer was correct. The plane was duly released and arrangements made for future Vortex flights. According to the Customs record, "Normal Customs procedures for incoming flights are expedited."

The friendly treatment of Palmer extended into the late 1980s. He was indicted in Detroit in 1986 for marijuana smuggling, and again in 1989 in Louisiana on charges of bringing 150 tons of marijuana into the US. Palmer used his CIA ties as a defense. Both cases were dropped. In Detroit the prosecutor said his office was acting "in the interest of justice." In Louisiana, federal prosecutor Howard Parker said he declined to prosecute Palmer because he wanted "to avoid a sideshow." The treatment of Palmer, a major marijuana shipper, contrasts vividly with the treatment of Rick Ross, the Los Angeles crack dealer put away for life. Looking back on Palmer's inviolability, US State Department man McNeil remarked sourly to the *Washington Post* in 1994, "The whole thing is too sleazy for words. It's not a happy chapter in US history."

In May and September 1986 the State Department gave more than $40,000 in NHAO contracts to an outfit called DIACSA operating in Costa Rica. Later, it was one of the companies that Oliver North used to launder money for the Contras. DIACSA was an interesting choice for this type of operation because six months before it had gained its State Department contract two of its principals, Alfredo Caballero and Floyd Carlton Casceres, had been indicted on charges of smuggling 900 pounds of cocaine into the US and laundering $2.6 million in drug profits. Caballero, president of DIACSA, was a veteran of the Bay of Pigs and a close friend of Mario Calero. He had been identified in January 1995 by DEA agent Daniel Moritz as using DIACSA as a front for his cocaine business. The firm, Moritz wrote, served "as a location for planning smuggling ventures, for assembling and distributing large cash proceeds from narcotics transactions and for placing telephone calls in furtherance of the smuggling ventures."

Caballero's partner in this cocaine enterprise, Floyd Carlton, was General Manuel Noriega's favorite drug pilot and became a star witness for the prosecution in Noriega's 1991 trial in Miami. According to Noriega's aide José Blandón, Carlton was also working for the Calí cartel flying numerous cocaine shipments for it in 1985 and 1986, the same period he was also flying Contra resupply missions.

In 1987 Carlton, hiding out in Costa Rica, phoned the DEA to offer to help bring Noriega to book in return for leniency for himself and protection for his family. Carlton said he gave the DEA details of Noriega's "money laundering, drugs, weapons, corruption, assassination." A few months later Carlton gave himself up. He faced nine counts of cocaine trafficking and money laundering charges that could have landed him a life sentence plus 145 years. Instead, he was given a 9-year prison sentence and was released after serving only 4.5 years. He was paid $211,000 for his testimony, as was his partner Caballero.

Manuel Noriega

On June 12, 1986, Seymour Hersh published a front-page story in the *New York Times* exposing General Manuel Noriega's twenty-year association with the Colombian drug cartels. The exposé appeared just as Noriega was in Washington to receive a medal of honor from the Inter-American Defense Board. The article alleged that Noriega was involved in money laundering, arms dealing and political assassinations, including the torture and murder by decapitation of his liberal opponent, Dr. Hugo Spadafora. The article, based on sources in the Defense Intelligence Agency, also accused Noriega of selling US technology to the Cubans and Eastern Bloc nations.

Hersh quoted from a 1985 House Foreign Affairs Committee report that called Panama "a drug and chemical trans-shipment point and money laundering center of drug money." That same investigation of Noriega prompted the NSC's Admiral John Poindexter to travel to Panama and have a session with Noriega, during which Poindexter claims he told the squat general to "cut it out." But it wasn't long before Elliott Abrams, assistant secretary of state, had bailed out Noriega by intervening in a policy debate within the Reagan administration to insist that only after the Sandinistas had been dealt with should any serious sanctions against Noriega be considered. Noriega was a vital component in the CIA's war against Nicaragua. At the request of the Reagan administration he had contributed more than $100,000 to Contras operating in Costa Rica, and in 1985 he had provided "an ordnance expert" for a North-planned operation that blew up a Sandinista military depot in Managua.

After the unflattering attention sparked by Hersh's article, Noriega called Oliver North seeking counsel in cleaning up his image. North agreed to meet with a Noriega emissary on August 23, 1986, and minuted the encounter in a computer-message to John Poindexter, later unearthed by the National Security Archive:

> You will recall that over the years Manuel Noriega and I have developed a fairly good relationship. It was Noriega who told me Panama would be willing to accept [Ferdinand] Marcos [the exiled former president of the Philippines]. ... Last night Noriega called and asked if I would meet w[ith] a man he trusts – a respected Cuban American – the president of a college in Florida. He flew in this morning and he outlined Noriega's proposal: In exchange for a promise from us to 'help clean up his [Noriega's] image' and a commitment to lift our ban on FMS [foreign military sales], he would undertake to 'take care of' the Sandinista leadership for us. I told the messenger that such actions were forbidden by US law and he countered that Noriega had numerous assets in place in Nicaragua that could accomplish many things that would be essential [to a] Contra Victory. Interesting. My

sense is that this is a potentially very useful avenue, but one which would have to be very carefully handled. A meeting with Noriega could not be held on his turf – the potential for recording this information is too great ... you will recall that he was head of Intelligence for the PDF [Panamanian Defense Forces] before becoming CG [commanding general]. My last meeting with Noriega was in a boat on the Potomac ... Noriega travels frequently in Europe at this time of year and a meeting could be arranged to coincide with one of my other trips. My sense is that this offer is sincere, that Noriega does indeed have the capabilities preferred and that the cost could be born by Project Democracy (the figure of $1M was mentioned) ... The proposal seems sound to me and I believe we could make the appropriate arrangements for reasonable OPSEC [operational security] and deniability. Beg advice.

Within minutes Poindexter had responded to North's suggestion that this murderous thug and drug smuggler be retained at a cost of $1 million to help in the Contra War. "I wonder what he means about helping him clean up his act," the admiral wrote. "If he is really serious about that we should be willing to do that for nearly nothing. If on the other hand he just wants us indebted to him, so that he can blackmail us to lay off, then I am not interested. If he really has access inside, it could be very helpful, but we cannot (repeat not) be involved in any conspiracy or assassination. More sabotage would be another story. I have nothing against him other than his illegal activities. It would be useful for you to talk to him directly to find out exactly what he has in mind with regard to cleaning up his act."

North cleared the meeting with Secretary of State George Shultz and Shultz's sidekick Abrams and then proceeded to London, where he hunkered down in a hotel with Noriega and reviewed plans to wreak mayhem on the Sandinistas, all in contravention of the express will of Congress. They reviewed plans for bombings of the Managua airport, attacks on phone lines and power plants and the destruction of an oil refinery. Noriega also pledged to create training camps for the Contras and the Afghan mujahedin, no doubt with advanced courses in accountancy, international banking practices and the covert movement of drugs and money.

In exchange North agreed to sign Noriega up with a New York PR firm. In his book *Panama: The Whole Story,* Kevin Buckley quotes an

American source who observed North and Noriega together. "To North, Noriega was a spymaster, an operator, a man who made things happen. To North, Noriega was like Brando, up the river in *Apocalypse Now.* No rules. Noriega thought North was a pipsqueak."

If North revered Noriega, North's patron William Casey, director of the CIA, had a coldly pragmatic appreciation of the usefulness of the Panamanian. Casey saw Panama as the key to US operations throughout Latin America, not only against Nicaragua but also Cuba. The relationship between Casey and Noriega was described by the latter's right-hand man, José Blandón, to documentary filmmakers Leslie and Andrew Cockburn: "The US had information that Noriega was involved in the drug trade for at least eight years. Yes, they knew about that. But for the White House, the Reagan administration, the Contras were so important that the drugs took second place. There was a very special relationship between Casey and Noriega. At least $3 million in support came from Casey. Whenever there would be an investigation of Noriega, Casey would stop it."

Actually the US had known about Noriega's drug trafficking since at least the late 1960s, and there was a history across nearly three decades of US military and intelligence agencies shielding Noriega from criminal investigation. He had been recruited by the Defense Intelligence Agency in 1959 and began working for the CIA in 1967. When the Bureau of Narcotics and Dangerous Drugs attempted to indict Noriega in 1971 for drug trafficking, the CIA intervened to protect their man in Panama. The BNDD continued to brood on ways to get rid of Noriega, including a procedure chastely described as "total and complete immobilization." But in the end the drug agency was overruled and ordered to work with the drug smuggler. Throughout the 1980s Noriega's star continued to rise. In 1976, for example, the CIA paid Noriega $100,000 for his work on behalf of the Agency. The director of the CIA at the time was George Bush. By 1985, at the height of the Contra War, Noriega's paycheck from the CIA had soared to $200,000 a year.

On October 5, 1986, a few weeks after the meeting in London, the bold plans explored by North and Noriega came crashing down in the wake of the similarly abrupt descent of a plane ferrying arms from Ilopango air base in El Salvador to Contra camps inside Nicaragua. As

Eugene Hasenfus, a veteran of the CIA's Air America operation in Laos, was kicking the supplies out of the back of a C-123K, a Sandinista gunner scored a direct hit and only Hasenfus managed to parachute down and into the world's headlines, offering incontrovertible proof of the Reagan administration's illegal shipments. Among the phone numbers in Hasenfus's notebook was that of George Bush's office.

In rapid order, Noriega's fervent supporters inside the Reagan administration lost favor. Then William Casey died. Noriega's star plummeted. He became a liability to George Bush, and it was not long before Noriega had been indicted as a drug smuggler, then became the target of an American invasion of Panama on December 20, 1989. Absurdly titled Operation Just Cause, the mission succeeded in killing plenty of Panamanian civilians but not Noriega, who found sanctuary in the house of the Papal Nuncio. Finally, on Christmas Eve, Noriega surrendered and in a Miami courtroom in 1990 learned what it was to fall from grace. The veteran of the CIA's payroll and a thousand forgiven drug shipments went down on a 45-year prison sentence, which as of 1998 he is serving in the state of Florida. His amusing memoir, *America's Prisoner,* detailing his career and relationship with the CIA, was not widely reviewed in the US press.

The greatest irony of all is that under the US-installed successor to Noriega, Guillermo Endara, Panama became the province of the Calí cartel, which rushed in after the Medellín cartel was evicted along with Noriega. By the early 1990s, Panama's role in the Latin American drug trade and its transmission routes to the US had become more crucial than ever.

Celerino Castillo, the DEA Man Who Worked Too Well

In the 1980s, Celerino Castillo III was one of the DEA's top agents, coordinating major busts in New York, Peru and Guatemala. But when he got to El Salvador at the height of the Contra War and reported that US agents under the control of Oliver North's NSC operation were running drugs, his superiors informed him that if he persisted he would be run out of town. "I was told my career would end because I was stepping on a White House operation," Castillo told us in the late summer of 1997. "I wrote dozens of reports but they disappeared into a black hole at DEA headquarters." Eventually Castillo was pulled out of Central America and placed under an internal investigation; he finally left the DEA in disgust.

Celerino Castillo was born in south Texas. His father had won the Bronze Star and the Purple Heart for heroism during World War II after being shot six times in the Philippines. "Cele," as he calls himself, won a Bronze Star during his tour of duty in Vietnam, a tour that persuaded him to pursue a career in anti-narcotics work. Prompting him to this decision was the sight of many of his comrades whacked out on heroin. "Every week we would send another overdose victim home in a green bag," Castillo recalled. "If the soldier was well liked someone would pump a bullet in the soldier's body. The family would be told he died a hero's death. If the consensus was that the dead soldier had been an asshole he would be sent home with nothing more than needle pricks in his arms."

After a stint in Texas working on the drug squad in the Edinburg police department, Castillo was hired by the DEA in 1979. He became the first Mexican American to work in the Agency's New York City office, at that time the largest DEA station in the US. Racism, Castillo remembers, was pervasive throughout the agency, which employed few Hispanics or other Spanish speakers even though it was busting Latin Americans on a daily basis. "Every Hispanic agent I knew fell into the same trap, and was assigned to wiretap monitoring, translations and sur-veillance. We worked long hours building cases against Dominicans and Puerto Ricans and would have to stand back while white paper-pushers took the credit."

Castillo broke through many of these barriers when he and his Latin American partner orchestrated one of the largest heroin seizures in New York history, a $20 million shipment of high-grade heroin that origi-nated in the poppy fields of Afghanistan. This bust earned Castillo a new assignment to lead a series of commando-style raids on cocaine labs in the forests of Peru. One such operation netted 4 tons of coca paste, three airplanes and a large cocaine refinery. But after a year in Peru, Castillo's cover was blown. "There was a picture of me taken during an operation that was in every newspaper in South America," Castillo says. "I left Peru and was assigned to work in Guatemala." In 1985 the Guatemala DEA station was run by Robert Stia who also oversaw DEA operations in Belize, El Salvador and Honduras. Castillo was given charge of El Salvador, and his assignment represented the first time the DEA had set up an operation in that country. Stia had some initial advice for Castillo: "One, stay out of trouble with the locals. Two, don't make the US government look bad."

Stia then brought up a touchy subject – the Contra supply project run by Oliver North's men out of Ilopango air base near San Salvador. "Be careful what you do down there. Don't interfere in their operations," Stia ordered Castillo, and told of persistent reports of drug running by Contras and the pilots supplying them with weapons. But, Stia insisted, those associated with the operation were off limits to the DEA.

Castillo responded that he wasn't going to be reluctant to investigate the Contras and their associates. "If I receive intelligence the Contra operation is trafficking," he told Stia, "I'll investigate and report it." Stia laughed and told Castillo he'd be quickly yanked out of Latin America if he interferred in the Contra resupply effort.

It didn't take long for Castillo to find evidence that those associated with Contra missions also had their hands in cocaine running. His first hard information came from a Cuban exile called Socrates Amaury Sofi-Perez, a Bay of Pigs veteran who worked as a freelance agent for the Guatemalan secret police and for the CIA. Sofi-Perez also ran a shrimp company in Guatemala City, which Castillo found out was being used to launder drug money for the Contras. According to Castillo, Cocaine from Colombia was delivered to Sofi-Perez's factory, where it was packed in with frozen shrimp and then shipped to Miami. Sofi-Perez had secured easy entry into the United States by paying off the US Customs. A share of the profits was duly turned over to the Contras. "We have to support the Contras fully," Sofi-Perez told Castillo in early 1986. "Nicaragua must be liberated from the Sandinistas at any cost, and if trafficking provides the means for that, so be it." Sofi-Perez went on to say that his operation paled next to what was going on at Ilopango under the nose of another Bay of Pigs veteran, Félix Rodríguez, aka Max Gomez.

THE CIA, DRUGS AND CENTRAL AMERICA

Rodríguez had been in some of the major hot spots associated with the CIA, from the Bay of Pigs to Bolivia (where he had been present at the capture and execution of Che Guevara in the 1960s, to Southeast Asia in the early 1970s. Rodríguez was also among the CIA men most deeply involved in planning operations against the Sandinistas. In March 1982 he drafted a proposal to create a mobile tactical squad, essentially an assassination team. This idea found great favor both at the CIA and in the National Security Council. Later in 1982 Rodríguez was assigned to oversee the Contra supply effort in El Salvador, which he did from 1982 to 1986.

Rodríguez had numerous ties to cocaine traffickers, perhaps most notoriously to Gerard Latchinian, an international arms dealer. In 1983 Rodríguez and Latchinian went into business together in a company known as Giro Aviation Corporation, headquartered in Florida. A year later, on November 1, 1984, Latchinian was arrested by the FBI at an airstrip in south Florida for his role in a $10 million cocaine deal. The money from the cocaine sale was scheduled to finance the assassination of the newly elected president of Honduras, Roberto Suazo Cordoba. Latchinian's partner in this project was General José Bueso Rosa, a man who had helped the CIA set up its Contra training base in Honduras.

In 1986 Bueso Rosa was arrested in the United States and, like Latchinian two years earlier, was convicted. But the US government, in the form of the NSC and CIA, intervened to have Bueso Rosa's sentence reduced. The brief on Bueso Rosa's behalf filed by General Robert Schweitzer of the NSC read, "General Bueso Rosa has always been a valuable ally to the United States. As chief of staff of the Honduran armed forces he immeasurably furthers the United States' national interest in Central America. He is primarily responsible for the initial success for the American military presence in Honduras. For this service he was awarded the Legion of Merit by the President of the United States, the highest award that can be presented to a foreign military officer."

In other words, North and the CIA were trying to save the ass of a drug smuggler and would-be assassin, a partner of a long-term CIA man who was on fairly close terms with former CIA director, and subsequently White House resident, George Bush. To quote North's memo when assistance to Bueso Rosa was being reviewed: "Look at options:

pardon, clemency, deportation, reduced sentence. Objective is to keep Bueso from ... spilling the beans." Poindexter e-mailed back to North: "you may advise all concerned that the President will want to be as helpful as possible to settle this matter." Bueso Rosa ended up doing a short stint in the minimum security prison at Elgin Air Force Base in Florida, known as Club Fed.

To continue with the unsavory circle of Félix Rodríguez, the CIA man with whom Castillo was now dealing. One of Félix Rodríguez's prime recruits in El Salvador was another man with a malodorous past: Luis Posada Carriles. Like Rodríguez, Posada was a Cuban exile who had been trained in anti-Castro terrorism by the CIA. He missed out on the Bay of Pigs since his anti-Castro brigade never left Nicaragua for the mission, but in the early 1960s he ran arms to anti-Castro cells in Cuba, supervised the sabotage of Cuban ships and planned terrorist assaults on Cuban embassies throughout Latin America. Through the 1960s he was working with another Cuban right-winger, Orlando Bosch.

By the late 1960s the CIA had placed Posada in the Venezuelan DISIP, the country's secret police. In that capacity he assisted the Chilean and Argentinian military regimes in some of the bloodiest repressions of the epoch. In 1976 Posada was called to a meeting of anti-Castro Cubans convened by Bosch in the Dominican Republic. A new wave of terrorism against Cuba began soon after, culminating in the October 6 mid-air destruction by bomb of a Cuban civilian airliner carrying seventy-three passengers, including a team of Cuban athletes. The police quickly arrested two men who had got off the plane at its last touchdown before it blew up. One confessed to planting the bomb and admitted that he worked for Posada. When Venezuelan police raided Posada's house in Caracas they found evidence linking him to the bombing, including flight schedules for the airline.

Posada was arrested but managed to avoid extradition and ultimately bribed his way out of prison in 1985. He made his way to Aruba, where he called his old comrade Félix Rodríguez. The CIA man promptly had him flown to El Salvador, gave him a new name, Ramon Medina, fixed him up with false papers and put him on a salary of $3,000 a month. The new job for this fugitive mass murderer was to work as chief of logistics at Ilopango air base in the Contra supply operation.

Posada arranged safehouses for the pilots who ferried weapons to the Contra bases and carried drugs back north to the United States on the return trip. He paid the pilots with cash flown in from banks in Miami and Panama and oversaw storage and transport of the weapons. In arranging the shipments of cash and weapons, Posada worked with another old Cuba hand, Luis Rodríguez, who ran a Costa Rican seafood company called Frigorificos de Puntarenas. This company had received more than $260,000 in State Department funds to provide humanitarian aid to the Contras, even though the US government had known since 1983 that the firm was little more than a front for Luis Rodríguez's cocaine trafficking. Indeed, in 1984, the FBI notified the DEA and the State Department that they believed Rodríguez was funneling cocaine profits to the Contras.

As DEA man Castillo began to compile reports on cocaine smuggling in El Salvador, he had an unexpected opportunity to alert Vice President George Bush to what was going on. Bush arrived in Guatemala City on January 14, 1986, and Castillo was among those at a US Embassy reception. Spotting Castillo's badge, Bush asked what he was up to, and Castillo replied that he was investigating cocaine trafficking in El Salvador. He advised the vice president that "there's some funny things going on with the Contras at Ilopango." Bush, Castillo says, smiled at him knowingly and walked away.

After Bush's visit, Castillo assembled all his notes on Contra drug running and turned them over to his boss, Robert Stia, saying, "This is too big. It's going to come back and bite us in the ass if we don't report it." Stia reluctantly signed the reports and sent them back to Washington. Months went by with no response from DEA headquarters. Castillo continued to dig and now developed a very useful informant in the person of Hugo Martinez, who was in charge of developing flight plans for the Contra resupply mission. Martinez told Castillo that most of the pilots ferrying arms from Ilopango to Contra camps in Honduras and Costa Rica were involved in the drug trade. He said that the pilots would brag about the fact that they worked for the CIA and that nobody could touch them. Martinez kept a list of the names of all the pilots he believed were running drugs on Contra missions. When Castillo ran the list through DEA computers he was shocked by the results: "Every one of them had a file," Castillo said.

In April 1986, Castillo got a cable from Bobby Nieves, a DEA man in Costa Rica. Nieves told Castillo that he believed cocaine was being smuggled from John Hull's large ranch on the Costa Rican side of the border with Nicaragua to Ilopango air base in El Salvador. He advised Castillo to investigate goings-on in Hangers 4 and 5 at Ilopango. The cable concluded, "We believe the Contras are involved in narcotics trafficking."

Soon thereafter Castillo was approached by Robert Chavez, the State Department's general counsel in El Salvador. Chavez explained his dilemma. As the man responsible for issuing visas to the United States, he'd been advised by the CIA to grant one to a Nicaraguan pilot named Carlos Alberto Amador. But, Chavez said, when he checked the files he'd found that Amador had a record for drug smuggling. What should he do? If he declined to issue the visa, he'd have the CIA on his neck. Castillo told him that of course he should refuse to grant the visa. In the end Chavez took this course. When the CIA duly raised a stink, Chavez said that he'd taken that action on the orders of Castillo. This was the moment, Castillo says as he looks back on the entire affair, that the CIA began to go after him seriously.

It wasn't long after this that Castillo got a visit from John Martsh, head of DEA operations in Latin America. "Cele, they're coming after you because of the Contra thing and the reports you wrote. They're trying to get rid of you, but they're going to do it very discreetly." Castillo didn't back down. He went on compiling dossiers on Contra airplanes and pilots. His source at Ilopango, Hugo Martinez, had told him about a Contra pilot named Francisco "Chico" Guirola who had made frequent cash runs to top up Contra bank accounts in the Bahamas. Martinez also believed that he was carrying cocaine to air bases in Florida and Texas. In 1985 Guirola was arrested in south Texas with $5.5 million in Contra cash, presumed to be drug profits. "That was a Contra operation," Castillo says. "He wasn't jailed; he was merely deported and the money returned to him." Guirola continued to work for the Contras in El Salvador.

Another Contra pilot whom Castillo had his eye on was Carlos Cabezas. Cabezas's role as a drug runner for the Contras has been detailed by the man himself in the CIA Inspector General's report, published at the end of January 1998. In that report Cabezas, now living in Nicaragua, says he attended a December 1981 meeting at a hotel in San José, Costa Rica. At this meeting, Cabezas told the Inspector General's staffers, the scheme was hatched to raise money for the Contras by selling cocaine. Present were Troilo Sánchez, Horatio Pereira, Julio Zavala, Zavala's wife Dora Sánchez, and Cabezas himself.

Cabezas says that Sánchez and Pereira first broached the idea of selling cocaine in California and cycling a share of the profits back to the Contras in Costa Rica. Zavala, the man who later had the $36,800 returned to him in the "Frogman" case in San Francisco, agreed to the plan and instructed Cabezas to serve as the go-between, collecting money from San Francisco street dealers and flying it back to Central America. Cabezas says his first money-raising trip for the Contras occurred in early 1982. He flew to San Pedro Sula in Honduras, where he met Pereira. Two days later, Cabezas says, they met a Peruvian who gave them several kilos of cocaine. Cabezas carried the cocaine back to San Francisco and distributed it to his network of street dealers, who sold it all within a few days. A week later Cabezas flew back to Honduras and gave Pereira $100,000 in cash for distribution to the Contras.

After this shake-down run, Cabezas set up a network of Contra "mules" to bring cocaine back into the United States. Usually Cabezas's couriers were airline attendants, who would carry one kilo at a time, concealed in woven baskets. Cabezas collected the baskets at the airport, sliced them open with an Exacto knife, extracted the cocaine, handed it out to the dealers and then collected the money from the sales. During 1982 alone, Cabezas remembers making more than twenty trips to Costa Rica and Honduras. He estimates that he delivered between $1 million and $1.5 million in cash to Sánchez and Pereira.

Then, in late 1982, so Cabezas told the CIA investigators fifteen years later, Troilo Sánchez instructed him to deliver a shipment of cash to his brother Aristides in Miami. Aristides was a leader of the FDN. Cabezas told the Inspector General's investigators that Aristides was "certainly aware that the money came from drug profits." In early 1984, Cabezas says he went to Danli, a Contra camp on the Nicaraguan–Honduran border, where Horatio Pereira gave several thousand dollars to

Contra commander Juaquin [CIA spelling] Vega. The money was used, so Cabezas says, to feed the troops and help support the families of Contra soldiers.

In May 1982, Cabezas recalled to the Inspector General's investigators, Pereira introduced him to a man called Ivan Gomez, who both Pereira and Gomez himself identified as the CIA's man in Costa Rica. Cabezas recalled that "Gomez was there to ensure that the profits from the cocaine went to the Contras and not into someone's pocket." Cabezas claimed that he met Gomez on one other occasion in the late summer of 1982, at the airport in San José, Costa Rica.

In 1997 the Inspector General of the CIA was obviously in an uncomfortable position when this smoking gun landed on his desk. Here was a Contra drug runner explicitly saying that a CIA man oversaw allocation of drug money for the Contras. The CIA's internal watchdog also had to deal with the uncomfortable fact, as his own report conceded, that "a CIA independent contractor used Ivan Gomez as an alias in Costa Rica in the late 1980s." The IG's report says lamely that the description of Gomez given by Cabezas in 1997 was wrong. Cabezas said that Gomez was a fluent Spanish speaker with curly black hair and an athletic build. The IG report claims that "the physical description of the CIA contractor is significantly different – although the CIA independent contractor has curly hair and speaks fluent Spanish. He is much shorter and of a slighter build than the person described by Cabezas." Thus the CIA tried to create a second Gomez out of the person Cabezas had seen fifteen years earlier on two separate occasions.

Castillo's last major target was a suspected cocaine-running pilot named Walter Grasheim. Castillo had been told by Martinez that Grasheim was flying drugs and weapons out of Ilopango. While Grasheim was away in New York City, Castillo and his men raided the pilot's house in San Salvador. They discovered a cache of US-made weapons, including M-16 rifles, rocket-propelled grenades, night-vision goggles and a case of C4 explosive. "This guy was a civilian," Castillo said. " He wasn't supposed to have this stuff. But we also found that all of his vehicles had US Embassy license plates. We found radios and weapons belonging to the US Embassy."

Castillo drafted a warrant for Grasheim's arrest, but his target was tipped off and never returned to El Salvador. Deeply angered, Castillo went off to see US Ambassador Edwin Corr. Castillo demanded to know why the embassy was furnishing such equipment to a drug runner. Corr told Castillo, "This is a covert operation. It's a White House operation. Stay away from it."

Soon after this exchange Castillo was suspended for three days and censured. The DEA's John Martsh told Castillo that he had become "too close" to his informants. He also reprimanded Castillo for using bad grammar in his reports and said that if he sent any more reports dealing with Contra drug running, he should use the word "alleged" when referring to such activities.

Castillo was still in the DEA in Central America when Senator John Kerry of Massachusetts launched his probe into allegations of the CIA's involvement in drug running. Despite a parade of witnesses, including convicted drug dealers and associates of Eden Pastora and Manuel Noriega, the Kerry hearings received little attention in the mainstream press. Castillo said in 1997 that he believes it was easy for CIA defenders in the press to discount the Kerry probe because so many of its sources were compromised by their criminal records. "They never brought people like me in to testify. I was the special agent in charge of El Salvador. I did all the investigation, and they never contacted me."

Similarly, Castillo says that none of the Iran/Contra committee investigators ever talked to him. But in 1991 he did meet secretly with Mike Foster, an FBI agent hired as an investigator for the Iran/Contra independent counsel, Lawrence Walsh. Castillo detailed for Foster his knowledge of the Contra drug operations and recalls that Foster told him after their first meeting, "Cele, if we can prove that the Contras and Oliver North were heavily involved in narcotics trafficking it would be like a grand slam home run." Foster filed what's known in the FBI as a 302 report, recording his interview with Castillo. "Castillo believes that North and the Contras' resupply operation at Ilopango were running drugs for the Contras," Foster wrote. "Many of the resupply pilots were drug traffickers."

Three days after Foster's report was filed, senior DEA officials contacted Walsh's office and tried to smear Castillo. Foster was asked to re-evaluate Castillo's credibility. The FBI man then wrote another memo to Craig Gillen, who was in charge of the "continuing investigations" part of Walsh's probe. In the memo, dated October 10, 1991, Foster wrote that "Castillo provides a lot of new background information and some significant leads that I think should be pursued." But the leads never were pursued, and Walsh's office decided that the drug trafficking allegations were outside the mandate of the independent counsel.

As for Cele Castillo, the failure of the Walsh probe was the last straw. He resigned from the DEA in December 1991, calling it "a corrupt agency." Back in Texas, seven years later, he was trying to recover his old reports to the DEA by suing the agency under the Freedom of Information Act.

Parry and Barger Break the Story

The first major story linking the Contras to drug running was written by Associated Press reporters Robert Parry and Brian Barger. It saw the light of day only by accident. The two reporters had been working on the story for months, to the growing discomfiture of their editors. After the usual editorial roadblocks had been thrown up – continual rewrites, revisions, clarifications and so forth – the story was ready to go, but was then held by an embargo from the higher-ups in the vast wire service. Then a Spanish-language editor translated the story, overlooked the embargo, and put it out on the AP's Latin American wire. On December 20, 1986, the story ran on front pages of Spanish-language newspapers throughout the world.

Three days later, a watered-down version went out on the English-language AP wire and then, amid the Christmas holidays, probably the slowest news days and the least read papers of the entire year, the *Washington Post* carried what Robert Parry later described as a cut-down version of the story, with extra denials from the Reagan administration inserted by the *Post*.

Even so, the compact story covered most of the bases and was a fine piece of journalism. "Nicaraguan rebels operating in northern Costa Rica," Parry and Barger began, "have engaged in cocaine trafficking in part to help their war against Nicaragua's leftist government, according to US investigators and American volunteers who work with the rebels." The story linked drug smuggling to both Eden Pastora's ARDE Contra group and the CIA-created FDN run by Adolfo Calero and Enrique Bermúdez. The story also disclosed that Contra leader Sebastian González Mendiola, head of a Contra splinter group known as the M-3, had been indicted in Costa Rica on drug charges.

Parry and Barger had also got information that much of the Contra-related cocaine running in Costa Rica was being overseen by members of the Cuban émigré group Brigade 2506, notorious in Miami and originally underwritten by the CIA to attack Castro. The story cited a classified National Intelligence Estimate prepared by the CIA, which charged that Eden Pastora had bought a helicopter and $270,000 worth of weapons with drug profits. Finally, Parry and Barger reported that a member of the Colombian cartel had donated $50,000 to the Contras for their help in securing safe passage for a 100-kilo shipment of cocaine. Parry and Barger followed up this story with a series of reports on Contra drug running, financial malfeasance and political corruption through the winter and spring of 1986.

The stories infuriated the Reagan administration, which lost no time in trying to shut off this embarrassing spotlight on its illegal activities. Early in 1986 an emissary from the Reagan White House contacted Parry and told him that his partner, Brian Barger, was a covert Sandinista propagandist. Parry was unimpressed. With the failure of this tactic, Elliott Abrams went after Parry. Abrams's press secretary, Gregory Lagana, sought out select members of the Washington press corps and dropped smears on Parry as a biased reporter who was out to undermine the Contra freedom fighters. There were even accusations that Parry and Barger had poisoned North's dog. (Iran/Contra investigators later cleared the two of the charges of dog assassination. North's pet had actually died of cancer.)

It turned out that North himself was deeply involved in the efforts to smear the two reporters. In his testimony to Iran/Contra prosecutors, Alan Fiers, the CIA man in charge of Latin America, said that North had enlisted the FBI's Oliver "Buck" Revell to harass Parry. The prosecutors' summary of their investigation was released in 1996:

The only activity Fiers is aware of by anyone in the government to in any way influence this case was North telling him [Fiers] that he [North] was going to call Oliver "Buck" Revell at the FBI and have him "do some things." Fiers recalls that on two or three occasions North told him he was having Revell either do something or not do something. Fiers thinks one of the calls from North to Revell was about North's concern about him [North] being hounded by Bob Parry the reporter.

When Parry contacted Fiers about this statement in 1997, Fiers told him, "That's right. You were the enemy."

Nor did Barger escape harassment. In the spring of 1986 the reporter discovered that his house in Washington was under round-the-clock surveillance. He reported the stake-out to the D.C. police, who confirmed he was being watched but refused to say who was involved.

Inevitably, pressure came down from the AP hierarchy. In the late spring of 1986 Parry went to Washington Bureau chief Charles Lewis to request authorization to write a series of stories about North, the Contras and drugs. Lewis nixed the idea, saying, according to Parry, "New York [AP headquarters] does not want to hear any more about the drug story. We don't think you should be doing any more of this." A few weeks later Lewis extended his prohibition to any coverage by Parry and Barger of the Contra War itself. "Nicaragua isn't a story any more," Parry remembers Lewis saying. This was a bit like a desk editor in Miami telling a reporter that Cuba wasn't a story any more, five months before the Bay of Pigs. In October of that year, Eugene Hasenfus's plane was shot down and the Iran/Contra scandal burst open.

It wasn't long before Parry was out of AP and working for Newsweek. Barger joined CBS. But any journalist discomfiting the Reagan administration on the Contra War invariably found trouble, and Parry had similar difficulties with Newsweek. The pair's signal triumph was to have gotten that original December story on the wires.

The Kerry Report

The main consequence of the Parry/Barger stories was the congressional investigation launched in April 1986 by Senator John Kerry of

Massachusetts, by far the most energetic probe in the 1980s of US government complicity in the Latin American drug trade. As his chief investigator Kerry selected Jack Blum, who had some years of experience in this kind of work for Senator Frank Church's Multinational Subcommittee, which had held some major hearings on corporate crookery in the late 1970s, most famously the Lockheed bribe scandal.

The Kerry investigation lasted two and a half years and heard scores of witnesses; it culminated in a report of some 400 pages with an annex of a further 600 pages of supporting documentation. Its main conclusion was unequivocal: "It is clear that individuals who provided support for the Contras were involved in drug trafficking. The supply network of the Contras was used by drug trafficking organizations, and elements of the Contras themselves received financial and material assistance from drug traffickers."

Contra members themselves were involved in drug trafficking, the report concluded. Drug traffickers played a key role in Contra supply operations and maintained business relationships with Contra organizations. Drug traffickers gave the Contras money, weapons, planes, pilots and supply services. The US State Department paid over $806,000 to known drug traffickers to carry humanitarian assistance to the Contras. In several cases the payments were made after the drug traffickers had been indicted by US federal prosecutors on drug charges.

The Kerry committee revealed that the Contras' complicity with drug traffickers went far beyond Eden Pastora's maverick operation in Costa Rica. Kerry charged that "[t]he largest Contra organization, the FDN, did move Contra funds through a narcotics trafficking enterprise and money-laundering operation." In addition, the Kerry report said, "The [US] military and intelligence agencies running the Contra war turned a blind eye to the trafficking." The report noted that investigators were unable to find a single drug case that was made on the basis of a tip or report by an official of a US intelligence agency. This despite an executive order requiring intelligence agencies to report trafficking to law enforcement officials and despite direct testimony that trafficking on the Southern Front was reported by CIA officials.

Kerry's committee concluded that the CIA and Oliver North's enterprise knew that drug traffickers had exploited "the clandestine infrastructures established to support the war and that Contras were receiving assistance derived from drug trafficking." Kerry's investigation concluded that "US officials involved in Central America failed to address the drug issue for fear of jeopardizing the war effort against Nicaragua."

These were damning conclusions, so far as the CIA was concerned, but Kerry's people felt that had it not been for constant government obstruction, they could have gone a great deal further.

Unsurprisingly (though of course illegally), the CIA had tried to sabotage the Kerry probe from the start. Evidence of this is found in the files of Lawrence Walsh, the independent counsel in charge of the Iran/Contra investigation. The information came from an interview with Alan Fiers, head of the CIA's Central America task force in the mid-1980s. As a memorandum of an interview conducted by one of Walsh's investigators put it, "Fiers was ... getting a dump on the Sen. Kerry investigation about mercenary activity in Central America from the CIA's legislative affairs people who were monitoring it." The Reagan administration also trumped up an ethics probe of Kerry for his temerity in smearing the Contras. Reagan, it will be recalled, had once honored these cut-throats as "the moral equivalent of the Founding Fathers."

Jack Blum has also described how the Reagan administration's Justice Department tried to undercut the Kerry investigation. The key player here was former Deputy Attorney General William Weld, a longtime political rival of Kerry's from Massachusetts. "Weld put a very serious lock on any effort we made to get information," Blum testified before Congress on October 23, 1996, during hearings into CIA/Contra drug ties prompted by Gary Webb's series. "There were stalls. There were refusals to talk to us, refusals to turn over data." Blum testified thus about ten days before the senatorial election in Massachusetts, where Weld was locked in combat with Kerry in a race that Weld ultimately lost by a narrow margin.

One of the subjects that Kerry and Blum wanted information on concerned the "Frogman" case in San Francisco, where – readers will recall from an earlier chapter – the CIA prevailed on the Department of Justice to return $36,800 seized in the drug raid on the grounds that the money, found in the bedroom of one of the Meneses gang, had been intended for the Contras. Weld's office refused to turn over the files.

US government lawyers also tried to keep one of Kerry's star witnesses from testifying. George Morales was a Colombian-born resident of Miami who had been convicted and sentenced to sixteen years in prison for cocaine trafficking. Justice Department lawyers offered Morales a lighter sentence if he would keep his mouth shut about his ties to the Contras. Morales declined the offer and told his story to Kerry and to Leslie Cockburn for her CBS documentary. Morales said that in 1984 the Justice Department had offered to suspend his indictment for drug trafficking if he would contribute $1 million a year to the Contras and furnish planes from his aviation company, based in Opa-Loka airport, Florida. The Contras, Morales explained, were low on funds at that time, and he had been invited to attend a meeting of Contra leaders at the Miami home of Marta Healey. Present were Octaviano César (a CIA asset) and Adolfo "Popo" Chamorro, former husband of Healey and also nephew of Violetta Chamorro, Nicaragua's future president. Chamorro and César were working to open up a second front in Costa Rica, aiming to take over operations from the uncontrollable Eden Pastora. At the Miami meeting they asked Morales to help them in their quest by providing planes, guns and cash. Both César and Chamorro said subsequently that the CIA had cleared the meeting with Morales. "I called our contact at the CIA, of course I did," Chamorro said. "The truth is, we were still getting some CIA money under the table. They said [Morales] was fine." César went on to say that he was told by a CIA agent that it was okay to be involved with Morales "as long as we didn't deal in the powder."

Morales recounted to the Kerry committee investigators how, over the next two years, he gave at least $3 million to the Contras in drug money. He described a trip in October 1984 to his bank in the Bahamas: Morales withdrew $400,000 in cash there and gave it to César, who noted the amount on a US Customs document.

Morales's story is backed up by two of his pilots. Gary Betzner, a former Navy flier from Arkansas, testified to the Kerry investigators that he had got a call from Morales in 1984 asking for Betzner's help with his indictment. "He [Morales] said that he made a deal with the CIA to supply them [the Contras] with money and with assistance," Betzner testified before Congress in 1987. "He wanted me to fly some guns and ammunition and stuff like that down to the Contras." Betzner says he made several flights in 1984 from Fort Lauderdale to airstrips in Costa Rica, one on the ranch of John Hull and the other nearby. None of these flights required any of the normal paperwork associated with an international flight. The plane was packed with M-16s, M-60 machine guns and C-4 explosive. Betzner says he unloaded the weapons and then put on the plane "seventeen duffle bags and five or six two-foot-six-square boxes filled with cocaine." Betzner recalls that he didn't worry much about being caught because Morales had told him that his flights were "covered." "Well, you know, if the Customs or DEA followed me in when I landed the aircraft I wouldn't have any problem. I mean, they wouldn't bother."

Betzner told Congress of two other pilots who flew drug/gun missions for Morales and the Contras: Geraldo Duran and Marcos Aguado, who – Gary Webb reported – had also done some runs for Norwin Meneses. Aguado claimed to be the head of the Contra air force on the Costa Rican front. He would later assert that he had been duped into working with drug traffickers, saying that people like Morales "fooled people. Unfortunately this kind of activity which is for the freeing of a people is quite similar to activities of the drug dealers." Duran was a Contra pilot from 1982 to 1985. Then, in early 1986, he was arrested in Costa Rica for transporting cocaine into the United States.

There are plenty of other confirmations of the use of Morales by the CIA. Eden Pastora's chief spokesman, Carol Prado, told *Wall Street Journal* reporter Jonathan Kwitny that it was his understanding that Octaviano César and Adolfo Chamorro had indeed told Morales that the CIA would assist him with his legal problems in exchange for his furnishing money and supplies. Furthermore, Oliver North's man in Central America, Robert Owen, testified during the Iran/Contra hearings that he had advised North of his belief that Prado, Aguado and Duran were all involved in the drug business themselves. They were as deep in the trade as Morales.

But some of the most damning information came from another of Morales's pilots, Fabio Ernesto Carrasco. On April 6, 1990, Carrasco was called as a government witness for the Justice Department in a drug trial in Tulsa, Oklahoma. The defense began to probe Carrasco's background and despite the frantic efforts of the federal prosecutor to suppress Carrasco's responses, the following facts emerged.

Carrasco testified that between 1984 and 1985 he flew more than five drug missions for Morales, carrying between 300 and 400 kilos of cocaine into the United States on each flight. He testified that he also flew on Contra resupply flights with Gary Betzner to Costa Rica, when weapons were offloaded and dope put on the plane for the return to Florida. Carrasco said that he believed the flights were authorized and protected by the CIA, and that the cocaine loaded on the planes was owned by Contra leaders Octaviano César and Mario Calero. Carrasco also testified that George Morales gave "several million dollars to César and Chamorro." He recalled making thirty to forty deliveries of cash to the Contra leaders in various "hotels, restaurants and George Morales's house."

The outlines of the Morales and Betzner stories had been publicly known since 1987, but they were derided by the *New York Times* and *Washington Post* as being the testimony of drug felons. *Newsweek* chided Senator Kerry as being a "randy conspiracy buff" for delving into such material. Walter Pincus and Douglas Farah did do a piece in the *Washington Post* in 1996, using the Carrasco testimony in Tulsa of six years earlier, even though this did not prompt the *Post*'s reporters to acknowledge that the earlier investigations by Kerry and by other journalists had been entirely on the mark. Those who doubt the self-serving nature of the journalistic trade as it is often practiced might care to study the tranquil effrontery of the *Washington Post* reporters, as they wrote on October 31, 1996 that stories of CIA ties to drug runners had "been around for more than a decade," but that a two-year congressional enquiry by Senator Kerry "caused little stir when its report was released." The *Post*, on which Walter Pincus was working when the Kerry report was published in 1989, buried it in a mocking story by Michael Isikoff twenty pages deep into the paper.

The *New York Times* didn't bother to cover Kerry's report at all. While Kerry's hearings were in progress, the *Times*'s Keith Schneider wrote a dismissive piece saying that no credence should be attached to the testimony of drug dealers looking to get lighter treatment. It's hard to grasp his reasoning here. Why would the Reagan-Bush Justice Department go easy on drug felons testifying against the administration to a committee controlled by Democrats? Only when Noriega became a target of the Bush administration did the press – notably the *Post* – suddenly start taking the testimony of Morales and others seriously.

After his hearings into CIA-Contra-drug ties, no reporters sought out Kerry on this topic until, in the wake of Gary Webb's series, an ABC News reporter asked Kerry his opinion. "There is no question in my mind," Kerry answered, "that people connected with the CIA were involved in drug trafficking while in support of the Contras. We had direct evidence that somewhere between $10 million and $15 million was going to the Contras. And I am quite confident that this was the tip of the iceberg. The Contras were desperate for money. So in a sense they took a bridge loan from anyone available and the drug lords were available."

The Man from the Medellín Cartel

Ramon Milian Rodríguez was the chief accountant for the Medellín cartel, handling $200 million in drug profits a month while shuttling between Panama, Miami and Colombia. He was another Cuban exile who got his start in anti-Castro drug politics working for Manuel Artime, the CIA-backed terrorist. Milian Rodríguez says one of his first major assignments was to deliver $200,000 in cash from Artime to some of the Cubans involved in the Watergate burglary organized by the Nixon White House in 1972. "I started in one scandal and landed in another," he recalled in a TV interview with Leslie and Andrew Cockburn. Milian Rodríguez says that in the mid-1970s he was asked by the CIA to funnel more than $20 million to the government of Anastasio Somoza to prop up his regime, which was then facing the Sandinista uprising. "If you have people like me in place it's marvelous. The Agency, quite rightly so, has things they have to do which they can never admit to an oversight committee. The only way they can fund these things is through drug money or other illicit funds that they can get their hands on."

In 1982 Milian Rodríguez, in his capacity as a money manager for the Medellín cartel, was approached by his old anti-Castro comrade and CIA man Félix Rodríguez to enlist the cartel in the Contra cause. The

CIA man, Milian Rodríguez says, asked him to contribute $10 million, which was duly delivered on a "per need basis" from 1982 to 1985. The question arises: did the CIA and the Contras know the source of Milian Rodríguez's money. "The Contra peasant didn't know," Milian Rodríguez told the Cockburns, who were doing a documentary broadcast by the PBS Boston PBS station WGBH. "But the men who made the contact with me did. I was under indictment at the time. But a tremendous patriot like Félix Rodríguez, all of a sudden he finds his troops are running out of money, for food, for medicine, for supplies. I think for Félix it was something he did out of desperation. He was willing to get it from any source to continue his war."

When Milian Rodríguez was finally arrested in 1985, the FBI seized his financial papers, including a spreadsheet of 1982 expenditures. The spreadsheet included a column titled "CIA," and recorded $3.69 million in payouts. One vehicle used by Milian Rodríguez to funnel money to the Contras was an outfit already encountered in this chapter, the frozen shrimp company Ocean Hunter, based in Miami and wholly owned by the Costa Rican–based firm Frigorificos de Puntarenas, which enjoyed a State Department contract to provide humanitarian aid to the FDN.

The cocaine accountant says that he was moving about $200,000 a month through Ocean Hunter during this period. Milian Rodríguez says the motives of Medellín cartel leaders were simple enough. The Colombian drug lords would supply the money and in return get protection from the DEA and also safe passage for their cocaine into the burgeoning US market, including the Meneses/Blandón operations in San Francisco and Los Angeles.

The deal with the Medellín cartel, Milian says, was approved by the CIA and certainly proved to be a profitable one for the Colombians. They saw repeated DEA investigations squashed. The amount of cocaine flooding into the US surged. Between 1982 and 1985, according to the DEA, US cocaine imports increased by 50 percen,t and cocaine became the most profitable illicit drug on the US market. The DEA estimated that the overall profits from these imports amounted to $30 billion. The Medellín cartel alone racked up $10 billion a year in sales, prompting *Forbes* magazine to put two of its leaders – Pablo Escobar and Jorgé Ochoa – on its list of the world's richest men in 1988. At the other end of the line from this affluence were the crackheads of South Central and other inner cities.

During the height of the Contra war, *Time* magazine agreed to send its reporter Lawrence Zuckerman to Central America to investigate the drug stories, and Zuckerman returned laden with documented accounts of Contra drug running. *Time* killed them all, and Zuckerman recalled being told by his editor, "*Time* is institutionally behind the Contras. If this story was about the Sandinistas and drugs you'd have no trouble getting it in the magazine."

Sources

With the trail now more than a decade cold, it's unlikely that Leslie Cockburn's book *Out of Control* will be surpassed as a work of original investigation into Contra drug running. The hearing record from the Kerry committee is brimming with unsavory details about CIA complicity in the Contra drug trade and was an important source for this chapter. Jonathan Marshall and Peter Dale Scott's *Cocaine Politics* is a richly documented overview of the relationship between drug traffickers and intelligence organizations throughout Latin America and was a book that we turned to often. Former DEA agent Celerino Castillo's book, *Powderburns*, is a courageous and informative work. The section of this chapter on Castillo is based on that account and interviews with him.

The best history of Manuel Noriega's tenure as the drug general of Panama is Kevin Buckley's *Panama: The Whole Story*. Michael Isikoff's reporting from Noriega's trial is also a useful record, though one his former paper, the *Washington Post*, seems to have forgotten. Noriega's own book is amusing and instructive. The treatment of Brian Barger and Robert Parry by their editors at the Associated Press is told in Mark Hertsgaard's *On Bended Knee*. In a series of books, Peter Kornbluh and Tom Blanton of the National Security Archive have produced the best record of the US war on Nicaragua and have also done much to force into the open the secret history of that war, including Oliver North's notebooks and incriminating e-mail traffic from Reagan's National Security Council. Robert Parry also continues to uncover the darker aspects of the Reagan/Bush policy toward Central America in his newsletter *The Consortium*. Lawrence Walsh's book *Firewall* is a riveting account of how difficult it was – even with a team of FBI agents, federal prosecutors and the power of subpoena – to get at the truth of the crimes committed during the Iran/Contra affair.

Adams, Lorraine. "North Didn't Relay Drug Tips; DEA Says It Finds No Evidence Reagan Aide Talked to Agency." *Washington Post,* Oct. 22, 1994.
Albert, Steve. *The Case Against the General*. Scribners, 1993.
Andreas, Peter. "Drug War Zone." *Nation*, Dec. 11, 1989.

Anderson, Jon Lee. "Loose Cannons." *New Outlook,* Feb. 1989.

Associated Press. "Noriega's Lawyer Claims 7 CIA Chiefs Sought Gun Deals." *Washington Post,* August 23, 1991.

Barger, Brian. "CIA Officer Linked to Surveillance on Two Reporters." AP Wire, Feb. 12, 1988.

Barger, Brian, and Robert Parry. "Nicaraguan Contras and Drugs." AP Wire, Dec. 20, 1985.

Bellamy, Christopher. "CIA Was Embroiled in Contra Drug Fund." *Independent,* Dec. 12, 1996.

Berger, Roman. "The Media's Double Standard: Who Deals Drugs?" *Covert Action Information Bulletin,* Summer 1987.

Bernstein, Dennis, and Howard Levine. "Snowblind." *Tucson Weekly.* Nov. 21, 1997.

Bernstein, Dennis, and Robert Knight. "DEA Agent's Decade Long Battle to Expose CIA-Contra-Cocaine Story." *Pacific News Service,* Oct. 4, 1996.

Bielski, Vince, and Dennis Bernstein. "NSC, CIA and Drugs: The Cocaine Connection." *Covert Action Information Bulletin,* Summer 1987.

Blanton, Tom, ed. *White House E-Mails: Top Secret Computer Messages the Reagan/Bush White House Tried to Destroy.* The New Press, 1996.

Bradlee, Ben, Jr. *Guts and Glory: The Rise and Fall of Oliver North.* Donald Fine, 1988.

Brinkley, Joel. "Contra Arms Crews Said to Smuggle Drugs." *New York Times,* Jan. 20, 1987.

Brooke, James. "Crackdown Has Cali Drug Cartel on the Run." *New York Times,* June 27, 1995.

Buckley, Kevin. *Panama: The Whole Story.* Simon and Schuster, 1991.

Carey, Peter. "Money Smuggling Charges Dropped Against Pilot." *Miami Herald,* June 13, 1985.

Castillo, Celerino III, and Dave Harmon. *Powderburns.* Mosaic Press, 1994.

Chamorro, Edgar. *Packaging the Contras.* Institute for Media Analysis, 1987.

Clarridge, Duane R., and Digby Diehl. *A Spy for All Seasons: My Life in the CIA.* Scribners, 1997.

Cockburn, Andrew, and Leslie Cockburn. *Dangerous Liaisons: The Inside Story of the US–Israeli Covert Relationship.* HarperCollins, 1991.

Cockburn, Leslie. *Out of Control: The Story of the Reagan Administration's Secret War in Central America and the Contra–Drug Connection.* Atlantic Monthly Press, 1989.

——."Flights of Fancy." (Letter) *Nation,* Sept. 1987.

Collier, Robert. "Honduras Drug Traffic Quietly Overlooked." *Pacific News Service.* May 20, 1988.

Corn, David. "Kerry's Drug Hearings: Can the CIA Lift the Veil?" *Nation,* April 30, 1988.

——. "From Contra War to Drug War." *Nation,* June 10, 1991.

——. "A Nod's as Good as a Wink." *Nation,* August 13/20, 1990.

——. *Blond Ghost: Ted Shackley and the CIA's Crusades.* Simon and Schuster, 1994.

Corn, David, and Jefferson Morley. "Beltway Bandits." *Nation,* March 15, 1989.

——. "Arias Strikes Back." *Nation,* April 1, 1989.

Cruz, Arturo. *Memoirs of a Counter-Revolutionary.* Doubleday, 1989.

Dillon, John, and Jon Lee Anderson. "Who's Behind Aid to the Contras?" *Nation,* Oct. 6, 1984.

Dinges, John. *Our Man in Panama.* Random House, 1990.

Draper, Theodore. *A Very Thin Line.* Simon and Schuster. 1991.

Emerson, Steve. *Secret Warriors: Inside the Covert Military Operations of the Reagan Era.* Putnam, 1988.

Engleberg, Stephen. "The US and Panama: Drug Arrest Disrupted CIA Operations in Panama." *New York Times,* Jan. 14, 1990.

——. "US Forgoes Trial of Panamanian." *New York Times,* Feb. 13, 1990.

Farah, Douglas. "Traffickers Said to Buy Contras' Arms; Colombia Also Probes Reported Deal Between Drug Lords, Europeans." *Washington Post,* Sept. 18, 1990.

——. "Drug Dealer Depicted as Contra Fund-Raiser." *Washington Post,* Oct. 4, 1996.

——. "CIA, Contras and Drugs: Questions on Links Linger." *Washington Post,* Oct. 31, 1996.

Gerth, Jeff. "The CIA and the Drug War: A Special Report; CIA Shedding Its Reluctance to Aid in Fight Against Drugs." *New York Times,* March 24, 1990.

Greve, Frank. "Some Latin Politicians Cashing In on Cocaine Smuggling Profits." *Miami Herald,* April 29, 1985.

Gutman, Roy. *Banana Diplomacy.* Touchstone, 1988.

Hatch, Richard. "Drugs, Politics and Disinformation." *Covert Action Information Bulletin,* Summer 1987.

Hersh, Seymour. "Panama Strongman Said to Trade in Drugs, Arms and Illicit Money." *New York Times,* June 12, 1986.

——. "Our Man in Panama." *Life,* March 1990.

Hertsgaard, Mark. *On Bended Knee: The Press and the Reagan Presidency.* Farrar, Straus and Giroux. 1988.

Hitchens, Christopher. "Minority Report." *Nation,* June 20, 1987.

——. "Minority Report." *Nation,* Dec. 18, 1989.

Hoffman, David. "Noriega Drug Questions Ignored, Report Says." *Washington Post,* April 9, 1989.

Honey, Martha. *Hostile Acts.* Univ. of Florida Press, 1994.

——. "Oh What a Tangled Web We Weave When First We Practice to Deceive." *Baltimore Sun.* Dec. 8, 1996.

Howard, Lucy, and Ned Zeman. "The Drug War: A Bad Report Card." *Newsweek.* Jan. 27, 1992.

Isikoff, Michael, and George Lardner, Jr. "Inquiry Sought in CIA's Alleged Use of Drug Ranch." *Washington Post,* July 6, 1990.

Isikoff, Michael. "Noriega Defense Team Vows to Detail Secret US Deals; Trial on Drug Charges Set to Begin Thursday." *Washington Post,* Sept. 3, 1991.

——. "US Witness Admits Contra Flights; Noriega Lawyers Begin Laying Groundwork for Defense." *Washington Post,* Oct. 1, 1991.

——. "Drug Cartel Gave Contras $10 Million, Court Told; Prosecution Witness Startles Noriega Trial." *Washington Post,* Nov. 25, 1991.

——. "Witness: Noriega Moved $19.3 Million Via BCCI; Funds Were Shifted After Drug Indictments." *Washington Post,* Dec. 10, 1991.

——. "US May Widen Anti-Drug Drive in the Caribbean; Pentagon Would Supply Copters to Combat Cocaine Traffickers." *Washington Post,* June 1, 1992.

——. "Noriega's Lawyers Seek Delay to Study Fresh DEA Documents." *Washington Post,* Dec. 16, 1991.

——. "US Probes Narcotics Unit Funded by CIA." *Washington Post,* Nov. 20, 1993.

Johnson, Haynes. "The Contradictions of Panama." *Washington Post,* Dec. 22, 1989.

Kagan, Robert. *A Twilight Struggle.* Free Press, 1996.

Kempe, Frederick. "The Noriega Files." *Newsweek,* Jan. 15, 1990.

Klare, Michael. "Scenario for Disaster: Fighting Drugs with the Military." *Nation,* Jan.

1, 1990.

Kornbluh, Peter. *Nicaragua: The Price of Intervention.* Institute for Policy Studies, 1987.

——, ed. "Contras, Cocaine and Covert Operations" (document packet). National Security Archive, 1997.

Kornbluh, Peter, and Malcolm Byrne. *The Iran–Contra Scandal: The Declassified History.* National Security Archive, 1993.

Kruger, Henrik. *The Great Heroin Coup.* South End Press, 1989.

Kurtz, Howard. "Question of Conflict at AP: Editor Had Met with North over Anderson." *Washington Post,* Dec. 14, 1991.

Kwitny, Jonathan. "Money, Drugs and the Contras." *Nation,* August 29, 1987.

——. "Kwitny Replies." (Letter) *Nation,* Sept. 1987.

——. *The Crimes of Patriots: A True Tale of Dope, Dirty Money and the CIA.* Norton, 1987.

Landau, Saul. "General Middleman." *Mother Jones,* Feb./March, 1990.

Lee, Martin A., and Norman Solomon. *Unreliable Sources: A Guide to Detecting Bias in the Media.* Lyle Stuart, 1990.

LeMoyne, James. "Military Officers in Honduras Are Linked to the Drug Trade." *New York Times,* Feb. 12, 1988.

Lindsay, Sue. "Man Citing Betrayal by CIA, Tells Story." *Rocky Mountain News,* March 1, 1987.

McAllister, Bill. "From Shriner to Smuggler: Witness Says He Made Millions Flying Drugs." *Washington Post,* April 8, 1988.

McNeil, Francis. *War and Peace in Central America.* Scribners, 1988.

Marquis González, Amida. "Aristides Sánchez Dies." *Miami Herald,* May 23, 1983.

Marshall, Jonathan, Peter Dale Scott and Jane Hunter. *The Iran/Contra Connection: Secret Teams and Covert Operations in the Reagan Era.* South End Press, 1987.

Marshall, Jonathan. "Nicaraguans Arrest Ex-Bay Man Linked to Cocaine, Contras." *San Francisco Chronicle,* Dec. 16, 1991.

Massing, Michael. "US Drug Policy on Trial: Noriega in Miami." *Nation,* Dec. 2, 1991.

Meldon, Jerry. "CIA's Latin Assets Cross the Cocaine Line." *I.F. Magazine,* July/August 1997.

Menges, Constantine. *Inside the National Security Council: The True Story of the Making and Unmaking of Reagan's Foreign Policy.* Simon and Schuster, 1988.

Millman, Joel. "Narco-Terrorism: A Tale of Two Sources." *Colombia Journalism Review,* Oct. 1986.

Morley, Jefferson. "Dealing with Noriega." *Nation,* August 27, 1988.

Mower, Joan. "Owen Criticizes Use of Plane, Crew with Shady Connections." AP Wire, May 19, 1987.

Moyers, Bill. *The Secret Government: The Constitution in Crisis.* Seven Locks Press, 1988.

Nairn, Alan. "The Eagle Is Landing." *Nation,* Oct. 3, 1994.

Nordland, Rod. "Is There a Contra Drug Connection?" *Newsweek,* Jan. 26, 1987.

Noriega, Manuel, and Peter Eisner. *America's Prisoner: The Memoirs of Manuel Noriega.* Random House, 1997.

North, Oliver, and William Novak. *Under Fire: An American Story.* HarperCollins, 1991.

Noyes, Dan, and Ellen Morris. "The Trouble with Father Dowling: The Strange Tale of San Francisco's Contra Priest." *Image,* Nov. 8, 1987.

Ostrow, Ronald. "Three Seized in Miami Cocaine Smuggling Linked to Nicaraguan

Interior Minister." *Los Angeles Times,* July 19, 1984.

Parry, Robert. "Dole Nearly Cited in Iran–Contra Report." *The Consortium,* Nov. 11, 1996.

———. "The Kerry–Weld Cocaine War." *The Consortium,* Nov. 11, 1996.

———. "CIA and Perception Management." *The Consortium,* Dec. 9, 1996.

———. "Contra–Cocaine: Big Media's Big Mistakes." *I.F. Magazine,* July/August 1997.

———. *Lost History: Contras, Cocaine and Other Crimes.* The Media Consortium. 1997.

Parry, Robert and Peter Kornbluh. "Iran/Contra's Untold Story." *Foreign Policy,* Fall 1988.

Perry, Mark. *Eclipse: The Last Days of the CIA.* Morrow, 1992.

Rasky, Susan. "North Urged Leniency for Honduran Linked to Assassination Plot." *New York Times,* Feb. 23, 1987.

Ridgeway, James. *The Haiti Files: Decoding the Crisis.* Essential Books, 1994.

Robinson, W. *A Faustian Bargain: US Intervention in Nicaraguan Elections and American Foreign Policy in the Post–Cold War Era.* Westview, 1992.

Rosenfeld, Seth. "Nicaraguan Exile's Cocaine–Contra Connection." *San Francisco Examiner,* June 23, 1986.

Satterfield, David. "Even Latest Fraud Trial Has Contra Tie." *Miami Herald,* Sept. 2, 1987.

Scott, Peter Dale, and Jonathan Marshall. *Cocaine Politics: Drugs, Armies and the CIA in Central America.* Univ. of California Press, 1991.

Shackley, Jacqueline. "True North." *Nation,* June 13, 1994.

Shannon, Elaine. "Confidence Games: How Venezuelan Traffickers Allegedly Colluded with the CIA to Smuggle Coke into the US." *Newsweek,* Nov. 29, 1993.

Sheehan, Daniel. "A Liberal's Dose of Facts." (Letter) *Nation,* Sept. 19, 1987.

Spannaus, Edward, and Jeffrey Steinberg. *Would a President Bob Dole Prosecute Drug Super-kingpin George Bush?* EIR News Service, 1996.

Trento, Susan. *Power House.* St. Martin's Press, 1992.

Uhrich, Kevin. "Contras Crop Up in LA Courts." *LA Weekly,* Oct. 4, 1996.

Umhoefer, Dave. "Fugitive Holds Key to Contra–Coke Mystery." *Milwaukee Journal Sentinel,* Dec. 22, 1996.

UPI. "Contra Accuses Other Rebels of Corruption, Drug Trafficking." UPI Wire, April 26, 1986.

———. "Report: CIA Received Cocaine Cartel Cash." *Washington Times,* June 30, 1987.

US Congress. Joint Select Committee on Iran/Contra. *Final Report.* Government Printing Office, 1987.

US Congress. House. Committee on Foreign Affairs. *US Narcotics Control Program Overseas: An Assessment.* Government Printing Office, 1985.

US Congress. Senate. Subcommittee on Security and Terrorism of the Committee on the Judiciary. *Hearings on DEA Oversight and Budget Authorization for Fiscal Year 1986.* Government Printing Office, March 19, 1985.

———. Subcommittee on Narcotics, Terrorism and International Operations. *Drugs, Law Enforcement and Foreign Policy.* Committee Staff Report, Dec. 1988.

———. Subcommittee on Narcotics, Terrorism and International Operations. *Drugs, Law Enforcement and Foreign Policy Volume I, The Report.* Government Printing Office, April 13, 1989.

———. Subcommittee on Narcotics, Terrorism and International Operations. *Drugs, Law Enforcement and Foreign Policy Volume II, The Exhibits.* Government Printing Office, April 13, 1989.

———. Subcommittee on Narcotics, Terrorism and International Operations. *Drugs, Law*

Enforcement and Foreign Policy: Hearings Transcripts, Part 1: May 27, July 15, and Oct. 30, 1987. Government Printing Office, 1988.
——. Subcommittee on Narcotics, Terrorism and International Operations. *Drugs, Law Enforcement and Foreign Policy. Hearings Transcripts, Part II: Feb. 8, 9, 10 and 11, 1988.* Government Printing Office, 1988.
——. Subcommittee on Narcotics, Terrorism and International Operations. *Drugs, Law Enforcement and Foreign Policy. Hearings Transcripts, Part III: April 4, 5, 6 and 7, 1988.* Government Printing Office, 1988.
——. Subcommittee on Narcotics, Terrorism and International Operations. *Drugs, Law Enforcement and Foreign Policy: The Cartel, Haiti and Central America. Hearings Transcripts, Part IV.*
——. Committee on Foreign Relations. *Report on Panama.* Staff delegation report, Dec. 8, 1987.
——. Subcommittee on Investigations of the Committee on Government Operations. *Drugs and Money Laundering in Panama.* Government Printing Office, 1988.
US District Court for the District of Colombia. *United States of America v. Oliver North.* (Stipulation of Facts.) 1988.
Walsh, Lawrence. *The Final Report of the Independent Counsel for Iran/Contra Matters.* Times Books, 1994.
——. *Firewall: The Iran/Contra Conspiracy and Cover-up.* Norton, 1997.
Washington Times, editorial. "Smearing William Weld." *Washington Times,* Oct. 25, 1996.
Weinstein, Henry. "Informant Put CIA at Ranch of Drug Agent's Killer." *Los Angeles Times,* July 5, 1990.
Worthington, Rogers. "Nicaraguan Woman Gets Three Years in Cocaine Case." *Chicago Tribune,* August 26, 1987.
Zaine, Maitland. "Cocaine Seized from Frogman at San Francisco Pier." *San Francisco Chronicle,* Jan. 18, 1983.

13

The Arkansas Connection: Mena

On March 16, 1986, President Ronald Reagan went on national television to make a desperate pitch for the restoration of congressional aid to the Nicaraguan Contras. This particular war had never been popular with Americans, who stubbornly remained indifferent to lurid scenarios proffered by the Great Communicator that the Sandinistas might sweep north through Guatemala and Mexico to menace Texas. So Reagan deployed a new tactic, denouncing the Sandinistas as a regime that had its hand in the drug trade.

For the previous six months, Oliver North and his colleagues at the National Security Council and the CIA had been leaking stories to the Washington press corps charging that the leadership of the Nicaraguan government, including Defense Minister Humberto Ortega, was in league with the Medellín cartel and with Fidel Castro in a hemisphere-wide cocaine-trafficking network. On that March evening, Reagan displayed a series of grainy photographs purporting to show Sandinista officials loading duffel bags of cocaine in a C-123K military transport plane destined for Miami, Florida.

"I know that every American parent concerned about the drug problem will be outraged to hear that top Nicaraguan government officials are deeply involved in drug trafficking," Reagan said. "This picture, secretly taken at a military airfield outside Managua, shows Frederico Vaughn, a top aide to one of the nine commandants who rule Nicaragua, loading an aircraft with illegal narcotics bound for the United States."

As that *Time* magazine editor told his reporter Lawrence Zuckerman, this was precisely the kind of drug story that would end up on the front pages of American newspapers. But it turned out to be a setup, part of an elaborate sting operation concocted by Oliver North, the CIA, George Bush's drug task force and a convicted drug runner named Barriman Alder Seal. It was Seal who had piloted the plane, equipped with CIA-installed cameras, to that Nicaraguan airstrip and brought the cocaine back to Homestead Air Force Base in Florida. In return for his services, Seal received more than $700,000 and a reduced sentence on pending drug convictions.

Years later the DEA admitted that Seal's CIA-sponsored mission was the only drug flight involving the Sandinistas it had any information about. To this day, Frederico Vaughn remains a figure clouded by mystery, with no one quite sure who he is or who he was working for. Seal wasn't around to answer any questions either. A few weeks before Reagan's television address, Seal was gunned down while in a federal witness protection program in Baton Rouge, Louisiana – a victim of Oliver North's press leaks.

Barry Seal was a veteran of both the drug trade and the intelligence business. Born in Baton Rouge, Seal was a bulky, athletic man with a beguiling presence. He was 5-feet-7-inches tall, weighed 250 pounds and wore thick muttonchop sideburns. He had a passion for cars, women and Snickers bars, though he neither smoked nor drank nor used cocaine.

Seal's first contact with the CIA came in the 1960s while he served as a pilot for the US Army's Special Forces division. He left the army in 1965 to become, at the age of twenty-six, a pilot for TransWorld Airlines, and it's apparent that Seal continued his relationship with the Agency during his employment with the airline. In 1972 Seal was busted by the US Customs Service for attempting to smuggle 14,000 pounds of C-4 explosives into Mexico. The bomb-making material was destined for a CIA-trained cell of anti-Castro Cubans. Seal lost his job at TWA but escaped prosecution when the CIA intervened. The Agency told the US Attorney's office that a trial would "threaten national security interests."

It wasn't long before Seal turned his considerable skills as a pilot and entrepreneur to Latin America's emerging black market in drugs and guns. In the mid-1970s he bought a small fleet of planes, recruited a network of ace pilots and mechanics (many of whom were veterans of the war in Vietnam and Laos) and developed ties to the leadership of the Medellín drug cartel.

By his own admission, Seal became the Medellín cartel's chief link to the cocaine markets of the southeastern United States. In federal court, Seal testified as a government witness in a drug trial that he earned more than $50 million smuggling cocaine and marijuana. But the pilot was most certainly being uncharacteristically modest. Investigators for the Arkansas State Police told the US Justice Department that they believed Seal's enterprise had raked in between $3 billion and $5 billion from the late 1970s up to his bloody death in 1986. Seal's bank records show that in 1981 he was making daily deposits of $50,000 in his favorite bank in the Bahamas. The drug money was reinvested in a variety of schemes, from hotels and casinos to a TV network and a drug company.

In 1982 Seal moved his base of operations from New Orleans to the small town of Mena in the Ouachita Mountains of western Arkansas. It was in this same year that Seal once again hooked up with his friends in the CIA, who were anxious to use Seal's fleet of planes to ferry supplies to Contra camps in Honduras and Costa Rica. The flight plans for Seal's drug enterprise provided the perfect cover for the illicit resupply missions. Seal's planes would fly from Mena to Medellín cartel airstrips in the mountains of Colombia and Venezuela, make refueling stops in Panama and Honduras, and then return to Mena, where the planes would drop parachute-equipped duffel bags loaded with cocaine over Seal-controlled farms near Mena. Seal's men would retrieve the drugs in pickup trucks and deliver them to the cartel's distributors in New Orleans, Miami and New York. Each flight packed between 200 to 500 kilos of cocaine, a load that would then fetch about $13 million on the street. By the early 1980s Seal's planes were making several flights a week.

In 1982, the CIA approached Seal about adding a new element to his flight plans. They wanted him to carry loads of supplies and guns on his trips to Central America. The quid pro quo seemed clear enough to Seal. If he would consent to help the US intelligence agencies, they would once again act as his protectors, keeping his planes from being hassled by US Customs and the DEA. In addition, the CIA agreed to outfit Seal's squadron of planes with the latest in high-tech aviation electronics. The CIA was familiar with at least some of Seal's aircraft, which by then included a Learjet, several helicopters and some large cargo planes, because many of them had been bought from CIA proprietaries, such as Air America and Southern Air Transport. The deal seemed to pay off for Seal. In the early 1980s, the US Customs Service backed off a drug investigation into one of Seal's pilots. In a memo to his superiors, a Customs agent noted, "Joe [name redacted] works for Seal and cannot be touched because Seal works for the CIA."

Some of the weapons Seal's plane flew to the Contra camps were manufactured by a Fayetteville, Arkansas gunmaker named William Holmes. Holmes specialized in the production of automatic pistols mounted with silencers, a weapon of choice for CIA executive actions. Holmes, who had been making guns for the CIA since the mid-1950s, testified in a federal court case that the Agency asked him to make 250 of the weapons for Seal. He later described Seal as "the ramrod of the Mena gun deal."

In 1983, Seal's luck with law enforcement seemed to run out. The DEA nailed him for smuggling 200,000 Quaaludes into a Fort Lauderdale airport, as part of a sting called Operation Screamer. After his indictment, Seal approached the DEA and offered his services as an informant. The DEA turned him down. Seal was convicted in February 1984 and faced the possibility of spending the next ten years in federal prison. Desperate to retain his freedom, Seal, apparently on the advice of his contacts in the CIA, made one last call, this time to Vice President George Bush's drug task force. The drug runner was swiftly granted an appointment. He fired up his Learjet and flew to Washington, D.C., where he met with a Bush staffer named Jim Howell. Howell, a former drug agent at US Customs, interviewed Seal and then took him to see a top DEA agent named Kenneth Kennedy. Howell vouched for Seal, and Seal complained bitterly that the DEA agents in Fort Lauderdale had brushed him off for personal reasons. Although the official position of the DEA was that Seal offered to help the agency gain information on the Medellín cartel, Kennedy recalls that Seal also boasted that he could help the Reagan administration expose the Sandinistas' role in the drug trade. Kennedy told a congressional committee that Seal informed him at their initial meeting that "officials of the Nicaraguan government are involved in smuggling cocaine into the United States, specifically the Sandinistas." Kennedy said that Seal promised to fly to Nicaragua, pick up loads of cocaine and bring them back to the United States.

Kennedy referred Seal to two Miami-based DEA agents, Ernst Jacobsen and Robert Joura. "After he was debriefed in Washington, a phone call was made to Group Six in the Miami Field Division," Jacobsen said in testimony before the House Judiciary Committee in 1989. "We were informed that Barry Seal was in D.C. and wanted to cooperate. I was asked if I wanted to work with Mr. Seal. I said I would."

Seal flew to Miami the next day, where he met with Joura, Jacobsen and Steve LeClair, an attorney with the US Justice Department. Seal told the DEA men that he could easily set up a delivery of 3,000 kilos of cocaine from Jorgé Ochoa's operation in Colombia. After this meeting, Seal was officially signed up as a confidential informant for the DEA: his DEA ID number was SGI-84-0028. The DEA agreed to pay him $800,000 a year for his services and postponed his sentencing on the Quaalude-smuggling conviction.

A few days later Seal called two of the Medellín cartel's top operatives in Miami, Felix Dixon Bates and Carlos "Lito" Bustamante, to let them know that he was back in business. Bustamante oversaw the distribution of Medellín cocaine in the US. Bates was a long-time pilot for the Ochoa network who specialized in smuggling exotic animals to Jorgé Ochoa's ranch in Colombia. Bustamante told Seal that Ochoa wanted him to ferry a Titan 404 plane from Miami to Medellín. Seal agreed to the plan and on April 4, 1984, he and Bates flew to Colombia. They were met at the airstrip by Jorgé Ochoa. Precisely what happened at this meeting is the subject of some controversy. DEA agents Joura and Jacobsen claim that it was at this session that the subject of Nicaragua first came up. They say that Ochoa told Seal that the cartel was moving most of its operations to Nicaragua because of increasing pressures on them in Colombia. This scenario seems far-fetched for a number of reasons, not least because at that time the cartel seemed to be operating with near impunity in Colombia, Panama, Honduras and Costa Rica. An alliance with the Sandinistas would only antagonize the US government, which the cartel was trying so hard to placate.

A more likely story is that Seal and Ochoa used this meeting to plan a sting operation against the Sandinistas designed to keep Seal out of prison and ensure the Medellín cartel the continued good graces of the US intelligence and law enforcement agencies.

Over the next week, Seal visited Panama and Guatemala before returning to Miami, where he conferred with Bustamante and other US representatives of the Medellín cartel. They set up plans for a series of drug flights from Colombia and Panama to Miami, and Seal invited the Colombians to come with him to Mena to inspect the planes that Seal was planning to use for the cocaine flights. The next day Seal flew four Colombians to Mena, where he treated the drug dealers to a lunch of Cajun food and took them for a spin in his new Lockheed Lodestar jet. The Colombians were duly impressed and gave the green light for the drug flights to begin.

The following day Seal relayed the plans to DEA agent Jacobsen, who got approval from the Colombian government for Seal to enter the country and pick up a load of cocaine. Before taking off for Colombia, Seal took the opportunity to make two trips to his bank in the Bahamas, where he deposited several hundred thousand dollars in cash.

A week before Seal was scheduled to fly to Medellín, he blew out an engine on his Learjet during a test run. The DEA paid to have the plane repaired. In the meantime, a DEA agent named S. B. Billbough passed on to the CIA Seal's contention that the Ochoa organization was preparing to move its base of operations to Nicaragua. According to a memo prepared by DEA agent Joura, the CIA expressed "considerable interest" in the Seal operation.

With his Learjet still in the repair hangar, Seal flew to Panama City on May 18 for a meeting with the equivalent of the board of directors of the Medellín cartel. At the session were Jorgé Ochoa, his brother Fabio Ochoa, Pablo Escobar, Bates, and Gonzalo Rodríguez Gacha. Seal arranged to trade one of his helicopters (previously owned by a CIA front) for a Merlin 3B owned by the cartel. It was also at this session that Seal said he was introduced to the mysterious figure of Frederico Vaughn.

The CIA would later claim that Vaughn was a "close associate" of the Sandinistas' interior minister, Tomás Borge. But Vaughn has long been suspected of having his own ties to the CIA. His cousin Barney Vaughn worked for the Popular Bank and Trust Company, once owned by Nicaraguan dictator Anastasio Somoza. The bank was also used by the CIA and Oliver North's operation to funnel money to the Contras. In addition, a telephone number Seal later claimed to be Vaughn's Managua home number turned out to be a line used by US intelligence assets from 1981 to 1986. The Sandinistas claimed that Vaughn had worked as an assistant manager of an import/export company in the capital after the revolution, but had left Nicaragua for Panama in 1983.

Seal said that he and Vaughn flew the next day on Copa Airlines to Managua, where Vaughn showed the pilot the 3,000-foot Los Brasiles airstrip northwest of Managua. Vaughn, Seal said, also pointed out the location of Sandinista anti-aircraft guns stationed throughout the capital. Seal spent the night at Vaughn's house and returned to Florida the next day, just in time for his long-delayed sentencing hearing in Fort Lauderdale on his Quaalude-smuggling conviction.

Seal was sentenced to ten years, but because of his cooperation in the drug operation the sentence was reduced to six months' probation. Federal Judge Norman Roettinger, a law-and-order conservative who had received letters on Seal's behalf from the DEA and the CIA, praised Seal for his work undermining the Sandinista regime.

These problems behind him, Barry Seal was cleared for his first DEA-sanctioned cocaine run. On May 28, Seal and his longtime copilot Emile Camp took off from Mena's Intermountain Regional Airport in Seal's retooled Lockheed Lodestar jet bound for Colombia. They arrived at a small airstrip in the mountains outside Medellín in a driving rainstorm that turned the dirt runway into a strip of mud. Seal nearly wrecked the plane on landing when the jet slid off the runway and into a ditch. The plane suffered damage to its landing gear and Seal was forced to run the return flight in a smaller plane owned by the Medellín cartel. This plane was the same Titan 404 that Seal and Bates had delivered to Medellín a month earlier. According to Seal, senior cartel executive Carlos Lehder himself was at the airstrip to meet his plane. From astride a white Arabian stallion, Lehder supervised a team of Indians who loaded the Titan with more than a ton of cocaine.

The smaller plane's limited range, Seal claimed, forced him to stop in Nicaragua for refueling. He landed at Los Brasiles airport, where he and Camp were greeted by Frederico Vaughn. The plane was quickly refueled and took off for Miami. But almost immediately, Seal told his DEA handlers, his plane was struck by anti-aircraft fire and he was forced to crash-land the plane at the Managua airport. One of Vaughn's associates arrived in a military-style truck and took the cocaine away for safekeeping. Seal and Camp were detained overnight by the Nicaraguan police. But once again, Seal said, in his thoroughly bizarre narrative of this episode, Vaughn came to their rescue, arranging their release from jail and providing them with a new plane to fly back to Florida. Seal claimed that this plane belonged to Pablo Escobar. Vaughn assured Seal that he would safeguard the cocaine until Seal could come back for it.

Seal arrived back in Miami and told his astounding tale to Joura and Jacobsen. Far from being a disaster, Seal told the DEA men, this created a great opportunity to move against the Sandinistas. Plans were swiftly made by the DEA and CIA for a return flight to Nicaragua. The first order of business was to get Seal a new plane. On June 10, Seal traded his Merlin 3B, recently acquired from Jorgé Ochoa, for a C-123K military cargo plane owned by a CIA contractor. Before it could be flown, however, the C-123K needed structural repairs and engine work. DEA agent Jacobsen arranged for the Pentagon to have the plane shipped to Rickenbacker Air Force Base outside Columbus, Ohio, where Air Force mechanics performed $40,000 worth of free work on Seal's plane. After the repairs were completed, the cargo plane was flown to Homestead Air Force Base outside Miami, where CIA technicians installed two hidden cameras, one in the plane's nosecone and the other in the rear cargo hold. The cameras were rigged so that Seal could use a remote control button hidden in his pocket to snap photos at will.

On the morning of June 25, Seal, Camp and their mechanic, Peter Everson, landed the C-123K at Los Brasiles airstrip. Although the CIA and President Reagan would refer to Los Brasiles as a military airbase, it was in fact a civilian runway used primarily by crop-dusters and other agricultural aircraft. Seal claimed that the plane was met by Frederico

Vaughn, Pablo Escobar, Gonzalo Rodríguez Gacha and some Nicaraguan soldiers, who helped carry more than 1,200 pounds of cocaine stuffed in duffel bags from a hangar into the rear of the plane. Seal clicked off a set of grainy and indistinct photos of the drug transfer.

The plane took off about an hour later, after taking on about 2,000 gallons of fuel. The next morning Seal landed his C-123K, nicknamed the Fat Lady, at Homestead Air Force Base, where the DEA took control of the cocaine and CIA agents rushed Seal's roll of film off to be developed in the Agency's photo labs.

Shortly after Seal returned to Florida, Ron Caffery, the head of the DEA's cocaine desk in Washington, D.C., received a call from his boss, David Westrate, assistant administrator of the DEA. Westrate instructed Caffery to brief members of the National Security Council and the CIA on Seal's mission. The next day Caffery met with Oliver North and CIA agent Dewey Clarridge at the Old Executive Office Building adjacent to the White House. He showed North and Clarridge blowups of Seal's photos and identified pictures of Seal, Camp, Vaughn and Escobar. But Caffery was surprised to discover that both North and Clarridge were already well-acquainted with the photos. Caffery recalled being somewhat unaware of Vaughn's background, but noticed that Clarridge seemed to be packing a dossier on the man. "The CIA representative told me that he [Vaughn] was an associate of a government officer, of the Nicaraguan government, which was news to me," Caffery told a congressional committee looking into the Seal affair.

The discussion between North, Clarridge and the DEA man rapidly turned to planning a new sting involving Seal. They decided that Seal should be sent back to Nicaragua with $1.5 million in DEA cash, along with assorted "toys" for Escobar and Vaughn, to arrange a new drug deal. At this point, Oliver North suggested that perhaps Seal could arrange a deal outside Nicaragua, so that Vaughn and Escobar could be arrested and the $1.5 million be turned over to the Contras. Caffery told North that the US Attorney's office would never countenance such a scheme. Then North suggested that perhaps it was time for the DEA to go public with Seal's photos. North told Caffery that "there was an important vote coming up on an appropriations bill to fund the Contras" and that information on Sandinista drug dealing could swing the vote in the administration's favor.

Again Caffery shot down North's idea. He told the North that release of any information on the Nicaragua flight would jeopardize their investigation of the Medellín cartel and place Seal's life at risk. But the information was already beginning to leak out as part of the Reagan administration's propaganda campaign to demonize the Sandinistas. On June 27, General Paul Gorman, head of the Pentagon's Southern Command, made an anti-Sandinista speech at a meeting hosted by the American Chamber of Commerce in El Salvador. Gorman claimed to have proof that the Sandinista leadership was involved in drug smuggling.

This exposure, however, didn't stop the DEA from sending Seal back to Nicaragua for another cocaine buy on July 7. The deal was apparently aborted at the last minute, when, Seal said, he was warned that the Sandinistas had learned about the mission.

By now the NSC and CIA were leaking reports of Seal's Nicaraguan exploits to their friends in the Washington press corps. The *Washington Times,* in a July 17, 1984 front page story by Edmond Jacoby, was the first to report on "evidence" of Sandinista drug trafficking. But Oliver North's diaries reveal that other reporters were also hot for the story. One of the first to lunge at the bait was Doyle McManus, the *Los Angeles Times* writer who savaged Gary Webb. In North's July 17 entry he wrote: "McManus, LA Times says NSC resource claims WH [White House] has pictures of Borge loading cocaine in Nic." McManus's source was dead wrong, of course. Borge had been nowhere near the Seal plane.

Within weeks all the major national papers and news magazines were running stories quoting "high-level" sources in the US government who claimed that they had hard evidence that the Sandinista leadership was "actively participating" in the drug trade. The two names most often cited in the stories were Borge and Defense Minister Humberto Ortega, brother of the president of Nicaragua, Daniel Ortega.

On September 7, with the Contra aid vote fast approaching, Senator Paula Hawkins, a right-wing Republican from Florida, convened a press conference in Washington at which she attacked the Sandinistas as "a brutal regime financed by the drug trade." Hawkins unveiled to the press four obscure photos taken on Seal's June 25 mission. She also displayed a high-altitude photo of the Los Brasiles "military airbase" taken by an

American U-2 spy plane. The photos were not released to the press, but her press conference put the story on the front page once again.

By now Barry Seal's cover as a secret drug agent was completely blown and he went back to what he did best, running drugs and guns. Fortunately for Seal, Congress was not persuaded to renew Contra funding in the fall of 1984 and instead enacted the Boland amendment prohibiting any direct military aid. This meant Seal still had a job shuttling lethal contraband for North's network from Mena to El Salvador, Honduras and Nicaragua. An Arkansas police officer investigating Seal's operation in August 1985 wrote in his report: "Every time Bari [sic] Seal flies a load of dope for the US govt., he flies two for himself."

In late December 1984, Seal was caught flying a load of marijuana into Louisiana. He was released the next day after he posted a $250,000 cash bond. Seal made a call to his friends in the DEA, and on January 7 he was interviewed by Special Agent Dale Hahn of the FBI. According to Hahn's notes, Seal offered to testify against low-level members of the Medellín cartel in exchange for a guilty plea and light sentence on the marijuana-trafficking charges. Over the next year, Seal testified in three major drug cases, helping the feds secure convictions. Seal was eventually sentenced to a six-month term in a halfway house in Baton Rouge.

Shortly after Seal's arrest in Louisiana, his old friend and co-pilot Emile Camp died when his Seneca plane, equipped with state-of-the-art navigational equipment, slammed into a mountain near Mena. Many of Camp's associates believe that his plane had been sabotaged and point out that he was one of the few to witness many of Seal's activities for the CIA and DEA.

In the summer of 1985, Seal decided to sell his C-123K cargo plane for $250,000. The buyer was the same CIA contractor, Harold Doan, from whom Seal had acquired the plane a year earlier. The plane later ended up in the service of Oliver North's Contra resupply program and entered aviation history on October 3, 1986, when it was shot down over Nicaraguan air space and its cargo kicker, Eugene Hasenfus, was taken into custody by the Sandinistas and paraded before the world as living proof of the Reagan administration's war against their country.

Although supposedly in a witness protection program, Seal said he considered himself "a clay pigeon." He was eventually tracked down by a team of assassins working for Jorgé Ochoa and Pablo Escobar. On February 19, 1986, Seal's body was riddled with hundreds of bullets as he sat in his white Cadillac outside the Salvation Army Center in Baton Rouge.

After Seal's death, IRS agents examined his bank records. They determined his estate owed more than $86 million in back taxes, but ended up forgiving much of the debt, citing Seal's "CIA-DEA employment."

By the mid-1980s, Arkansas was an important staging post in the Contra War against Nicaragua being run from Washington. One scheme for maintaining a cover-up for Oliver North's network was, it appears, played out in the Governor's Mansion in Little Rock, Arkansas occupied by a young Bill Clinton.

Among the occupants of that same mansion was Buddy Young, the man in charge of Clinton's security. According to court documents filed by Terry Reed, a former CIA asset involved in North's Contra resupply effort, Young was a pivotal figure in a case designed to land Reed in prison not long after Reed had walked out of an arms-for-drugs operation in Guadalajara, Mexico, where he had been working with CIA man Félix Rodríguez.

Arkansas's role in the Contra War and in an arms-for-drugs supply network goes back to the early 1980s and the airport at Mena. A federal investigation aided by the Arkansas State Police established that Barry Seal had his planes refitted at Mena for drug drops, trained pilots there and laundered his profits partly through financial institutions in Arkansas. Seal at this time was in close contact with North, who acknowledged the relationship in his notebooks and his memoir.

Among those recruited by North was – so the man subsequently asserted in court papers – Terry Reed, formerly with Air America in Thailand. Reed says he was working for North in 1983. North put Reed in touch with Seal, and by 1984 Reed had established a base at the hamlet of Nella, ten miles north of Mena in the Ouachita National Forest. There Nicaraguan Contras and other recruits from Latin America were trained in resupply missions, night landings, precision airdrops and similar maneuvers. Reed, familiar with the commercial affairs of Mena, asserts that large sums of drug money were being laundered through leading

Arkansas bond brokers, an allegation also being considered by a federal investigator just as his researches were abruptly terminated.

One of Reed's contacts in North's network was William Cooper, another Air America veteran then working for Southern Air Transport. Cooper was at the controls of the C-123K once owned by Seal that was shot down by a Sandinista soldier in October 1986. That plane had been serviced at Mena. Cooper died in the crash. His crewman, Eugene Hasenfus, survived.

Back in 1985, Cooper had suggested to Reed that he go to Mexico and set up an operation expanding the supply network. Reed agreed, traveled to Vera Cruz for discussions with Félix Rodriguez and, in July 1986, set up a front company, Machinery International, in Guadalajara.

Three months later Cooper was dead and Hasenfus was being paraded by the Sandinistas before the Managua press corps. Reed says that Machinery International's business, "trans-shipping items" in "support of our foreign politics," was put on hold until January 1987, this at a time when the Iran/Contra cover-up was pressing forward in Washington. Seven months later, Reed says, he became aware that drugs were part of the shuttle passing through Machinery International's premises in Guadalajara and that he himself was a likely candidate for fall guy if things came unglued.

Reed says he confronted Rodriguez and told him he was quitting. By early September 1987 he had returned to the United States. A month later Governor Clinton's security chief, Buddy Young, was activating – from the governor's mansion – a sequence of events seemingly designed to land the potentially troublesome Reed in prison.

The instrument at hand was a plane owned by Reed.

On March 24, 1983, Reed's plane had been stolen from a repair shop in Joplin, Missouri (Reed's home state). Prior to this, Reed says, Oliver North had asked him to contribute this same plane to Project Democracy, a scheme by which individuals would allow their fully insured planes and boats to "disappear" for the sake of counterrevolutionaries in Nicaragua. Reed claims he had refused the request. At all events, the plane was removed while Reed was out of town. Reed duly reported the theft to his insurance company and received compensation. He says that in 1985 North's people contacted him in Mena, told him that his plane was being returned after having been in Central America for two years and asked that he not report its return because they might need to "borrow" it again. Reed consented. He had the plane stored at his hangar in the North Little Rock Airport and left for Guadalajara soon thereafter.

On October 8, 1987, Tommy Baker, a former Arkansas State Police officer and longtime friend of Buddy Young, says he happened to be passing Reed's hangar when a powerful gust of wind blew the door open, revealing a plane. Baker said he thought the plane looked "suspicious" and so called his pal Young at the Governor's Mansion. Young later claimed in testimony that he contacted the National Crime Information Center to check if the plane's registration number came up on a list of stolen planes, found no record of this and then instructed Baker to check if the plane's markings had been changed, a common practice of plane thieves (also a routine practice at Mena and in North's Project Democracy). Baker established that they had been altered, and by October 21, the two claim, they turned the case over to the FBI.

Under scrutiny, the sequence of events as set out by Baker and Young did not stand up. On October 5, three days before that fortuitous gust blew open the hangar door, Young was phoning Reed's parents masquerading as an old friend of their son, according to legal papers filed by Reed. Young had called in the plane's correct registration number to the National Crime Information Center – so the center's records show – on October 7, before Baker had, by his own account, even set eyes on the plane (and before Young had called in with the doctored number). That same evening Young had called Joplin to inquire about the plane's original disappearance. In June 1988, Reed was indicted on mail fraud charges in connection with his 1983 insurance claim on the plane.

Reed accused Young and Baker of preparing and presenting false evidence for the purpose of furthering a false prosecution. This much is clear. In efforts to discredit someone familiar with the Mena operation, Buddy Young made his calls from Bill Clinton's mansion. Young and Baker have admitted to entering Reed's hangar three times without a warrant. They have also admitted to tampering with the plane. When they finally did obtain a warrant, it was on the basis of misrepresentations. According to court documents, they subsequently made false statements to a federal grand jury as well as, on more than one occasion, in hearings related to *United States* v. *Reed.* Finally, evidence that might have helped Reed's case was secreted in Young's office in Clinton's mansion when it was supposed to have been in federal court. A federal judge involved in the case, Frank Theis, declared that Baker and Young had acted with "reckless disregard for the truth." Reed was acquitted when the court determined that the government did not have enough legitimate evidence to convict him.

Three months before his assassination Barry Seal described in sworn testimony to federal and state investigators a nexus of airstrips, front corporations, "legitimate" Arkansas companies and banks participating in the shipment of drugs and laundering of drug profits. His interrogators – IRS agent Bill Duncan and Russell Welch of the Arkansas State Police – had hoped to get Seal to gradually detail the bigger picture and were frustrated in their efforts when Seal, then under a drug conviction in Louisiana, was returned to that state for sentencing. When he was killed, one important path toward uncovering the Contra resupply operation in Arkansas turned cold.

Nevertheless, Duncan and Welch were determined to continue their investigation and follow the trails leading out from Mena into the rest of the state. Where the money trail ultimately led, the investigators never were able to discover fully because their investigation was abruptly halted. One alleged money launderer, conspicuous in Arkansas's politico-financial world and profitably involved in state business, was – according to a source whose information had proved reliable in the past – in receipt of large sums of drug money from Seal. Duncan and Welch eventually prepared a 3,000-page file on Mena, documenting widespread money laundering and drug running. Duncan prepared thirty-five indictments for the US Attorney, but they were never acted upon and in 1988 the Arkansas State Police began shredding its Mena files, including all documents linking Oliver North to Seal and Seal's associate Terry Reed.

There is every indication that many of the illicit activities linking intelligence agencies to drug traffickers continued into the 1990s. An IRS report from the fall of 1991, three years after Duncan left the agency, notes that the "CIA has ongoing operations out of Mena, Arkansas airport ... one of the operations at the airport is laundering money."

Duncan, a special agent in the IRS's criminal division, was assigned to the Mena investigation in 1983. In 1989, he was called to testify before the House Judiciary Committee about the goings-on at Mena. The committee had convened to probe the lack of criminal indictments and the possible hampering of the investigations by the CIA and Clinton's gubernatorial staff in Little Rock. Another agency under scrutiny was the US Attorney's office, which had been empowered to convene a grand jury and bring indictments in the affair, but did not do so.

Duncan had learned of an alleged payoff to US Attorney General Ed Meese by suspects in the Mena investigation. He was told by the IRS's attorneys to deny to congressional investigators that he had any knowledge of this allegation and to state that he had "no opinion" on the reluctance of the US Attorney to convene a grand jury. He refused. Shortly thereafter Duncan was transferred from his IRS job to a position with the Subcommittee on Crime of the House Judiciary Committee, where he continued to probe Mena. Later that year, Duncan was arrested at the Capitol Building in Washington for possession of a concealed weapon (his service pistol) as he tried to enter his office. The case went to the US Attorney General's office, where it was held in limbo for more than a year, effectively preventing Duncan from pursuing the Mena case. He quit the House Judiciary Committee and went to a position with the Arkansas Attorney General's office.

Russell Welch also suffered a similarly rocky career. He had been a criminal investigator for the Arkansas State Police and had worked closely with Duncan on the Mena case since 1983. When the federal government closed down its inquiry, Welch's superiors in Arkansas also took him off the case. Welch claims that an attempt was made on his life in 1991 while he was meeting with Duncan in Little Rock.

In 1992 Clinton spokeswoman Max Parker was asked why Clinton had never responded to the 1990 request of Deputy Prosecutor Charles Black for assistance in forwarding a state inquiry into "the rather wide array of illegal activities" centering on the Mena airport. Black, whose jurisdiction includes Mena, suspected a federal cover-up of activities there. Parker claimed that Black was merely a subordinate in the prosecutor's office and that Clinton went straight to the top. She said Clinton told State Police commander Tommy Goodwin that he would allow

$25,000 to be released to the chief prosecutor in Black's district, Joe Hardagree. Hardagree, Parker said, rejected Clinton's offer of funds as proffered by Goodwin, presumably (according to Parker) because $25,000 was insufficient for such a probe.

But this claim contradicts what Hardagree said in a 1992 letter to Mark Swaney of the Arkansas Committee, a group of citizens looking into the Mena affair: "During my tenure as prosecuting attorney, I did not receive $25,000 in State funds, or any part of this amount of money, nor did I hear anything concerning these State funds, from Colonel Goodwin or anyone at Arkansas State Police or anyone in the Governor's office. The only investigation that I am aware of which has expended funds or resources has been the Grand Jury investigation of the Federal Court for the Western District of Arkansas."

In October 1991 the US Congress appropriated another $25,000 upon the intervention of Arkansas Representative Bill Alexander. The money languished unused in the State Police headquarters. Parker said that it was just a matter of completing some paperwork and that Goodwin would straighten everything out.

But Goodwin was less than forthcoming on the matter in an interview during the 1992 election season. Where once the policeman had been enthusiastic about the resumption of an investigation, now he said he wasn't sure there would be any "value" to it, adding that even if the Mena investigation was to proceed, the chief investigator, Duncan – who was at that time sequestered from reporters' inquiries by his superiors in the Attorney General's office – would not have subpoena power.

Hardagree said that it looked as if political pressure had been exerted on Goodwin. "These are all good people, but they are too involved in politics," Hardagree said. "I think the world of Tommy Goodwin, but someone's put the heat on him."

At a crucial stage in the Contra War, Governor Bill Clinton's personal creation, the Arkansas Development Finance Authority, made its first industrial development loan. The year was 1985, and the recipient of the loan was Park on Meter, Inc., or POM, a parking meter manufacturer based in Russellville, Arkansas. POM, it has been alleged by Michael Riconosciuto, a computer expert serving a prison sentence on drug charges in Washington state, was under secret contract to make components of prototype chemical and biological weapons for use by the Contras, as well as special equipment for C-130 transport planes. Such planes were at that time ferrying drugs and weapons in and out of Mena, which is just a few miles away in western Arkansas. Clinton's state was thus an important link in the Contra supply chain at a time when military aid to the Contras had been banned by Congress.

About a mile north of the airport in Russellville on Highway 331 sits POM's headquarters and factory in a low building made of corrugated metal. POM began making parking meters at this site in 1976. Except for some superficial alterations, its premises are the same ones once owned and occupied by defense giant Rockwell International. Back when POM took over the site from Rockwell, its property covered a little more than thirty-six acres. But between 1976 and 1992 a complicated series of real estate transactions (the county court documents fifteen mortgages or deeds concerning this property over this period) left POM itself owning only about eight acres. The remainder of the property POM deeded to a partnership called MBVG. In 1990, one of the partners in MBVG, a man named Mac Van Horn, leased a portion of this property to the US Army Reserve. A plot of land northwest of POM's property housed the 354th Chemical Company of the 122nd Army Reserve Command.

When Mark Swaney of the Arkansas Committee investigated the site he saw two camouflaged trucks with trailers mounted with what looked like generators for creating smoke screens, along with some military transport trucks and a number of industrial drums. Swaney talked to some of the soldiers there, who told him that they were part of a "smoke unit." A few days later former IRS investigator Bill Duncan took a trip out to Russellville. Duncan saw the drums sitting next to two corrugated metal sheds without windows or markings of any kind. Duncan also saw what he described as "chemical tanker trucks" at the Army Reserve Post. In short, here in a scruffy corner of Russellville was a kind of military/industrial landscape, a setting appropriate to our tale.

Southwest of Russellville there is another kind of military/industrial landscape, this one in a wooded valley that surrounds Mena. So far we have described Mena as a center for covert operations involving Contra training and resupply missions, as well as drug smuggling and money laundering. Mena was also important as a base for aircraft maintenance and retrofitting.

We come now to Michael Riconosciuto, a former contract employee of the CIA, who says he worked at Mena on and off between 1980 and 1989. Riconosciuto was arrested on drug charges shortly after being named as a witness in the Inslaw Corporation's case against the US government for the latter's alleged unauthorized use of the PROMIS software, which Riconosciuto wrote for Inslaw. Riconosciuto claims he was set up. He is now in prison in Washington state.

According to Riconosciuto, Mena was part of a network of bases that evolved over time, rising and receding in importance with the changing needs of US covert operations. He says that at the time he was involved, Mena was crucial because of its central location relative to other bases, because of its retrofitting and maintenance facilities and because of its role as the administrative center of the operations. Finally, he says, Mena was the main drop-off point for narcotics shipments, the other bases serving as distribution points or as "nesting facilities" for the aircraft, mainly a fleet of about thirty C-130 transport planes.

Thus Riconosciuto is the third person who stepped forward with details of the covert military and narcotics operations at Mena, corroborating information already supplied by Barry Seal and Terry Reed. But unlike Seal, who was primarily a drug smuggler, and Reed, who supervised the training of pilots and participated in resupply operations, Riconosciuto served in a technical and administrative capacity that gave him a broader picture of the whole operation. He came to Mena with a background in computer technology and programming as well as intelligence experience, gained from working with the Wackenhut Corporation, a private security firm whose imbrication with the intelligence world is well known. In Mena, Riconosciuto supervised the transshipment of high-tech equipment (including infrared gun scopes and night-vision goggles) to the Contras, maintained the administrative computer network and developed accounting software to facilitate the electronic transfers of funds for the money-laundering side of the operation.

Riconosciuto says that to his knowledge no drugs were ever unloaded at the Mena airport itself. As with Seal's setup in Louisiana, planes flying at low altitude would use drag chutes to drop containers of drugs in the surrounding countryside. Sometimes the dope would be dropped onto clearcuts in the Ouachita National Forest. More often it would be dropped onto farmland outside Mena. The drugs would be picked up by helicopter or truck and taken to a loading area, from which they would be sent to distribution points via truck or two-engine plane. He described a constellation of support facilities for both the shipment of drugs and for the manufacture of airplane parts. Independent sources for parts were especially necessary both to ensure a ready supply of equipment without attracting undue attention and to provide equipment that could not be easily traced if a plane crashed or was captured.

Riconosciuto's account of these support facilities matched, in many of its particulars, the evidence gathered by state and federal investigators who were on the trail of the Mena operation from 1983 to 1988. But in the same way that his story augmented the picture drawn from Seal and Reed, so it extends the line of supporting actors beyond the environs of Mena. Which brings us back to the headquarters of POM.

POM, according to Riconosciuto, was not merely in the business of making parking meters. He says that beginning in 1981, the company also made ferry drop tanks – external fuel canisters – for use on C-130s. Drop tanks are essentially nothing more than aerodynamic metal containers, well within the production capabilities of a company set up to make parking meters. These tanks, attached to pylons on the wings and jettisoned when empty, are necessary to fuel long-range transport missions. While standard on C-130s and other military aircraft, they are virtually unknown in civilian use.

To this point, most of our discussion of Mena has centered on conventional weapons delivery and more or less conventional training. But Riconosciuto points to other, even more sinister, tactics that began to take shape in Arkansas. By 1983, he says, it was clear to US intelligence that the Contras were unable to inflict real damage on the Sandinista troops and needed a tactical advantage – either through the use of high-tech weaponry and equipment, such as the infrared and night-vision devices mentioned above, or through unconventional weaponry. To this end, Riconosciuto says, POM was enlisted in a project with the Stormont Labs of Woodland, California, and the Wackenhut Corporation to develop chemical and biological weapons that could be deployed in guerrilla warfare. POM was assigned the task of producing the munitions themselves.

Recall the configurations on the ground in that corner of Russellville described above. According to Riconosciuto, the Army Chemical unit had an arrangement to provide POM with the chemical agents once the prototypes had become advanced enough for testing. These prototypes were meant to be fairly simple devices – a hand-held grenade, a mortar shell, a small bomb – all of which could have been produced with the machinery on hand at POM.

Stormont confirmed in 1992 that in the early 1980s it was approached by Wackenhut in connection with the development of biological weapons, but denied that anything went beyond the talking stage. Wackenhut denied any involvement with Stormont, POM or Riconosciuto. When asked in 1992 about allegations by Riconosciuto that POM built aircraft drop-tanks and had been engaged to produce bio-chem munitions, "Skeeter" Ward, boss of POM, said breezily to Bryce Hoffman of the *Nation,* "Hell no. What we make is re-entry nose cones for the nuclear warheads on the MX missile and nozzles for rocket engines." He also said, "We have got a contract with McDonnell Douglas to make aircraft parts, but I don't even know what that's about." "Skeeter" Ward is the brother-in-law of Webster Hubbell, Clinton's disgraced assistant attorney general. POM was founded by Seth Ward Sr., the father of Hubbell's wife, Suzie. While an attorney at the Rose Law firm, Hubbell had shepherded POM's application to become the first company to receive an industrial development loan from the Arkansas Development Finance Authority. This loan for $2.75 million was rushed to completion in the closing hours of 1985.

The Arkansas Development Finance Authority came into being in April of that year as part of Clinton's sweeping Economic Development Initiative. What had previously been the Arkansas Housing Development Agency, which offered low-interest loans to develop single-family housing, was now revamped into a kind of full-service financial institution charged with attracting capital into the state for the purposes of industrial development, job creation, agricultural and even aquacultural financing. It advertised itself as an agency especially helpful to small companies "who have traditionally been excluded from the bond market by high issuance costs and servicing fees" but which under the umbrella of ADFA bond issues would be able to trim such costs.

The crux of ADFA's mission was to offer companies long-term loans financed through the sale of tax-exempt bonds. Companies in need of capital would come to ADFA, which in turn arranged for the issuance of a bond from a private bondholder, which ADFA then offered for sale. (The state of Arkansas did not guarantee these bonds, but by virtue of ADFA's involvement the bonds receive tax-free status.) When the bonds were sold, ADFA delivered the indenture and a record of the bond owners to a bank, which became the trustee of the deal. ADFA thus served as a kind of middleman in a deal between the trustee and the companies. The trustee was responsible for collecting the payments on the loan and interest and was also responsible for paying out dividends and ultimately the principal to the bond holders. In turn, the trustee bank was allowed to invest the money it got from the bond issue in Treasury bills, CDs, money market accounts, or even time deposit accounts at other banks.

The trustee had huge latitude in deciding where to invest these funds. According to ADFA's standard contract the trustee was limited only by the stipulation that wherever the money was invested, it had to be guaranteed by the US government in some way. However, this stipulation was not always honored. There are records of a deal in which a trustee invested in Fuji Bank's Grand Cayman Islands branch, a favorite depository of drug dealers.

Many of the beneficiaries of ADFA deals bore the aroma of Clinton's inner circle. Among underwriters of the agency's bond issues, Stephens Inc. featured prominently. The company's chairman, Jackson Stephens, and his son Warren helped Clinton raise more than $100,000 for his 1992 campaign. In January of that year, the bank Stephens has a controlling interest in, Worthen National, extended to Clinton a $2 million line of credit. The name of the Worthen bank, represented by Hillary's Rodham Clinton's Rose Law firm on several occasions, appeared among institutions that have from time to time had liens on POM.

Another familiar name on the bond issues was the now-defunct Lasater and Co. Dan Lasater, who headed the company, is a long-time friend of Clinton and his brother, Roger. Both Roger Clinton and Lasater were convicted on cocaine charges.

Thus ADFA was at the center of financial dealings in which large amounts of money could be moved around easily and, it would seem, discreetly. Because ADFA was not subject to legislative oversight – being solely within the purview of the governor's office – and because of the loose strictures upon the trustee bank, it also opened the gate for questionable, possibly illicit financial dealings. As IRS man Bill Duncan explained, theoretically, bonds could be issued to provide a loan to a company involved in laundering drug profits. That loan represented clean money. The loan could in turn be paid back with drug profits, slowly over time and in small increments. In this way drug money could be successfully filtered into the legitimate financial system. If the company in question did nothing more with the loan than redeposit it into its bank account, then the company had lost nothing but it had gained clean money. Thus, in effect, ADFA could serve as a washing machine – dirty money could be cleaned simply by passing through its system. Duncan suggested that it would also be possible for ADFA clients never to repay a loan and for the money simply to be circulated through the trustee's investment end of the arrangement.

In the case of POM, records concerning the $2.75 million loan were curiously incomplete. One ADFA document stated that twenty-four jobs had been created; another cited total wages paid of $2.56 million. No repayment records for POM were available in 1992, when ADFA's operations were under our scrutiny, though ADFA officials said that POM had paid off the loan in 1991, two years ahead of schedule.

The Mena story was going critical in the spring of 1992 amid Clinton's bid for the Democratic nomination. The major networks were poised to do big probes. Then beneath the banner headline "Anatomy of a Smear," *Time* took up the Mena saga in its April 15, 1992 issue. *Time*'s reporter, Richard Behar, took a full page to suggest that the story was all nonsense and that Governor Bill Clinton had been maligned.

Leaving aside for the moment the matter of Behar's motives, *Time*'s story was ludicrous, claiming that all reports of Contra resupply and CIA activities in western Arkansas stemmed from allegations by Terry

Reed, the former pilot, trainer of the Contras and associate of George Bush's pal Félix Rodríguez. Reed, according to Behar, said that the drugs and arms "enterprise" in Mena was "personally supervised" by Clinton. Reed had never said that to anyone. In an extensive clip file on Mena, including many stories in the Arkansas press dating back to 1987, no trace of any such claim can be found, even in the form of dismissals of assertions too silly to be taken seriously.

But *Time*'s hit piece was successful. The networks abandoned the story in those important weeks. Later one of *Time*'s senior editors, Strobe Talbott, was appointed to a high-level post in the Clinton State Department. Talbott's wife, Brooke Shearer, also landed a job in the administration.

The suppression of the Mena story did not end with the election of Bill Clinton. In 1994, while researching a book on Bill and Hillary Clinton, investigative reporter Roger Morris came across a mound of new information on Mena, including Barry Seal's notebooks, tax filings and bank records. Morris was a former National Security Adviser to Richard Nixon who resigned his position in protest of the invasion of Cambodia. He went on to write a biography of Nixon, as well as trenchant books on Henry Kissinger and Alexander Haig.

To pursue the Mena story, Morris joined forces with another investigative reporter, Sally Denton. Denton was the author of *The Bluegrass Conspiracy,* a gripping account of political corruption and drug dealing in Kentucky. By the fall of 1994, Morris and Denton had amassed a 2,000-page file on Seal, Clinton and Mena. They wrote up part of the story and submitted it to the op-ed page of the *New York Times.* The story was swiftly rejected. When Morris asked the *Times*'s op-ed page editor, Michael Levitas, why the paper turned down the article, Levitas replied that this was a *"Wall Street Journal* kind of story." Levitas also pointed out that the *Times*'s news staff had looked at Mena and declined to cover it.

So Morris and Denton took their piece to the Outlook section of the *Washington Post,* whose deputy editor, Jeffrey Frank, accepted the story, praising the authors for writing an explosive and extraordinary article. But the story ran into innumerable roadblocks. Over the next eleven weeks the article was edited, re-edited, fact-checked and reviewed by the *Post*'s legal team. Morris and Denton were subject to detailed questioning from *Post* reporters and editors from the news section. Finally, on January 25, 1995, the story seemed ready to go. The galleys were set, contracts were signed and the story was scheduled to run on Sunday, January 29, 1995.

As the Outlook section was headed to press, Jeffrey Frank called Morris, leaving a message on his answering message to the effect that the *Post*'s managing editor, Robert Kaiser, had killed the story. Morris called Kaiser for an explanation, but the *Post* editor refused to take his call. Kaiser's secretary told the exasperated writer, "He doesn't want to talk to you."

Why did Kaiser kill the piece? Morris doesn't know. But a former *Washington Post* staffer tells us that Walter Pincus, the paper's long-time intelligence reporter, had dismissed the story as "garbage." Editors at the *Post* had leaked the substance of Morris and Denton's story to both the White House and the CIA, which furiously denied the story.

Eventually, Morris and Denton's excellent article appeared in *Penthouse* magazine and hardly met with the explosive reception that such a story deserved. A similar fate awaited Morris's book on the Clintons, *Partners in Power,* which was greeted by reviewers in the mainstream press with a mixture of indifference and hostility.

For his part, Bill Clinton has studiously avoided the subject, mentioning Mena in public only once since being elected president. His statement came in response to a question at an October 1994 press conference from the Associated Press White House correspondent, Helen Thomas, who asked the president what he knew about the use of Mena as an outpost for gun/drug runners associated with the Contra War. "They didn't tell me anything about it," Clinton said. "The state really had next to nothing to do with it. The local prosecutor did conduct an investigation based on what was in the jurisdiction of state law. The rest of it was under the jurisdiction of the United States attorneys who were appointed successively by previous administrations. We had nothing – zero – to do with it."

But Clinton's claim of ignorance didn't ring true. One of his state prosecutors, Charles Black, brought the issue to Clinton's attention in 1988, emphasizing its role as a nexus for international drug operations.

Five years before that there was a federal investigation into drug money laundering at Mena – an investigation joined by Clinton's own state police. As part of that investigation, a federal grand jury was assembled. This grand jury was eventually dismissed, and the local press carried reports that members of the panel had been prevented from seeing crucial evidence, hearing important witnesses and even seeing the 29-count draft indictment on money laundering drawn up by an attorney with the Justice Department's Operation Greenback. In 1989 Clinton received petitions from Arkansas citizens demanding that he convene a state grand jury and continue the investigation. Winston Bryant made Mena an issue in his successful campaign for attorney general in 1990. A year later Bryant turned over the state files involving Mena, along with petitions from 1,000 citizens, to Iran/Contra prosecutor Lawrence Walsh. Later that year, on August 12, 1991, Clinton's adviser on criminal justice wrote to a concerned citizen to say that Clinton understood the matter of criminal activity in Mena was being studied by Bryant, Walsh and Arkansas Representative Bill Alexander.

Yet with all this knowledge Clinton did nothing. The state attorney general did not have the power to conduct an investigation, but the state prosecutors did. When Charles Black urged Clinton to allocate funds for such an investigation, Clinton refused his request. The Arkansas State Police were taken off the case and their files shredded.

Clinton's protestations of ignorance on the matter also don't square with the story told by a former Clinton friend and Arkansas state trooper L. D. Brown. Brown worked on Clinton's security detail in the 1980s. He says that in 1984 Clinton encouraged the 29-year-old trooper to apply for a position with the CIA. Clinton, Brown claims, even helped prepare a writing sample to accompany his application to the intelligence agency. The paper was an analysis of Marxist movements in El Salvador and Nicaragua. Brown says the essay took a hard-line Reaganite approach and did not display any sympathy for the cause of the Sandinistas or the Salvadoran revolutionaries.

In a 1995 court case, Brown testified that he was contacted by the CIA in October 1984 and instructed to meet with Barry Seal at the Cajun Wharf restaurant outside Little Rock. At the meeting, Seal asked Brown to fly with him on a mission to Central America. Brown testified

THE ARKANSAS CONNECTION: MENA

that he and Seal left Mena airport on October 23 in Seal's C-123K transport, dropped cartons of M-16s over Contra base camps and landed for refueling at an airstrip in Honduras. There, Brown said, he saw Seal take on board more than a dozen duffel bags, which were kicked out of the plane over fields near Mena on the return flight. Brown later learned these bags were filled with cocaine.

After two more of these flights, Brown says he confronted Clinton about Seal's operation. Clinton, Brown testified, didn't seem surprised, telling the trooper, who was an admirer of George Bush, "Your hero Bush knows about it." Of the cocaine coming into Mena, Brown testified that Clinton snapped, "That's Lasater's deal." The reference appears to have been to long-time Clinton intimate Dan Lasater, the Little Rock–based bond magnate who was one of the governor's biggest campaign contributors. Lasater had also been convicted of distributing cocaine and was suspected, according to Roger Morris's account, of using his deals with ADFA to launder some of his drug profits.

Like Clinton, the CIA kept a low profile during the decade of controversy over Mena. The Agency repeatedly denied any activities at Mena, claiming at most that it was "a Rouge operation of the DEA." Then, in 1995, with the Republicans newly in charge of Congress, Rep. Jim Leach of Iowa used his position as chairman of the House Banking Committee to launch a new investigation into money laundering, drug-running and intelligence operations at Mena. One of Leach's first orders of business was to request that the CIA's Inspector General, Frederick Hitz, review the agency's files and prepare a report on Mena.

The report was completed in November 1996. It remains classified, but a summary of the report was released by Leach. Though still a whitewash, the IG report for the first time admitted that the CIA did have a sustained presence at Mena through the 1980s and early 1990s. According to Hitz's report, the CIA conducted "authorized and legal activities at the airport." These activities included contracts for "routine aviation-related services." They also involved a still top-secret "joint training operation with another federal agency." The other federal agency is almost certainly the National Security Council, which the Inspector General's report claims handled the "interface with local officials." The investigation also confirmed L. D. Brown's claim that he applied for a position with the Agency in 1984.

The confession that Leach finally extracted from the CIA regarding its operations at Mena received scant notice from the press, with only the *Wall Street Journal* covering the report in any detail. The *Post*'s Walter Pincus wrote a short item on the report, faithfully echoing the CIA's line that it had no involvement in "money laundering, narcotics trafficking, [or] arms smuggling."

Christopher Reed, a reporter with the *Guardian,* recalls asking a senior news executive at the *Los Angeles Times* if the paper had investigated the allegations of drugs and arms smuggling at Mena. "Yes," the executive told Reed. "But nobody in authority would confirm it."

Such passivity on the part of the press allowed the CIA and Bill Clinton to portray the Mena scandal as, in the words of White House spin doctor Mark Fabiani, "the darkest backwater of right-wing conspiracy theories."

Sources

The background for this chapter comes largely from a series of interviews by the authors and their colleagues Bryce Hoffman and JoAnn Wypijewski. The interviewees included Bill Duncan, Larry Nichols, Russell Welch, Terry Reed, Michael Riconosciuto, Mark Swaney, Skeeter Ward, Charles Black, Joe Hardagree, Tommy Goodwin, Rep. Bill Alexander and David Orr. Most of the background for Seal's history as a smuggler and DEA/CIA agent during the 1980s comes from a chronology of Seal's movements prepared by the DEA for Rep. William Hughes's hearings on Seal. The story of how Seal was hired as an informant comes from testimony to the Hughes committee by his DEA handlers. Roger Morris and Sally Denton's story, and Morris's book, provided a key source for Seal's life and his adventures in Arkansas. Their *Penthouse* article also details their encounters with the *New York Times* and the *Washington Post.* Jonathan Kwitny's early story in the *Wall Street Journal* effectively dismantled the Reagan administration's attempt to use Seal to link the Sandinistas to the drug trade. Bill Duncan's tumultuous career at the IRS is recounted in congressional hearings investigating the retaliatory actions by senior officers at the agency.

Allen, Charles F., and Jonathan Portis. *Bill Clinton: Comeback Kid.* Carol, 1992.
Anderson, Jack, and Dale Van Atta. "Intrigue in the Ozarks." *Washington Post,* March 1, 1989.

——. "Legacy of a Slain Drug Informer." *Washington Post,* Feb. 28, 1989.
——. "Medellín Cartel Targets DEA Agents." *Washington Post,* Sept. 16, 1988.
——. "Kings of the Medellín Cartel." *Washington Post,* August 24, 1988.
Arbanas, Michael. "Hutchinson Knew in '83 of Seal Probe, Ex-IRS Agent Says." *Arkansas Gazette,* Sept. 19, 1990.
——. "Truth on Mena, Seal Shrouded in Shady Allegations." *Arkansas Gazette,* Dec. 22, 1990.
——. "FBI Apparently Investigating Mena, Seal." *Arkansas Gazette,* May 24, 1991.
Bowers, Rodney. "Slain Smuggler Used Airport." *Arkansas Gazette,* Dec. 14, 1987.
——. "House Investigators Open Mena Probe." *Arkansas Gazette,* Dec. 17, 1987.
Byrd, Joann. "Put on Hold." *Washington Post,* Feb. 12, 1995.
Cockburn, Alexander. "Say It with Flowers." *Nation,* Feb. 10, 1992.
——. "Chapters in the Recent History of Arkansas." *Nation,* Feb., 24, 1992.
——. "The Secret Life of a Parking Meter Manufacturer." *Nation,* April 6, 1992.
——. "Clinton Cocaine Scares." *Nation,* April 20, 1992.
——. "*Time's* Attack on *Nation,*" May 4, 1992.
Cockburn, Leslie. *Out of Control.* Atlantic Monthly Press, 1987.
Crudele, John. "Drugs and the CIA – A Scandal Unravels in Arkansas." *New York Post,* April 21, 1995.
——. "Bombshell in Arkansas Investigations Brings Both Parties the Jitters." *New York Post,* August 14, 1995.
Eddy, Paul, Hugo Sabogal and Sara Walden. *The Cocaine Wars.* Norton, 1988.
Epstein, Edward Jay. "On the Mena Trail." *The Wall Street Journal,* April 20, 1994.
Evans-Pritchard, Ambrose. "Airport Scandal Set to Crash into White House." *Daily Telegraph.* March 27, 1995.
Gutman, Roy. "The World That Made Cocaine." *Washington Post,* May 21, 1989.
Haddigan, Michael. "'Fat Man' Key to Mystery." *Arkansas Gazette,* June 26, 1988.
——. "The Kingpin and His Many Connections." *Arkansas Gazette,* June 27, 1988.
Henson, Maria. "Testimony Reveals Leak in Drug Probe: Cost Seal His Life Witness Says." *Arkansas Gazette,* July 29, 1988.
Isikoff, Michael. "Noriega Lawyer Scores Prosecution." *Washington Post,* April 12, 1992.
——. "Dispatches from the Drug Front." *Washington Post,* July 1, 1990.
Kwitny, Jonathan. "Dope Story: Doubts Rise on Report Reagan Cited in Tying Sandinistas to Cocaine." *Wall Street Journal,* April 22, 1987.
Lardner, George. "Ex-CIA Airline Tied to Cocaine." *Washington Post,* Jan. 20, 1987.
Lewis, Charles, Alejandro Benes and Meredith O'Brien. *The Buying of the President.* Avon Books, 1996.
Maranis, David. *First in His Class: The Biography of Bill Clinton.* Simon and Schuster, 1995.
Mermelstein, Max. *The Man Who Made It Snow.* Simon and Schuster, 1990.
Morris, Roger. *Partners in Power: The Clintons and Their America.* Henry Holt, 1996.
Morris, Roger, and Sally Denton, "The Crimes of Mena." *Penthouse,* Feb. 1995.
Morris, Scott. "Clinton: State Did All It Could in Mena Case." *Arkansas Gazette,* Sept. 11, 1991.
Morrison, Micah. "Mena Coverup? Razorback Columbo to Retire." *Wall Street Journal,* May 10, 1995.
——. "Mysterious Mena." *Wall Street Journal,* June 29, 1994.
——. "Mysterious Mena: CIA Discloses, Leach Disposes." *Wall Street Journal,* Jan. 29, 1997.

Nabbefeld, Joe. "Evidence on Mena/CIA Ties to Go to Walsh." *Arkansas Gazette,* Sept. 10, 1991.

Norman, Jane. "Arkansas Airstrip Under Investigation." *Des Moines Register,* Jan. 26, 1996.

North, Oliver, and William Novak. *Under Fire: An American Story.* HarperCollins, 1991.

Parry, Robert. *Fooling America: How Washington Insiders Twist the Truth and Manufacture the Conventional Wisdom.* Morrow, 1992.

Pincus, Walter. "Hitz Says Arkansas Town Not a Secret CIA Base." *Washington Post,* Nov. 9, 1996.

Reed, Terry, and John Cummings. *Compromised: Clinton, Bush and the CIA.* Shapolsky Publishers, 1994.

Robinson, Deborah. "Unsolved Mysteries in Clinton Country." *In These Times,* Feb. 12–18, 1992.

Sharkey, Jacqueline. "True North." *Nation,* June 13, 1994.

Snepp, Frank. "Clinton and the Smuggler's Airport." *Village Voice,* April 14, 1992.

Starr, John Robert. *Yellow Dogs and Dark Horses: Thirty Years on the Campaign Beat.* August House Books, 1987.

Tyrell, R. Emmett Jr. "The Arkansas Drug Shuttle." *American Spectator,* August 1995.

US Central Intelligence Agency. *Inspector General's Report on CIA Activities at Mena, Arkansas* (Declassified Summary). Central Intelligence Agency, Nov. 1996.

US Congress. House. Subcommittee on Crime of the Committee on the Judiciary (Hughes Committee). *Enforcement of Narcotics, Firearms, and Money Laundering Laws. Appendix I. – Chronology of Seal's Role as Drug Trafficker and Confidential Informant for the Drug Enforcement Administration.* Government Printing Office, 1989.

——. Subcommittee on Crime of the Committee on the Judiciary (Hughes Committee). *Enforcement of Narcotics, Firearms, and Money Laundering Laws. Testimony of Ernst Jacobsen, Drug Enforcement Field Agent. Ron Caffery, Chief of the Cocaine Desk in 1984, DEA; Frank Monastero, Former Assistant Administrator DEA; and Dave Westrate, Assistant Administrator DEA.* Government Printing Office, 1989.

——. Commerce, Consumer and Monetary Affairs Subcommittee of the Committee on Government Operations. *Continued Investigations of Senior-Level Employee Misconduct and Mismanagement at the Internal Revenue Service.* Government Printing Office, 1991.

US Executive Office of the President. "Transcript of Questions Asked of President William J. Clinton." White House Press Office, Oct. 7, 1994.

14

The Hidden Life of Free Trade: Mexico

The bulk of this book has addressed the collusion between the CIA and drug producers and traffickers. We have described how the political imperative of the Agency has guided it from the very moment of its inception into criminal associations. But as we have stressed earlier, it is always a mistake to regard the CIA as somehow a "rogue agency": whether in recruiting Nazi scientists, in saving war criminals like Klaus Barbie, in nourishing the Southeast Asia drug crops, in protecting the transfer of drugs from Latin America northward, the Agency has always been following national security policy as determined by the US government. The Mexican saga and the role of the US banks display not just the collusion of a spy agency in narco-trafficking, but of the US banking industry as well. The looting of Mexico, the corruption of its institutions, was no distant affair, something mysterious like political corruption in Bangkok. Even as the Mexican state was on display as an entity as lawless as Chicago in 1928, even as a tsunami of drugs and drug money was coming north, the US government, backed by almost the whole of the US press, was loudly praising the Mexican kleptocracy run by the Salinas family as "reform-minded" and urging even closer ties.

So though this book is mostly about the CIA, it would be unfair to the Agency not to stress that the patrons, facilitators and benefactors of the drug trade extend far into those US institutions in whose interest – to take the long view – the CIA toils so diligently. On the other side of the coin, the US government that has been bolstering the drug billionaires has also been assisting diligently in repressing popular movements of resistance, as we describe below.

Around noon on February 7, 1985, Enrique "Kiki" Camarena, one of the DEA's top agents in Mexico, locked his badge and his service revolver in his desk drawer, left his office in the US consulate and headed out for a lunch appointment with his wife, Geneva. His wife waited at the restaurant for two hours, but Camarena never showed. She didn't report his absence until the following morning, thinking he had been detained at work. Later the next day the DEA office in Guadalajara got a call from an anonymous tipster saying that Camarena had been kidnapped by a drug cartel headed by Miguel Félix Gallardo, Ernesto Fonseca Carrillo and Rafael Caro Quintero. These were the same narco-traffickers whom Camarena had been investigating for the previous two years.

Two witnesses were rounded up who reported that as he left the consulate Camarena was surrounded by five gunmen and shoved into the back seat of a waiting car. The witnesses said the gunmen appeared to be members of the Mexican secret police, the DFS. Another informant told the DEA that he had heard talk that the Gallardo-Quintero cartel was planning to kill "a lawman."

Two days later, the DEA learned that Rafael Caro Quintero was at the Guadalajara airport ready to board a private plane bound for Mexico City. The agents contacted the Mexican Federal Judicial Police and converged on the airport. The jet was surrounded by ten men carrying AK-47s, and Caro Quintero was approached by police Commandante Armando Pavón. To the astonishment of the DEA agents, Pavón and Caro Quintero shook hands, talked warmly and the plane was permitted to depart. Pavón told the American agents that everything was under control, because the armed guards were actually DFS agents who had been assigned to Caro Quintero by the secretary of the interior. The DEA later learned that Caro Quintero had offered Pavón $300,000 to permit his plane to take off.

As the DEA later reconstructed the events, Camarena and his pilot, Alfredo Zavala Avelares, who had also been captured, were driven to a remote ranch owned by Félix Gallardo. Over the next thirty hours both men were subjected to savage beatings as the drug lords attempted to learn how much the DEA agent knew about their enterprise. Camarena was given repeated injections of amphetamines to keep him conscious throughout the session. The interrogation and the torture were tape-recorded by the drug gang and their associates in the DFS.

Camarena, who was scheduled to be reassigned in March of that year, had become a major threat to the Guadalajara cartel. In the previous months he had directed stunning raids on two of their largest marijuana plantations. But more troubling, Camarena had also begun to unravel the ties between the cartel, the Mexican secret police and ranking politicians in the PRI.

Finally, sometime on February 9, Camarena and Zavala were killed. Camarena apparently died when a Phillips-head screwdriver was shoved through his skull. Their corpses were discovered a month later in a shallow pit on a ranch in Michoacán state. The bodies were wrapped in plastic, the hands and feet bound. The DEA later determined that the two bodies had been dumped on the ranch after a bizarre raid by the DFS in which four rival drug lords where killed. They speculated that Camarena's corpse had been left in Michoacán to implicate leftist politician Cuauhtémoc Cardenas in the murders.

The Guadalajara cartel controlled Mexico's largest marijuana operation and dabbled in opium production. But the cartel's most profitable venture was its direct pipeline to Colombian cocaine. After stepped up interdiction efforts in south Florida in the early 1980s, the Colombians turned to Mexico as a transshipment point for their cocaine destined for US markets. Instead of merely taking a fee for hauling the cocaine across the border, the Guadalajara cartel took a share of the cocaine, often as much as 50 percent. This swiftly made them big players in the cocaine business and brought in a torrent of money. By some counts, the Félix Gallardo/Fonseca/Caro Quintero network was making $5 billion a year. In 1982, the DEA learned that Félix Gallardo himself was moving $20 million a month through a single account at the Bank of America in San Diego. The drug agency asked for the CIA's help in investigating the money-laundering scheme, but the Agency refused.

Indeed, the DEA was soon convinced that the forces behind the

Camarena murder went far beyond the drug traffickers and corrupt Mexican police to include the CIA itself. Some agents at the DEA continue to believe that the CIA may have actually eavesdropped on the torture of Camarena.

The first clues to a wider involvement came when investigators found two witnesses who said they had been present at meetings during which Camarena's kidnapping and murder had been planned by cartel leaders and members of the Mexican security apparatus, the DFS. Also present at these sessions was Juan Matta Ballesteros, the Honduran drug king with ties to the CIA whom we encountered in a previous chapter.

One witness, Hector Cervantes Santos, was at an October 1984 meeting when cartel leaders discussed how to deal with Camarena. Cervantes said it was clear to him that the cartel had fairly detailed knowledge of Camarena's goings and comings and his key contacts. The DEA concluded that the cartel either had a mole inside the Guadalajara office or that the office had been bugged. Cervantes recalled that at one point during the meeting Matta suggested that Camarena should be captured and killed. "Silence is golden," Matta said.

Matta was the cartel's principal contact with the cocaine barons of Colombia. He had introduced Félix Gallardo's predecessor, Alberto Sicilia-Falcon, to Colombia's largest cocaine wholesaler, Santiago Ocampo. Ocampo, was a progenitor of the Calí cartel, and was said by the DEA to be the mastermind of the "biggest cocaine ring in US history." Matta, a Honduran chemist and transportation whiz, oversaw Ocampo's logistics network and arranged political pay-offs in Panama, Honduras, Mexico and the United States. A DEA agent described Matta as being "at the same level as the rulers of the Medellín cartel."

As we described in a previous chapter, at the very moment when Matta was plotting the abduction and murder of Camarena, his company, SETCO Inc., was one of the key Contra transport companies. SETCO was hired by the Contras using CIA money to ferry weapons, soldiers and supplies to camps in Honduras and Costa Rica. Even after Matta had been fingered in the Camarena case, his companies continued to receive funding from the US State Department, taking in $186,000 for carrying "humanitarian" assistance to the Contras.

Another DEA witness, Enrique Plascencia Aquila, says he saw Matta at a meeting at Ernesto Fonseca's house in December 1984, where Camarena's photograph passed around the room. Plascencia says the drug lords also reviewed a file on Camarena compiled by the DFS. According to Plascencia, the details of Camarena's kidnapping were planned at this meeting.

The DEA officers investigating Camarena's death thus knew that the drug agent's murder was a joint operation between the drug cartel and the DFS, an agency with intimate ties to the CIA. "The CIA didn't give a damn about anything but Cuba and the Soviets," said retired DEA agent James Kuykendall, who worked alongside Camarena in Mexico. "Indirectly, they [the CIA] have got to take some of the blame."

Kuykendall claims that the CIA protected the DFS for decades, even though they knew the agency had been corrupted by the narco-traffickers. "They didn't want their connection with the DFS to ever go away," Kuykendall said. "The DFS just got out of hand." Among the top DFS agents tied to Camarena's murder were Miguel Aldana and Sergio Espino Verdin. The DEA also had evidence linking two other high-ranking Mexican officials to the Camarena abduction: Manuel Ibarra, director of the Federal Judicial Police, and Ruben Zuño Arce, brother-in-law of Luis Echeverría, the former president of Mexico.

Much of the DEA's information on the ties of top-level Mexican officials to the Camarena kidnapping came from reports of an interrogation of drug lord Rafael Caro Quintera by Sergio Saavedra Flores, a special assistant to Manuel Ibarra. Saavedra was a Cuban exile whom DEA agents believe had ties to CIA-backed anti-Castro groups operating in Mexico. Before becoming Ibarra's right-hand man at the Mexican Judicial Police, Saavedra had been a ranking officer in the DFS. Immediately after his arrest, Caro Quintero had received soft treatment from the Mexicans and was allowed to continue running his drug empire via a cellular phone in his prison cell. Under mounting pressure from the US, Saavedra finally questioned Caro Quintero about Camarena's murder. To compel the drug dealer to talk, Saavedra employed a method of torture called *el tehuacanazo,* after Mexico's popular brand of sparkling water. Saavedra forced carbonated water laced with jalapeño peppers up Caro Quintero's nose. It didn't take the drug dealer long to spill his guts, revealing the names of top Mexican officials on the cartel's payroll.

Prominent among the names given up by Caro Quintera was José Antonio Zorrilla Pérez, the commander of the DFS. Like other heads of the DFS, Zorrilla Pérez enjoyed the indulgence of the CIA.

Though never charged in the Camarena case, Zorrilla was arrested in 1989 for his involvement in the May 1984 murder of Mexico's top political columnist, Manuel Buendía. When he was gunned down, Buendía had been in the midst of an investigation into the ties between the DFS and the drug cartels. The Buendía assassination and subsequent cover-up were part of a DFS project called Operation News.

Caro Quintero's connections to the top leaders of the DFS and Mexican Interior Department apparently convinced Saavedra that it might be more prudent to switch sides. He promptly joined in the cover-up of the Camarena case, helping Matta Ballesteros evade arrest in Mexico and escape to the safe haven of Cartagena, Colombia. Saavedra soon left Mexico for Los Angeles, where he took a well-paying position with the Mexican television network, Televisa. Televisa, which then enjoyed a near monopoly on Mexico's television market, is closely associated with the ruling PRI party and is run by "the richest man in Mexico," billionaire Emilio Azcarraga. The DEA tracked down Saavedra in 1988 and asked for his cooperation in the Camarena case. A few days later Saavedra and his family disappeared.

He wasn't the only missing witness. At least thirteen people connected to the Camarena case were murdered during the course of the investigation, including three of the twenty-two defendants and several police detectives. Other potential witnesses were picked up by the DFS and Mexican Judicial Police and held, so the DEA believed, to keep them silent.

One of the DEA's most explosive witnesses was a Californian named Lawrence Harrison. Harrison was a former student at the University of California at Berkeley, where he says he dabbled in left-wing politics and helped organize anti-war rallies before heading to Mexico in the early 1970s. There Harrison eventually landed a position as a communications specialist with the DFS and the Mexican Interior Ministry's Office of Political and Special Investigations. Harrison says his job was to install high-tech electronic bugging systems for the two intelligence agencies.

The blond 6-feet-7-inch Californian was known to his Mexican colleagues as Torre Blanca, the White Tower. He says in the early 1980s he learned of the DFS's close relationship to the Guadalajara cartel. According to Harrison, DFS agents served, in effect, as the cartel's private army, protecting them from arrest and suppressing rival operations. In 1983 Harrison says he was instructed by his bosses at the DFS to set up a sophisticated telecommunications and electronic surveillance system for the Guadalajara cartel.

During two trials in Los Angeles, Harrison testified that he spent from July to January of 1984 at the Guadalajara house of drug kingpin Ernesto Fonseca, where he installed and managed a bugging operation. Among his other duties, Harrison claims to have developed a system to monitor Camarena's office at the DEA.

He says he recorded hundreds of conversations between the drug traffickers and their associates in the DFS in Mexico City. "As systems engineer," Harrison testified, "I listened to the system and had full control of it 24 hours a day during the entire time that it was installed and operated."

Harrison recalled a conversation with Félix Gallardo in which the drug trafficker told him that the cartel's operations in the United States enjoyed a high-degree of protection because they were sending weapons and money to the Nicaraguan Contras. A DEA report from February 1989 says that Harrison also told investigators that Félix Gallardo's ranch near Vera Cruz had been used by the CIA to train Guatemalan troops. The report quotes Harrison as saying, "Representatives of the DFS, which was the front for the training camp, were in fact acting in consort with major drug overlords to ensure a flow of narcotics through Mexico into the US." The report says Félix Gallardo's ranch was the target of a marijuana raid in the early 1980s by the Mexican Federal Judicial Police, who were unexpectedly confronted by the Guatemalan troops and slaughtered. "As a result of the confrontation, 19 MFJP agents were killed," the DEA report says. "Many of the bodies showed signs of torture. The bodies had been drawn and quartered."

Of course, the CIA promptly denied it had ever used the Vera Cruz ranch as a training ground. But Harrison wasn't finished. He testified during the trials of the Camarena defendants that CIA agents had visited the leaders of the cartel. While Harrison was working at Fonseca's house, he said two Americans showed up to arrange a drug deal. Harrison says he warned them to be careful taking the drugs back across the US border. But the two men chuckled and said they didn't have much to worry about because the drug run was protected by the CIA. "We're working with the Contras," they told Harrison.

Harrison also identified another American visitor to Fonseca's house as Theodore Cash, a former Air America pilot. In a separate drug case, Cash testified as a government witness and admitted that he had worked for the CIA for ten years. Cash was apparently running drugs and guns for the Guadalajara cartel, including several weapons drops to Contra camps in Honduras.

Attorneys for the defendants in the Camarena case believed that Harrison himself was a CIA contact, a suspicion shared by several DEA agents. "The CIA obviously was cultivating a very powerful and efficient arms transport network through the cartel," said Gregory Nicolaysen, one of the defense lawyers. "They didn't want the DEA screwing it up." Nicolaysen described Harrison as "the liaison between the agency and the cartel."

Harrison left Mexico in 1988 and went on the DEA's payroll as an informant. Matta Ballesteros was tracked down in Colombia, arrested, and convicted of conspiracy charges for his role in Camarena's abduction and death. Félix Gallardo and Caro Quintero and more than a dozen others were tried and convicted in Mexico.

The CIA's ties to Mexico's drug lords far predate the Camarena case. The Mexico City station has long been the CIA's most important base of operations in Latin America. Despite a somewhat rocky relationship with Mexican politicians, the Agency has always maintained and cultivated a cozy partnership with Mexico's military and internal security apparatus. Indeed, the DFS, founded in 1946, was largely a creature of the CIA, which has contributed a substantial portion of the outfit's budget since the 1950s and has kept many of its senior officers on its payroll.

The CIA viewed the DFS as an important component of the US intelligence network. It served as a source of information on the activities of the Soviets, Cubans and Eastern Bloc officials in Mexico, provided intelligence on popular insurgencies throughout Latin America, and protected some of the CIA's most problematic associates, particularly the growing cadre of anti-Castro Cubans. One of the Cuban exiles who enjoyed the indulgences of the DFS was Alberto Sicilia-Falcon. Sicilia-Falcon was flamboyant and cruel. By the mid-1970s, the Cuban was regarded as the pre-eminent drug smuggler in the Western Hemisphere, a fame that won him the favors of many high-ranking Mexican politicians, including Maria Ester Zuño de Echeverría, the wife of Mexican president Luis Echeverría. Señora Echeverría's family had its own links to the drug trade, including ties to European heroin operations. Her brother, Rubin, would later be convicted of involvement in the slaying of Enrique Camarena.

Sicilia-Falcon fled Cuba after the revolution in 1959, landing in Miami. He says he was trained by the CIA in Miami for several night raids on Cuba, delivering weapons to anti-Castro troops on the island. In the late 1960s, Sicilia-Falcon moved to Mexico and got involved in the marijuana trade. He entered the cocaine business in the early 1970s after being introduced by Juan Matta Ballesteros to Calí cocaine lords Santiago Ocampo and Benjamin Herrera Zuelta, known as the "black pope of cocaine."

Soon Sicilia-Falcon was a billionaire, living in a fortified compound outside Tijuana called the Roundhouse. The premises were guarded by a contingent of DFS troops armed with AK-47s. From the Roundhouse, Sicilia-Falcon commanded his $5-billion-a-year drug enterprise, an international arms-smuggling network and a team of thugs, ready for use against rival drug outfits or incorruptible cops.

One of Sicilia-Falcon's closest associates was a Bay of Pigs veteran and CIA-trained operative named José Egozi Bejar. Egozi, a financial wizard, inhabited the twilight world where intelligence agencies, private armies and organized crime intersect. Since the Bay of Pigs, Egozi had worked off and on for the CIA. He had also lent his considerable talents to the DFS and maintained cordial relations with the mob in Las Vegas.

During their investigation of Sicilia-Falcon, DEA agents interviewed Egozi. He admitted that he had introduced Sicilia-Falcon to "political contacts" in the Mexican elite, helped him set up a network of bank accounts to launder his drug proceeds and had once given the drug lord a

CIA catalogue of weapons. They also worked together in an attempt to finance the Morgan super-rifle, a high-powered gun made by a Los Angeles–based firm that the CIA wanted put in the hands of its covert armies in Latin America. In 1974, Egozi and Sicilia-Falcon arranged a $250 million weapons shipment for a CIA-supported coup attempt against the recently elected socialist parliament in Portugal.

Sicilia-Falcon's other connection to the CIA came in the person of Miguel Nazar Haro, the head of the DFS from the mid-1970s to 1982. After Sicilia-Falcon's arrest by Mexican police and the US DEA in 1976, Nazar intervened, keeping the Cuban drug trafficker from being tortured during interrogation. Nazar's judicious intervention also, of course, kept Sicilia-Falcon from exposing his connections to Mexican politicians and intelligence agencies.

Nazar had been on the CIA's payroll for years and headed a CIA-financed counterinsurgency team called the Guardias Blancas, the White Brigade, notorious for its bloody suppressions of populist uprisings. The security chief's interests also extended to more traditional criminal enterprises. The DEA produced witnesses at two drug trials in the 1980s who fingered Nazar as ordering his DFS troops to serve as security details for Mexico's leading narcotics traffickers. The witnesses also testified that Nazar himself had made a fortune in the drug trade.

In 1979, Nazar came under investigation by the FBI for running a car-theft ring out of his office in Mexico City. According to the FBI, car thieves would steal cars in Los Angeles and San Diego, drive them across the border and drop them off at the DFS office in Tijuana. The hot cars were then driven by DFS agents to Mexico City for Nazar's personal inspection, after which they were sold. By no means was this a small-time operation. The FBI estimated that this car-theft ring had stolen more than 4,000 cars.

A grand jury in San Diego indicted Nazar and some of his collaborators. But the CIA came to the rescue of its Mexican protégé. Warnings were issued to the Justice Department saying that Nazar was "an essential repeat essential contact for the CIA station in Mexico City." The Agency insisted that prosecution of Nazar would deal a "disastrous blow" to the "security of the United States." The CIA claimed that Nazar was its "most important source in Mexico and Central America."

The CIA got its way. Deputy Attorney General Lowell Jensen intervened to block Nazar's prosecution. The move outraged William Kennedy, the US Attorney for San Diego, who disclosed to a reporter the CIA's heavy-handed tactics in the Nazar case. For this impertinent act, Kennedy was promptly fired by Ronald Reagan.

Two of the other DFS officers indicted but not tried in the auto theft case, Juventino Prado Hurtado and Raúl Pérez Carmona, were later arrested in Mexico for their involvement in the 1984 slaying of Mexican journalist Manuel Buendía. The DFS was finally disbanded in 1985, following revelations of high-level involvement in the Camarena case. But many of its key operators simply switched agencies, ending up in similar positions in the equally corrupt and brutal Federal Judicial Police or the military. As for Nazar, he disappeared for a while but resurfaced in 1989 when Mexico's new president, Carlos Salinas, picked him to head up his new Police Intelligence Directorate.

NAFTA, Carlos Salinas and the Rise of the Mexican Cartels

Carlos Salinas de Gortari was selected as the PRI candidate for the 1988 Mexican presidential election. The Harvard-trained economist enjoyed the enthusiastic backing of the US government and press. Salinas came from the ruling elite of Mexico. His father, Raúl Salinas Lozano, had long served as Mexico's minister of industry and commerce. Since 1982, Carlos Salinas had been the architect of the Mexican economy, overseeing the wild fluctuations of the peso from his post as cabinet secretary for programs and budgets.

The ruling PRI party, which Salinas now headed, had not lost its grip on the Mexican presidency for more than seventy years. But during the 1988 elections, Salinas was pitted against the left-populist candidacy of Cuauhtémoc Cardenas. As the first votes began to be tallied, Cardenas appeared to be winning. Then Interior Minister Manuel Bartlett Diaz ordered a suspension of the counting. Bartlett, a long-time powerbroker in the PRI who had been accused of involvement in the Camarena kidnapping, claimed that the electoral computer system had crashed. Ten days later Salinas was declared the winner with 52 percent of the vote.

Over the next month, official vote sheets were found to have been altered by the placement of additional zeros in Salinas's PRI column. More than 20,000 ballots that favored Cardenas were found in waste dumps or floating in riverbeds. An independent analysis of the vote estimated that Cardenas had in fact won with 42 percent, against Salinas's 36 percent.

Washington was delighted with Salinas's triumph. An April 13, 1989 editorial in the *Washington Post* is typical of the kind of reception Salinas received in the American press: "When Mexican President Carlos Salinas de Gortari took office last December, he was known as a technocrat with three degrees from Harvard and an interest in economics – not exactly a scintillator. That, together with the relatively narrow margin by which he won the election, seemed to indicate a distant and cautious style of leadership. Instead, Mr. Salinas has been enforcing the law and, not incidentally, asserting presidential power, with a ferocity that Mexicans have not seen for a generation."

The great project of the Salinas regime was to privatize the Mexican economy. Land reform initiatives in rural Mexico were rolled back and the heritage of the revolution ruthlessly dismembered. Salinas and his cronies also moved swiftly to suppress the Mexican labor movement. One of his first actions was against Joaquín Hernández Galicia, the head of the powerful Oil Workers Union, who had campaigned on behalf of Cardenas. Less than three weeks after taking office, Salinas ordered the arrest of Hernández on bogus charges of stockpiling weapons. Later that year, Salinas sent 5,000 paratroopers to crush a strike at the Cananea copper mine in Sonora. The US Embassy showed a particular fondness for Salinas's secretary of labor, Arsenio Farrell, who cracked down mercilessly on labor unions and striking workers. "Farrell has maintained his reputation as a formidable labor opponent," exulted a US Embassy report on Mexican labor trends under the Salinas government. "He has maintained pressure on the labor sector in an effort to hold the line on wage demands. Farrell has not hesitated in declaring a number of strike actions illegal, thus undercutting their possibility for success."

In 1992, Salinas responded to concerns voiced by American factory owners doing business in northern Mexico that Agapito Gonzáles, the 76-year-old leader of the Day Laborers and Industrial Workers Union in

Matamoras, was making life difficult by agitating for higher wages. Salinas had Gonzáles picked up on charges of tax evasion, later found to be groundless.

While Salinas as opening up Mexico to a flood of foreign investment, he was also engaged in the biggest disposal of government-owned businesses in the history of Mexico. In his six years in office, Salinas sold off 252 state-owned companies, including the national telephone firm and the nation's eighteen largest banks, a $23 billion stream of revenues to the PRI insiders and intimates of Salinas, who were able to profit first from the looting of Mexico's public assets. The bonanza produced a new crop of billionaires. This largesse did not go unappreciated. In February 1993, when the PRI coffers were running low and the leftist opposition was gaining strength, the Mexican Twelve, the country's top billionaires, gathered for a fund-raiser, where Carlos Salinas pleaded with them to dig deep in their pockets. By the end of the meeting the twelve businessmen had ponied up $750 million. Emilio Azcarraga, head of the Mexican television network Televisa, alone pledged $50 million.

The crowning achievement of Salinas's reign was his successful negotiation of the North American Free Trade Agreement, or NAFTA. Salinas worked closely with both Bush and Clinton to navigate the agreement around opponents on both sides of the border. The US poured money into Mexico to lobby the Mexican public for the trade pact. The National Endowment for Democracy, a foundation with long-standing ties to the CIA, channeled more than $1 million into Mexico in 1990 to build support for NAFTA. Some of the money no doubt returned to the United States as part of the millions that Mexico spent to lobby members of the US Congress who were reluctant to support a pact that might entice even more US companies to relocate American jobs to Mexico.

Questions about human rights, the environment, money laundering and drug trafficking were brushed aside. In fact, both the DEA and the US Customs Service were prohibited by the Bush and Clinton administrations from raising the subject of drugs during the NAFTA negotiations. "They said we could not make drugs part of the debate," said Carol Hallen, US customs commissioner during the Bush presidency. "I think it was a terrible mistake not to tie the two together."

It would not have been hard to do. Evidence of the involvement of the

Mexican police and military in the drug trade was glossed over by the US government during the period when the terms of NAFTA were being ironed out. When seven Mexican drug agents were gunned down in an ambush by 100 members of the Mexican army on the payroll of a drug cartel, US Ambassador John Negroponte dismissed the slaughter as "a regrettable incident." The slaughter had been videotaped by the DEA from another plane, which had also been strafed by the army unit.

Robert Nieves, the former chief of the DEA's international operations, said that his agency could never get an audience for its concerns about how NAFTA might serve as a boon to drug traffickers. "Drugs have never been the number one issue as it relates to Mexico," Nieves said. "It ranks somewhere below the North American Free Trade Agreement, economic bailout and other bilateral trade and commerce issues."

But the drug agents had good cause for concern. The reign of Carlos Salinas witnessed an astounding expansion of the Mexican drug trade. By 1990, more than 75 percent of all cocaine entering the United States came through Mexico. Mexico remained a major producer of marijuana, and was well on its way to becoming a leading source of heroin and methamphetamines. The Mexican government itself estimated that the illicit drug business was generating more than $30 billion a year. Other reviews of the trade put the figure at closer to $50 billion.

The drug business in Mexico was dominated by four multibillion dollar cartels. The old Guadalajara cartel, started by Sicilia-Falcon, splintered into two operations after the 1989 arrest of Félix Gallardo, one based in Sinaloa and another headquartered in Tijuana. The Tijuana cartel was run by the violent Arellano-Félix brothers, who were behind more than 200 drug-related slayings in Tijuana in 1992 alone. Many of its victims were tortured and dismembered. In 1993, the Arellano-Félix gang ordered the assassination of Cardinal Juan Jesus Posadas Ocampo at the Guadalajara airport. The four gunmen surrounded the cardinal's car, opened the door and filled his body with bullets. The killers then walked into the airport, flashed badges identifying them as members of the Federal Judicial Police and got on an AeroMex flight to Tijuana. Since this brazen evidence of drug violence and corruption might have had an adverse impact on the NAFTA debate, the killing was touted as a mystery, alien to Mexico's normal manner of doing business.

In 1996, another Federal Judicial Police unit working for the Arel-lano-Félix gang was linked to the murders of Tijuana's top drug investigators, Ernesto Ibarra Santes and Jorgé García Vargas. Ibarra Santes was gunned down a month after purging 700 corrupt police officers from his unit. Around the same time, García Vargas, Tijuana's anti-drug chief, was kidnapped at the Mexico City airport, tortured and strangled. His mutilated body was found in the trunk of a car.

The Juárez cartel, headed by Amado Carillo Fuentes until his death on July 4, 1997 from complications following plastic surgery, was perhaps the most profitable of the Mexican drug enterprises. Some estimates showed the Carillo operation to be generating more than $20 billion a year in cocaine sales. Carillo, who was a relative of the Ochoa family, flew huge amounts of cocaine from Medellín and Calí, Colombia on the cartel's own fleet of Boeing 727 planes: he became known as "Lord of the Skies."

The drug enterprise with the most intimate ties to the Salinas government was the Gulf cartel, based in Tamaulipas and headed, until his arrest in 1996, by Juan García Abrego. Abrego got his start in the drug business in the mid-1970s exporting Mexican marijuana to Texas, Louisiana and Florida. In the early 1980s, García Abrego turned to cocaine. His major innovation was to change the terms on which Mexican cocaine couriers received payment from the Colombian cartels. Instead of accepting the usual $1,500 per kilo as a transport fee, García Abrego demanded a 50 percent share of the Colombians' cocaine shipments. This allowed him to set up his own distribution networks and dramatically increase his profits and political influence. A 1994 DEA report pegged Abrego's revenues from the cocaine business at more than $10 billion a year.

By 1990, this flood of drug money had saturated the Salinas administration. The Mexican daily *El Financero* claimed that during the Salinas years upwards of 95 percent of those working in the attorney general's office had been bribed by the drug cartel. There's no better example than Javier Coello Trejo, the man Salinas picked to head the anti-narcotics wing of the attorney general's office. Coello Trejo, who referred to himself as the Iron Prosecutor, was praised by the US for his tough measures. But according to Eduardo Valle, an investigator in

Coello Trejo's own department, the attorney general was on the payroll of García Abrego to the tune of more than a million dollars a year. One of Coello Trejo's aides alone pocketed more than $50 million from the drug trade, Valle said. The office's drug enforcement operations tended to focus on rivals of the Gulf cartel.

In 1994 García Abrego's cousin and partner in the cocaine business, Francisco Pérez Munroy, testified in a Texas drug trial that he had personally delivered money and expensive gifts to the attorney general and his wife. "Well, the suits and the money," Pérez testified, "they were so that he wouldn't be bothered with the movement of drugs."

The attorney general's alliance with drug dealers never seemed to concern either Salinas or the US government. But Coello Trejo did land in hot water when four of his bodyguards were convicted of raping nine women in Mexico City. Under pressure from religious groups, Coello Trejo resigned, accompanied by expressions of regret by the US Embassy. "He's been great," a state department official told the *Los Angeles Times*. "This is a blow."

But Coello Trejo didn't languish long in the unemployment lines. Salinas soon appointed him to the post of federal attorney for consumer affairs. In 1995, the Mexico City paper *La Reforma* reported that Coello Trejo was serving as an adviser to Mexico's new internal security apparatus, the Coordinación de Seguridad Pública de la Nacíon.

The Clinton administration did everything in its power to conceal the criminality saturating the Mexican state apparatus. In October 1996, the Clinton White House invoked executive privilege to keep from turning over to Congress an April 1995 memo written by FBI director Louis Freeh and DEA administrator Thomas Constantine. The memo excoriated the administration's drug policy, particularly regarding Mexico. According to a report in the *New York Times,* Freeh and Constantine charged that the Clinton drug policy was "adrift," "lacked any true leadership," and was being sabotaged by competing agencies, including the CIA, the Department of Commerce and the NSC.

An internal State Department memo written two years after the passage of NAFTA reached similar conclusions. It identified Mexico as "one of the most important money laundering centers in the Western Hemisphere" and cited it as the "principal transit route for cocaine entering the United States." The report concluded that "no country in the world poses a more immediate narcotics threat to the US than Mexico."

The Fall of the House of Salinas

Carlos Salinas's six-year term as president of Mexico ended in a blaze of gunplay. On March 23, 1994, Salinas's hand-picked successor, Luís Donaldo Colosio, was shot in the head and killed during a campaign stop in Tijuana. Although Colosio was close to Salinas, he had recently angered many PRI hard-liners by vowing to clean out corrupt government officials and take action against the drug cartels. Colosio was killed two days before he was scheduled to meet with Mexican drug investigators looking into ties between the Gulf cartel and the Salinas government. A few days before his murder, Colosio had ordered Humberto García Abrego, Juan's brother and an executive of the Gulf cartel, removed from the list of attendees at a PRI fundraising event, a move that angered the drug lords.

"I have no doubt that Colosio was killed by narco-politicians or poli-narcos," said Eduardo Valle, the former head of a Mexican drug task force targeting the García Abrego operation. Valle's investigation was shut down by Carlos Salinas, and Valle fled to safety in the United States in August 1994.

The Salinas administration blamed Colosio's assassination on a deranged gunman named Mario Aburto Martínez. But Mexican police unearthed evidence that many others may have been behind Colosio's killing, including the drug cartels and members of Salinas's government. The police had some suspicion that an officer in Center for Investigation and National Security (an agency thoroughly penetrated by the Gulf cartel) might have aided Aburto in Colosio's murder. In the end, the attorney general's office released all suspects other than Aburto, reportedly on the orders of Carlos Salinas.

After Colosio's death, Salinas tapped Ernesto Zedillo Ponce de León as the new PRI presidential candidate. The PRI had groomed Zedillo from an early age. He was sent to study in England and to Yale, where he received a doctorate in economics. He served a stint as a banker, and then in 1988 he was appointed by Salinas to the important post of secretary of programming and budget. After supervising the Salinas privatization scheme, Zedillo became secretary of education. A 1995 CIA psychological profile of Zedillo described him as "cold, hard, rigid and humorless."

To assist Zedillo in his run for the presidency, Salinas turned to an old friend and former brother-in-law, José "Pepé" Ruiz Massieu. Ruiz Massieu was appointed the new secretary general of the PRI and was set to be majority leader of the Mexican congress. But Massieu had been a good friend of Colosio's and used his position to push for a more thorough investigation of the slain candidate's assassination. Massieu also began to take up Colosio's unnerving talk about reform. He gave speeches suggesting it was time to shake up the PRI leadership, cut some of its ties to the Mexican business elite, and pursue a more progressive agenda.

On September 28, 1994, Ruiz Massieu got into his car outside the Casablanca Hotel in downtown Mexico City. A 28-year-old farm worker named Daniel Aguilar stepped up to the car and shot him in the neck with an Uzi submachine gun. Ruiz Massieu died an hour later. Aguilar was nabbed by a guard at the scene and wasted little time in telling the police that he had been hired for the hit on Ruiz Massieu by Fernando Rodríguez. Rodríguez was a senior aid to Manuel Muñoz Rocha, a PRI politician from Tamaulipas, the headquarters of the García Abrego cartel. Rodríguez said Muñoz Rocha and a García Abrego associate, Abraham Rubio Canales, ordered him to arrange the assassination.

To quell suspicion of another government cover-up, Carlos Salinas appointed Pepé Ruiz Massieu's brother, Mario, to lead the investigation into his death. Mario Ruiz Massieu was an assistant attorney general with a reputation as a political reformer and a battler against corruption. US intelligence agencies had known otherwise for years, but apparently neither the CIA nor the Defense Intelligence Agency told any Mexican law enforcement officials that the deputy attorney general was on the payroll of the Gulf cartel until after Mario fled Mexico for the United States, where he had stashed away more than $7 million in the Texas Commerce Bank. Aside from the CIA's routine monitoring of Ruiz Massieu's activities, the Texas bank had informed the feds of the prosecutor's suspicious deposits in March 1994. No action was taken until Ruiz Massieu showed up in New Jersey in January 1995.

Instead of probing the forces behind his brother's murder, Mario Ruiz Massieu had apparently covered up the involvement of the Mexican president's brother, Raúl Salinas, and his associates in the Gulf cartel in Pepé's slaying. It turns out that the key witness in the case, Fernando Rodríguez, had fingered Raúl as the "intellectual author" of Pepé's assassination. Even stranger, Rodríguez had asserted that Carlos Salinas himself was present at the March 1993 meeting when Pepé Ruiz Massieu's murder was planned by Raúl Salinas and Muñoz Rocha.

Raúl Salinas was arrested on murder charges on February 28, 1995. His brother Carlos, a man who had been the toast of the town, honored with a slot on the board of the Dow Jones Company, parent company of Salinas's greatest admirer, the *Wall Street Journal*, and promoted as the heavy favorite to head the World Trade Organization, fled Mexico for the life of a furtive itinerant, scuttling between a Cuban compound and an estate in Ireland.

Raúl's Dirty Money

While Raúl Salinas was sitting in a Mexican jail – where, at least as of the spring of 1998, he remains – his wife, Paulina Castañon, was seized by Swiss drug enforcement authorities while trying to withdraw money from a bank account in which Raúl had no less than $90 million under the name Juan Guillermo Gómez Gutierrez.

An interesting account of Raúl Salinas's banking habits appeared on the front page of the June 4, 1996 *New York Times* in a story written by Anthony de Palma and Peter Truell. Presumably basing their account on information from Mexican state investigators and from PRI sources around embattled President Ernesto Zedillo – who have no love for the Salinas family – the *New York Times* reporters gave an account of how Raúl had received special treatment from Citibank as he went about the business of transferring enormous sums from Mexico to secret accounts abroad. The bizarre aspect of an altogether fascinating story was that in an article of 4,200 words the phrase "money laundering" was used a total of two times, neither of them in connection with Citibank. The word "drugs" was similarly inconspicuous, with cautious language from the intrepid journalists to the effect that there were "rumors but no evidence" that what Mexican prosecutors had termed Raúl's "inexplicable enrichment" had come from the drug trade. De Palma and Truell did note that "US laws bar banks from knowingly accepting money or turning a blind eye from crimes such as drug dealing."

Raúl Salinas, on an official salary of $190,000 a year, had approached Citibank's private banking unit, described by the *Times* as a "bank within a bank, reserved for the very rich." Here Salinas placed himself and his fortune in the capable hands of a Cuban American woman named Amy Elliot, a vice president of Citibank in charge of private accounts.

Elliot pampered the Mexican tycoon, making ten to twelve trips a year to Mexico for consultations on how Raúl's torrent of pesos – whose origins she apparently never questioned – would be steered to off-shore accounts in the Caymans, the Bahamas and kindred secret sanctuaries before ending up in the placid harbor of Switzerland. Elliot later said that inquiring into the source of the Salinas's millions "would be like asking the Rockefellers where they got their money." From 1992 on, there was lavish reporting in the Mexican press of how Raúl had amassed his criminal fortune. His methods included shakedowns of contractors, sale of access to his brother, and partnerships with the Mexican and Colombian drug cartels, by whom he was known unflatteringly as "the leech."

But Amy Elliot was not a rogue operator at Citibank. "Elliot didn't do anything on her own," a federal banking investigator told the *Miami Herald* in 1996. "Citibank's top management was behind everything she did." She told investigators that her boss, Edward Montero, and a Citibank lawyer, Sandra Lopez Bird, had approved the Salinas account and the transfers to Switzerland. Elliot testified to federal investigators that after Raúl Salinas's arrest, Montero had instructed her to give his account information to his brother Carlos, who was waiting in a limousine outside Elliot's Citibank office in New York.

Sometimes Raúl Salinas's money would spring from Banco Cremi in Mexico City, be transferred into a Citibank account, also in Mexico

City, and then be dispatched directly to a Citibank unit in Zurich called Confidas. There were many other paths, but they all added up to the same thing: the brother of the Mexican president was taking in an immense hoard of ill-gotten money and hiding it abroad. Raúl later told Swiss investigators that he was stashing his money in off-shore accounts in order to avoid "political scandal."

The virtue of the *New York Times* article was that it showed the minutiae of money-laundering procedures: one can imagine a Third World predator, or a First World one for that matter, studying the text and then thoughtfully reaching for the phone to have a chat with Citibank. What the *Times* piece did not do was place Raúl's operations in the context of his overall activities in Mexico, or suggest that operations described in such detail might throw useful light on the ties between the US banking industry and the international traffic in heroin and cocaine.

The *Times*'s reporters offered no explanation of where the $90 million might have come from. In fact, the figure of $90 million itself is a grotesque underestimate of an operation that has been reckoned by Mexican authorities to have garnered Raúl more than $1 billion during the six years his brother held office.

Raúl Salinas, aka Mr. Ten Percent, derived his power and his money from the fact that he was head of the state food distribution network Conasupo. Raúl was also the co-owner of a tuna-canning operation in Ensenada. Place these items in conjunction with the well-established fact that one of the prime methods of smuggling cocaine and heroin north from Colombia and Venezuela is on tuna boats, and the origin of at least some of Raúl's fortune becomes explicable.

By 1993, the Mexican press was already detailing the way in which Conasupo – under Raúl's supervision – was used as a distribution network for illegal drugs and as the embarcation point for the long process of laundering drug money. Raúl dumped on the long-suffering Mexican people radioactive milk, some of which apparently made its way north to US schoolchildren. He used US food credits to buy powdered milk that had been contaminated by the Chernobyl nuclear disaster. The newspaper *La Reforma* has also noted that Raúl Salinas was suspected of having "diverted high-quality US corn, bought with US foreign aid credits and meant for Mexico's poor, for sale as tortillas in US supermarkets." Instead of the corn meal, Salinas palmed off animal feed to the Mexican poor. These scams alone are estimated to have put $20 million into Raúl Salinas's private bank accounts.

The Mexican newspaper *El Financero* and the US Drug Enforcement Agency have produced estimates of how much money goes from the narco-traders to bribe PRI officials: half a billion dollars a year in 1995. *El Financero* reported that it reckons an equivalent amount goes north of the border each year to corrupt US officials and private citizens.

So much for Raúl, just one of tens of thousands of powerful people around the world stealing the resources of poor countries and raking in millions from the drug trade. Turn now to the US banking industry. In fourteen years of the War on Drugs that began in Ronald Reagan's first term, it has apparently never crossed the minds of US editors and reporters that the US banking industry cannot be unaware of the fact that it is handling large amounts of hot money. The DEA reckons that from Mexico alone $30 billion in drug profits enters the US.

It certainly has crossed the minds of some US politicians. Henry Gonzalez, the fiery Texas populist who was, until 1995, Democratic chairman of the House Banking Committee, held hearings on money laundering and drug trafficking back in 1994. Entered into evidence in those hearings was a US State Department watch list of countries handling drug money in particularly large quantities. The list ran from Aruba, the Caymans, Colombia, Hong Kong, Mexico, Nigeria, Switzerland and Venezuela to the US. One homegrown example cited by Gonzáles was the Beverly Hills branch of the American Express Bank, where two officials were indicted for helping Raúl Salinas's associate Juan García Abrego launder $100 million. The bank was fined $950,000 by the Federal Reserve. But Gonzalez wryly noted the bankers probably still made money on the transaction.

These Gonzalez hearings also established that the overseas subsidiaries of multinational banking concerns, such as Citibank, did not regard themselves as bound by US laws on money laundering, but by the money-laundering laws of the countries in which they were doing business. "Moreover," the report continued, "bank, privacy and data protection laws in some of those countries [namely Switzerland, France and Mexico] serve to prevent US regulators from conducting on-site examinations of the US bank branches within their borders." No doubt this is why Citibank gave the name Confidas to its Swiss subsidiary.

Gonzalez's hearings and subsequent investigations presided over by his successor as House Banking Committee chairman, Rep. Jim Leach of Iowa, concluded that the "banks within banks" – similar to the Citibank operation described by the *New York Times* – are conduits for hot cash, primarily from narco-trafficking.

So much for the "War on Drugs." As a method of social control and political subversion it has been very effective in putting away troublesome poor people and feeding federal pork to the prison lobby. Meanwhile, there has never been the slightest attempt to interfere with the operations of the large and powerful US financial institutions handling the profits, part of which are regularly remitted to US politicians, in the form of campaign contributions from the US banking industry.

Back in 1987 Andrew Cockburn interviewed Ramón Milian Rodríguez in Butner Federal Penitentiary in North Carolina. Milian Rodríguez was serving forty-two years, having been arrested by a south Florida task force while carrying $5 million on a plane, money which he – while working for the Colombian cocaine cartels – described casually as "walk around" cash or tips. Milian Rodríguez told Cockburn that all the major US banks had "special representatives" who would greet people like himself as they came north, provide entertainment, women and covert cash for $100 million denomination certificates of deposit.

"Who did they think you were?" Andrew asked.

"A major drug money launderer, of course," Milian Rodríguez answered, laughing heartily.

In the Kerry hearings on drugs and the Contras, Milian Rodríguez testified that he gave $10 million to the Contras at the request of Reagan administration operatives. Indeed, his account books, which were seized by the FBI at the time of his arrest, showed as much. During his testimony, one congressman told him that he "must be very clever." "Well," Milian Rodríguez answered, "First Boston [caught up in the laundering charges and now partly owned by Crédit Suisse] paid a fine of $25,000 and I'm doing forty-two years. Who do you think is cleverer?"

On June 6, 1996, the British news agency Reuters reported that another Swiss bank account under the control of Raúl Salinas had been

identified. It held $240 million. It now appears that Raúl Salinas control-
led more than seventy different off-shore accounts. Citibank, whose top
officials knew well the enormous scale of their bank's transactions with
Salinas and who no doubt were also sensitive to the overwhelming like-
lihood that his millions were criminally acquired, continued to do business with the imprisoned murder suspect after his arrest, since Raúl
deployed money through Citibank accounts using a phone from his
prison cell.

Ten months after Salinas's arrest, Ann Wexton, an internal investigator at Citibank charged with monitoring "questionable" currency transactions, began to take an interest in possible improprieties in the handling of the Salinas account. It was later reported that her investigation
was quickly blocked by senior officials at the bank. Wexton quit Citibank and went to work for General Electric in its capital unit.

But Raúl Salinas's millions may be just the icing. By 1996, the Mexican press was circulating reports that former president Carlos Salinas
may have left office with a private hoard amassed during his six-year
term of as much as $5 billion, thus putting him on the A-list of Third
World looters. The Salinas family was indeed uniquely well-placed for
thievery on a grand scale, though it should be noted that Carlos Salinas,
unlike his brother, has not been charged with any crime.

At the period of its political ascendancy two torrents of money were
sluicing into Mexico. From the north came billions in US loans, bond
purchases and corporate bribes to capture the richest pickings of privatization. Suddenly there were more billionaires in Mexico than in Canada. Simultaneously Mexico had become the prime staging area for
drug shipments sent north from the Calí and Medellín cartels, with billions in drug money irrigating the Mexican elites. Citibank was
uniquely positioned to enjoy the benefits of this confluence. From the
1940s throughout most of the 1980s, it was the only US bank with
branches in Mexico, and its executives, who had led the negotiations on
two rounds of Mexican financial bailouts, spent many evenings carous-
ing with Carlos Salinas and associates.

On April 14, 1998, one of the biggest business mergers in the world
was unveiled: a proposed union between Citicorp and the Travelers
Group, an insurance conglomerate. This cleaving was valued at $76 bil-

lion, and the only factors that threatened a smooth marriage ceremony were the Glass-Steagall Act of 1933, inhibiting cross-ownership between the banking and securities industries, and a Justice Department criminal probe of Citibank, a Citicorp subsidiary, for washing drug money.

The Justice Department began this investigation into Citibank's handling of Raúl Salinas's money in 1996. But in news reports of the Citicorp/Travelers merger, it was emphasized that the Federal Reserve would not factor possible criminal conduct by one of the marriage partners into its assessment. In other words, drug billions could effortlessly flow into Citibank without a squeak from the prime banking regulator.

This is the point on which Maxine Waters, US Representative from South Central Los Angeles, seized. It was Waters who had been the fiercest critic of the CIA in the wake of Gary Webb's series in the *San Jose Mercury News*. In speeches from the floor of Congress in April 1998, she took on not only the CIA and the drug lords but also the international banking houses, who make money handling their business. Waters understood that these colossal financial mergers aren't good for ordinary people. It's going to be even harder for the poor to find banking services at competitive rates, and what little credit is available in poor urban areas will instead flow into the Wall Street money mart, jostling for investment opportunities with the criminal drug millions garnered by exploitation of such markets as South Central L.A.

Zedillo, Guns and Money

While lacking the flare of the Salinas regime, the government of Ernesto Zedillo, who trampled Cuauhtémoc Cardenas in the 1994 presidential election, continued the neoliberal economic and political agenda of his patron, auctioning off public businesses, opening Mexico ever more widely to foreign corporations and financial houses, and bearing down hard on dissidents, all the while exhibiting complaisance toward Mexico's $35 billion annual drug trade.

There was a report in the Colombian press that the Calí cartel was so enthusiastic about Zedillo that it funneled $70 million into the campaign coffers of the PRI. This story was followed by a February 1997 account in *La Reforma* of a videotape, secretly recorded by Mexican prosecutors, of a lawyer for Carlos Salinas boasting that Mexican fugitive banker Carlos Cabal Peniche had given $40 million to the Zedillo campaign. Cabal Peniche is suspected by US and Swiss banking authorities of using his banks to launder drug money.

Zedillo entered office promising reform. He said he wanted to make Mexico "a nation of laws." And there were some high-profile arrests early in his term, including the capture of Juan García Abrego. But mostly the drug cartels continued to flourish with the indulgence of the government. "It's a joke for the people of Mexico and the US who think Mexico is fighting drugs," said Ricardo Cordero Ontiveros, a former drug investigator in the Mexican attorney general's office. "The only thing they are fighting is to make them disappear from the newspapers."

Cordero said he brought his frustrations to Mexico's new attorney general, Antonio Lozano. Lozano told Cordero to stop whining. "People would pay $3 million to have your job," the attorney general said.

Bill Clinton also saw things differently from Cordero. Under mounting pressure to decertify Mexico as a vigilant fighter against drug trafficking, Clinton praised Zedillo's government. "They are taking steps to address a problem they inherited," Clinton said. "We'll help them in every way appropriate." One of the remarkable aspects of this observation is Clinton's dulcet admission – after two years of furious denials – that there had in fact a drug problem under the Salinas government.

Critics of Clinton accused the president of a double standard when it came to Mexico. They noted that in 1996 Clinton had imposed harsh economic sanctions against Colombia after decertifying it as a drug-fighter, though Mexico's record was equally poor. "Of course it's a double standard," said Peter Hakim, director of the Inter-American Dialogue, a Washington policy center. "Imagine decertifying your partner in NAFTA just one year after you lent it $13 billion to help it recover from an economic crisis."

The major feature of Zedillo's counter-narcotics strategy was to use the allegations of corruption to transfer much of the drug enforcement work (and budget) from the police to the Mexican military. To further this realignment, Zedillo picked General Jesús Gutierrez Rebollo as the chief of his new anti-drugs unit. Gutierrez Rebollo, a well-regarded military commander from Jalisco state, had been vetted by the CIA and had received training by the US Army. In his first two months in office, the general met frequently with US intelligence officers to share information on the Mexican drug trade. General Barry McCaffery, the US Drug Czar, knew Gutierrez Rebollo from McCaffery's stint as head of the US Southern Military Command. McCaffery declared his unflinching confidence in the general's ability, saying, "He's a guy of absolute unquestioned integrity."

The main US contribution to Zedillo and Gutierrez Rebollo's new militarized approach was to step up military aid and training to Mexico. In the summer of 1996, the Pentagon launched a $28 million program to train more than 1,100 Mexican soldiers a year at US bases. At the same time, the CIA embarked on a plan to bring ninety Mexican intelligence officers to the US for training at Langley and at Bolling Air Force Base's intelligence unit near Washington, D.C. In consequence, US anti-drug aid to Mexico shot up from $10 million in 1995 to $78 million in 1997. The Mexican army accounted for the largest share of foreign troops getting US military training.

The instruction classes were assigned to seventeen US military bases, including the School of the Americas at Ft. Benning, Georgia, and the helicopter school at Ft. Rucker, Alabama. Officers of the new Mexican drug strike force, a unit called Airmobile Special Forces or GAFE, were sent to Ft. Bragg, North Carolina, where they underwent an intense twelve-week course given by the US 7th Special Forces Group, an army unit specializing in covert operations. The GAFE troops were trained in helicopter assault methods, bomb-making, counterinsurgency operations and intelligence techniques.

The Pentagon claimed that the GAFE training program was intended solely for purposes of anti-narcotics operations and not intended to bolster the Mexican army's counterinsurgency capability. Moreover, the US military has asserted that the instructional sessions conducted by the Special Forces Group include "a substantial human rights component."

These assertions are disputed by Mexican defense analyst Raúl Benitez. "The GAFE are not just for the drug war," Benitez told the *Guardian*. "They are for everything."

To date, the GAFE graduates of Ft. Bragg don't have much to show for their American education. A 1997 report on the program by McCaffery's office could not identify a single large seizure of cocaine or an arrest of a major drug baron by the special forces units. That's not to say the GAFE unit was inactive on its return to Mexico. In September 1997, eighteen members of the new Mexican counter-narcotics strike force were arrested after being caught flying a military plane loaded with cocaine from Chiapas to Mexico City. The two pilots involved in the crime had just completed training in the United States.

More disturbing have been persistent reports of torture and assassination by GAFE squads. In Jalisco state, twenty-eight GAFE officers were jailed for their involvement in the abduction and torture of six young men. One boy, Salvador Jiménez Lopez, was beaten, had his tongue pulled out and was ultimately murdered by members of the GAFE. The Pentagon later admitted that some of the officers involved in the torture and killing of Jiménez had been trained at Ft. Bragg, saying dismissively "some soldiers sought retribution for the theft of a watch."

Another incident occurred in September 1997, when six young men from Colonia Buenos Aires, an impoverished area in Mexico City, were kidnapped and killed. Their mutilated corpses turned up a few days later in two remote areas. The Mexican newspaper *La Jornada* cited police sources as saying GAFE members had carried out the killings.

The Clinton administration has admitted that there is little or no review over how US counter-narcotics aid is spent or what the US-trained forces do after they go back to Mexico. Reports of abuses and corruption did not dent Drug Czar McCaffery's faith in Mexico's program. "It should not be my business how foreign countries organize for their counter-narcotics strategy."

McCaffery's judgment has been somewhat less than unerring in these matters. In late January 1997, McCaffery invited his Mexican colleague, General Gutierrez Rebollo, to Washington, D.C. The Mexican general toured the capital, met with members of Congress, visited the Pentagon and lunched at the White House. At a White House ceremony, McCaffery stood shoulder to shoulder with the general from Mexico City. "General Gutierrez Rebollo has a reputation of being an honest man who is a no-nonsense field commander of the Mexican army who's now been sent to bring the police force the same kind of aggressiveness and reputation he had in uniform," McCaffrey said. "We are not unaware of the progress that they have made at enormous personal sacrifice."

But the man McCaffery praised so extraordinarily had a more nuanced concept of sacrifice. Five days later, General Gutierrez Rebollo was under arrest in Mexico City, on charges that he had accepted more than a million dollars in bribes from drug lord Amado Carillo Fuentes. Investigators for the Mexican Defense Ministry became suspicious about the general after discovering that he was living in an expensive apartment in an exclusive section of Mexico City. The apartment had been rented by a ranking member of the Carillo Fuentes cartel. That's not the only favor the general received. He was also given an apartment for his mistress, several cars, a jeep, an encrypted cellphone that allowed him to communicate freely with his drug cartel patrons, and several thoroughbred horses.

The US government expressed shock at this turn of events, although Clinton said he remained confident that the Mexican military was a good "antidote, a counterweight" to the drug corruption problem. Ernesto Zedillo claimed that he was "fully deceived" by the general. He called the arrest the "most difficult, saddest, bitterest moment of my administration."

But neither the US nor Zedillo were being entirely forthright. Both had plenty of advance warning about the general. Indeed, Zedillo's attorney general, Antonio Lozano, said that he had warned Zedillo personally about Gutierrez Rebollo's ties to the Juárez cartel before the general was appointed to head Zedillo's National Institute to Fight Drug Trafficking.

While the CIA prepared highly complimentary profiles of Gutierrez Rebollo, calling him a "soldier's soldier," the DEA had compiled a much different assessment of the general. It had amassed evidence showing that his drug suppression strikes had almost exclusively targeted small operators or Carillo Fuentes's hated rival, the Tijuana-based Arellano-Félix gang.

From his jail cell in Mexico City, the imprisoned general had a few surprises of his own. He claimed to have evidence linking "government officials and their relations at the highest levels of Mexican politics" to the cocaine trade. Gutierrez said among those profiting from the drug trade were "former presidents, the current president's family and top officials at the Ministry of Defense." To back up his claim, the general produced tape-recorded phone calls purporting to link members of the Guadalajara cartel to Fernando Velazco Silva, the father of Ernesto Zedillo's wife, Nilda Patricia Velazco.

The Drug War Hits Chiapas

Shortly after Thanksgiving 1996, the first twenty of a planned seventy-three Huey helicopters were shipped in cargo planes out of Goodfellow Air Force Base in San Angelo, Texas, headed for Mexico. The Hueys were part of a weapons and reconnaissance package worth $50 million, military equipment sold, loaned or given by the Clinton administration to the Mexican armed forces. The official pretext was that the arms were for use in the drug war and to combat illegal immigration.

The true purpose harked back to a famous recommendation made by Chase Bank in 1994 regarding threats posed by an uprising of Mayan Indians in southern Mexico. At that time a Chase vice president circulated an advisory to the bank's clients saying that "the Zapatistas must be eliminated." Though an embarrassed Chase Bank later disowned the very sentiment it had promulgated, the Clinton administration saw no need to back off that urgent imperative. Any threat to the ruling elites in Mexico was by extension a threat to US interests. Insurgency in Mexico is always of the most urgent concern to the US government.

Donald E. Schulz, a professor of national security at the US Army's War College, put it this way: "A hostile government could put the US investments [in Mexico] in danger, jeopardize access to oil, produce a flood of political refugees, and economic migrants to the north. And under such circumstances the United States would feel obligated to militarize the southern border."

In fact, throughout the last decade the southern border has been diligently militarized. Since 1988, six years before the Zapatistas rose up out of the Lacandón forest in Chiapas on New Year's Day 1994, the Pentagon has been dispatching arms and reconnaissance aircraft south of the border, using the same excuse of drug interdiction, a rationale accompanying similar shipments to the Colombian military. The DEA has helped out in the operation, sending twelve agents to Chiapas, even though the region is not a major trafficking area.

During the Bush years, the US shipped $212 million worth of military supplies to Mexico, more US military aid than Mexico had received in the previous thirty years combined. This figure will be more than eclipsed by the end of the Clinton era. In addition to the seventy-three Huey helicopters, in the past seven years the US has given to Mexico four C-26 reconnaissance planes, 500 bullet-proof armored personnel transports, $10 million worth of night vision and C^3 equipment (command, control and communications), global positioning satellite equipment, radar, spare parts for thirty-three helicopters, machine guns, semi-automatic rifles, grenades, ammunition, flame-throwers, gas masks, night sticks, uniforms, rations and two *Knox*-class attack boats.

Although the rationale is drug interdiction, the arms listed above have a wider purpose. A June 1996 report from the General Accounting Office titled "Drug Control: Counter-narcotics Efforts in Mexico" offers evidence that the Mexican government used the US arms officially designated for counter-narcotics operations to suppress insurgencies. "During the 1994 uprising in the Mexican state of Chiapas," the report says, "several US-provided helicopters were used to transport Mexican military personnel to the conflict, which was a violation of the transfer agreement." More than 150 indigenous peasants were killed in those operations.

The GAO placed most of the blame for this on the US government, which, it suggested, connived in the misuse. "The US embassy [in Mexico City] relies heavily on bi-weekly reports submitted by the Mexican government that typically consist of a map of specific operational records – US personnel have little way of knowing if the helicopters are being properly used for counter-narcotics purposes or are being misused. Embassy officials told us that helicopter operational records have been requested and received on only one occasion in the past eight months [that is, from November 1995 to June 1996]." US-built helicopters were also used to suppress peasant farmers in southern Mexico protesting low corn prices brought about by NAFTA.

According to a May 1996 story in the Mexico City paper *La Jornada,* the US State Department assured the Zedillo regime that the arms shipments did not have to be exclusively used in anti-drug operations. The State Department informed the Mexican government that its "aviation advisers" would only inspect the location and condition of the helicopters once a year and would always give prior notice of their trips.

Across the summer of 1996, the uprising by the Popular Revolutionary Army (EPR) in Guerrero state prompted James Jones, the US ambassador to Mexico and former president of the New York Stock Exchange, to declare at a telecommunications conference in Cancún on September 9, 1996 that the US was willing to provide increased military aid, intelligence, and training to Mexico to fight the rebels. "Whatever they need," Jones said, "we will certainly support." Jones added a comparison: "The United States has much experience tracking right-wing militias, which could be of great use to Mexico. Like armed militias, [the ERP] has weapons and munitions capabilities. Terrorist groups operate much the same all over."

Colonel Warren D. Hall, a top aide to General Barry McCaffery when he was head of the US Southern Command, spoke bluntly about the dual-use nature of US anti-drug aid. "It's unrealistic to expect the military to limit its use of the equipment to operations against narco-traffickers," Hall said. "The light infantry skills US Special Operations forces teach during counter-drug training deployments can be used for counterinsurgency as well."

Cross-border collusion extended, naturally enough, to the CIA and FBI. In February 1995, the CIA boasted to its friends in the US press that it had lent important assistance to efforts to unmask Subcomandante Marcos, the Zapatista leader. The FBI maintains a huge border force and one of its largest foreign offices in Mexico City, where it trains Mexican police and intelligence forces.

The US military has also spent hundreds of millions of dollars over the past five years in increased surveillance in Mexico with insubstantial results in terms of halting the flow of drugs, according to a recently released report written by the Inspector General for the Defense Department in 1994. "Although the Pentagon has significantly expanded US monitoring and detection of cocaine smugglers, this expanded capability has come with a hefty price tag and has yet to reduce the flow of cocaine onto American streets," the report concluded. "The portion of the federal drug budget earmarked for military surveillance has quadrupled during the past five years, without measurable goals or results to show that the increases were warranted ... the fact that cocaine remains affordable and readily available in the United States strongly suggests that surveillance is not producing results commensurate with its costs."

But assuredly the US military is putting the surveillance information to use. In fact, there is plenty of evidence that the Pentagon is readying itself for intervention in Mexico sometime in the near future, with Department of Defense analysts drafting worst-case scenarios. In 1994, a year which ended with the collapse of the Mexican peso, a Pentagon briefing paper, declassified under the Freedom of Information Act, concluded that it was "conceivable that a deployment of US troops to Mexico would be received favorably if the Mexican government were to confront the threat of being overthrown as a result of widespread economic and social chaos. In such a scenario the intelligence and security services would probably cooperate with US intelligence forces to identify threats to Mexico's internal stability."

As Clinton's former Defense Secretary William Perry put it in a speech in October 1995, "When it comes to stability and security our destinies are indissolubly linked."

On December 22, 1997, Mexican paramilitary troops using US-made weapons executed a bestial raid on the Acteal refugee camp in Chiapas, massacring forty-five Tsotzil Indians, mostly women and children. The methodical butchery of the raid followed the same pattern by which the CIA-backed Guatemalan military and allied death squads, year after year, wiped out Indian villages suspected of rebel sympathies.

Immediately after the killings, the Mexican government reacted to a huge popular outcry across Mexico by deploring the massacre and by arresting some of the actual participants (though none of the "intellectual authors" of the crime). But with the New Year and a new minister of the interior, Francisco Labastida Ochoa, Mexican federal troops kept moving forward, ultimately surrounding Zapatista strongholds. The army troops threatened to disarm the rebels forcibly, though the latter had not used their guns since the cease-fire on January 12, 1994, less than two weeks after the rebellion began with the seizing of the town of San Cristóbal on New Year's Day.

Labastida, the new man at the Interior Ministry, excused these troop movements against the Zapatistas by claiming that the plan was to demilitarize the state of Chiapas. But the troops did not move against the paramilitaries nor did they operate in the area where the massacre took place. Rather, they headed eight hours' march away from the Acteal area toward the Zapatistas' central base in the Lacandón forest.

There's never been any doubt that the PRI government and its international advisers had from the start yearned to rid themselves of the Zapatistas, an impudent affront to the Mexican state and the PRI's entire neoliberal economic program. (This same program spelled doom to the Indian farming communities in southern Mexico, which is why the Zapatistas rebelled in the first place.) From the first days the government was deterred from full-blown military attack only because of strong public concern in Mexico and throughout the world, where the Zapatistas have been seen as a bright spark of hope in a drear political landscape. This was why the Mexican government, with the encouragement of the US, opted for its low-intensity strategy of arming and training paramilitary groups who harried and occasionally killed Indian villagers seen as pro-Zapatista, to such a degree that places like Acteal became de facto refugee camps. The local elites in Chiapas, who had seen their power threatened and their land taken, were hoping that the massacre they helped to organize would survive, not as a horrible memory but as an agreeable lesson in how rural rebellion should be dealt with. It's not an exercise in hyperbole to invoke the specter of a Guatemalan-style program of annihilation of Indians. After all, the Mayans on the Mexican side of the border are not that different from the Mayans on the Guatemalan side.

"US-provided helicopters have been used in the past by the Mexican military to attack unarmed populations," said Cecelia Rodríguez, spokesperson for the Zapatistas in the US. "The Mexican armed forces have been accused by human rights monitors of murders, disappearances, kidnapping and rape. Nonetheless their requests for military equipment and expertise have been granted time and time again. Under the guise of fighting drug traffickers, the US government has bolstered an anti-democratic and corrupt Mexican government with a laundry list of high-tech military equipment that has been used to violate the basic human rights of the people of Mexico." This is what the drug war looks like on the ground. As the Indians of Chiapas well know, and as the poor of South Central Los Angeles also well know, "drug war" is a code phrase for social control and repression.

Sources

The reporting of the Mexican newspapers *La Jornada* and *La Reforma* have been extraordinary and far superior to any coverage of Mexico/US relations in the States. The writings of Andrew Reding proved to be a useful guide to the treacherous and shifting waters of Mexican politics. Former DEA agent Michael Levine's books, *The Big White Lie* and *Deep Cover,* provide an insider's account of what it was like to work in Mexico against drug dealers, corrupt politicians, bureaucrats and the CIA. Frank Bardacke and Cecelia Rodríguez helped us more fully appreciate the forces behind the Zapatista rebellion and subsequent retaliation by the US-backed Mexican military in Chiapas. Andres Oppenheimer's book, *Bordering on Chaos,* and his reporting for the *Miami Herald* were valuable sources. Several reporters for national papers have done fine work on Mexico. Particularly useful were the reporting of Sam Dillon at the *New York Times,* Douglas Farah at the *Washington Post,* and Laurie Hays at the *Wall Street Journal.* Tim Golden's 1997 article in the *New York Times* on what the US intelligence agencies knew about the narco-penetration of the Salinas and Zedillo regimes contained a trove of new information, though Golden soft-pedals the CIA's complicity in the corruption of the Mexican intelligence and security appartus. The DEA's public affairs office must be thanked for supplying background information on the life and death of Enrique Camarena.

Americas Watch. *Human Rights in Mexico: A Policy of Impunity.* Americas Watch, 1990.
Anderson, John Ward. "Mexico Fires Anti-Drug Czar in Bribe Probe." *Washington Post,* Feb. 19, 1997.
——. Anderson, John Ward, and William Branigan. "Flood of Contraband Hard to Stop." *Washington Post,* Nov. 2, 1997.
Baker, Peter. "White House Claims Executive Privilege on Drug Memo." *Washington Post,* Oct. 2, 1996.
Bardacke, Frank. ed. *Shadows of Tender Fury: The Letters and Communiqués of Subcomandante Marcos. Anderson Valley Advertiser* broadsheet edition and Monthly Review Press, 1995.
Barker, Jeff. "US Failing to Halt Drugs, Key Aide Says." *Arizona Republic,* Nov. 23, 1997.

Bennet, James. "Clinton Says Mexico's Firmness Is Bright Side of Drug Scandal." *New York Times,* Feb. 17, 1997.

Branigan, William. "Trial in Camarena Case Shows DEA Anger at CIA." *Washington Post,* July 16, 1990.

———. "Mexican Writer's Death Laid to Ex-Police Chief." *Washington Post,* June 13, 1989.

Camp, Roderic. *Who's Who in Mexico Today.* Westview Press, 1993.

———. The Zedillo Cabinet: Continuity, Change or Revolution? Center for Strategic Studies, 1995.

Castañeda, Jorgé. *The Mexican Shock: Its Meaning for the US.* New Press, 1995.

Cordoba, José. "In Mexico, General Says Top Officers Got Bribes." *Wall Street Journal,* Oct. 2, 1997.

———. "Miami Trial Probes Cocaine Links Between Calí Cartel and Mexico." *Wall Street Journal,* May 30, 1997.

Crawford, Leslie. "Mexico Admits Drug Traffickers Bought Bank." *Financial Times,* March 17, 1998.

Detmer, Jamie. "Border Wars." *Insight,* May 17, 1997.

Dillon, Sam. "Mexico Drug Dealer Tried to Buy Way Out, General Says." *New York Times,* Sept. 20, 1997.

———. "A Fugitive Lawman Speaks: How Mexico Mixes Narcotics and Politics." *New York Times,* Dec. 23, 1996.

Dillon, Sam, and Craig Pyes. "Court Files Say Drug Baron Used Mexican Military." *New York Times,* May 24, 1997.

Falk, Pamela. "Drugs Across the Border: A War We're Losing." *Washington Post,* Sept. 24, 1997.

Farah, Douglas, and Molly Moore. "Trilateral Suspicion: Mistrust Complicates Case Against Raúl Salinas." *Washington Post,* Nov. 20, 1997.

Farah, Douglas, and Dana Priest. "Mexican Drug Force Is US-Bred." *Washington Post,* Feb. 26, 1998.

Fineman, Mark. "Remains Found at Ranch Owned by Raúl Salinas." *Los Angeles Times,* Oct. 10, 1996.

Golden, Tim. "Mexico and Drugs: Was US Napping?" *New York Times,* July 11, 1997.

Gunson, Phil. "Mexican Drug Force Linked to Torture." *The Guardian,* April 22, 1998.

Hays, Laurie. "Swiss Interview Witnesses in US About Salinas Case." *Wall Street Journal,* Nov. 26, 1997.

———. "Mexican Cartels Used Citibank Accounts to Launder Drug Money, US Alleges." *Wall Street Journal,* Sept. 26, 1997.

———. "New Testimony Links Raúl Salinas to Drugs." *Wall Street Journal,* March 13, 1998.

Hays, Laurie, Joel Millman and Craig Torres. "Raúl Salinas Linked to Big Cash Deposits." *Wall Street Journal,* May 29, 1997.

Hays, Laurie, and Michael Allen. "Mexico Drug Lords Exploit NAFTA, Report Says." *Wall Street Journal,* Feb. 11, 1998.

Isikoff, Michael. "Mexican Ex-Officer Guilty in Murder of DEA Agent." *Washington Post,* Sept. 23, 1988.

Jones, Robert. "Narcomania Knocks." *Los Angeles Times,* March 19, 1997.

Kerry, John. *The New War: The Web of Crime That Threatens America's Security.* Simon and Schuster, 1997.

Klare, Michael, and Cynthia Arnson. *Supplying Repression.* Institute for Policy Studies, 1981.

Levine, Michael. *The Big White Lie*. Thunder's Mouth, 1993.
——. *Deep Cover*. Delacorte Press, 1990.
Lupsha, Peter. *Drug Lords and Narco-corruption: The Players Change But the Game Continues*. Paper for symposium at University of Wisconsin, 1990.
——. "Under the Volcano: Narco-Investment in Mexico." *Transnational Organized Crime Journal*, Spring 1995.
McConahay, J. "Mexico's War on Poppies – and Peasants," *New Times*, Sept. 3, 1976.
Marshall, Jonathan. *Drug Wars: Corruption, Counterinsurgency and Covert Operations in the Third World*. Cohen and Cohen, 1991.
Mills, James. *The Underground Empire*. Doubleday, 1986.
Oppenheimer, Andres. *Bordering on Chaos: Guerrillas, Stockbrokers, Politicians and Mexico's Road to Prosperity*. Little, Brown. 1996.
——. "Jailed General: Mexican Elite Tied to Drugs." *Miami Herald*, July 8, 1997.
——. "Drug Money Hidden in US Banks, Officials Say." *Miami Herald*, Sept. 14, 1997.
——. "Raúl Salinas Scandal: Grilling His Bankers." *Miami Herald*, Sept. 16, 1996.
Orme, William A., Jr. *Continental Shift: Free Trade and the New North America*. Washington Post Company, 1993.
Paternostro, Silvana. "Mexico as a Narco-Democracy." *World Policy Journal*, vol. 12, no. 3, 1995.
Payne, Douglas. "Ballots, Neo-Strongmen, Narcos and Impunity." *Freedom Review*, Feb. 1995.
Poppa, Terence. *Druglords*. Pharos Books, 1990.
Preston, Julia. "US Trying to Smooth Mexico Path for Clinton." *New York Times*, April 20, 1997.
Pyes, Craig. "Legal Murders," *Village Voice*, June 4, 1979.
Reding, Andrew. *Democracy and Human Rights in Mexico*. World Policy Papers. World Policy Institute, 1995.
——. "Mexico Under Salinas: A Facade of Reform." *World Policy Journal*, Fall 1989.
——. "A Drug Bust That Was Just for Show." *Sacramento Bee*, Jan. 28, 1996.
——. "Mexico at a Crossroads: The 1988 Election and Beyond." *World Policy Journal*, Fall 1988.
——. "How to Steal an Election." *Mother Jones*, Nov. 1988.
Reuter, Paul, and David Ronfeldt. *Quest for Integrity: The Mexican/US Drug Issue in the 1980s*. Rand Corporation, 1991.
Riding, Alan. *Distant Neighbors*. Random House, 1984.
Robinson, Jeffrey. *The Laundrymen*. Arcade, 1996.
Ross, John. *Rebellion from the Roots: Indian Uprising in Chiapas*. Common Courage Press, 1995.
Schulz, Donald. *Mexico in Crisis*. Strategic Studies Inst., US Army War College, 1995.
Scott, Peter Dale, and Jonathan Marshall. *Cocaine Politics*. Univ. of California Press, 1991.
Shannon, Elaine. *Desperados: Latin Drug Lords, US Lawmen, and the War America Can't Win*. Viking, 1988.
Sheridan, Mary Beth. "Mexico Declares War on Drug Cartel." *Los Angeles Times*, March 10, 1998.
Solis, Dianne. "Mexico Replaces Its Disgraced Drug Czar." *Wall Street Journal*, March 11, 1997.
Stares, Paul. *Global Habit: The Drug Problem in a Borderless World*. Brookings Institution, 1997.
Sullivan, Brian. "International Organized Crime." *Strategic Forum*, May 1996.

Thomas, Pierre. "US/Mexico Trade May Outweigh Anti-Drug Concerns." *Washington Post,* Feb. 23, 1997.

Torres, Craig. "Mexican Skeleton May Hold Key to Solving a Mystery." *Wall Street Journal,* Oct. 14, 1996.

US Department of State. *International Narcotics.* Government Printing Office, March 1996.

US Drug Enforcement Administration. "Debriefing Report on Lawrence Harrison," Sept. 26, 1989.

——. *Drug Control Along the Southwest Border.* Government Printing Office. July 31, 1996.

US House Committee on Foreign Affairs. *US Narcotics Control Program Overseas: An Assessment.* 1985.

——. Select Committee on Narcotics Abuse and Control. *Study Mission to Central America and the Caribbean.* Government Printing Office, 1989.

——. *Narcotics Control in Mexico.* Government Printing Office, 1988.

Wager, Stephen, and Donald Schulz. *The Awakening: The Zapatista Revolt and Its Implications for Civil-Military Relations and the Future of Mexico.* Strategic Studies Institute, US Army War College, 1994.

Walker, William III. *Drug Control in the Americas.* Univ. of New Mexico Press, 1989.

Washington Post, editorial. "The Mexican Surprise." *Washington Post,* April 13, 1989.

Weinstein, Henry. "Honduran Guilty of Conspiracy in Camarena Death." *Los Angeles Times,* July 27, 1990.

Whalen, Christopher. "Narcosistema II: The Salinas Cartel." *The Mexico Report,* Sept. 3, 1996.

Willson, Brian. "US Military Moves into Mexico." *Earth Island Journal,* Spring 1998.

Witkin, Gordon, and Linda Robinson. "Drugs, Power and Death." *US News and World Report,* August 4, 1997.

15

The Uncover-up

Down the decades the CIA has approached perfection in one particular art, which we might term the "uncover-up." This is a process whereby, with all due delay, the Agency first denies with passion, then concedes in profoundly muffled tones, charges leveled against it. Such charges have included the Agency's recruitment of Nazi scientists and SS officers; experiments on unwitting American citizens; efforts to assassinate Fidel Castro; alliances with opium lords in Burma, Thailand and Laos; an assassination program in Vietnam; complicity in the toppling of Salvador Allende in Chile; the arming of opium traffickers and religious fanatics in Afghanistan; the training of murderous police in Guatemala and El Salvador; and involvement in drugs-and-arms shuttles between Latin America and the US.

The specific techniques of the uncover-up vary from instance to instance, but the paradigm is constant, as far back as Frank Wisner and his "mighty Wurlitzer" of CIA friendlies in the press. Charges are raised against the CIA. The Agency leaks its denials to favored journalists, who hasten to inform the public that after intense self-examination, the Agency has discovered that it has clean hands. Then, when the hubbub has died down, the Agency issues a report in which, after patient excavation, the resolute reader discovers that, yes, the CIA did indeed do more or less exactly what it had been accused of. Publicly, the Agency continues to deny what its report has reluctantly admitted. The accusations are initially referred to in the CIA-friendly press as "unfounded" or "overblown" or "unconfirmed," or – the final twist of the knife – "an old story." After the CIA denials, they become "discredited accusations" and usually, when the fuss has died down, they revert to their initial status of "unfounded" or even "paranoid" charges, put about by "conspiracy-mongers."

Faithful to the "uncover-up" paradigm, the CIA passionately denied the allegations made by investigators including Gary Webb about the Agency's alliance with drug-smuggling Contras, its sponsorship and protection of their activities in running cocaine into the United States. Then came the solemn pledges of an intense and far-reaching investigation by the CIA's Inspector General. In his 1996 series of denials, CIA director John Deutch had promised that the Agency's Inspector General, Frederick Hitz, would conduct an internal review of all Agency files relevant to the issue and swiftly place the facts before the American people because of "the seriousness of the allegations and the need to resolve definitely any questions in this area."

Inspector General Hitz went to work. At first, Deutch pledged that Hitz would present his findings within three months. Hitz was unable to meet this schedule. For almost a year and a half there was silence, except for intermittent news tidbits in the *Washington Post* from the CIA's erstwhile apprentice Walter Pincus to the effect that the Inspector General's probe was turning up nothing on Norwin Meneses.

Then, on December 18, 1997, stories in the *Washington Post* by Walter Pincus and in the *New York Times* by Tim Weiner appeared simultaneously, both saying the same thing: Inspector General Hitz had finished his investigation. He had found "no direct or indirect" links between the CIA and the cocaine traffickers. As both Pincus and Weiner admitted in their stories, neither of the two journalists had actually seen the report whose conclusions they were purporting to relay to their readers. These two news stories were promptly picked up by the networks, all of which made great play with the news that the CIA was clean. It was at this point that Gary Webb announced that after negotiation, he and his newspaper, the *San Jose Mercury News,* were parting company.

Then, fully six weeks later, George Tenet, the CIA's new director, declared that he was releasing the Inspector General's report. Anyone listening to Tenet's announcement could have reasonably concluded that Weiner and Pincus had been accurate in their anticipatory news stories. Tenet boasted that "this has been the most extensive investigation ever undertaken by the Inspector General's office, requiring the review of 250,000 pages of documents and interviews with over 365 individuals. I am satisfied that the IG has left no stone unturned in his efforts to uncover the truth. I must admit that my colleagues and I are very concerned that the allegations made have left an indelible impression in many Americans' minds that the CIA was somehow responsible for the scourge of drugs in our inner cities. Unfortunately, no investigations – no matter how exhaustive – will completely erase that false impression or undo the damage that has been done. That is one of the most unfortunate aspects of all of this."

Tenet's assertions were duly reported. The actual report itself, so loudly heralded, received almost no examination. But those who took the time to examine the 149-page document found Inspector General Hitz making one damning admission after another.

The report described a cable from the CIA's Directorate of Operations dated October 22, 1982, describing a prospective meeting between Contra leaders in Costa Rica for "an exchange in [the US] of narcotics for arms."

The CIA's Directorate of Operations instructed its field office not to look into this imminent arms-for-drugs transaction "in the light of the apparent involvement of US persons throughout." In other words, the CIA knew that the Contras were scheduling a drugs-for-arms exchange, and the Agency was prepared to let the deal proceed. How did the Inspector General handle this cable, which on its face confirmed the central accusation made by investigators going back to Robert Parry, Brian Barger and Leslie Cockburn's first reports?

The episode is buried deep in the report, itself written in sedative prose, and the Inspector General triumphantly concludes that the CIA was conducting itself in a proper manner, since any action against US citizens involved in the Costa Rica meeting would have breached the prohibition on activities by the CIA within the United States.

Among those set to attend this Costa Rican rendezvous were leaders of two of the main Contra groups, the FDN and the UDN, US arms dealers and one Renato Peña, who was a lieutenant in Norwin Meneses's drug ring importing cocaine from Latin America to the United States and marketing it on the West Coast. Peña was also chief spokesman for the Contras in San Francisco. Peña was interviewed by the CIA's Inspector General, to whom Peña admitted he had made as many as eight trips in California between 1982 and 1984, ferrying money and drugs from Meneses's cocaine ring. On each trip, Peña told the Inspector General, he would take $600,000 to $1 million in cash to Los Angeles and return to San Francisco with 6 to 8 kilos of cocaine. Peña said he had met Meneses at a 1982 San Francisco meeting of the FDN. Eventually, Peña became the "military representative of the FDN in San Francisco," a position he owed, so Peña told the CIA Inspector General, to Norwin Meneses's close relationship with Enrique Bermúdez, the CIA-paid military commander of the FDN. Peña further told Hitz that he had been told by Colombian wholesalers that a percentage of the profits from Meneses's cocaine sales were being funneled to the Contras.

Thus did Peña confirm to the Inspector General that a major drug smuggler was also a Contra high-up; and that the CIA knew that there was a Contra arms-for-drugs shuttle and did nothing to stop it.

Reading further into the Inspector General's report, we find that six months after the CIA cable traffic concerning the Costa Rica meeting, there was another CIA cable from the Latin American division station, alluding to a Nicaraguan expatriate who, in October 1982, said he was "hoping to contact a friend named Norbin [sic] [Meneses] in Miami who would direct him to the counter-revolutionary training camps in south Florida and eventually to join Miskito combat units in Honduras." The CIA report thus discloses more evidence that the CIA knew of links between Norwin Meneses, identified as a drug smuggler as early as 1978, and the Contras.

When Hitz's staff finally interviewed Meneses himself in the Nicaraguan prison where he is serving a forty-year sentence for drug smuggling, the report notes that Meneses made haste to declare that he had been a Contra "recruiter," but had never been involved in the cocaine business. Hitz uses this blatantly untruthful statement as proof that drug smuggling and Contra activity never overlapped.

As for Danilo Blandón, Rick Ross's cocaine supplier in Los Angeles and the cocaine ring associate of Meneses: the Inspector General's interview with Blandón, now a timber merchant in Nicaragua, records that Blandón declared he entered the cocaine business in 1981 and that during the time he was a cocaine wholesaler he met with FDN military commander Enrique Bermúdez at least four times. On each occasion Bermúdez said that he was desperate for money and urged the Nicaraguan to do what he could to help the Contra cause. "The ends justify the means," Blandón recalled the Contra commander telling him. Blandón admits that Bermúdez was aware that Meneses was involved in criminal enterprises.

Somewhat undercutting the credibility of Meneses, Blandón described a meeting with Bermúdez in Honduras that occurred as Blandón and Meneses were in the midst of a drug run to Bolivia. Blandón said he'd met with Bermúdez again in Fort Lauderdale in late 1983. The significance of these meetings is that Blandón, a confessed drug smuggler, had an ongoing relationship with the CIA's top Contra military commander.

Blandón told the Inspector General that he gave about $40,000 to the Contra cause in 1981 and 1982 and that Meneses gave a similar amount. In other words, the Contras were getting drug money. Blandón had an even closer relationship to the Contra commander Eden Pastora, so the Inspector General's report notes. Blandón told the CIA probers that he had allowed Pastora to live "rent free in one of his houses in Costa Rica from 1984 to 1987." This is a period when Blandón admits that his income was coming almost solely from his cocaine business. Blandón recalled to CIA investigators that Pastora asked everyone he came in contact with to raise money for the Contra cause. Blandón said he gave Pastora $9,000 in cash in 1985 and also two trucks in 1986.

Hitz's investigators checked out Blandón's story with Eden Pastora, who acknowledged the generosity of Blandón and then added some disclosures of his own. Pastora confessed that he had received at least $40,000 and two planes, including a C-47 cargo plane, from cocaine trafficker George Morales. Pastora also admitted to receiving two helicopters and $60,000 in cash from two Cuban exiles also linked to the drug trade. He acknowledged receiving another $25,000 from Manuel Noriega.

Even more damning, the Inspector General's report ekes out the admission that the Agency requested the Justice Department to return $36,800 to a member of the Meneses drug ring. This was money that had been seized by the DEA in the famous "Frogman raid" on the San Francisco waterfront in which the drug agents captured Meneses's men unloading 200 kilos of cocaine. The raiding party then proceeded to the home of Julio Zavala, one of Meneses's lieutenants who had been arrested. In a bedside table the police discovered $36,800 and confiscated the money as evidence.

The CIA immediately went to bat on Zavala's behalf. A memo in the CIA file quoted in Hitz's report says that "At OGC's [the CIA's Office of General Counsel] request the US Attorney has agreed to return the money to Zavala." The CIA's Inspector General said the Agency wanted the money returned "to protect an operational equity, i.e. a Contra support group in which it [the CIA] had an operational interest."

An August 22, 1984 CIA memo, also quoted in the Inspector General's report, talks of the need for secrecy in the whole Frogman affair. Under the name of Lee S. Strickland, assistant general counsel of the CIA, the memo says in part, "I believe the station must be made aware of the potential for disaster. While the allegations [that is, drugs for Contra guns] might be entirely false, there are sufficient factual details which would cause certain damage to our image and program in Central America."

One familiar feature in the "uncover-up" paradigm is the frequently made statement by CIA-friendly journalists that "no smoking gun" has been detected in whatever probe is under review. The CIA's successful request that $36,800 be returned to a gang of drug smugglers because the CIA had an "operational equity" in it is an obviously smoking gun, although to say this is to scant the larger truth that the whole of Inspector General Hitz's report is a smoking gun.

If one were to look for another spectacularly smoking gun, in the narrower sense of the phrase, the account of Carlos Cabezas, a drug pilot who was making drug/arms runs between San Francisco and Costa Rica, is a suitable candidate. As we described it in Chapter 12, the Inspector General's report has to confront the fact that Cabezas told CIA investigators how he had gone to Costa Rica in the spring of 1982 with money for the Contras. There he met with Horatio Pereira and Troilo Sánchez, who were Contra leaders and also partners with the Contra/drug smuggler Norwin Meneses. In the company of these two, Cabezas recalled, was a curly-haired man who said his name was Ivan Gomez. Pereira identified Gomez to Cabezas as the CIA's "man in Costa Rica." Cabezas told the Inspector General that Gomez said he was there to "ensure that the profits from the cocaine went to the Contras and not into someone's pocket."

Struggling with this damning statement, the Inspector General concedes that indeed the CIA did have a "contractor" in Costa Rica using the name "Ivan Gomez." But, the Inspector General bravely adds, though Cabezas's description of a man he had seen twice fifteen years earlier was accurate to the extent that the CIA's contractor did indeed have dark curly hair, his overall appearance was "significantly different," that is, the "real" Ivan Gomez was shorter and slighter in build than Cabezas's memory of him.

Six weeks after his report (heavily censored in its declassified version) was released, Inspector General Hitz went to Capitol Hill to testify before a House committee. There he made even more damaging admissions. For the first time the Inspector General of the CIA disclosed that his Agency knew that "dozens of people and a number of companies connected in some fashion to the Contra program" were involved in the drug trade. He said the CIA knew that drugs had been going back along the Contra supply lines into the United States and added, "Let me be frank. There are instances where the CIA did not in an expeditious or consistent fashion cut off relationships with individuals supporting the Contra program who were alleged to have engaged in drug trafficking activity or take action to resolve the allegations."

Even more damaging was Hitz's revelation that in 1982 the CIA had signed a memorandum of understanding with Ronald Reagan's attorney general, William French Smith, freeing the Agency from any requirement to report allegations of drug trafficking involving non-employees. The non-employees, according to Hitz (who refused to release the entire memo), were described as paid and non-paid "assets, pilots who ferried supplies to the Contras as well as Contra officials and others."

Thus, in 1982, as it was mounting its covert Contra supply operation, the CIA was evidently aware enough of the nature of the traffic it was supervising to make sure that it would not have to report the drug-trafficking activities of any Contra leaders, contract pilots, businessmen, etc. with whom it was doing business. Only in 1986, after the flow of congressional funds to the Contras had been restored, was the agreement with the Justice Department modified to require the Agency to stop paying "assets" whom it believed to be involved in the drug trade. The agreement was officially ended in 1995.

This kind of arrangement typifies the extralegal mindset of the CIA. "In an Agency that employs pressure and 'national security' to hide violations of law, incompetence, politically unacceptable facts, and an assortment of malfeasance, you need the highest degree of accountability," observes former CIA officer Ralph McGehee. "What you have is the opposite – a system that defends itself at all costs – no matter what the transgression."

So much for uncover-up. As the CIA turned fifty in 1997, it attempted to define its role in a world no longer containing the Soviet Union. What it came up with was a plan to combat something it had done so much to encourage over the first half-century of its existence: international crime! Among the CIA's proposed targets for preserving its slice of the $27 billion intelligence budget were money laundering, illegal immigration, drug smuggling and chemical and biological terrorism. Only three years earlier the CIA was still enjoying an exemption from reporting the drug activities of any of its associates. If they were alive to read the CIA's prospectus for the third millennium, the ghosts of Lucky Luciano, Meyer Lansky, Chiang Kai-shek, George Hunter White, Barry Seal and thousands of others would surely have laughed at the effrontery of their old partner in crime.

Sources

The tender topic of which journalists have been on the CIA's payroll has been touched upon from time to time by investigators. In 1977 Carl Bernstein attacked the subject in *Rolling Stone*, concluding that more than 400 journalists had maintained some kind of alliance with the Agency from 1956 to 1972. In 1997 the son of a well-known senior CIA man in the Agency's earlier years said emphatically, though off the record, that "of course" the powerful and malevolent columnist Joseph Alsop "was on the payroll."

At the fiftieth anniversary of the CIA, President Bill Clinton outlined his vision of the CIA's future. "Our first task is to focus our intelligence resources in the areas most critical to our national security – the areas where, as Director Tenet has said, we simply cannot afford to fail. Two years ago I set out our top intelligence priorities in the Presidential Decision Directive. First, supporting our troops and operations, whether turning back aggression, helping secure peace or providing humanitarian assistance. Second, providing political, economic, and military intelligence on countries hostile to the United States so we can help to stop crises and conflicts before they start. And, third, protecting American citizens from new transnational threats such as drug traffickers, terrorists, organized criminals, and weapons of mass destruction."

Has the CIA changed? There isn't much evidence of it. In March 1998, the Agency responded angrily to a move by the Congress to enact whistle-blower protection provisions for CIA employees. Director George Tenet duly trotted out the refrain that to do so would pose a "grave" threat to national security. Similarly, in May the Agency denounced legislation that would have required it to open up its files about its relationships to murderous police gangs in Latin America. The CIA's Lee Strickland, the man who tried to cover up the Frogman case, testified that the Agency was able to decide on its own which documents should be disclosed to the public without any interference from Congress.

Beamish, Rita. "CIA Uses Intelligence Briefing to Tout Role in Battling Drugs." AP Wire, June 28, 1995.

Bernstein, Carl. "The CIA and the Media." *Rolling Stone*, Oct. 20, 1977.

Cockburn, Alexander, and Jeffrey St. Clair. "Crack-Up: The CIA Probe." *Counter-Punch*, Feb. 1–15, 1998.

Honey, Martha. "Don't Ask, Don't Tell: The CIA's Complicity with Drug Traffickers Was Official Policy." *In These Times*, May 17, 1988.

Parry, Robert. "Contra-Coke: Bad to Worse." *The Consortium*, Feb. 16, 1998.

Pincus, Walter. "CIA Finds No Link to Cocaine Sales." *Washington Post*, Dec. 18, 1997.

——. "Probe Finds No CIA Link to L.A. Crack Cocaine Sales." *Washington Post*, January 30, 1998.

——. "Inspector: CIA Kept Ties With Alleged Traffickers" *Washington Post*, March 17, 1998.

Tenet, George J. "Statement on Release of Inspector General's Report." USCIA Public Affairs Office, Jan. 29, 1998.

US Central Intelligence Agency. Office of Inspector General. *Report of Investigation*

Concerning Allegations Between CIA and the Contras in Trafficking Cocaine to the United States. USCIA Inspector General's Office, Jan. 29, 1998.

US Executive Office of the President. "Remarks of President William Jefferson Clinton on the 50th Anniversary of the Central Intelligence Agency." White House Press Office, Nov. 4, 1997.

Weiner, Tim. "Aging Shop of Horrors: The CIA Limps to 50." *New York Times*, Nov. 16, 1997.

——."CIA Says It Has Found No Link Between Itself and Crack Trade." *New York Times*, Dec.19, 1997.

Index